Introduction to the Philosophy of Sport

ELEMENTS OF PHILOSOPHY

The Elements of Philosophy series aims to produce core introductory texts in the major areas of philosophy, among them metaphysics, epistemology, ethics and moral theory, philosophy of religion, philosophy of mind, aesthetics and the philosophy of art, feminist philosophy, and social and political philosophy. Books in the series are written for an undergraduate audience of second- through fourth-year students and serve as the perfect cornerstone for understanding the various elements of philosophy.

Titles in the Series

Moral Theory: An Introduction (third edition 2022), by Mark Timmons

An Introduction to Social and Political Philosophy: A Question-Based Approach, by Richard Schmitt

Epistemology: Classic Problems and Contemporary Responses, by Laurence BonJour

Aesthetics and the Philosophy of Art: An Introduction, by Robert Stecker

Aesthetics Today: A Reader, edited by Robert Stecker and Ted Gracyk

Introduction to Ethics: A Reader, edited by Andrew J. Dell'Olio and Caroline J. Simon

Introduction to the Philosophy of Sport (second edition 2022), by Heather L. Reid

Introduction to the Philosophy of Sport

Second Edition

Heather L. Reid

ROWMAN & LITTLEFIELD
Lanham • Boulder • New York • London

Acquisitions Editor: Natalie Mandziuk
Acquisitions Assistant: Sylvia Landis
Sales and Marketing Inquiries: textbooks@rowman.com

Credits and acknowledgments for material borrowed from other sources, and reproduced with permission, appear on the appropriate pages within the text.

Published by Rowman & Littlefield
An imprint of The Rowman & Littlefield Publishing Group, Inc.
4501 Forbes Boulevard, Suite 200, Lanham, Maryland 20706
www.rowman.com

86-90 Paul Street, London EC2A 4NE

British Library Cataloguing in Publication Information available

Library of Congress Cataloging-in-Publication Data

Names: Reid, Heather Lynne, 1963- author.
Title: Introduction to the philosophy of sport / Heather L. Reid.
Description: Second edition. | Lanham, Maryland : Rowman & Littlefield, 2023. | Series: Elements of philosophy | Includes bibliographical references and index.
Identifiers: LCCN 2022034021 (print) | LCCN 2022034022 (ebook) | ISBN 9781538156193 (cloth) | ISBN 9781538156209 (paperback) | ISBN 9781538156216 (epub)
Subjects: LCSH: Sports--Philosophy.
Classification: LCC GV706 .R4395 2023 (print) | LCC GV706 (ebook) | DDC 796.01--dc23/eng/20220718
LC record available at https://lccn.loc.gov/2022034021
LC ebook record available at https://lccn.loc.gov/2022034022

Contents

Acknowledgments

I remain grateful to my teachers, students, and colleagues for their encouragement and inspiration over the years. I would also like to thank the organizations and foundations that have supported my scholarship, including the National Endowment for the Humanities, Andrew W. Mellon Foundation, American Academy in Rome, U.S.-Italy Fulbright Commission, Harvard Center for Hellenic Studies, the Sharon Walker and VerSteeg programs at Morningside College, and the Exedra Mediterranean Center in Siracusa, Sicily. Comments and suggestions instrumental to the second edition came from Jesús Ilundáin-Agurruza, Francisco Javier Lopez Frias, Georgios Mouratidis, and Rafael Mendoza. I also received important feedback from Sarah Teetzel, Pam Sailors, and anonymous reviewers at Rowman & Littlefield. I thank again those who helped with the first edition: Susan Brownell, Daniel Campos, Christos Evangeliou, Warren Fraleigh, John Gleaves, Drew Hyland, Scott Kretchmar, Bill Morgan, Jim Parry, Graham Priest, Mark Holowchak, and Sherry Swan. Most of all, I thank my husband, Larry Theobald, for more than thirty years of patience with and support of my passion for the philosophy of sport.

Introduction

Why Study the Philosophy of Sport?

Like many of those reading this book, I have done extraordinary things out of love for sport. We can leave aside the hours training in the rain, the nights spent on strangers' couches, the thousands of miles on interstate highways, and the scarred knees and elbows of my cycling career—for these might be explained by the enthusiasm of youth and the intoxicating dream of competing in the Olympic Games. But what about the things I have done as an adult, as a philosophy professor trained in logic and value theory, presumably able to distinguish what is important from what is not? I have curled my toes into a rough, stone starting block and then raced barefoot across the ancient track of Greece's Nemean Games. I have ridden my road bicycle up a steep alpine climb and then waited shivering on the side of the mountain to cheer the exhausted racers of the Giro d'Italia as they struggled past. Crazier than that, I then rode the bike back down the hill, threading my way through the crowd of wobbling spectators, my thin tires skittering on the bumpy dirt road. Where does this come from? Why do I care? Why did I get up at four in the morning to watch an Olympic opening ceremony from Italy? These may seem like crazy things, but I am not crazy, and I am hardly alone in my passion for sport. There are reasons behind these passions, and they are not trivial. Neither is sport.

Sport is a significant human activity. Its origins reach back into the depths of history, and its contemporary practice reaches across cultures and continents. Sport, further, is a meaningful human activity. Some people devote large portions of their lives to it, many people practice it on a regular basis, and most people at least watch it on television—especially when the Olympic Games come around. It is surprising, given the importance so many people attribute to sport, that philosophers have historically neglected it as a subject of serious inquiry. Despite sport's metaphysical relationship with art and play, despite its ethical association with virtue and fairness, despite its educational potential, political influence, and even despite Socrates's comparison of himself to an Olympic athlete, serious philosophical discussion of sport did not take hold until the latter part of the twentieth century. There are probably good—or, at least interesting—explanations for this. But the purpose of this book is not to discover why sport hasn't been studied philosophically in the past. Rather, its purpose is to demonstrate why sport should be studied philosophically now and in the future.

We can learn much from the philosophical study of sport—not just about sport but also about ourselves, about society, and about philosophy. Because sport has important metaphysical, ethical, epistemological, and sociopolitical dimensions, philosophers of sport must engage with a variety of philosophical disciplines to study it properly. And because students are often familiar with and curious about sport, the philosophy of sport is an excellent platform from which to launch into the general study of philosophy. Students' experience as athletes, or even simply playing games, provides a foundation for discussion of metaphysical issues such as the relationship between games and play, mind and body, and even sport and art. Sport can also serve as a moral laboratory in which theories such as deontology, consequentialism, and virtue ethics can be experienced and tested in a controlled environment. Finally, sport is a social experience through which we encounter political issues such as democratic responsibility, social categorization, and the challenges of seeking peace in a globalizing world.

A good philosophical understanding of sport can also help teachers and scholars to communicate difficult philosophical concepts. Philosophers as varied as Plato, Thomas Hobbes, and Jacques Derrida have used sports metaphors to explain important parts of their philosophy. As a young scholar of ancient philosophy, it was Plato's use of athletic examples and metaphors that connected with my own sports experience and gave me insight into his theory of moral education, the subject of my doctoral dissertation. As a professor, sport philosophy has pushed me beyond the comfort zone of my academic specialty and invited me to interact with scholars and concepts from across the philosophical spectrum—not to mention related disciplines such as archaeology, history, and kinesiology. Just as sport improves athletes by subjecting them to challenges, philosophy of sport improves scholars by challenging them to think seriously about this rich and complex human practice.

In this book I have endeavored to provide an introduction to the philosophical study of sport that not only covers the charted terrain but also looks up to survey the horizon and suggest future paths for this discipline. I have tried to create a structure that reflects the traditional division of philosophy into metaphysical, ethical, epistemological, and sociopolitical issues. I have also endeavored to link them together, carrying metaphysical approaches over to ethical theories and then applying them to concrete issues surrounding education, gender, and politics. Rather than arguing for particular solutions to problems such as doping, violence, risk in youth sport, transgender eligibility, and national team allegiance, I try to set the stage for intelligent and informed classroom discussions of these issues. A good philosophical analysis of something like the amateur regulations in intercollegiate athletics, for example, depends on a justified understanding of the purpose of the activity, which demands sensitivity to the epistemological and ethical issues involved, issues that are based on the metaphysics of the practice. This book begins at the roots of sport philosophy, with its ancient history and Olympic heritage, then works its way through metaphysics, ethics, education, social epistemology, and finally politics to arrive, hopefully, at the flower of improved understanding.

Although I carve up the philosophy of sport according to traditional philosophical divisions, my aim is to achieve a whole much greater than the sum of its parts. What we have in this book is not only an outline of this fledgling academic discipline and a summary of much of its pioneering work, but also an invitation to join the conversation by connecting these issues to one's own athletic experience. It will be obvious that some topics have attracted more interest than others; in several cases, I have not been able to provide a full survey of the important literature on that subject. It will be obvious as well that I have my own perspective on the field. I have inevitably left out essays, books, or even entire topics that some of my colleagues might deem essential. I can only reply that I have done my best to provide an organized and readable introduction to the discipline that looks both at its past and toward its future, but most of all inspires the reader to think about sport philosophically here and now. Sport is a significant human activity that, beyond its intrinsic worth, has enormous educational potential. It is only by achieving a deeper understanding of sport that we can help it to function in service of the human good.

PART I

History and Heritage

We begin with history and heritage not only because philosophical studies should be informed by the history of their subjects but also because an important link exists between the history of sport and of philosophy. The obvious connection is that the two practices share a common birthplace in ancient Greece, but there is also a sense in which the knowledge-seeking spirit characteristic of philosophy was originally exhibited in Olympic-style sport. Before the advent of open contests, athleticism seems to have functioned primarily as a political tool for demonstrating a leader's divine favor and worthiness to lead. We find this function in Homer when Agamemnon claims victory in the javelin event without taking a throw or Odysseus takes back his kingdom by winning an archery contest and stringing the royal bow. But Homer also describes Olympic-style sport, in which the outcome is uncertain and left to the contest to decide—at the risk of challenging existing social hierarchy.

I call this familiar style of sport "Olympic" because I believe it was competing claims to honor among the diverse tribes present at the Panhellenic sanctuary of ancient Olympia that motivated the use of a fair and impartial mechanism for choosing someone to light the sacrificial flame—the mechanism of a footrace. Just as early Olympic sport sought answers through impartial testing rather than preexisting belief, early philosophy sought answers about the world through the testing of ideas rather than the passive acceptance of mythology or orthodox beliefs. Just as sport is essentially blind to social assumptions and distinctions, philosophy sought to liberate truth from cultural tradition. Sport further revealed that excellence could be trained and was not merely a matter of birth, perhaps inspiring philosophers such as Socrates and Plato to find ways of training virtue through competitive debate. From these roots sprang also the phenomenon of democracy, and its values remain embedded in sport. Philosophy, democracy, and the Olympic Games are commonly counted among Greece's gifts to the modern world. The spirit of sport is visible in all of them.

The Olympic Games were revived at the end of the nineteenth century as a deliberate expression of philosophy. This philosophy, called Olympism, was not based on the ideas of Plato and Aristotle so much as on the beliefs of the European Enlightenment. Further, it was not the work of professional philosophers but, rather, a group of idealistic enthusiasts, led by the French pedagogue Pierre de Coubertin. Its lack of analytic rigor and precision raises the question of whether Olympism is really a philosophy, but it may also explain Olympism's success as the guiding principle of such a complex and multicultural organization as the Olympic Movement.

Taking a flexible approach, we can discern in Olympism the main branches of philosophy: metaphysics, ethics, and politics. Olympism's metaphysics posit a conception of an ideal human that exalts body as well as mind and emphasizes balance and harmony, but the portrait is not so specific as to exclude any gender or ethnicity. Olympism's ethics refer to universal fundamental principles without spelling out what they are—a weakness that turns into a strength when facing the challenges of multiculturalism. Sport provides the common culture that unites the diverse individuals in the Olympic Movement, and the structure of sport reflects such moral values as equality of opportunity and the pursuit of excellence. Sport also serves as the foundation for Olympism's political goal of peace. By requiring people to put aside their differences, treat one another as equals, and tolerate their differences, the Olympic festival creates a model for peaceful coexistence that depends not on a civilizing authority but, rather, on cooperation. Olympism, to be sure, is a thin philosophy, but it is one intimately connected to sport that has withstood the test of time.

Chapter 1

The Ancient Hellenic Heritage

Imagine yourself at the conclusion of a conference championship game in college basketball. The gymnasium is packed full with euphoric fans, the victorious players writhe on the floor in glee, and the coaches shake hands and exchange solemn words as the ritual of cutting down the net begins. Now imagine that the microphone is given to a famous sports commentator who has been asked to say a few words about the historic victory. He stands at center court as a hush comes over the stands. He looks up toward the heavens and then begins his speech:

> Creatures of a day!
> What is someone? What is no one? A dream of a shadow is man.[1]

These poetic-philosophical lines are part of an ancient Greek athlete's victory hymn, but how out of place would they seem in sports today? The arena may stand on a university campus, and the building may be full of students, but philosophers, poets, and other intellectuals are usually sequestered in ivy-covered stone buildings—they don't wander into the gymnasium. If we were in ancient Greece, however, the philosophers would be running the gymnasium, and poets would staff the sports information office. Athletics and philosophy were close enough in ancient Greece that the great poet Pindar not only described men philosophically as "dreams of shadows," but he linked sport with the pursuit of knowledge, nicknaming Olympia, site of the famous Games, "Mistress of Truth."[2]

It is not coincidence that philosophy, democracy, and Olympic-style sport share a common birthplace in ancient Greece. These three things share important conceptual resemblances, and it should not be forgotten that the eldest of the family members is, in fact, athletics. The conventional date for the founding of the Olympic Games is 776 BCE, although the first contest there happened much earlier. Philosophy arrived on the scene hundreds of years later, sometime in the sixth century BCE, whereas democracy showed

3

up even later, near the end of that century. The resemblance between these three practices begins with their ability to sort out competing claims to virtue, truth, and governance—without capitulating to existing social hierarchies or resorting to the use of violent force. Indeed, sport seems to have helped the ancient Hellenes to question the validity of natural aristocracy and the truth value of mythology. These seeds of doubt were sown partly by intercultural exchange between the diverse tribes and intellectual ideas present at the Olympic Games, as well as the foreign cultures contacted through overseas trade. The evidence that even lower-class athletes could achieve excellence through training likely inspired the educational activities of Socrates, Plato, and Aristotle, which were based in gymnasia. Sport may not have been the subject of serious philosophical reflection in ancient Greece, but philosophy itself was closely linked with sport.

HEROES AND HIERARCHIES

When looking for the origins of what we now call sport, we arrive inevitably at the epics of Homer. The *Iliad* and *Odyssey* are foundational in many ways, but their often overlooked accounts of athletics offer important clues not only for understanding the nature of sport today but also for providing perspective on how sport has changed since those ancient times. Homer describes athletics more or less as they existed in his own era, around the eighth century BCE, though he purports to be recounting events that happened much earlier. And in fact, Homer's contests have much in common with the athletic practices of earlier civilizations such as the Mesopotamians, Egyptians, Minoans, and Hittites.[3] The most important commonality is the perceived link between athleticism and human virtue, specifically the worthiness to lead.

As early as the third millennium BCE, the athletic ability of ancient leaders was taken as evidence of divine favor or at least partially divine status. In Greek mythology, mortals with divine ancestry such Heracles (Latin: Hercules) were called heroes. Like all heroes, Heracles was known for his *athla*, amazing feats of strength and intelligence that served communities by defeating monsters and tyrants. In English, we call these "labors," but heroic *athla* provide the conceptual model for athletes and athletics.[4] Sport, in fact, was born in ancient Greece as an imitation or emulation of the *athla* of ancient heroes—or, more specifically, of the *aretē* (excellence or virtue) those heroes displayed in such feats.[5]

In the early days, however, these emulated "feats" were not recognizable as sport. They appeared as religious rituals designed to activate the hero's life-giving spirit[6] and as political propaganda in fanciful stories or unchallenged displays designed to make leaders appear heroic to their subjects.[7] It isn't until the time of the Homeric epic that we find athletic *contests* containing that crucial element of sport: the risk of losing.

The funeral games dedicated to Patroclus in the twenty-third book of Homer's *Iliad* ends with an "uncontested" victory. King Agamemnon is named winner of the javelin event and awarded the prize without ever making a throw. As supreme leader, his superior athleticism is presumed and honored without having to be subject to a test. This turn of events contrasts sharply with the overall theme of the poem, however, which revolves around a dispute over Agamemnon's worthiness to lead and his refusal to subject his authority to any kind of challenge. What we have in the *Iliad* is a novel situation in which many kings—Achilles, Odysseus, and their peers are all the supreme leaders of their individual tribes—have been removed from their familiar homeland hierarchies and asked to join together as equals to fight for a common cause. The situation provokes competing claims to *aretē*, or a "crisis of value," in which each man's claim to social honor must be renegotiated.[8] The athletic contests staged in book 23 provide a kind of model for that: a relatively open process for (re)distributing honor according to merit.

In the *Iliad*'s games we recognize many familiar aspects of sport: a (relatively) open call for voluntary participation, a common understanding of the rules, a uniform starting line, responsible referees, the resolution of disputes about fairness, the selection of victors, and the awarding of prizes. The games also have important differences: only members of the upper echelon are allowed to compete, prizes are not always awarded according to contest results, and gods and goddesses interfere with the contest to help their favorites and hinder rivals. The competitive spirit is clearly recognizable, however, and as it does today, the competitive nature of Homeric society extends well beyond sport. The Homeric conception of *aretē*, or more precisely, *aristeia*, is inherently competitive: it can be neatly expressed in the oft-quoted phrase "being the best and outdoing all others."[9]

What is revolutionary in Homer in contrast with earlier forms of sport, however, is that one's *aretē* is not presumed on the basis of social status or ancestry; rather, it must be publicly demonstrated through action—in war, in government, or even in athletic contests. In this context, sport begins to resemble in some measure a form of inquiry rather than propaganda, and so it begins to acquire what I call its "philosophical" or truth-seeking nature.[10]

ANCIENT OLYMPIC PHILOSOPHY

Like philosophy, sport should begin in wonder and uncertainty.[11] When contestants line up on a starting line in Homer's *Iliad*, there is usually uncertainty—an authentic question about who will prevail. In the *Odyssey*, the Homeric epic that describes Odysseus's decade-long return home after the Trojan War, sport is used to prove *aretē* and worthiness to lead. The journey-worn hero overcomes doubt about his nobility by performing athletic feats on the island of the Phaeacians and wins back his queen and his kingdom in Ithaca by triumphing in an archery contest. So, in the *Odyssey* there is doubt, but sport still affirms the aristocratic status quo in a way not so very far removed from the uncontested "feats" of political propaganda. It was with the advent of the ancient Olympic Games that sport would seriously dissociate itself from man-made hierarchies and exhibit authentic philosophical wonder and uncertainty, by embracing the possibility of failure and leaving questions about virtue and worthiness up to the contest itself.

The motivation for this change was ultimately religious. Long before athletes began to compete at Olympia, the site was a Panhellenic sanctuary that honored all the gods and served all the tribes of Greece. As in Homer's *Iliad*, the bringing together of diverse tribes for a common cause—even the religious cause of worship—was not without its conflicts. Each tribe brought its own social hierarchy to the officially neutral sanctuary, so when the time came to select someone to light the sacrificial flame, the choice was not as easy as simply pointing at the king. Further, it mattered to everyone that someone pleasing to the god was chosen for this honor because the benefits believed to be provided by the gods—such as successful harvests and recovery from disease—were thought to depend upon divine propitiation through such rituals. The process can be regarded as a kind of gift exchange between humans and gods through the ritual of sacrifice; the currency of exchange was *aretē*.[12]

The first athletic event contested at Olympia seems to have been a footrace from the edge of the sanctuary to the altar, where the winner was given the honor of lighting the sacrificial flame.[13] The athletic victor became a kind of symbolic sacrifice or dedication to the god; the olive wreath, palm branch, and ribbons awarded to Olympic champions were also associated with sacrificial animals and priests.[14] By demonstrating his *aretē* athletically, the victor proved he would be most pleasing to the god and, therefore, most deserving of the religious honor.

By using a footrace to select a suitable honoree—or perhaps by staging a footrace to allow the god to select his favorite—Olympia was both preserving the traditional association among athleticism, virtue, and divine favor and introducing the novelty of letting the contest, rather than existing social hierarchies, decide the results. The process reflects, in many ways, the emergence of philosophy in Hellenic Ionia during the sixth century BCE. The so-called pre-Socratic philosophers, such as Thales, Xenophanes, and Anaximenes, distinguished themselves from earlier mythological and poetic forms of truth seeking by insisting on some amount of argument and evidence to support their claims.[15]

Philosophy is a process of truth seeking that acknowledges the fallibility of existing beliefs and structures as a relatively rational and impartial process for finding a universally acceptable answer, all under the scrutiny of a watchful public. Indeed, I think that the Olympic Games' association with peace derives less from the so-called truce (*ekecheiria*) that protected athletes and spectators traveling to the festival, and more from the pacifying and unifying effects of bringing together diverse people to engage in a fair and transparent decision-making process.[16]

The unsurpassed prestige and longevity of the ancient Olympic Games (more than a thousand years) depended heavily on the perceived accuracy and justice of its results. Olympia never allowed subjectively judged events and carefully policed the integrity of both athletes and officials. In wrestling, boxing, and *pankration* (similar to mixed martial arts), pairings for the "heavy" events (so called because there were no weight classes and so bigger, heavier athletes dominated) were drawn by lot, and care was taken to avoid unfair advantages. The boxing events, for example, were staged near noon, to avoid fighters being blinded by the sun. A starting gate called the *hysplex* was developed to reduce the chance of "jumping the gun" in the sprints. And in the horse races, starts were staggered to compensate for the difference in distance from the various starting gates to the central turning post. Violations of the rules were considered affronts to the gods, and stories of divine retribution levied against cheaters were reinforced by the row of *zanes*—statues of Zeus erected with the money from fines paid by cheaters—that lined the entrance to the stadium and reminded passersby that "Olympic victory is to be won not by money but by swiftness of foot or strength of body."[17]

FROM ARISTOCRACY TO DEMOCRACY

The motivation for all this attention to fairness was at least partly religious—selecting anything less than the worthiest victor might displease the god—but the practical effect seems to have been widespread public confidence in the validity of the results. Eventually this confidence became strong enough to create doubt about the validity of existing social hierarchies, whereas pre-Olympic sport had merely reinforced them. Some claim, in fact, that Olympic-style athletics provided a foundation for the invention of democracy.[18] Athletics in ancient Greece had originally been embraced by the aristocracy as a way to justify their privileged political position—to demonstrate that *aretē* was a matter of heredity, not hard work. As Nigel

Nicholson explains, "If quality was not inherited, there was no reason power should be either."[19] In order for the upper classes to keep dominating the Games, however, they were forced to rely increasingly on the competitive edges that wealth can provide: time to train and travel, private gymnasia, personal coaches, top-flight race horses, and professional charioteers. But even as these advantages helped to win crowns for the wealthy, they inevitably eroded the very idea of genetic *aristeia* that such victories were intended to protect. People knew the difference between a victory earned with sweat and one earned with wealth.

Meanwhile, the relatively equal opportunity and merit-based rewards that athletic games provided, combined with the prestige and divine favor associated with victory, motivated cities to look past their internal class distinctions in search of potential champions. The success of the social underdog seems to have fascinated the ancient world no less than it does today. The first official Olympic champion, from 776 BCE, is said to have been a cook.[20] Aristotle remarks that a later Olympic champion was a fishmonger.[21] In reality, it is hard to know the social class of Olympic victors because most of our surviving evidence comes from families wealthy enough to erect memorial statues or commission famous poets such as Pindar to write victory odes. But even if non-aristocratic Olympic champions were relatively few in the ancient world—as gold medalists from poor countries are today—the fact that they existed at all reflects the democratic impetus built into the structure of sport.

Democracy, which emerged in Athens more than two centuries after the Olympic Games began, shares with sport at least two fundamental values: liberty and equality. The Greek word for liberty, *eleutheria*, represented first and foremost the coveted distinction of being a free person rather than a slave. Later, it became more closely associated with freedom from tyranny. Part of *eleutheria*'s association with athletics comes from the athletic duo Harmodius and Aristogeiton, who became a symbol of the democratic spirit in Athens after they killed the tyrant Hipparchus in the Panathenaic Games of 514 BCE.[22] The Greek word *dēmokratia* (democracy) suggests government by the many, but the real ruler in a democracy is the law, to which all of the people willingly subject themselves. It is likewise characteristic of sport that competitors willingly subject themselves to the rules of the game. The fact that diverse people managed to subject themselves to a single set of sports rules at Olympia might indeed have inspired the democratic idea that citizens of diverse classes could coexist under the authority of a common law.

Not only did ancient athletes subject themselves to common rules in sport, but they also understood that they were considered equal under those rules, no matter what their social rank might have been at home. Stephen G. Miller argues that this fact about ancient athletics inspired the Greek concept of *isonomia*, equality before the law[23]—a concept so closely linked with democracy that Herodotus indicates "rule of the many" by the term *isonomia*.[24] A second democratic concept, *isēgoria*, meaning equal access or opportunity to participate in public debates as a free citizen, is also associated with sport, albeit less clearly. Females, slaves, and foreigners were explicitly excluded from the Olympic Games (though women competed in other games), and participation was more difficult for the poor than the rich. Likewise, Greek democracy limited full participation to a certain subset of eligible males. Nevertheless, it was revolutionary in its time because it reduced the overwhelming gap between rich and poor, noble and commoner.[25]

ATHLETICS AND PHILOSOPHY IN GREEK EDUCATION

Perhaps the greatest legacy of the social changes inspired by sport in ancient Greece was the focus that even diehard aristocrats such as Plato placed on education. Because the *aretē* traditionally associated with athletic success was revealed to be something cultivated through training rather than an entitlement of birth or divine favor, the idea emerged that the *aretē* associated with citizenship could also be gained through *ponos* (effort). Indeed, it is tempting, given the sixth century BCE proliferation of gymnasia, to recognize ancient Greece as the originator of physical education.

Of course, the Greeks would never have used that term because their metaphysical understanding of persons was quite different from our own.[26] Most ancient Greeks conceived of the human being as a combination of *sōma* (body) and *psychē*, a word commonly translated as "soul" but also encompassing our modern ideas of life, mind, spirit, and emotion.[27] The *psychē* is conceived as the source not only of human thought and creativity but also of physical movement and, indeed, of life itself. In Homer, a *sōma* without a *psychē* is nothing more than a corpse.[28]

For Socrates, only the *psychē* can initiate motion.[29] So, intentional movement of the body originates in the *psychē*, and *gymnastikē*, the kind of training and exercises associated with the gymnasium, were understood as education of the whole person and not just the body. In Plato's *Republic*, Socrates goes so far as to say that *gymnastikē* serves the soul even more than the body, concluding that its purpose is to stretch and relax "the spirited and wisdom-loving parts of the soul itself, in order that these may be in harmony with one another."[30]

Socrates himself seems to have adapted the competitive spirit and methods associated with athletics to the explicitly educational purpose of cultivating *aretē*, which he identified with wisdom rather than Olympic victory. His preferred educational milieu was the gymnasium or *palaestra* (wrestling school),[31] probably because it was a good place to find the young men he liked to wrestle with—occasionally in the athletic sense, but more important, in the intellectual sense. Socrates spent so much time at the gymnasium that when his friend Euthyphro finds him at the court house in Plato's dialogue of the same name, one of the first things he asks is why the philosopher is not at his usual haunt: the Lyceum gymnasium.[32] Philosophers' presence in gymnasia goes back a century before Socrates to Pythagoras who is said to have recruited a young athlete to philosophy, first by paying him to study and then by eventually enticing him to pay for lessons.[33] But Socrates certainly was not after money; he took it as part of his service to the city of Athens and the god Apollo to win over the youth to philosophy—turning their natural and competitive love of victory (*philonikia*) into the love of wisdom (*philosophia*).[34]

There was in Socrates's time no public higher education for the young men of Athens. Instead, wealthy families would hire "wise men" called sophists to educate their sons privately in the skills they would need to be successful as free men—skills such as rhetoric and effective argument. Competition among the sophists was predictably fierce. They would attract clients by giving erudite lectures, answering questions on any subject, and sometimes debating one another. Eventually a kind of verbal contest called *eristic* emerged in which a questioner would try to force his opponents to contradict themselves. Publicly observed victory in *eristic* was no doubt good for a sophist's pedagogical business and, even though Socrates denied being a sophist (or a teacher at all) based on the fact that he never collected fees, Plato depicts him in several dialogues challenging and defeating even famous sophists at their own game.[35]

Such defeats, no doubt, were bad for the sophists' business and were probably at least part of the motivation for putting Socrates on trial in 399 BCE. Socrates defends himself by arguing that he is making these wise men and all Athenians better by showing them that they don't know as much as they thought they did; after all, he says, it is better to be as he is and not believe oneself to be wise when one is not.[36] He argues that what he deserves from the city as recompense for his service is the reward given to Olympic victors, because "the Olympian victor makes you think yourself happy; I make you happy."[37] This criticism of the civic rewards afforded athletes recalls the earlier philosopher Xenophanes, who said, "It is not right to prefer strength to my good wisdom" because victorious athletes do not "fatten the storerooms of the city."[38] But Socrates's point is not that philosophy will bring the city wealth or even prestige; on the contrary, he exhorts Athenians to be ashamed of caring for such things instead of *aretē*, "the best possible state of one's soul."[39]

So, Socrates's competitive defeat and shaming of the sophists are aimed at exposing their ignorance, thereby seducing them and, more important, their would-be students to the study of philosophy. A philosophical education with Socrates still involves competitive argument, and even some mild forms of shaming, to reveal false conceit. But Socrates regards this intellectual wrestling as a kind of friendship—a cooperative contest in which one opponent's challenge improves the other opponent's strength. This is the very attitude toward competition espoused by enlightened athletes, who use sport as a means not just to win contests, prestige, or even prizes but also to make themselves better persons through the experience.[40] As Socrates tells his interlocutor Protarchus, "We are not contending here out of love of victory for my suggestion to win or yours. We ought to act together as allies in support of the truest one."[41]

By improving the participants' mutual understanding of virtues such as piety, courage, or self-control, Socratic conversations help to cultivate *aretē*. Achieving the wisdom characteristic of *aretē* is a struggle (*agōn*), and so gymnasium conversations modeled on athletic contests (*agōnes*) must have seemed like a good way to accomplish it.

THE ACADEMIC GYMNASIUM

When we look back today at what Socrates was doing, we might say he was bringing academics into sport or maybe adapting athletic methods to academic uses, but we would deny that his methods are "physical education." In stating that, however, we might forget that the very word "academics" derives precisely from one of Socrates's favorite gymnasiums: the Academy on the outskirts of Athens where Socrates's student Plato set up his famous school.

It is important when we imagine ancient gymnasia that we don't think of buildings with grandstands and basketball courts. Ancient gymnasia were more like modern parks: open-air spaces with easy access to water and room for running, wrestling, and other sports. Sometimes they included covered colonnades to protect athletes from the sun and rain. They might also have had facilities for undressing and oiling the skin, as well as storage rooms and bathing facilities. Besides the tradition started by Pythagoras and Socrates of philosophers plying their trade in gymnasia, Plato may have set up his school in one because he thought *gymnastikē*—exercises such as running, jumping, and wrestling—were just as important a part of education as philosophical debate. In fact, Plato seems to have embraced the customary gymnasium values of military preparedness, athletic beauty, and even erotic partnerships—but with a twist. Plato tries to redirect these traditions away from the body and world, toward the soul and abstract ideals.[42]

There are scholars who explain the entirety of Greek gymnastics and athletics in terms of military preparedness and simulated battle. This is part of the story, but far too restrictive. As an admirer of the gymnastic education in Sparta—a state almost completely devoted to military excellence—Plato clearly understood that many benefits of athletic training were useful in war. He recognized the value not just of physical qualities such as strength but also of moral virtues such as courage. In fact, in Plato's dialogue "Laches," two generals debate appropriate training for soldiers and discover that Socrates's philosophical *aretē*—as evidenced by his performance in the Peloponnesian War—trumps training in armor or even military experience.[43] Socrates's military valor turns out to be nothing more than a kind of wisdom—as do all of the other virtues explored in Plato's dialogues. So Plato's gymnasium would not eliminate military or physical exercises, but it would look for a way to put them ultimately in the service of wisdom and, therefore, *aretē*.

In Plato's *Republic*, this is precisely the function that athletic training and contests serve. They are used to educate and to select the kind of people who will have the self-discipline, psychological endurance, and civic dedication to serve the community as guardians and eventually philosopher-kings (and queens).[44] Plato thought that the same virtues that lead to success in athletics—for example, courage, endurance, and indifference to wealth and fame—also lead to success in philosophy, because the road toward wisdom and virtue is "long and steep." Athletes who train for superficial goals, such as a beautiful appearance, gathering admirers, or even winning fame and riches in the games, are effectively letting their souls go to waste. In Plato's later political dialogue, *Laws*, only education aimed at *aretē* is taken to be worthy of the name. "A training directed to acquiring money or a robust physique, or even to some intellectual facility not guided by reason and justice, we should want to call coarse and illiberal, and say that it had no claim whatever to be called education."[45] It is not the means so much as the ends that distinguish Plato's virtue-based gymnastics from the more superficially aimed activities typically called "physical education."

Another decidedly nontraditional thing to be found in Plato's gymnasium is the presence of females. In both *Republic* and *Laws*, girls and women take part in gymnastic training and athletic games as well as more robust forms of citizenship than were current at the time.[46] Reports show that Plato's real-life Academy had at least two female students: Axiothea of Philius and Lasthenia of Mantinea.[47] In fact, ancient Greece has a long tradition of athletic women, including the mythological heroine Atalanta, who refused to marry any suitor unable to beat her in a footrace. We have early evidence of running rituals for girls, and Sparta had an organized program of gymnastic education for them—gymnastic even in the sense that they exercised nude.[48] It is possible that Plato's inclusion of women in his gymnasium was inspired by these traditions, but the metaphysical rationale is the same as for all of his other educational innovations: a focus on the soul, which he views as sexually neutral.[49]

Aretē, as excellence of the soul, was the same for men and women in Plato's view and could be trained through athletic activity.

ARISTOTELIAN ATHLETES

Plato's most famous student, Aristotle, also set up his school in a gymnasium, though no report indicates whether the Lyceum admitted women. A close look at the relationship between sport and Aristotle's idea of education for virtue, however, suggests that gymnastic training might be ideal for males and females alike. Like Plato, Aristotle divides the soul into rational and nonrational parts. It is the nonrational parts that convert rational commands into behavior, and Aristotle therefore assigns them different particular virtues—and different types of training—than the rational parts. Specifically, he thinks the lower parts of the soul are educated through training: habituation into the proper state (*hexis*) by repeated intentional action. As he says in *Nicomachean Ethics*, "Virtue of character (*ēthos*) results from habit (*ethos*); hence its name 'ethical,' slightly varied from 'ethos.'"[50] Aristotle then points to training for athletic contests as an example of *ethos*,[51] though he doesn't prescribe *gymnastikē* as a form of moral training as Plato does. His understanding of *aretē* as a *hexis* achieved by training—a sort of moral fitness—does suggest that gymnastic contests in *philoponia* (love of effort) and *euexia* (good condition) may have been judged on the state of the students' souls and not just their bodies.[52]

Aristotle is very explicit that *aretē*—not unlike fitness—must be expressed in activity.[53] This cuts the last thread holding the aristocratic understanding of *aretē* as a passively inherited state that need not be tested or proven. He uses an athletic example to reinforce his point: "Just as the Olympic prizes are not for the finest and strongest, but for the contestants—since it is only these who win—the same is true in life; among the fine and good people, only those who act correctly win the prize."[54] On the other hand, Aristotle thinks that too much athletic activity is harmful—especially for the youth. He chides "the city-states that are thought to be most concerned with children [but] turn them into athletes, and thus distort the shape and development of their bodies" and accuses Sparta of "brutalizing" their youth by subjecting them to rigorous exertion "without training in what is necessary."[55]

"What is necessary" seems to be mostly an ability to discern noble (*kalon*) ends and to determine the "golden mean"—the midpoint between excess and deficiency—when aiming to perform a virtuous action.[56] At first glance, and in light of Aristotle's criticisms of those who subject children to excessive training, athletics would not seem to be the kind of activity associated with nobility and moderation.[57] But the lesson of avoiding excess and deficiency is one often learned in sport, where performance suffers both from under- and overtraining. Aristotle uses the athletic examples of proper diet and archery (or perhaps javelin throwing) to illustrate the need for balance and aim.[58] In fact, Aristotle regards athletic training as a particularly well-developed science, which requires the same sort of apprehension of noble ends and deliberation about proper means such as medicine and ethics.[59] Although he does not discuss it at length, athletic training is consistent in many ways with the underlying principles of Aristotle's ethics.

What is likely is that athletics, as practiced in Aristotle's fourth century BCE Athens, was characterized more by blind excess and pursuit of such ignoble ends as wealth and fame, rather than the training for virtue valued by Aristotle, Plato, and their prime inspiration, Socrates. Most modern sport philosophers and physical educators would make similar criticisms of sport and its role in education today. But just because sport often fails to live up to its potential as education for virtue does not mean that striving to understand and appreciate that potential is a waste of time. What is more, our contemporary separation of academics and athletics—a result of the modern segregation of body and mind, discussed in chapter 7—deserves to be revisited considering the close connections between philosophy and athletics in the golden age of Greece.

By the same token, the ancient Olympic discovery of sport's potential to challenge social hierarchies is likewise worth remembering as we continue to struggle with issues of privilege, class, race, and gender. The ancient Greek heritage reveals a genuine link between athletics and philosophy, especially ethics and moral education. It also provides an inspiring example of sport's educational and political potential today—as long as its connection with philosophy is preserved.

DISCUSSION QUESTIONS

1. In ancient times, athleticism was used to demonstrate rulers' worthiness to lead. Is athletics relevant to leadership in the modern world?
2. The religious context of the ancient Olympic Games inspired a truth-seeking attitude toward sport that emphasized impartial judging and accuracy of results. What would be the effect of a more religious approach to modern sport?
3. Ancient sport is said to have inspired democracy in part by revealing the worth of people from lower classes. Does sport today provide a similar opportunity for poor people to show their worth, or does it tend to favor the wealthy?

4. Plato promoted athletics for females because he viewed athletics as a form of moral education. What would he say about female participation in school sports today and equal opportunity laws such as the United States' Title IX?
5. Aristotle's ethics emphasizes activity and training. Do you think training for sports can also be a kind of moral education?

NOTES

1. Pindar, "Pythian 8," in *Olympian Odes, Pythian Odes*, trans. William H. Race (Cambridge, MA: Harvard University Press, 1997), 95–97.

2. Pindar, "Olympian 8," in *The Complete Odes*, trans. Anthony Verity (Oxford: Oxford University Press, 2007), 1.

3. For a full comparison, see Heather L. Reid, "Athletic Heroes," *Ethics and Philosophy* 4, no. 2 (2010): 125–35. Reprinted in *Athletics and Philosophy in the Ancient World: Contests of Virtue* (London: Routledge, 2011), chap. 1.

4. On the link between *athla* and *athletics*, see Heather L. Reid, "Heroic *Mimēsis* and the Ancient Greek Athletic Spirit," *CHS Research Bulletin* 7 (2019). Published online at http://nrs.harvard.edu/urn-3:hlnc.essay:ReidH.Heroic_Mimesis_and_the_Ancient_Greek_Athletic_Spirit.2019.

5. Gregory Nagy, *The Ancient Greek Hero in 24 Hours* (Cambridge, MA: Harvard University Press, 2013), 8§43; Heather L. Reid, "Performing Virtue: Athletic *Mimēsis* in Platonic Education," *Politics and Performance in Western Greece*, ed. Heather L. Reid, Davide Tanasi, and Susi Kimbell (Sioux City: Parnassos Press, 2017), 265–77, argues that athletes' *mimēsis* is more precisely of the heroes' *aretē*.

6. On the link between athletics and hero cult, see Nagy, *"Ancient Greek Hero,"* 7A§4–7, and Sarah C. Murray, "The Role of Religion in Greek Sport," in *A Companion to Sport and Spectacle in Greek and Roman Antiquity*, ed. Paul Christesen and Donald Kyle (Malden, MA: Wiley-Blackwell, 2014), 309–19. For a detailed argument, see Heather L. Reid, "The Ecstasy of *Aretē:* Flow as Self-Transcendence in Ancient Athletics," *Studies in Sport Humanities* 15 (2014): 6–12, reprinted in *Olympic Philosophy*, 147–60.

7. See Reid, "Athletic Heroes," especially 12–15.

8. According to Ben Brown, "The crisis of social value in the *Iliad* is a crisis within the pre-monetary economy of peer relations. The *Iliad* focuses upon a society composed of many *basileis*, great warriors who find themselves outside of the comfortable hierarchies of home. This world of warrior peers—*homoioi*—is by no means stable. The relations of equality and the claim to deserve recognition must be founded on each man's daily concern for his own time, the complex of his social worth." Ben Brown, "Homer, Funeral Contests and the Origins of the Greek City," in *Sport and Festival in the Ancient Greek World*, ed. David J. Phillips and David Pritchard (Swansea: Classical Press of Wales, 2003), 129.

9. The Greek phrase *aien aristeuein kai upeirochon emmenai allōn* is said twice, at *Iliad* 6.208 and 11.784.

10. For a full exploration of this thesis, see Heather L. Reid, "Sport, Philosophy, and the Quest for Knowledge," *Journal of the Philosophy of Sport* 36, no. 1 (2009): 40–49.

11. Aristotle, "Metaphysics," in *Complete Works*, ed. Jonathan Barnes (Princeton, NJ: Princeton University Press, 1984), 1.2, 982b12–21: "Whoever is puzzled and in a state of wonder believes he is ignorant (this is why the lover of myths is also in a way a philosopher, since myths are made up of wonders). And so, if indeed they pursued philosophy to escape ignorance, they were obviously pursuing scientific knowledge in order to know and not for the sake of any practical need."

12. For more on the "economics" of ancient Greek religion, see J. Mikalson, *Ancient Greek Religion* (Malden, MA: Blackwell, 2005), 25.

13. Philostratos, "Gymnastics," in Stephen G. Miller, *Arete: Greek Sports from Ancient Sources* 38 (Berkeley: University of California Press, 1991). For a detailed analysis of the passage, see Panos Valavanis, "Thoughts on the Historical Origins of the Olympic Games and the Cult of Pelops in Olympia," *Nikephoros* 19 (2006): 141.

14. For more on the connection between athletic victors and religious sacrifice, see Walter Burkert, *Greek Religion*, trans. John Raffan (Cambridge, MA: Harvard University Press, 1985), 56; and David Sansone, *Greek Athletics and the Genesis of Sport* (Berkeley: University of California Press, 1988).

15. In *Metaphysics* (1000a9–20), Aristotle distinguishes philosophers from theologians by saying that the former offer argument (*apodeixis*) to support their views, whereas the latter offer only stories or speak *mythikōs*.

16. For a full account of these arguments, see Heather L. Reid, "Olympic Sport and Its Lessons for Peace," *Journal of the Philosophy of Sport* 33, no. 2 (2006): 205–13.

17. Pausanias, *Description of Greece*, trans. Peter Levi, 2 vols. (New York: Penguin, 1979), 1:5.21.2–4.

18. See, for example, Stephen G. Miller, "Naked Democracy," in *Polis and Politics*, ed. P. Flensted-Jensen and T. H. Nielsen (Copenhagen: Festschrift, 2000), 277–96.

19. Nigel James Nicholson, *Aristocracy and Athletics in Archaic and Classical Greece* (Cambridge, UK: Cambridge University Press, 2005), 134.

20. The social class of Olympic victors is a matter of controversy among historians. For a full discussion of the debate, see David Young, *The Olympic Myth of Greek Amateur Athletics* (Chicago: Ares, 1984); and Mark Golden, *Greek Sport and Social Status* (Austin: University of Texas Press, 2008).

21. Aristotle, "Rhetoric," in *Complete Works*, 1.1364a20, 1367b18.

22. The story is told, in slightly different versions, by Thucydides, *History of the Peloponnesian War*, trans. B. Jowett (Oxford, UK: Clarendon, 1900), 6.56–59; and Aristotle, *The Athenian Constitution*, trans. Sir Frederic G. Kenyon (Washington, DC: Merchant Books, 2009), 18.

23. Miller says, "This equality before absolute standards of distance and speed and strength—as measured by those of the other competitors present—that are subject to the interpretation of no man is basic *isonomia*" ("Naked Democracy," 279).

24. Herodotus, *Histories*, trans. A. D. Godley (Cambridge, MA: Harvard University Press, 1920), 3.80–82.

25. Ian Morris, "Equality and the Origins of Greek Democracy," in *Ancient Greek Democracy*, ed. Eric W. Robinson (Malden, MA: Blackwell, 2004), 63.

26. The term "physical education" is often used by modern translators to render the Greek term *gymnastikē*, which does refer to training exercises not unlike what we now call physical education, but the Greek term does not imply that it is the body rather than the soul, or more accurately, the whole person, that is being educated.

27. See, for example, Aristotle, "De Anima," in *Complete Works*, 415b.

28. For an excellent discussion of these terms and ideas, see Bruno Snell, *The Discovery of the Mind in Greek Philosophy and Literature* (New York: Dover, 1982), 8–22.

29. Plato, *Phaedrus*, 245e.

30. Plato, *Republic*, trans. G. M. A. Grube (Indianapolis: Hackett, 1992), 410b–11e.

31. Plato sets *Charmides* in the Palaestra of Taureas (153b), in *Euthydemus* we find Socrates with *pankratists* at the Lyceum, and in *Lysis* Socrates is on his way from one gymnasium (the Academy) to another (the Lyceum) when he is pulled aside into a new wrestling school (203–4a). *Theaetetus* is also set in a gymnasium, as indicated by Theaetetus and his friends oiling themselves down before the conversation (144c), and it is likely that *Sophist* and *Politicus* share the same setting—although it's not obvious from the text.

32. Plato, "Euthyphro," in *Complete Works*, ed. John M. Cooper (Indianapolis: Hackett, 1997), 2a. This is the same Lyceum that would become the site of Aristotle's school, but as of the dramatic time (and probably when the dialogue was written), it was simply a gymnasium.

33. Iamblichus, *The Pythagorean Life*, trans. Thomas Taylor (London: Watkins, 1818), 6–7.

34. For a detailed account, see Heather L. Reid, "Wrestling with Socrates," *Sport, Ethics and Philosophy* 4, no. 2 (2010): 157–69. Reprinted in *Athletics and Philosophy in the Ancient World: Contests of Virtue* (London: Routledge, 2011), chap. 4.

35. Plato, *Apology*, trans. G. M. A. Grube (Indianapolis: Hackett, 1980), 19d. See especially, *Protagoras*, *Euthydemus*, and *Gorgias*.

36. Plato, *Apology*, 22d–23b.

37. Plato, *Apology*, 36de.

38. Xenophanes, quoted in Athenaeus, "The Deipnosophists," in *The Smell of Sweat: Greek Athletics, Olympics, and Culture*, ed. W. B. Tyrrell (Wauconda, IL: Bolchazy-Carducci, 2004), 413c–f.

39. Plato, *Apology*, 30b.

40. This understanding of sport is explained by Drew A. Hyland in "Competition and Friendship," *Journal of the Philosophy of Sport* 5 (1978): 27–37.

41. Plato, "Philebus," in *Complete Works*, 14b.

42. For more details, see Heather L. Reid, "Plato's Gymnasium," *Sport, Ethics and Philosophy* 4, no. 2 (2010): 170–82. Reprinted in *Athletics and Philosophy*, chap. 5.

43. Plato, "Laches," in *Complete Works*, 181b.

44. This is the central argument in Heather L. Reid, "Sport and Moral Education in Plato's *Republic*," *Journal of the Philosophy of Sport* 34, no. 2 (2007): 160–75.

45. Plato, *Laws*, trans. Trevor Saunders (London: Penguin, 1970), 643e.

46. For an analysis, see Heather L. Reid, "Plato on Women in Sport," *Journal of the Philosophy of Sport* 47, no. 3 (2020): 344–61.

47. Diogenes Laertius, *Lives of Eminent Philosophers*, vol. 1, trans. R. D. Hicks (Cambridge, MA: Harvard University Press, 1972), 3.46.

48. For more on Sparta's educational programs, see Nigel M. Kennell, *The Gymnasium of Virtue: Education and Culture in Ancient Sparta* (Chapel Hill: University of North Carolina Press, 1995).

49. For a full analysis, see Nicholas D. Smith, "Plato and Aristotle on the Nature of Women," *Journal of the History of Philosophy* 21, no. 4 (1983): 467–78.

50. Aristotle, *Nicomachean Ethics*, 2nd ed., trans. Terence Irwin (Indianapolis: Hackett, 1999), 1103a17–18.

51. Aristotle, *Nicomachean Ethics*, 1114a8–10.

52. For an overview of the evidence, see Nigel B. Crowther, "*Euexia, Eutaxia, Philoponia*: Three Contests of the Greek Gymnasium," *Zeitschrift für Papyrologie und Epigraphik*, Bd. 85 (1991): 301–4.

53. Aristotle, *Nicomachean Ethics*, 1120a16–17.

54. Aristotle, *Nicomachean Ethics*, 1099a3–6.

55. Aristotle, *Politics*, trans. C. D. C. Reeve (Indianapolis: Hackett, 1998), 1138b–39b.

56. Aristotle, *Nicomachean Ethics*, 1106a27–34.

57. This perhaps is why David Young says Aristotle sees physical and mental training as enemies of one another in "Mens Sana in Corpore Sano? Body and Mind in Greek Literature," *Proceedings of the North American Society for Sport History* (1998): 61. Moderate physical activity, however, is not derided as contrary to intellectual development.

58. Aristotle, *Nicomachean Ethics*, 1106b.

59. Aristotle, *Nicomachean Ethics*, 1112b. For a more detailed account of Aristotle's view on sport, see Heather L. Reid, "Aristotle's Pentathlete," *Sport, Ethics and Philosophy* 4, no. 2 (2010): 183–94.

Chapter 2

The Modern Olympic Revival

The ancient Greek connection between sport and philosophy emerged again in modern times with the nineteenth-century revival of the Olympic Games. The award-winning movie *Chariots of Fire* offers a glimpse of sport in this period and shows both how much and how little it had changed since ancient times. The story revolves around two British sprinters, a Jew named Harold Abrahams and a Christian named Eric Liddell, both of whom face challenges derived from issues of class and diversity. Abrahams, a Cambridge University student, employs a professional coach to improve his technique. This is considered unethical by the college dons because it runs contrary to the ethos of the gentleman amateur who should rely on his natural athletic gifts and not take sport too seriously. Eric Liddell, meanwhile, finds himself torn between a very strong commitment to his faith and the practical demands of his sport. When the Olympic final for his best event turns out to be on the Sabbath, he chooses not to run, despite a personal appeal to his patriotism by the Prince of Wales. In the end, Abrahams wins his event, foreshadowing the demise of amateurism. And Liddell, buoyed partly by a note of support from American competitor Jackson Scholz, gains an unexpected victory in his weaker event, the 400 meters—sweet reward for his unwavering dedication to his faith.

On the one hand, these scenes seem very far removed from the Olympic Games of ancient Greece; the equipment, venues, even the contests themselves are different. On the other, we can recognize issues such as religious dedication, aristocratic entitlement, transcendence of social class, and competitive encouragement familiar from our study of ancient Greek sport in chapter 1. Historian Allen Guttman lists the key differences between ancient and modern sport as secularism, equality, specialization, rationalization, bureaucratization, quantification, and a focus on records.[1]

We will return to these principles when we discuss the nature of sport. But what of sport's close association with philosophy? What about its role in education? In fact, sport did find its way into schools and universities in Great Britain, Canada, and the United States in the modern era. Philosophy had its place in the curriculum as well, but it was now kept separate from sport. College athletics came to be regarded as something detached from academics, and philosophers generally shunned sport as a subject unworthy of serious inquiry. It would not be until the 1970s that the philosophical study of sport was recognized as a legitimate academic field.

I think it is fair to claim, nevertheless, that the ancient link between philosophy and sport born in ancient Greece was "revived" with the founding of the modern Olympic Games in 1896—an event that shaped the values and governance of sport as we know it today. Indeed, the modern Olympic Games may represent the first time in history that a sporting event was self-consciously driven by philosophy. The Games' primary founder, Pierre de Coubertin, and his colleagues were interested not only in promoting a sporting event but also in promulgating a set of philosophical ideals that they thought would improve the world. Drawing on ideas from ancient Greece, as well as the contemporary European Enlightenment and British pedagogical thought, Coubertin coined the term "Olympism" to describe this philosophy.

Coubertin was not a professional philosopher, and Olympism, arguably, is not a philosophical system, but it does present definite philosophical guidelines for the practice of sport. What is more, these guidelines have endured despite the more than one-hundred-year history of the modern festival and its unprecedented global reach—almost every sport practiced today has a governing body within the Olympic Movement. Modern Olympism's continued appeal is testament, I believe, to the profound link between sport and philosophy discovered in ancient Greece.

An interesting question arises from the study of Olympism as a philosophy of sport—or perhaps from the study of the Olympic Games as a manifestation of that philosophy: what does it mean in practice to adopt a philosophy of sport, and, more specifically, how can a movement spanning so many different epochs and cultures be guided by a single philosophy? Philosophies, like sports, are generally thought to be the products of particular cultures, epochs, and even particular lives. We speak of Confucianism or Kantianism, referring to specific people. Even philosophies with more general names, such as Daoism or utilitarianism, are easily linked with a particular time, place, and thinker or group of thinkers. Olympism, in a way, is linked with the time and place of the ancient Olympic Games—but it is not an effort to impose ancient Greek culture and values on the modern world. Rather, it is an attempt at a universal philosophy based on values common to everyone in the world and expressed in their practice of sport. In the same way that people all over the world can play the game of soccer, people all over world are supposed to be able to embrace Olympism. Is it possible for sport to generate a universal philosophy?

OLYMPISM AS A PHILOSOPHY

First, we must ask whether *philosophy* itself can be universal, and before we can answer that question, we have to ask what is meant by the term. The primary tenet of Olympism, which can be traced to Pierre de Coubertin,[2] clearly presents itself in philosophical terms: "Olympism is a philosophy of life, exalting and combining in a balanced whole the qualities of body, will and mind. Blending sport with culture and education, Olympism seeks to create a way of life based on the joy of effort, the educational value of good example and respect for universal fundamental ethical principles."[3]

Self-declaration does not make something a philosophy in the strict academic sense, and Olympism can be criticized for its lack of systematic propositions.[4] Philosophy—at least in the context of the European Enlightenment familiar to the Olympic founders—should involve a series of clear propositions established through reason and knowledge.

Coubertin's countryman René Descartes is a good example of this conception of philosophy. Descartes developed a philosophical method based on rejecting all previous traditions or opinions and then reconstructing knowledge by solely rational means from the cornerstone of one logically irrefutable truth.[5] This understanding of philosophy would have appealed to the Olympic founders' interest in internationalism because it took itself to be culturally transcendent. Descartes regarded himself as a "citizen of the world"[6] and believed the power of reason was "naturally equal in all men."[7] According to this way of thinking, philosophical propositions based on reason demonstrated through logic are universally valid and applicable across cultures. The problem, however, is that not all cultures and systems of thought regard such clear propositions to be philosophy's goal. The Chinese classic *Daodejing*, for example, seeks to understand the "Way" (*Dao*) but asserts at the beginning that this understanding cannot be explained or even "named."[8]

It seems fair to say that modern Olympic leaders did not have Daoism in mind when they drafted the "Fundamental Principles of Olympism," but it would not be fair to deny that Daoism is indeed a philosophy. After all, Olympism defines its goal as creating a certain "way of life" right after it declares itself to be a philosophy. Indeed, if we define philosophy according to its ancient Greek meaning as the love (*philia*) of wisdom (*sophia*), or characterize it as a disposition for learning and contemplation following Pythagoras (who is said to have coined the word),[9] our understanding becomes compatible not only with European rationalism but also with Chinese Daoism and, most important, with a flexible interpretation of Olympism itself.[10] Olympism may be criticized for changing over time, but other forms of philosophy (i.e., process philosophy) are continual negotiations.[11] Olympism might be eclectic, but eclecticism is itself a nineteenth-century European philosophy that seeks to consolidate and conciliate diverse systems. Olympism need not be the same kind of philosophy as rationalism or empiricism in order to be a philosophy.

In fact, the qualities that make Olympism seem weak when tested against some strict definitions of philosophy can explain the strength and endurance of the Games on a global scale. One of these paradoxical strengths comes from the lack of a detailed and definitive text—no book in any language spells out Olympic philosophy at length.[12] If Olympism can be said to have a text, it would be the *Olympic Charter*, or more specifically, the page in the *Olympic Charter* that lists the "Fundamental Principles of Olympism," only the first of which (quoted above) can be said to be specifically philosophical. Olympism's principles are sometimes vague and always open to multiple interpretations. Nevertheless, one can discern within Olympism elements of philosophy's traditional branches of metaphysics, ethics, and politics. Each of these branches is discussed more fully in subsequent sections of this book, but a brief discussion of Olympism in terms of them will help us to see the relationship between philosophy and sport.

OLYMPISM AND METAPHYSICS

Metaphysics is the branch of philosophy that examines the fundamental nature of things. What are Olympism's metaphysics? Within the description of Olympism as a philosophy that exalts and combines "in a balanced whole, the qualities of body, will and mind," we recognize a humanistic viewpoint that posits an idealized metaphysics of mankind. It is this aspect that motivated professional philosopher and Olympic gold medalist Hans Lenk to interpret Olympism as a philosophical anthropology (i.e., a philosophy concerned with the nature and status of humanity).[13] The lack of any clear definition of just what this ideal Olympic human being would be, however, might seem to keep the philosophical anthropology of Olympism from having much normative force (i.e., the ability to bind a person morally to that ideal). How can we use the ideal Olympian as an ethical guide when it is unclear what the ideal Olympian is?

Coubertin, no doubt, was inspired by the Hellenic idea of *aretē* and the images of heroism to be found in ancient Greek poetry and mythology—images like that of Heracles, Achilles, and Odysseus. But any attempt to draw a portrait or even point to an example of the ideal Olympian would run up against the immense diversity of individuals who have exemplified the Olympic ideal over the history of the modern Games. Coubertin's ideal was probably a strapping European male, but tiny female gymnasts and lanky

African marathoners have come to exemplify the ideal, as have lithe male figure skaters and husky female shot-putters. The point here is that the *lack* of a strict definition has allowed for a variety of interpretations of the ideal without leaving it devoid of meaning. In a similar way, the simple definition of a goal in soccer can accommodate a variety of playing styles and strategies without sacrificing the notion of excellence.

The language of a balanced "body, will, and mind," on the other hand, seems to evoke a specifically Western metaphysics of mankind derived from medieval Christian philosophy and the Muscular Christianity of Victorian England. In fact, the "ancient Greek" adage of a "sound mind in sound body" only makes sense as a tenet of Olympism when reinterpreted through the eyes of modern British pedagogical thought—where it appears as the slogan on a gymnasium in Henry Fielding's popular novel *The History of Tom Jones*. The Latin saying *mens sana in corpore sano* came from the Roman satirist Juvenal, who was talking about prayer—it originally had nothing to do with sports or even exercise.[14] Olympism's ability to reinterpret Juvenal's words into a motto for a physically as well as mentally active lifestyle, however, stands as further evidence for the importance of philosophical flexibility. We can clearly affirm that Olympism is a philosophy that values humanity generally—after all, it identifies as a goal "the harmonious development of mankind"[15]—without definitively articulating the exact image of humanity it promotes.

Indeed, Olympism's failure to define its vision for humankind might have inspired its commitment to nondiscrimination. Among the current "Fundamental Principles of Olympism" is the following statement: "Any form of discrimination with regard to a country or a person on grounds of race, religion, politics, gender or otherwise is incompatible with belonging to the Olympic Movement."[16] This declaration flies in the face of modern Olympic Games history. Coubertin himself wished to bar females from the Games, and discrimination and exclusions of all kinds can be found throughout Olympic history. But philosophical ideals should not be derived from the practices of flawed human beings; rather, they should serve as a guide and inspiration to improve those practices over time. The ever-increasing diversity of athletes participating in the Olympic Games today reveals the power of a vague and sketchy philosophical ideal not only to accommodate a variety of interpretations but also to expand our collective conception of an ideal human being. If Olympism is to be a globally relevant philosophy, the ideal image of humanity it presents is best left vague enough to accommodate a variety of interpretations across cultures and over time.

OLYMPISM AND ETHICS

The next question to ask of Olympism as a philosophy is whether its soft metaphysics can support any kind of meaningful ethics. Ethics—the branch of philosophy concerned with right and wrong action—traditionally depends for its normative force on a clear metaphysics. For example, Immanuel Kant's metaphysical understanding of human beings as essentially ends in themselves leads him to assert that it is a moral imperative to always treat humanity, others as well as oneself, as ends and never merely as means to some end.[17] It may be charged that Olympism fails to present a philosophical anthropology or that the image of the ideal human it does present is too vague to have ethical force. But Kant's characterization of human beings as ends in themselves is likewise vague and open to interpretation. Olympism's promotion of an inclusive and holistic ideal of mankind that values harmony and balance as well as excellence is sufficient to support the kinds of ethical principles inscribed in the logic of sport—principles such as equality and fairness.

The first Fundamental Principle of Olympism demands "respect for universal fundamental ethical principles" without ever articulating what these principles are. Some would say that ethical principles are always the product of a particular culture, so there can no more be universal ethical principles than there can be a universal culture. Even very general moral guidelines such as the Golden Rule or Kant's categorical imperative (discussed in chapter 9) cannot capture the moral beliefs of every culture under the Olympic umbrella. There is something common to all members of the Olympic Movement, however—a sincere value for sport. Sport-related moral principles, such as equality of opportunity and reward according to merit, may therefore be considered universal within the Olympic community. These principles are manifest in the rules of sport. In the 100-meter dash, for example, runners must start from the same line at the same time (equality of opportunity), and the gold medal is awarded to the first athlete across the finish line in the final heat (reward according to merit).

It can be dangerous, however, for Olympism to try to codify these general moral principles into rules and regulations beyond sport. As the sad history of Olympic amateurism shows, some noble ideals quickly lose their moral force once they become written regulations. The ideal of the amateur is an athlete who competes for the love of the sport rather than any external reward—especially money. By defining amateurs in terms of income sources rather than motivation, however, the Olympic Movement promoted a culture of greedily "gaming the system" rather than valuing sport as something to be appreciated as an end in itself. Individual athletes and entire nations responded to amateur regulations by finding clever ways to pay athletes—for example, by giving them special government jobs. Athletes for whom sport was strictly an avocation found it difficult to compete in this environment. And soon the rule designed to *remove* the influence of money on Olympics put money at the center of athletes' and coaches' concerns.

Eastern philosophy could have predicted amateurism's demise. The *Daodejing* of Laozi warns that increasing prohibitions and rules only increases the commission of crimes, and Confucius observes that most people respond to legislation by thinking only about exemptions.[18] Although sports depend for their existence upon rules, Olympism's "universal ethical principles" are better left as general ideas than codified into a specific set of rules. This allows for universal agreement about the importance of ethics, and even about the value of general principles such as equality and fairness, without privileging the specific interpretation of any particular culture. The enduring debate about female participation from conservative Muslim countries (discussed further in chapter 15) illustrates the complexity of such issues. Olympism declares sport to be a human right and demands that it be practiced "without discrimination of any kind and in the Olympic spirit, which requires mutual understanding with a spirit of friendship, solidarity and fair play."[19] But does forcing a country such as Saudi Arabia to send a certain number of female participants to the Games show friendship and understanding?

Since the postmodern turn in twentieth-century philosophy, there has been a return to the ancient tradition of virtue ethics—a form of moral thought that focuses on persons rather than principles (as in Kantianism) or consequences (as in utilitarianism). A key benefit of virtue ethics for Olympism is that it has roots in both the ancient Greek tradition of Socrates, Plato, and Aristotle and the ancient Chinese tradition of Laozi and Confucius. It even plays an important role in contemporary feminist ethics of care. Perhaps more important, an ethical emphasis on virtue rather than legislation better reflects Olympic values, not least because it looks inward toward personal perfection, rather than outward toward the correction and control of others.[20] Virtue is understood as a kind of "moral force" that is contrasted favorably with physical (and especially violent) force. Virtue is conceived not as a social construction but as an innate disposition that is cultivated, like athletic talent, through intentional training and inspiring examples—a model that well reflects Olympism's professed promotion of the "educational value of good example."

Of course, specific conceptions and lists of virtues vary inevitably across history and cultures. Even though specific virtues typically demanded by Olympic sports—for example, courage and self-control—are universally valued, how these values are expressed might vary from culture to culture. Thus, there is more room for cross-cultural consensus on the question of virtue than may first appear.[21] Olympism may affirm that certain virtues are universal while allowing for different expressions of them within different activities. A judo player's courage in facing an opponent's charge is different, for example, from a gymnast's courage in facing the parallel bars—but they are both forms of courage, and they are valued in Eastern and Western sports alike. Virtue ethics—as we will see in chapter 10—can help Olympism to accommodate Western demands for philosophical rigor while respecting Eastern philosophy's (as well as postmodern philosophy's) skepticism about hard and fast rules.

OLYMPISM AND POLITICS

Finally, we must acknowledge Olympism's explicitly political dimension in addition to its metaphysics and ethics—despite the Olympic Movement's frequent attempts to dissociate itself from politics. International Olympic Committee (IOC) members swear an oath to keep themselves free of any political influence.[22] National Olympic committees are instructed to resist political pressure.[23] Political demonstrations are barred from Olympic sites or venues.[24] And part of the "Mission and Role of the IOC" is "to oppose any political or commercial abuse of sport and athletes."[25] Another part, however, is "to place sport at the service of humanity and thereby to promote peace."[26] Because it promotes a particular vision of community, this is an explicitly political goal—one that reflects the fundamental principles of Olympism's stated goal of "promoting a peaceful society concerned with the preservation of human dignity."[27] What is distinctive about Olympism's politics, not unlike its ethics, is its connection to sport. The IOC wants to use sport rather than conventional governmental means to achieve the political goal of peace.

This approach might be unusual, but I would not call it innovative. Indeed, I think it derives from the ancient Olympic Games, whose own association with peace seems not to have originated as a political decree but, rather, grown out of the unifying and pacifying effects of multicultural competition—specifically the ability to set aside differences, treat others as equals, and tolerate differences.[28] Of course, the ancient Olympic Games—in stark contrast to the modern festival—were initially open only to Greeks, more specifically free, male Greeks with enough wealth and leisure time to train and travel to competitions. But there were real cultural differences between the loosely organized collection of Greek tribes and city-states—the frequently cited contrast between Athens and Sparta is just one example. What is more, these tribes were constantly competing for resources and very often at war with one another.

What the Olympic festival did was to give them a religious reason to set aside their differences, declare a temporary truce (*ekecheiria*), and come together on neutral ground to worship a common deity. As we saw in chapter

1, the first footrace was staged at Olympia to select an honoree to light the sacrificial flame.[29] Obviously each tribe would have its own best candidate for the honor; I believe that the footrace functioned as a mutually acceptable way to make this selection without resorting to established social hierarchies or to violence. In order for the selection made by the footrace to be valid (and therefore pleasing to the all-knowing deity), each contestant needed to be given a fair chance—all needed to be treated as equals for the purpose of the race, no matter how much they hated each other outside the sanctuary. In addition, they had to tolerate their differences long enough to live and dine together for the duration of the festival. No doubt there was friendly sharing of songs, stories, food, and wine brought from back home, and it is likely that some of them came to value their differences. In this way, the Olympic Games taught ancient Hellenes a political lesson about peace, even though their original purpose was religious.

Because engaging in sport requires us to set aside conflict, treat others as equals under a common set of rules, and at least tolerate if not appreciate our differences, it lays the groundwork for peaceful coexistence. And because the modern Olympic Games do this on a global scale with the whole world looking on, they, too, can place sport in the service of peace—as the "fundamental principles of Olympism" declare. This political philosophy conflicts somewhat with tradition because it relies not on the authority of a civilizing force but, rather, on the need for cooperative decision making in the absence of a single authority.

Western philosophers such as Thomas Hobbes understand law as something imposed by an authority to overcome our uncivilized and violent natural state. Eastern thought tends to associate violence with law and authority and seeks peace by "going back" either to Confucianism's remote and idealized past or to Daoism's uncorrupted natural state. What is important for Olympism is not to promote peace through the force of authority, even the IOC's own authority but, rather, to focus on staging the Games and promoting sport for all, because sport functions as a vehicle for promoting peace precisely by gathering diverse groups together and treating them all as equals in an open, publicly observed forum.

Sport's metaphysical structure provides a better model for Olympism's political goals than does the Games' troubled history. Nationalistic abuse of the Olympic festival by host governments, competing nations, and even terrorist groups has interfered with the movement's larger political goal. The practice of boycotting the Olympic Games—which reached its peak in the 1980s with the Moscow and Los Angeles protests—hampers the Olympics' peace-promoting potential by preventing diverse athletes from interacting. The current practice of housing athletes outside the Olympic Village to avoid distractions that could harm performance has an analogous effect.

Other political uses of the Games, such as Tommie Smith and John Carlos's 1968 protest against civil rights abuses in the United States—captured in the famous image of the barefoot athletes raising gloved fists on the Olympic medals stand—can be interpreted as part and parcel of the Olympic promotion of peace. The United Nations now declares a modern Olympic truce, but its principles are widely violated, as when the United States hosted the Salt Lake Games while fomenting war in Iraq, or when Russia invaded Georgia nearly simultaneously with the opening ceremony of the Beijing Games.

Despite such frustrations, what Olympism demands is a nonviolent and nonauthoritarian philosophy of peace that rejects hegemony and embraces diverse interpretations. It demands Coubertin's notion of a sincere internationalism, which embraces cultural differences while seeking common ground, rather than the paradigm of hegemonic cosmopolitanism, which seeks to impose a single "superior" culture upon all.[30] The ideal is neatly captured in the contemporary concept of multiculturalism, but the political dimension of Olympism should perhaps allow even more interpretations than those limited to the discourse of nations. For example, the IOC has committed itself to the principle of global environmental sustainability—a commitment easily interpreted as an outgrowth of Olympism's peace-promoting philosophy.

The political philosophy of the Olympic Games depends on the "Olympic spirit" that the "fundamental principles of Olympism" define in terms of mutual understanding, friendship, solidarity, and fair play. These terms, like the rest of Olympism's language, must be open to translation in hundreds of languages and to interpretation across history and culture. Such flexibility and vagueness may disqualify Olympism from the status of a legitimate philosophy in the academic sense, but an enduring international phenomenon such as the Olympic Movement needs philosophical principles flexible enough to express common values that can be interpreted in different ways without losing their meaning. Just as Olympic athletes from diverse cultural backgrounds compete in a common arena, diverse understandings of Olympism can find common ground. Understanding Olympism as a philosophy, both derived from and expressed through sport, demands a multicultural approach. In this sense it can teach us something about the problem of philosophy—and its relation to sport—in the age of globalization. Olympism is not the only philosophy of sport to emerge in the modern era, however. Philosophical approaches to sport depend ultimately on metaphysics—what we think sport *is*. That is the question we will discuss in the next section.

DISCUSSION QUESTIONS

1. It has been charged that Olympism is not really a philosophy because it does not have systematic propositions and it offers only a short and vague written text. Do you think Olympism should be developed into a more traditional philosophy, or do you think it works well as it is?
2. Olympism is said to promote a particular human ideal. Try naming some people who reflect that ideal. Do they have to be of a certain race, sex, or ethnicity? What do they have in common?
3. Olympism suggests that sport promotes "universal fundamental ethical principles"; a common example is fairness. Can you think of another fundamental ethical principle that is universal (i.e., common across cultures)? Can you think of an ethical principle that is specific to certain cultures and does not cross over?
4. Olympism's political goal is to promote peace, partly by bringing diverse athletes together in an atmosphere of friendship. Do you think this atmosphere is expressed in today's Olympic Games? Are there aspects of the Olympic Games that work against the goal of peace?

NOTES

1. Allen Guttmann, *From Ritual to Record: The Nature of Modern Sports* (New York: Columbia University Press, 1978).

2. Though Coubertin is certainly the origin of the philosophy, the specific authors of the "Fundamental Principles of Olympism" that appear in the *Olympic Charter* are not clear. According to Olympic scholar Rafael Mendoza, the conversation about these principles started in the late 1970s and evolved in response to such challenges as doping, Olympic boycotts, and actions against the spirit of amateurism. In the 1991 *Olympic Charter*, Olympism is officially presented as the philosophy that guides the Olympic Movement.

3. International Olympic Committee, "Fundamental Principles of Olympism," in *The Olympic Charter* (Lausanne, Switzerland: Author, 2010), 11.

4. For a full discussion of Olympism's legitimacy as a philosophy, see Lamartine DaCosta, "A Never-Ending Story: The Philosophical Controversy over Olympism," *Journal of the Philosophy of Sport* 33, no. 2 (2006): 157–73.

5. For a full account, see René Descartes, "Discourse on Method," in *The Philosophical Writings of Descartes*, ed. J. Cottingham, R. Stoothoff, and D. Murdoch (Cambridge, UK: Cambridge University Press, 1985), 1:111–51.

6. In at least one of his early writings, Descartes used the pseudonym "Polybius, citizen of the world." René Descartes, "Preliminaries," in *Philosophical Writings of Descartes*, 1:2n1.

7. Descartes, "Discourse on Method," 111.

8. Lao-Tzu, *Tao Te Ching*, trans. S. Addiss and S. Lombardo (Indianapolis: Hackett, 2003), 1.1.

9. The story is related in Marcus Tullius Cicero, *Tusculan Disputations*, trans. J. King (Cambridge, MA: Loeb, 1927), 5.8s.

10. For a more detailed account of Olympism's relationship to Eastern and Western philosophy, see Heather L. Reid, "East to Olympia: Recentering Olympic Philosophy between East and West," *Olympika: The International Journal of Olympic Studies* 19 (2010): 59–79.

11. DaCosta, "A Never-Ending Story," 166.

112. There is, however, a collection of essays by Pierre de Coubertin titled *Olympism: Selected Writings*, ed. Norbert Müller (Lausanne, Switzerland: International Olympic Committee, 2000); a collection of philosophical essays about the Olympic Games: Heather L. Reid and Mike W. Austin, eds. *The Olympics and Philosophy* (Lexington: University Press of Kentucky, 2012); and most recently, Heather L. Reid, *Olympic Philosophy: The Ideas and Ideals behind the Ancient and Modern Olympic Games* (Sioux City: Parnassos Press, 2020).

13. Hans Lenk, "Towards a Philosophical Anthropology of the Olympic Athletes and the Achieving Being," in *International Olympic Academy Report* (Ancient Olympia, Greece: 1982), 163–77.

14. David C. Young, "*Mens Sana in Corpore Sano?* Body and Mind in Greek Literature," *Proceedings of the North American Society for Sport History* (1998): 60–61.

15. International Olympic Committee, "Fundamental Principles," 11.

16. International Olympic Committee, "Fundamental Principles," 11.

17. Immanuel Kant, *Groundwork for the Metaphysic of Morals*, trans. H. J. Paton (New York: Harper and Row, 1948), 96.

18. Lao-Tzu, *Tao Te Ching*, 57; Confucius, *Analects*, trans. E. Slingerland (Indianapolis: Hackett, 2003), 4.11.

19. International Olympic Committee, "Fundamental Principles," 11.

20. For a comparison of Eastern and Western conceptions of virtue applied to sport, see Heather L. Reid, "Athletic Virtue: Between East and West," *Sport Ethics and Philosophy* 4, no. 1 (2010): 16–26.

21. Mike McNamee, "Olympism, Eurocentricity, and Transcultural Virtues," *Journal of the Philosophy of Sport* 33, no. 2 (2006): 174–87.

22. International Olympic Committee, *Olympic Charter*, 31.

23. International Olympic Committee, *Olympic Charter*, 62.

24. International Olympic Committee, *Olympic Charter*, 98.

25. International Olympic Committee, *Olympic Charter*, 15.

26. International Olympic Committee, *Olympic Charter*, 14.

27. International Olympic Committee, "Fundamental Principles of Olympism," 11.

28. Heather L. Reid, "Olympic Sport and Its Lessons for Peace," *Journal of the Philosophy of Sport* 33, no. 2 (2006): 205–13.

29. Philostratos, "Gymnastics," in *Arete: Greek Sports from Ancient Sources*, ed. Stephen G. Miller (Berkeley: University of California Press, 1991), 38. For a detailed analysis of the passage, see Panos Valavanis, "Thoughts on the Historical Origins of the Olympic Games and the Cult of Pelops in Olympia," *Nikephoros* 19 (2006): 141.

30. This distinction is explained by William J. Morgan, "Cosmopolitanism, Olympism, and Nationalism: A Critical Interpretation of Coubertin's Ideal of International Sporting Life," *Olympika* 4 (1995): 88.

PART II

Metaphysical Issues in Sport

Socrates typically began philosophical discussions with a "What is x?" question—an initial attempt to conceptualize or even define the subject. Metaphysical questions ask about the fundamental nature of things, and so the first question Socrates would ask in a discussion of sport would be simply "What is sport?" When I ask my own students this question, they usually answer by listing examples: football, basketball, tennis, high jumping, and so forth; but this approach quickly runs into obstacles. First, there is debate about whether some activities, such as fishing, cheerleading, bowling, and video games, are sports. Then, in order to answer that question, we need to agree upon the characteristics we take to be essential to sport. We need a definition that lists the necessary and sufficient conditions for something to qualify as a sport. So perhaps we go back to the list of things we all agreed to be sports and start looking for characteristics that they all have in common. Do all sports have written rules? Do they all have competition? Do they all require physical prowess?

The question and the process we use to answer it are important because our metaphysical understanding of what sport is directly influences our normative conception of it (i.e., our account of what sport should be). Before we can claim that it is wrong to break the rules, to take performance-enhancing drugs, or to run up the score against weaker opponents, we first need an understanding of the nature and purpose of the primary activity. At the same time, in the pursuit of a metaphysical understanding of sport, we must always keep an open mind. Sport may have multiple or constantly changing natures and purposes. For every serious attempt to conclusively define sport, there is a serious contention that sport is, by nature, indefinable.

Some say that an accurate definition of sport is not only impossible but also undesirable—first, because we can understand things without defining them (indeed, we need a preexisting understanding just to test the definition); and second, because thinking that we do have a definition might lead to the conclusion that we already understand sport and, therefore, have no need to think about it further. The lesson here is that it is much more important to ask and explore the question "What is sport?" than it is to find a perfect answer. Just as dribbling, shooting, and passing comprise the "fundamentals" of basketball, the debate about what is and is not a sport, the negotiation of characteristics essential to sport, and the comparison of theories about the nature and purpose of sport comprise the "fundamentals" of sport philosophy.

Applying Socrates's famous "What is" question to sport and athletes yields a variety of answers. In this section we will explore the relationships between sport and play, games, art, and virtue-centered social practices. Sport has important metaphysical relationships with all of these things, but at the same time it is identical to none of them, and to understand it metaphysically we need to consider how these various facets fit together to create sport as we experience it today. We will also consider the metaphysical nature of athletes and observe how contrasting views in the Eastern and Western traditions might affect the practice and understanding of sport. From the metaphysical foundations that we establish in this section we will go on to explore the ethical, educational, and political aspects of sport. The foundational activity of trying to understand what sport is prepares us to discuss the real-world questions about how it should be practiced.

Chapter 3

Sport and Play

One of the first and most influential answers to the metaphysical question "What is sport?" is that sport is a form of play. On some level, this link seems undeniable. No matter how seriously cultures or individuals take their sports, we never seem able to tear them away from the roots of play completely. We *play* games, competitors are called *players*, and even the most complex and orchestrated movement in sport is called a great *play*. When a serious professional such as Serena Williams plies her trade, we say that she is *playing* the *game* of tennis. At the same time, what Williams is doing seems a far cry from the paradigm of lighthearted child's play.

When I was a kid, I used to play with model horses, building them barns out of cardboard boxes, "feeding" them breakfast cereal, and repairing their broken legs with electrical tape bandages. It can be hard to see anything more than a linguistic connection between "playing" model horses and "playing" middle linebacker in America's National Football League. But philosophers make a good case for a metaphysical link between sport and play, even if they disagree about what that link is and whether it should be preserved. What is clear is that we cannot deny, and should not ignore, sport's connection to play. Sport may not be identical to play, or even a specific subset of it, but in order to understand what sport is we must first try to understand play.

Reactions to the idea that sport is a form of play are generally of two kinds. First, there are those who believe that it debases or trivializes sport. Sports today, they say, are serious business, in both the psychological and the economic sense. People may play around with sports by tossing a ball in the backyard or staging an informal soccer game on the beach, but competitive sport demands planning, dedication, toil, and persistence. The kind of spontaneous, lighthearted frolicking we associate with play contrasts sharply with the sports ideal of superlative achievement earned through years of training and practice. In real sports, winning is the most important thing, not pleasure. True athletes are not consoled by the refrain "It's only a game!" Sport is rightly taken seriously because it is an instrument that provides important educational and economic benefits. Student-athletes play sports to finance their educations. Professional athletes dedicate themselves to sport just as doctors and lawyers dedicate themselves to medicine and law. They make sacrifices, strive for excellence, and earn a living, sometimes even a fortune. It is not child's play. On this view, linking sports with play belittles the efforts of serious athletes and ignores the social importance of athletics. Modern sports, from this perspective, seem to be almost the opposite of play.

On the other hand, there are those who believe that thinking of sport as play actually elevates or ennobles it. In fact, both Plato and Aristotle exalted play as something higher and better than practical business: things like music, art, even religion. Aristotle defined as most noble those actions that are done for their own sake.[1] Most of human activity is done to satisfy our needs, but gods have no needs, and so they have the luxury of doing whatever seems pleasant or intrinsically worthwhile. Because humans should privilege their divine rather than their animalistic impulses, they should strive to engage in intrinsically worthwhile activities. Plato declared that "man is made God's plaything, and that is the best part of him." In *Laws*, it is concluded that the best life is one of play:

> Therefore every man and woman should live life accordingly, and play the noblest games and be of another mind from what they are at present. For they deem war a serious thing, though in war there is neither play nor culture worthy of the name, which are the things we deem most serious. Hence all must live in peace as well as they possibly can. What, then, is the right way of living? Life must be lived as play, playing with certain games, making sacrifices, singing and dancing, and then a man will be able to propitiate the gods, and defend himself against his enemies, and win in the contest.[2]

In this view, play is among the highest human functions. The practical business of earning a living, winning honors, and advancing socially are all lower concerns—linked to the survival instinct we share with animals. In fact, in an ideal world where all of our needs are satisfied, we would do nothing but play. The educational and economic benefits of sport would no longer be needed, and our games would be uncorrupted by such concerns. In the end, both philosophers who believe that play trivializes sport and those who believe that play ennobles sport seek to understand the metaphysical link between the two. As philosophers we believe that making the world better begins by understanding it better.

THE CHARACTERISTICS OF PLAY

In attempting to understand sport as a form of play, many philosophers look to Johan Huizinga's 1944 book *Homo Ludens* (Man the Player). Using a historical and sociological approach, Huizinga surveys the play element in culture and notes at the outset that play is, in fact, older than culture and engaged in by animals and not just human beings.[3] Huizinga discusses modern sports near the end of his book, acknowledging that they have been taken with increasing seriousness since the end of the nineteenth century (i.e., the period of the revival of the Olympic Games) and, therefore, that "something of the pure play-quality is inevitably lost."[4] It is not Huizinga's discussion of sport on which philosophers focus, however, but rather his definition of play, which is presented in the first chapter.

> Summing up the formal characteristics of play we might call it a free activity standing quite consciously outside "ordinary" life as being "not serious," but at the same time absorbing the player intensely and utterly. It is an activity connected with no material interest, and no profit can be gained by it. It proceeds within its own proper boundaries of time and space according to fixed rules and in an orderly manner.[5]

Here, Huizinga describes play using a kind of *via negativa* similar to the method some medieval philosophers used to describe God—that is, he defines it primarily by specifying what it is not. Play is not necessary, not serious, not ordinary, and not materially productive. Later, Huizinga offers a more positive definition: "Play is a voluntary activity or occupation executed within certain fixed limits of time and place, according to rules freely accepted but absolutely binding, having its aim in itself and accompanied by a feeling of tension, joy, and the consciousness that it is 'different' from 'ordinary life.'"[6]

In 1958, Roger Caillois evaluated Huizinga's characterization of play critically, taking issue with, among other things, its disconnection from material interest.[7] Caillois then turned Huizinga's summary into a six-point list. Play, he says, is "defined as an activity which is essentially

Free: in which playing is not obligatory; if it were, it would at once lose its attractive and joyous quality as diversion;

Separate: circumscribed within limits of space and time, defined and fixed in advance;

Uncertain: the course of which cannot be determined, nor the result attained beforehand, and some latitude for innovations being left to the player's initiative;

Unproductive: creating neither goods, nor wealth, nor new elements of any
    kind; and except for the exchange of property among the players, ending
    in a situation identical to that prevailing at the beginning of the game;
Governed by rules: under conventions that suspend ordinary laws, and for
    the moment establish new legislation, which alone counts; and
Make-believe: accompanied by a special awareness of a second reality or
    of a free unreality, as against real life.[8]

It was Caillois's list that John W. Loy Jr. used as a starting point for his
1968 effort to define the nature of sport.[9] Paul Weiss then incorporated both
Huizinga and Caillois into his own discussion of play, sport, and games in his
book *Sport: A Philosophic Inquiry*.

Philosophers quickly recognized, however, that a philosophical approach
to the question of play would have to go beyond external descriptions of the
activity itself and account for the internal experience of the agent (the person
who plays)—that is, the phenomenology of play. As David Roochnik puts it,
"Play is a quality of activity; it is a vibrant experience that each one of us has
had at some time or another. To deal with it as an objective thing is to contradict what it is, and thus destroy it."[10] Roochnik goes on to characterize play as
an orientation toward the world; a kind of chosen attitude or "stance." "Play
is a mode of being. It is a way of comporting oneself, a way of approaching
and extending oneself to the world. It is a phenomenon that frequently arises
in various human activities. But when taken self-consciously, when chosen
as the best way to be, play can become more than a sporadic phenomenon;
it can become a stance."[11] Drew Hyland picks up on this idea and goes on to
develop a theory of play that defines its stance as one of "responsive openness," a combination of being open and sensitive to anything that might happen, and being prepared to respond quickly and forcefully.[12] But Hyland's
was not the final word, and the discussion continues.[13] To this day, the philosophy of sport literature contains no universally accepted definition of play.

What we can say, however, is that philosophical accounts of play need to
synthesize the agent's internal experience with the activity's external qualities. As Angela Schneider puts it, "play is a mode of performing actions rather
than a type of action."[14] If we revise Huizinga's and Caillois's lists of (mostly)
external qualities according to the internal approaches that such theorists as
Roochnik, Hyland, Klaus Meier, Schneider, and Randolph Feezell adopted,
we might generate a new characterization of play as voluntary, extraordinary,
autotelic, absorbing, and fun. Let us examine each of these as they have been
discussed in relation to sport.

VOLUNTARY

"First and foremost," says Huizinga, "all play is a voluntary activity. Play to order is no longer play: it could at best be but a forcible imitation of it."[15] The claim that play must be voluntary is rarely disputed.[16] The paradigm case of play as spontaneous frolic clearly occurs at the will of its participants. Even in more formal activities, it is difficult to imagine what it could mean to play against one's will. We do know of children forced by overbearing parents to play little league baseball, but surely this example is "play" only in a manner of speaking—an unfortunate choice of words that fails to capture the true spirit of play. Once I watched my brother in a youth soccer game happily spearing dried leaves on the spikes of his shoes in an isolated corner of the field. He was playing, but not playing soccer. The child on the baseball diamond and the soccer player on the field might, at some point, "get into the game" and *begin* to play despite his initial reluctance, but until he willingly engages in the activity, he is not playing. As Paul Weiss concludes, "Play . . . must be freely accepted, even when it is not freely entered into or freely ended; it is free in the sense that it is carried on by the player only while he desires to engage in it."[17]

Caillois, in the definition quoted above, describes play as "free" rather than "voluntary." Is there any difference? Caillois says that sport is free in the sense that it is "not obligatory" and explains that players are "free to leave whenever they choose by saying, 'I am not playing anymore.'"[18] Huizinga also seems to equate freedom and voluntariness, by describing play "first and foremost" as "voluntary" and then identifying its first "main characteristic" as freedom.[19] But there are important philosophical differences between the conceptions of freedom and voluntariness. The most obvious is that "freedom" better describes external facts, whereas "voluntariness" describes internal attitudes. If we think of freedom "negatively" simply as the absence of constraints—as when a person is freed from prison or a student-athlete is declared eligible and therefore free to compete—we do not capture the sense in which play is free. The playing of games entails the imposition of constraints—specifically, the constraints spelled out by the rules of the game—not the elimination of them. Even most forms of child's play, as when I played with my model horses or my brothers played at being "superheroes," require an acceptance of the constraints imposed by the make-believe world.

Freedom in play is not so much an external fact as an internal attitude—a *sense* of freedom that is gained, paradoxically, by the voluntary acceptance of boundaries and constraints. According to Hyland, the experience of freedom for finite human beings "must take place within a set of limiting conditions."[20] Sport provides these limiting conditions by marking off a particular place and time, such as the boundaries and time limit of a soccer game, within which we play. Players feel free because these constraints allow them to concentrate fully on the unpredictable events that take place within that time and space. Hyland explains it thus: "The boundaries and time limits of a game perhaps most clearly of all do allow us to focus our consciousness and our bodies in such a way as to pursue to the end a set of possibilities, and so a realm of freedom."[21] There is a sense, as Caillois observes, in which players' actions are free within the limits set by the rules.[22]

Realistically, however, athletes' possibilities are limited: I could respond to a tip-off in basketball by performing a backflip—it would even be athletic—but I wouldn't be playing basketball. The freedom we experience by playing sports is primarily *psychological* freedom that depends on voluntary attitudes, not the elimination of external barriers.

This distinction is important for philosophy because we must consider the possibility that all events, including our personal actions, are predetermined. It could be that our course of life is already programmed, and we experience it like we experience a movie, under the illusion that the characters are free to do whatever they choose. Freedom, in that case, can be nothing more than a feeling. John Locke illustrated this possibility with the image of a man unknowingly locked in a room with an old friend. He willingly stays to chat with his friend, oblivious to the external fact that he is imprisoned. Locke concludes that liberty is nothing more than being able to do what we choose to do.[23]

Perhaps the sense of freedom in sport depends precisely on the choice to play. If so, conscious choice might also transform obligation into freedom as with Albert Camus's Sisyphus, condemned by the gods as his eternal punishment to roll a heavy rock up a mountain, only to have it roll back down to the bottom. Camus imagines Sisyphus liberating himself from his punishment, not by refusing to push the boulder, but by *choosing* to do it.[24] Likewise, a person "made to play," as Weiss says, can play freely if "he willingly does what he must."[25]

Of course, true voluntariness and the sense of freedom that comes from it may not be such an easily controlled choice as Camus makes it out to be. Randolph Feezell, who emphasizes the enjoyment inherent in play, links the experience of freedom not just with willingness but also with an individual's ability to identify with the activity.[26] He thinks that we feel free within the time and space provided by play because it gives us the chance to be who we really are.[27] Drew Hyland likewise believes that we identify with the play experience because it fulfills our human nature as "incomplete and overfull, both given to dominance and to submission, both monadic and relational."[28]

The feeling of freedom, characteristic of play, according to both, depends on its voluntariness, and its voluntariness depends on our ability to embrace and identify with what we are doing. Freedom in play is an internal perception more than an external reality.[29] And in rule-governed activities such as sport, the sense of freedom depends paradoxically upon the voluntary acceptance of the limitations and constraints that the rules impose.

EXTRAORDINARY

Huizinga's second defining characteristic of play is that it is "not 'ordinary' or 'real' life, but rather a stepping out of 'real' life into a temporary sphere of activity with a disposition all its own."[30] The distinction between play and ordinary life, on the one hand, reflects the observations of Plato and Aristotle that things done for their own sake are importantly different from things done to satisfy worldly needs and desires—things done because they have to get done. The idea goes back to the ancient Greek myth of Prometheus, who gave humans the spark of divine intelligence so that they could transcend the realm of animals, which is focused only on survival, and create beautiful things such as poetry, music, and dance. In this view, play is separate from—and nobler than—work. It is a view at odds with modern industrialism, which tends to privilege work and production. Industrial societies value play only insofar as it refreshes and restores people to a state where they can work more.[31] We might even say that the view of play as nobler than work is not much in favor with modern sports, where a serious approach is demanded, hard work is expected, and financial reward is often sought. Despite this culture (which will be discussed further), the modern sports world does seem to be distinct from ordinary life. As Paul Weiss affirmed, "Sport, athletics, game, and play have in common the idea of being cut off from the workaday world."[32]

How exactly is play "cut off" or "separate" from the ordinary world? A common answer is through spatial and temporal boundaries. Says Caillois, "In effect, play is an essentially separate occasion, carefully isolated from the rest of life, and generally engaged in with precise limits of time and space."[33] Huizinga also associates play's "secludedness" with its "limitedness."[34] He emphasizes here the spatial separation from ordinary life, which in sport is often represented by visible boundaries. The lines that mark off a football field, the plastic tape that carves a mountain-bike course through the woods, and the walls that surround a handball court serve not only to contain the space of play but also to exclude ordinary life. As Huizinga explains, "A closed space is marked out for [play], either materially or ideally, hedged off from the everyday surroundings. Inside this space play proceeds, inside it the rules obtain. Now, the marking out of some sacred spot is also the primary characteristic of every sacred act."[35] The stipulation that the boundaries may be "ideal" and the connection to sacred acts betrays the fact that play's apparent separateness, like its apparent freedom, exists more within the mindset of players than objective reality. The physical boundaries and barriers are symbolic and, like the religious rituals, they serve to get participants into the right mood. Play itself is as much a part of real life as anything else. It is the attitude of the players that makes it extraordinary.

Roochnik insists on this last point and denigrates those who would discount the importance of play by deeming it illusory or separate from the real world. He notes that the feeling of seclusion we experience in play is our own doing and not exclusive to the play activities. "A full involvement in any situation will give rise to a unique world of distinctive temporality and spatiality."[36] Play is extraordinary because we view it as extraordinary or, more accurately, because it is a stance or attitude that is distinct from the stance of ordinary life. Hyland says that in the stance of play "we have a particular relationship with space, time, others, our equipment, etc."[37] He describes this relationship as one of openness (a heightened awareness of our surroundings) and responsiveness (the ability to respond to what happens in those surroundings).[38]

It is, of course, the bounded nature of the play world that makes such a focused stance possible; by setting aside the concerns of everyday life, we can give all our attention to the task at hand. "Play is full commitment of body and spirit to the activity," Roochnik reminds us; "it is immersion in the world that is here and now, and it is only this kind of immersion that does full justice to the powers of man to encounter the world."[39] Understood in this way, not as a particular activity but, rather, as a focused and committed approach to almost any activity, play is neither illusory nor trivial. In fact, it permits the utmost seriousness within its limited boundaries.[40] Play, then, is extraordinary, both in the sense that it lies beyond the ordinary and that it is something special that deserves to be valued.

AUTOTELIC

The Greek word *telos* signifies a purpose or end. Aristotle claims that we always act for the sake of some end, and that every end terminates in the final end of happiness (*eudaimonia*), which is desired for its own sake.[41] A thing desired for its own sake, then, is *autotelic*—an end in itself. Play is generally characterized as autotelic because it aims at no end beyond itself—that is, no external or extrinsic end. The goods sought in play are said to be internal and intrinsic to the task—such as the pleasure gained by playing a good game of ping-pong. Further, play's internal goods should not satisfy preexisting needs or obligations. If I go for a run because I need to release some stress, my activity is not strictly autotelic. As Huizinga explains, "Play is superfluous. It is never imposed by physical necessity or moral duty. It is never a task. It is done at leisure, during 'free time.'"[42]

Early on, autotelicity was widely accepted by philosophers as characteristic of play and valued as a quality of truly worthwhile sport. Later, however, the nature and scope of autotelicity were called into question, especially as they apply to sport. If a game is played for the sake of pleasure, is it truly autotelic? What about schoolchildren let out to play at recess so that they can concentrate better when they return to the classroom? Could professional sports ever be autotelic? Caillois revised Huizinga's claim that play should have no material interest to the stipulation that it be "unproductive," thereby including casino games but excluding professional sports.[43]

Paul Weiss interprets autotelicity to exclude gamblers, professional athletes, and even fitness buffs. "If engaged in for the sake of health or money," he claims, "play ceases to be play at the point where these objectives dictate what is done."[44] Embedded in Weiss's apparent stringency, however, is an important caveat: it is only when external objectives "dictate" the action that play ceases to be play. Autotelicity, like voluntariness, depends on internal attitudes rather than external circumstances. I may take up tennis in order to improve my health, and in that sense, it won't be play. But nothing precludes me from becoming pleasantly absorbed in the activity and thereby achieving a state of play somewhere along the line. The difference is not the activity so much as how I think about it.

We might even say of the first case that I am *using* tennis (to get in shape) rather than *playing* tennis (for no external purpose). Bernard Suits has helped to clear up much of the confusion here.[45] He employs the term "instrumentalism" to describe the use of games to achieve external goods, including but not limited to prizes and salaries.[46] But he distinguishes between instrumental and autotelic activities, not on the basis of the activity, but rather on the motivations of the participant. Echoing erstwhile Olympic ideology, he endorses the amateur attitude of playing "out of love of the game" rather than "love of what the game can produce."[47]

But Suits here makes the same mistake that the Olympic Movement did in thinking that external circumstances can reveal internal motivations. The fact that someone dedicates much of her life to achieving excellence in an activity, the fact that she is praised, rewarded, and even paid for performing it publicly, does not entail that she is doing it for the money. In fact, the pursuit of excellence and performance of a task with which one identifies and finds intrinsically rewarding is the hallmark of . . . a professional. We have all done jobs for the money, but serious careers are a matter of passion. Most philosophy professors I know believe this. Feezell states that teaching philosophy is, for him, "more like play than work."[48] Why should we hold athletes to a different standard?

Perhaps we believe that play-type activities lose some of their value when taken too seriously. Suits complains that Olympic athletes, even though technically amateur (in his day), are playing because they are under immense pressure to win—pressure that is simply absent from informal contests such as pickup basketball. He argues that "acting under such a compulsion, rather than the desire to win simply because winning defines the activity one is undertaking, is what turns a game that could be play into something that is not play."[49] Athletes often say that no one puts more pressure on them than they put on themselves. I think the pressure Suits has in mind here is external—the pressure to win for the sake of one's team, for the sake of one's country, or for the sake of the honor attached to an Olympic medal.

On the other hand, if we require play to have absolutely no external *telos*, it may end up that hardly anyone ever really plays. Engaging recent research in action theory and psychology, Stephen Schmid argues that the autotelicity of play requires both a player's goal (i.e., climbing a rock) and the goal motivation (because it provides a rewarding challenge) to be intrinsic.[50] In reality, most of us have mixed, even complex, sets of reasons for playing sports, which include at least some extrinsic goods.

Autotelicity remains an important characteristic for play, but perhaps it is better regarded as an ideal than a requirement. Instead of insisting that motivations for play be purely autotelic, we might focus on their value or defensibility. Education, for example, is an excellent reason to play sports, and it might be that achieving the responsively open stance of play is one of sports' great educational benefits. Hyland shares this view, but he warns that we undermine the educational benefits of play by making education our explicit goal. "[If I say,] 'Today I will play basketball in order to learn about myself': not only am I unlikely to learn much, I almost certainly will fail to attain genuine play."[51]

Although it is clear that extrinsic goals can compromise or even destroy the experience of play, it is not clear that all extrinsic goals always do. I have met several student-athletes who regard their sports as distracting drudgery—something they do only for the scholarship dollars that make their educations possible. I also know student-athletes completely engaged in and enthralled by their sports experience. They embody the spirit of play while earning just as many scholarship dollars as those doing sports for the money. As Roochnik concludes on the question of autotelicity, "Play is a stance to be taken and . . . it is characterized by immersion. It does not follow from this that we should be utterly oblivious to the future. Play does not preclude having a *telos*."[52]

FUN

The most obvious intrinsic reason for engaging in play is simply that it is fun. Many philosophies, including Epicureanism and utilitarianism,[53] posit pleasure as the highest good, yet philosophers of sport identify pleasure as a primary characteristic of play less often than one might expect. An exception is Feezell, who says, "We choose to play our games or engage in such activities for no other reason, in many (or most) cases, than the intrinsic enjoyment involved."[54] Pleasure does not appear in Caillois's definition of play or in Huizinga's most frequently quoted summaries of play. But Feezell points out that Huizinga, at one point, calls the fun element "the essence of play."[55]

Fun is perhaps overlooked because it is such an obvious feature of play. If I say that I played around all day, the implication is that I had fun. If I say that I played baseball or soccer all day, the implication is not clear because I may just be using the verb "play" as a manner of speaking. Sports, sometimes, are not fun at all—and we know that going in. But insofar as sports are or can be a form of play, it seems like they should be fun. Sports completely devoid of fun surely are disconnected from play. Feezell claims, in fact, that once pleasure goes out of sports, an athlete will quit playing.[56] This observation seems to be confirmed by the popular athletic saying "I'm going to play until it quits being fun." Fun is essentially pleasant.

Where exactly is the fun in play? We say "baseball is fun," but two kids could be playing the exact same game and one is miserable while the other is happy. Is fun a quality of the activity or of the person participating? Feezell suggests that enjoyment is something intrinsic to play itself. He claims, "Play is engaged in for the sake of the intrinsic enjoyment of play itself" and that this enjoyment makes play "intrinsically valuable."[57] Feezell takes his account to affirm play's autotelicity, but he is challenged by Schmid who claims that it begs the question (i.e., it assumes as true what it is trying to prove). On the one hand, to argue that autotelic play is intrinsically valuable because it does not depend on anything else extrinsic to the activity is essentially to say that "autotelic play is intrinsically valuable because it is intrinsically valuable."[58] On the other hand, if play is valued because it produces fun or enjoyment, then "these psychological states are what is intrinsically valuable and one's participation in a sport is a means to this end."[59]

Schmid's challenge seems to reflect Aristotle's claim that happiness is the only thing pursued for its own sake, but in fact Schmid argues that we *can* engage in activities for their own sake quite independently of any pleasure or enjoyment gained. His real point is that pure autotelic play requires purely intrinsic reasons for participating; pleasure and fun are extrinsic reasons. This doesn't mean, however, that fun and pleasure aren't good reasons to engage in playful activities, or even that they aren't essential elements of play. As Feezell admits, it is "from the standpoint of the lived experience of the player [that fun] appears as the irreducible and essential element of his activity."[60] We have returned again to the idea that play is an attitude or stance adopted by a person rather than an externally observable quality of some activity. We further note, with Hyland, that "fun is not the *telos* of sport; [but] when sport works, when it is the best it can be, it is fun. Fun, too, is a distinctive characteristic of that [stance of] responsive openness which informs our sporting play."[61]

ABSORBING

If we accept fun as a distinctive characteristic of play, and we value play as a mode of participation in sport, the question naturally arises, what is it about playful activities that generates fun? Perhaps the connection lies in play's ability to absorb us completely. Huizinga characterized play as "utterly absorbing" in his initial summary, but this characteristic was left off Caillois's list, perhaps because, again, he was trying to describe play as something external rather than an attitude or stance. Weiss recognized that "play is all-absorbing both for the child and the athlete,"[62] but it is the theory of play as a stance that provides the greatest insight into play's capacity to absorb. In Hyland's characterization of play as the stance of responsive openness, we can see how the need to remain open and to respond to whatever happens requires absorption in the activity. Games and sports in particular create the uncertainty identified by Huizinga[63] and the doubt identified by Caillois[64] as features of play activities that grab our attention and pull us away from the ordinary—even away from self-consciousness.

There is a sense in which play demands that we leave behind self-conscious intentions and calculations and simply abandon ourselves to the flow of the activity. As Weiss observes, "He who wants to be refreshed through play must forget about refreshing himself, and just play."[65] Even the early twentieth-century philosopher R. G. Collingwood recognized that play required "capriciousness" in the sense of making decisions "spontaneously or out of habit without any conscious process of reasoning."[66] In 2008, Seth Vannata applied Edmund Husserl's phenomenological insight to play, declaring its "defining trait" to be thoughtlessness. "Like the mundane activities of reading out loud or even finishing a spoken sentence," Vannata explains, "once you are overly conscious of the act, you stumble. In this light, playing can be said to be 'unconscious.'"[67] Absorption in the flow of play activity often manifests itself in sport as the phenomenon of "flow" or "the zone"—a feeling of perfect control and effortlessness even while performing difficult athletic tasks. In fact, psychological studies reveal that the experience of "flow" or "being in the zone" occurs when an athlete's skills reach perfect balance with the challenge presented by the activity.[68] One cannot force oneself, or even will oneself, into flow—it must arise spontaneously.

On the other hand, an athlete must prepare herself to reach the level of skill necessary to experience flow. In Eastern philosophy, the concept of *wu-wei* implies a similar kind of effortlessness, one that comes out as result of training and understanding. The *Daodejing* of Laozi reminds us that

> The most supple things in the world run roughshod over the most rigid. That which is not there can enter even when there is no space. This is how I know the advantages of *wu-wei*! The teaching that is without words,
> The advantages of *wu-wei*
> Few in the world attain these.[69]

Getting beyond the self and "not thinking" are likewise important ideas in Eastern philosophy that can be applied to sport. Vannata recognizes this, adding that the Western tradition of phenomenology, specifically Husserl's idea of passive synthesis, which recognizes the contribution of our pre-reflective consciousness to experiences such as play, get to the heart of our absorption in play.[70] Approached from an Eastern or Western perspective, absorption seems to be an important characteristic of play.

Hopefully this chapter has improved our understanding of play as a phenomenon related to sport. One thing clear from the discussion is that play isn't always sport and sport isn't always play. But insofar as sport shares some important characteristics with play, we might ask whether those characteristics can have normative application—that is, can they make sport better?

- First, the connection between voluntariness and the quality of the sports experience is clear. Forcing a child or even oneself to participate in sport is unlikely to result in a positive experience. At the same time, it is possible to willingly accept something forced upon you, as Sisyphus did. But it is always important, in the first place, to understand and value the principle of voluntary participation.
- Second, we should appreciate the extraordinariness of play and try to make sport a special place apart from ordinary life—even if it is a job.
- Third, the principle of autotelicity should be viewed as an ideal that might be experienced within play—even if our motivations for entering into sport are mixed and can be directed at other extrinsic goals. The point is that focusing on those external goals can corrupt the value of play.

- Fourth, fun is essential to play but not essential to sport. By finding a way to play in sport, we are more likely to have fun and maybe to succeed.
- Fifth, play is all absorbing, as is sport performed at the highest levels—especially in "flow." In sport, unlike child's play, this absorption depends on a proper balance between challenge and skill, but it is never a bad idea for an athlete to practice not thinking and just abandon herself to the game.

So, sport's relation to play helps us to understand some of its hereditary characteristics, but we still need to discover what is metaphysically distinctive about sport itself. The first step toward that goal is exploring the nature of games.

DISCUSSION QUESTIONS

1. The term "play" is more often applied to team sports such as soccer than individual sports such as swimming. Do individual sports have the philosophical characteristics of play?
2. Have you ever felt forced to play a sport against your will? How did it affect your experience? Has sport ever seemed like work to you?
3. Do you think athletes perform better when they are having fun, or does the experience of fun come from playing well?
4. Have you ever experienced "flow" or "being in the zone" in sport? Did the experience have any of the play characteristics (voluntary, extraordinary, autotelic, absorbing, and fun) discussed in this chapter?

NOTES

1. He repeats the theme in several places—for example, Aristotle, *Politics*, trans. C. D. C. Reeve (Indianapolis: Hackett, 1998), 7.1325b20.
2. Plato, *Laws*, trans. Trevor Saunders (London: Penguin, 1970), 803ad.
3. Johan Huizinga, *Homo Ludens: A Study of the Play Element in Culture* (Boston: Beacon Press, [1944] 1955), 1.
4. Huizinga, *Homo Ludens*, 197.
5. Huizinga, *Homo Ludens*, 13.
6. Huizinga, *Homo Ludens*, 28.
7. Roger Caillois, *Man, Play, and Games*, trans. Meyer Berlash (Urbana: University of Illinois Press, [1958] 2001), 5.
8. Caillois, *Man, Play, and Games*, 9–10.

9. John W. Loy Jr., "The Nature of Sport: A Definitional Effort," *Quest* 10, no. 1 (May 1968): 1–15. Loy accepted Caillois's definition and added such elements as competition and physical skill.

10. David L. Roochnik, "Play and Sport," *Journal of the Philosophy of Sport* 2, no. 1 (1975): 37.

11. Roochnik, "Play and Sport," 39. See also Klaus Meier, "An Affair of Flutes: An Appreciation of Play," *Journal of the Philosophy of Sport* 7, no. 1 (1980): 25.

12. Drew Hyland, "The Stance of Play," *Journal of the Philosophy of Sport* 7, no. 1 (1980): 90.

13. For a recent account, see Francisco Javier Lopez Frías, "Does Play Constitute the Good Life? Suits and Aristotle on Autotelicity and Living Well," *Journal of the Philosophy of Sport* 47, no. 2 (2020): 168–82.

14. Angela J. Schneider, "Fruits, Apples, and Category Mistakes: On Sport, Games, and Play," *Journal of the Philosophy of Sport* 28, no. 2 (2001): 152.

15. Huizinga, *Homo Ludens*, 7.

16. It figures prominently in Bernard Suits's highly influential definition of games (discussed in chapter 4), and Meier identifies it as one of only two necessary and sufficient conditions for play (the other is autotelicity; "Affair of Flutes," 25).

17. Weiss, *Sport: A Philosophic Inquiry* (Carbondale: Southern Illinois University Press, 1969), 134.

18. Caillois, *Man, Play, and Games*, 3.

19. Huizinga, *Homo Ludens*, 8.

20. Drew A. Hyland, *Philosophy of Sport* (New York: Paragon, 1990), 134.

21. Hyland, "The Stance of Play," 95.

22. Caillois, *Man, Play, and Games*, 8.

23. John Locke, *An Essay Concerning Human Understanding* (Oxford, UK: Clarendon, 1975), 238.

24. Albert Camus, *The Myth of Sisyphus and Other Essays*, trans. Justin O'Brien (New York: Random House, 1955), 88–91. For an extended discussion of the arguments made in this paragraph, see Heather L. Reid, *The Philosophical Athlete* (Durham, NC: Carolina Academic Press, [2002] 2019), chap. 3.

25. Weiss, *Sport: A Philosophic Inquiry*, 134.

26. Randolph Feezell, *Sport, Play, and Ethical Reflection* (Urbana: University of Illinois Press, 2006), 23.

27. Feezell, *Sport, Play*, 25.

28. Drew A. Hyland, *The Question of Play* (Lanham, MD: University Press of America, 1984), 102.

29. This is confirmed by empirical psychology according to Stephen Schmid, "Reconsidering Autotelic Play," *Journal of the Philosophy of Sport* 36, no. 2 (2009): 250.

30. Huizinga, *Homo Ludens*, 8.

31. Meier says, "If play is utilized as a break in routine for the purpose of returning recuperated to work, it is merely another utilitarian link in the chain, serving as a handmaiden to the productive enterprise, and thereby demonstrating essentially a work orientation and structure" ("Affair of Flutes," 28).

32. Weiss, *Sport: A Philosophic Inquiry*, 134.
33. Caillois, *Man, Play, and Games*, 6.
34. Huizinga, *Homo Ludens*, 9.
35. Huizinga, *Homo Ludens*, 19.
36. Roochnik, "Play and Sport," 41.
37. Hyland, "The Stance of Play," 88.
38. Hyland, "The Stance of Play," 89.
39. Hyland, "The Stance of Play," 88.
40. A fact admitted by Huizinga, *Homo Ludens*, 45, and Weiss, *Sport: A Philosophic Inquiry*, 136.
41. Aristotle, *Nicomachean Ethics*, 2nd ed., trans. Terence Irwin (Indianapolis: Hackett, 1999), 1097b21–2.
42. Huizinga, *Homo Ludens*, 8.
43. Caillois, *Man, Play, and Games*, 5–6.
44. Weiss, *Sport: A Philosophic Inquiry*, 139.
45. Suits, "Words on Play," 119–22.
46. Bernard Suits, "The Tricky Triad: Games, Play, and Sport," *Journal of the Philosophy of Sport* 15, no. 1 (1988): 9.
47. Suits, "Tricky Triad," 8.
48. Feezell, *Sport, Play*, 26.
49. Suits, "Tricky Triad," 9.
50. Schmid, "Reconsidering Autotelic Play," 25.
51. Hyland, *Question of Play*, xv.
52. Roochnik, "Play and Sport," 41.
53. At least Jeremy Bentham's version of utilitarianism.
54. Feezell, *Sport, Play*, 11.
55. Huizinga, *Homo Ludens*, 3.
56. Feezell, *Sport, Play*, 14.
57. Feezell, *Sport, Play*, 14.
58. Schmid, "Reconsidering Autotelic Play," 243.
59. Schmid, "Reconsidering Autotelic Play," 244.
60. Feezell, *Sport, Play*, 23.
61. Hyland, *Philosophy of Sport*, 139.
62. Weiss, *Sport: A Philosophic Inquiry*, 140.
63. Huizinga, *Homo Ludens*, 10.
64. Caillois, *Man, Play, and Games*, 7.
65. Weiss, *Sport: A Philosophic Inquiry*, 137.
66. Spencer K. Wertz, "The Capriciousness of Play: Collingwood's Insight," *Journal of the Philosophy of Sport* 30, no. 1 (2003): 164.
67. Seth Vannata, "A Phenomenology of Sport: Playing and Passive Synthesis," *Journal of the Philosophy of Sport* 35, no. 1 (2008): 63–72.
68. Susan A. Jackson and Mihaly Csikszentmihalyi, *Flow in Sports* (Champaign, IL: Human Kinetics, 1999), 6.

69. Laozi, "Daodejing," in *Readings in Classical Chinese Philosophy*, 2nd ed., ed. P. Ivanhoe and B. Van Norden (Indianapolis: Hackett, 2001), 184.

70. Vannata, "Phenomenology of Sport," 71.

Chapter 4

Sport and Games

The American cyclist Lance Armstrong won seven Tours de France, two more than anyone else in history. He has admitted to doping in all of those races by using, among other things, a banned drug called erythropoietin (EPO). To many, the allegation is not surprising because EPO is believed to have been used widely in the sport as a relatively safe and undetectable crutch to make it through grueling three-week stage races.[1] Based on our knowledge that Armstrong intentionally broke the rules at these Tours, what may we conclude? Should we say that he is still the legitimate winner of the races, because such rule-breaking was generally accepted and widespread among pro cyclists at that time? Should we say that he is not the legitimate winner because he intentionally violated the rules and therefore failed to "play the game" of cycling, which is defined by its rules? Perhaps we can argue that anti-doping rules are not "essential" to sport, or that it is consistent with the true "spirit of sport." Our approach to ethical questions such as these depends ultimately on metaphysical beliefs. Does sport have an essence, and if so, what (and who) determines it? In contrast with other forms of play, games and sport are distinguished by their formal rules. Is that, fundamentally, what (or perhaps all) they are?

SUITS ON GAMES AND RULES

One of the most common answers to the metaphysical question "What is sport?" is that it is a set of rules. The most influential correlation between rules and sport is made by Bernard Suits in the process of defining games. In his seminal work *The Grasshopper*, Suits identifies the elements of a game as (1) the goal, (2) the means of achieving the goal, (3) the rules, and (4) the "lusory" attitude.[2] At first glance, this account makes it seem as though rules are only one among four distinct elements of a game, but it turns out that the other three elements all depend on the rules. First, there is a game's goal (i.e., putting a ball in a net or crossing the finish line first), a state of affairs that Suits designates as "prelusory" because it can be described independently of a game. But of course, this state of affairs derives its meaning from the rules that designate it as a way of winning the game, thereby transforming it into a "lusory" goal.[3] Game ends are inseparable from rules for Suits. "If the rules are broken, the original end becomes impossible of attainment, since one cannot (really) win the game unless one plays it, and one cannot (really) play the game unless one obeys the rules of the game."[4] His point here is metaphysical; he is trying to describe the nature of games, though such descriptions have implications for the ethics of sport as well.

Game rules do more than give meaning to otherwise meaningless game goals (such as putting a ball into a net); they make the activity possible. On the face of it, this seems fairly obvious. I cannot play football without obeying any of the rules. I may be playing with an object called a football, I may be running around on a field, kicking a ball, and so on, but I will not be playing the game of football unless I willingly obey the rules of the game. This feature of game rules makes them different from, say, moral rules such as the Bible's Ten Commandments, which I may choose to follow, but my following them does not make my engagement in the activity (i.e., loving my neighbor) possible. I'm perfectly capable of loving my neighbor without such rules. The Ten Commandments designate rather than define actions. As Suits concludes, "In morals obedience to rules makes the action right, but in games it makes the action."[5]

This aspect of game rules not only makes games seem to be essentially sets of rules but also captures the sense in which playing games must be voluntary. Play, as we saw in chapter 3, must be voluntary; and to play games we must voluntarily obey the rules. What is more, our voluntary acceptance of rules can be withdrawn at any time. As Suits says, "There is always the possibility of there being some non-game rule to which the game rule may be subordinated"—as when continuing to play might violate some rule of morality.[6] Suits gives the example of a race car driver who drives off the track to avoid hitting a baby that has crawled into his path. Of course, the driver at this point has quit playing the game, not just because his obligation to avoid running over children is more serious than the game but also because he has voluntarily ceased to obey the rules of the game.

Not all games are instances of play, says Suits,[7] but he does believe that games grow out of play. "[A] game is when unsophisticated play, i.e., kicking a can, is transformed into a sport, i.e., soccer or hockey."[8] Games, however, cease to be play, according to Suits, once they become "instruments for external purposes (most obviously for acquiring money, as in the form of salaries drawn by players)."[9] Such "instrumental" purposes violate the autotelic character of play, but professional athletic games are not exactly work either, in

Suits's view, because work is something characterized by the employment of efficient means, and game rules are distinctive precisely in that they forbid efficient means.[10]

If I work at a brewery loading beer barrels onto trucks, I will be forgiven for and even expected to use levers, forklifts, and any other efficient means I can find to accomplish my task. But when beer-barrel loading becomes a game, as it does in some strongman competitions, such efficiencies are explicitly forbidden by the rules. This sense in which athletic games require the voluntary adoption of inefficient means also has important ethical implications for the use and regulation of performance-enhancing technologies. Not only are sports justified in prohibiting certain means of improving performance, but prohibiting efficient means is also a fundamental part of what sport is (this will be discussed further in chapter 9).

Despite their origin in play, difference from work, and link with voluntary choice, games can be (and often are) played with the utmost seriousness. Such seriousness, observes Suits, is a characteristic of the player and not of the game.[11] Nevertheless, Suits does build a psychological condition into his definition of games. He calls it the "lusory attitude" and says it is needed to explain "that curious state of affairs wherein one adopts rules which require one to employ worse rather than better means for reaching an end."[12] As in our discussion of play in chapter 3, the mind-set of the agent turns out to be essential to any understanding of the activity. Indeed, Suits's final and extremely influential definition of a game does not describe an object so much as a way of acting—a way of acting that can only be understood within the context of rules:

> To play a game is to attempt to achieve a specific state of affairs [prelusory goal], using only means permitted by the rules [lusory means], where the rules prohibit use of more efficient in favour of less efficient means [constitutive rules], and where the rules are accepted just because they make possible such activity [lusory attitude].[13]

Suits's definition of games, then, when applied to sport, links sport metaphysically with rules of a certain type and with a participant's willingness to accept those rules. It shows that rules provide a context without which sport can make no sense. But what is the relationship between rules, games, and sport?

FROM GAMES TO SPORTS

Even if we recognize that games are made possible by the existence and acceptance of rules, more needs to be said about the difference between sport and games. Suits's initial thought was that a game could become a sport by meeting certain requirements, namely "(1) that the game be a game of skill, (2) that the skill be physical, (3) that the game have a wide following, and (4) that the following achieve a certain level of stability."[14] In an article titled "The Tricky Triad," Suits illustrates the relationships among games, play, and sport with a Venn diagram of three intersecting circles that illustrate, among other things, that not all sports are games.[15] For the area of the diagram representing sports that are not games, Suits has in mind performance sports, such as diving and gymnastics.[16] Because these kinds of events are judged rather than refereed, they seem less defined by their rules and therefore more similar to competitions in art, music, or even beauty contests (the relationship between sport and art is discussed in chapter 6). Nevertheless, he judges them to be sports because of their emphasis on physical skills. In "Tricky Triad," Suits redefines sports as "competitive events involving a variety of physical (usually in combination with other) human skills, where the superior participant is judged to have exhibited those skills in a superior way."[17]

Physical skill is widely regarded as an essential element of sport. It clearly distinguishes sports games such as basketball from non-sport games such as poker or chess. However, the rise of eSports has called this criterion into question. It is clear that even if a game such as chess should happen to involve physical skills—as it would when played by moving heavy, life-size pieces around on a giant outdoor board—it would remain a game and not a sport on Suits's definition because the outcome is not dependent on the superior demonstration of physical skills. Are the skills that lead to victory in computer games "physical" in the relevant way?[18]

Meanwhile, if someone were to protest that eSports are sports because they appear on television sports networks or are discussed in the sports section of the newspaper, we would have to wonder what the metaphysical difference between a sport and game could be. Competitive computer gaming certainly can satisfy Suits's requirement that sports have a wide following, but is that criterion essential? The International Olympic Committee (IOC) requires that potential Olympic sports be "widely practiced by men in at least 75 countries and on four continents and by women in at least 40 countries and on three continents,"[19] but the IOC is not here defining the term "sport"; rather, it is setting up criteria for the kinds of events that should be included in the Olympic Games. Activities such as eSports can certainly be sports without being Olympic sports—but what exactly makes them sports?[20]

We might demand that sports be institutionalized in the sense of having established norms, codified rules, formal associations, and specific administrative bodies.[21] But the question immediately arises of what such an activity is before it becomes institutionalized. Are we to say, for example, that wrestling was not a sport until some official body was developed to oversee it? Homer's epics depict wrestling events centuries before the Olympic Games were supposed to have begun, and even at the height of ancient athletics, rules seem to have varied between one festival and another. Rationalization and bureaucratization were among Guttman's key distinctions between ancient and modern sport. Indeed, the codification of rules and the establishment of modern sports' governing bodies (such as FIFA, the international soccer association) took place after the nineteenth-century revival of the Olympic Games revealed that a common understanding was needed. The American discus thrower Robert Garrett, for example, did not know the weight of the discus he would throw in those first modern Games.[22] Institutionalization certainly facilitates quantification and record—two other characteristics of modern sport on Guttman's list. But are such things essential? Rules seem to be metaphysically necessary for games and sport in ways that institutions are not.[23]

Even if we agree that rules are essential to sports, does it follow that sports are essentially sets of rules? You can't play volleyball without any rules, but what about activities such as figure skating or diving, which can be understood and performed without rules? Aren't they sports?

Suits himself claimed at one point that such "performance sports" lacked "constitutive rules,"[24] the kind of rules without which a game could not exist, or at least it wouldn't be the same game. For example, if the rule against handling the ball were eliminated from soccer and players were allowed to pick up the ball and run with it, we would no longer have a game of soccer. Constitutive rules are those upon which, in William Morgan's words, "the very existence of the game is logically dependent."[25] Even though activities such as swimming and running can be performed without rules, to become sports they have to be turned into a game—most often a race. Even judged sports such as gymnastics are games with constitutive rules, as Meier observed,[26] and further, they satisfy Suits's original four defining characteristics of games: goal, means, rules, and lusory attitude.[27] In fact, the gymnastic event of balance beam is an excellent example of a game whose rules stipulate the inefficient requirement that certain moves be performed on a narrow platform elevated off the ground.[28]

It seems, in the end, that the only thing required to transform a game into a sport is, in Meier's words, "the additional characteristic of requiring physical skill or prowess to be demonstrated by the participants in the pursuit of its goal."[29] Sports, on this view, are essentially types of rule-based games that demand physical skills.

FORMALISM AND ITS LIMITS

The metaphysical understanding of sports as games defined exclusively in terms of their formal rules is part of an approach called "formalism" that carries important normative implications for how games should be played. Explains William J. Morgan, "[For formalists] what it means to engage in a game, to count as a legitimate instance of a game, to qualify as a bona fide action of a game, and to win a game is to act in accordance with the appropriate rules of that game. All instances and actions that fall outside the rules of the game, therefore, do not count as legitimate instances or actions of a game."[30] This implies that an intentional rule violation, such as Diego Maradona's infamous "hand of god" goal in the 1986 World Cup or even the common practice of fouling to stop the clock in basketball, are effectively failures to play the game that negate the outcome and may even have the result of transforming that activity from a game into something else. Predictably, this implication has caused much debate about formalism and especially about the ethics of rule breaking (which we'll discuss in chapter 9). If sports exist metaphysically only on account of rules, does breaking one of those rules make the sport cease to exist? How about breaking two of them? We may agree that you can't break *all* of the rules and still call the activity a sport, but where do we draw the metaphysical line?

One response goes back to the concept of "constitutive" versus "regulative" rules.[31] Maybe fouling someone to stop the clock in basketball doesn't nullify the game's existence, but handling the ball in soccer does. In the basketball example, additional rules anticipate such violations and prescribe appropriate penalties. The basketball player who commits the violation does so in full expectation of being penalized; in fact, her whole motivation for fouling is that the clock will be stopped to assess the penalty. She seems to be working within the framework of the rules and therefore legitimately playing the game. Other rules, such as the prohibition on handling the ball in soccer, seem constitutive in that they define the game in question and distinguish it from other games. If a soccer player catches the ball and starts running with it, we are likely to say that he is playing a different game, perhaps rugby, rather than soccer. The temptation is to say that the handball rule is constitutive because it somehow defines the game of soccer, whereas the basketball fouling rule is merely regulative, because it simply regulates actions within the game. However, it is not always easy to distinguish "constitutive" from other types of rules. Suits identified constitutive rules with those that stipulate the inefficient means central to his definition of games. Performance-enhancing technology regulations (such as doping bans) also prohibit more efficient means—yet they hardly define or distinguish particular games.

Perhaps the difference between essential and inessential rules is to be found not in the rule itself but rather in how it is used. Graham McFee argues that the same rule may be used in a regulative or in a constitutive way. The handball rule can be used to (partially) define soccer, or it can be used to regulate action within a game through the use of penalties.[32] So, a game in which handling of the ball is allowed is not a game of soccer, but a game in which the ball is handled on occasion and appropriately penalized is still a legitimate game of soccer. McFee's distinction challenges formalism as a metaphysical account of games because it shifts the emphasis in understanding sport away from the formal nature of the rules and toward the way human beings *use* those rules at particular times.

This means that we cannot define an entire game or sport in terms of its written rules. What we can do is refer to those rules, along with several other factors, in trying to determine whether a particular event counts as a soccer match. Formalists might contend that Maradona's "hand of god" goal or Lance Armstrong's use of banned substances invalidates the result—or the entire legitimacy—of their contests. But questions about the limits of formalism remain. Does it matter what kind of rule was broken? Does the infraction need to be detected and called during the event? Should awards, records, and public recognition of the winner be withdrawn? If no rules are in place to answer such questions, to what can a formalist appeal?

THE LETTER VERSUS THE SPIRIT

One response to the logical incompatibility puzzle produced by formalist metaphysics (i.e., that you cannot intentionally break a rule and play the game at the same time) is that sports and games should be understood not just in terms of written rules but also in terms of unwritten rules—the spirit of sport that underlies the written rules. Fred D'Agostino calls this the "ethos" of games. He describes it specifically as "that set of unofficial, implicit conventions which determine how the rules of a game are to be applied in concrete circumstances."[33] The distinction employs a Platonic approach to metaphysics in which perfect ideals (sometimes called forms) are contrasted with inevitably imperfect instantiations in real life. So, the written rules may describe an ideal notion of what a perfect game of baseball should be, even if that ideal is never achieved in practice. In the real world, games can accommodate a certain (but not infinite) amount of imperfections such as rule breaking without ceasing to count as an instance of the ideal.

D'Agostino's favorite example is baseball's spitball, a very difficult pitch to hit because of the action achieved by pitchers illegally moistening the ball before they pitch it. For some pitchers, such as Gaylord Perry, the spitball was a specialty, and players expected him to use it even though it was illegal. According to a strict reading of formalism's logical incompatibility thesis, spitballs cannot be part of the game of baseball, and games in which spitballs were thrown are not true instances of the sport. If we focus on the unwritten rather than written rules, however, the illegal spitball can nevertheless be "part of the game" as long as it is accepted as such by the players.

D'Agostino's challenge to the strictly formalist metaphysics of games has intuitive appeal, not just because it offers a solution to the logical incompatibility thesis but also because it seems to reflect the actual practice of sports as we experience them. The ethos theory of sport raises epistemological and ethical issues, however. If we identify the essence of sport with unwritten rules, conventional practice, or what is generally accepted by players, we are left with little independent basis for discerning a legitimate instance of a game, not to mention a good from a bad game.

When the maximum speed limit in the United States was fifty-five miles per hour on the highway, drivers routinely broke the rule without being ticketed by police. Because the written rule was ignored and the enforced rule was neither posted nor consistent on any given highway on any given day, it became a dangerous guessing game to see how fast one could drive before being pulled over. Perhaps an "ethos" of appropriate speeding, say sixty-five miles per hour, was adopted. But it seems absurd for a driver breaking the law at sixty-five to rebuke as a scofflaw someone who passes him at seventy miles per hour. Without any publicly known universal standard such as written rules, how can we distinguish acceptable from unacceptable actions in sport?

William Morgan describes the problem thus: "By taking as its point of departure convention rather than the internal logic of the game, as revealed by its rules, the critics [of formalism] collapse any meaningful distinction between theory and ideology."[34] Morgan admits that games played in the real world rarely live up to a Platonic ideal in which every written rule is followed perfectly, but he wonders whether we should stop short of simply accepting these defects as part of the game because rule-breaking behavior is often caused by extraneous economic or political concerns—as such, it is a form of contamination.[35] According to Morgan, we can grant "that games are more than their rules, and that games are played out in rich social textures it would be foolish to ignore," without giving up the metaphysical importance and moral force of constitutive rules:

> An awareness of the social fabric of baseball [does not explain] why a game in which spitballs are thrown is still a game of baseball. We already know the answer to that question: spitball-baseball is a legitimate game because it does not violate the constitutive rules of baseball. The conventions of American baseball may well explain the greater incidence and matter of fact acceptance

of such rule violations in this culture as opposed to other cultures, for example Japanese baseball, but it is the formal rule-governed structures of these games that explain to us why both are in fact baseball games.[36]

The insight here is that sports have an internal logic expressed by the formal rules, which spell out in a public way what the sport is supposed to be. It is this logic that allows us to identify a legitimate instance of a game, despite conventionally accepted rule violations such as spitballs and offensive holding in American football.

BROAD INTERNALISM

A common response to the limits of metaphysical formalism is to identify sports with this internal logic that is expressed by the rules but not reducible to them. This view, generally called broad internalism, holds that sports have a universal essence that transcends any particular social or historical context. Sport may be something that human beings create, but it contains an essence or spirit that makes it what it is—and can be used to interpret particular instances of it. Formalism itself is an internalist theory, but broad internalist theories include more in sport's essence than the written rules. There is, as we have been saying, the "spirit" of the rules, or rather the spirit of sport. Indeed, the World Anti-Doping Association (WADA) uses "the spirit of sport," along with safety and performance enhancement, as the criteria for determining whether a substance or technique should be banned. They claim that it represents "the intrinsic value of sport."[37] It is the only "internal," sport-specific criterion they have for making the rules that regulate performance-enhancing technologies. But even if we agree on its importance and claim to know what it is, defining the spirit of sport has proven elusive. We have discussed the relationship between sport and play, as well as Suits's idea of "a voluntary [physical] effort to overcome unnecessary obstacles." What else can be said about the enduring essence of sport?

The general approach of broad internalists is to look for common principles embedded in the logic of sports.[38] In an article titled "Are Rules All an Umpire Has to Work With?" John Russell used a historical baseball example in which a runner who had just scored stayed on the field and interfered with the catcher to help a teammate score. There was no specific rule against the action, but the umpire called the runner out by appealing, argues Russell, to the principle that "the excellences embodied in achieving the lusory goal of the game are not undermined but are maintained and fostered."[39]

We can hear the echo of Suits's definition here, especially in the term "lusory goal," but Russell has gone beyond things defined by the rules and put the concept of "excellence" at the center of the essence of sport. We should recall from chapter 1 that the cultivation of excellence, called *aretē*, was also at the center of ancient Greek sport. Further, the purpose of Suits's inefficient means was precisely to create the kind of challenges that promote such excellence. Excellence is also at the center of Robert Butcher and Angela Schneider's idea of respecting the integrity of a game.[40] "The pursuit of human excellence through the dedicated perfection of each person's natural talents" is even part of WADA's explanation of its "spirit of sport" criterion.[41] Is excellence an essential concept without which we cannot make sense of sport?

A very influential account of sport espoused in Robert Simon's book *Fair Play: Sports, Values, and Society* is that sport is a "mutual quest for excellence through challenge."[42] This form of broad internalism, sometimes called "mutualism," admits up front that it is a Platonic-style ideal or what sport should (and can) be, rather than a description of what it often is. For example, mutualists admit that the rule-based object of a sports game is victory, but they claim that its *purpose* is to achieve excellence by meeting the challenge—a benefit available to winners and losers alike.[43] By incorporating principles beyond the scope of the rules, this approach allows values such as education and human flourishing to be part of the essence of sport, which gives that essence some of the normative force that formalism lacked.

Further, the idea that the quest for excellence must be mutual emphasizes the cooperative, social nature of sport. As Warren Fraleigh points out, sports are made possible not by the existence of rules but, rather, by the players' agreement to follow them.[44] This mutual agreement, he continues, incorporates both the spirit and the letter of the rules. "If participants understand only the letter of the rule, they have a limited base from which to determine how to follow the rules."[45] The same holds for officials, journalists, and record keepers. We need some metaphysical conception of what sport is—or at least an idea of what it should be—to make judgments about what counts as a sport, what actions should be permitted within a sport, and what differentiates a better from a worse instance of sport.

Returning to our original questions about Armstrong's Tours de France, we can appeal to metaphysical criteria such as inefficiency, challenge, and excellence to answer them—without accepting the formalist conclusion that they weren't Tours de France at all. Sports are more than rules, though it is clear that rules, both in letter and spirit, play an essential role in our metaphysical understanding of them. The *ethos* of sport, the unwritten rules, and the spirit of sport that underpins its rules all metaphysically matter. Still, sport's essence remains hard to pin down.

According to Graham McFee, the problem stems from trying to define sport narrowly according to one thing or another, rather than recognizing it as a complex human activity that simply takes account of rules and spirit.[46] In his view, the metaphysical relationship between rules, games, and sports depends not on the intrinsic nature of these things but, rather, on how people use them. To be sure, we cannot understand things such as "sport" or "rugby" without involving the concept of rules, but it seems clear that we need to add people into the mix. Without players who follow them, rules are nothing more than words on paper. Sports are not rules but rather rule-governed activities—something perhaps better understood as social conventions.

DISCUSSION QUESTIONS

1. Name a game that is definitely not a sport; then name a game that definitely is a sport. What seems to be the essential difference? Do activities such as fishing and hunting have to be turned into games with winners and losers to be considered sports?
2. The prohibition on handling the ball seems like a constitutive rule in soccer; can you identify a rule in your sport that is similarly constitutive? How is it different from one that is not constitutive?
3. Give an example of rule breaking that is socially accepted in your sport (i.e., fouling to stop the clock in basketball). Do you think the sport would be better if people quit breaking that rule? Would it be worse?
4. You can learn a sport's rules by reading them, but how does a player learn the spirit of a sport? Are rules, in fact, learned in a similar way?

NOTES

1. See Eric Moore, "Was Armstrong a Cheat?" *Sport, Ethics and Philosophy* 11, no. 4 (2017): 413–27, and the response from Jon Pike and Sean Cordell, "Armstrong Was a Cheat: A Reply to Eric Moore," *Sport, Ethics and Philosophy* 14, no. 2 (2020): 247–63.

2. Bernard Suits, *The Grasshopper: Games, Life, and Utopia*, 2nd ed. (Peterborough, Ontario: Broadview, [1978] 2005), 50.

3. Suits, *Grasshopper*, 51.

4. Suits, *Grasshopper*, 39.

5. Suits, *Grasshopper*, 46.

6. Suits, *Grasshopper*, 42.

7. Bernard Suits, "The Tricky Triad: Games, Play, and Sport," *Journal of the Philosophy of Sport* 15, no. 1 (1988): 7.

8. Suits, "Tricky Triad," 5. See also, Suits, "Words on Play."

9. Suits, "Tricky Triad," 8.

10. Suits, *Grasshopper*, 37.

11. Suits, *Grasshopper*, 42.

12. Suits, *Grasshopper*, 52.

13. Suits, *Grasshopper*, 54–55.

14. Bernard Suits, "The Elements of Sport," in *Philosophic Inquiry in Sport*, ed. W. J. Morgan and Klaus V. Meier (Champaign, IL: Human Kinetics, 1988), 43.

15. The diagram also implies that not all games are play, not all sports are play, and the reverse of these statements, a position Suits reaffirms in "Venn and the Art of Category Maintenance," *Journal of the Philosophy of Sport* 31, no. 1 (2004): 6.

16. Suits, "Tricky Triad," 2.

17. Suits, "Tricky Triad," 3.

18. This question is addressed by Ivo van Hilvoorde and Niek Pot, "Embodiment and Fundamental Motor Skills in eSports," *Sport, Ethics and Philosophy* 10, no. 1 (2016): 14–27.

19. International Olympic Committee, *Factsheet on the Olympic Programme* (Lausanne, Switzerland: Author, 2007), 5.

20. For a discussion of this question, see Jim Parry, "E-Sports Are Not Sports," *Sport, Ethics and Philosophy* 13, no. 1 (2019): 3–18.

21. This is Klaus V. Meier's interpretation of one of Suits's requirements (which he goes on to reject), "Triad Trickery: Playing with Sport and Games," *Journal of the Philosophy of Sport* 15, no. 1 (1988): 16. On the link between eSports and the institutionalization requirement, see Cem Abanazir, "Institutionalisation in E-Sports," *Sport, Ethics and Philosophy* 13, no. 2 (2019): 117–31.

22. Thomas P. Curtis, "Amusing Then Amazing: American Wins 1896 Discus," *Technology Review*, July 24, 1924, reprinted in *MIT News*, July 18, 1996, http://web .mit.edu/.

23. Concludes Meier in "Triad Trickery," "Any recourse to institutionalization, as an integral, necessary component of the essential nature of sport, is arbitrary, as well as erroneous and counterproductive; consequently, it should be actively rejected" (17).

24. Suits, "Tricky Triad," 5–6.

25. William J. Morgan, "The Logical Incompatibility Thesis and Rules: A Reconsideration of Formalism as an Account of Games," *Journal of the Philosophy of Sport* 14, no. 1 (1987): 3. Despite such clear declarations, however, the concept of constitutive rules is hard to apply with precision. Warren P. Fraleigh, *Right Actions in Sport: Ethics for Contestants* (Champaign, IL: Human Kinetics, 1984), 69, for example, counts the specifications for a sport contest's area and duration as well as the allowable equipment and materials among the constitutive rules (69). Suits, however, wants to classify such things as "pre-event" rules, admittedly part of performance sports but distinct from the constitutive rules that characterize game sports ("Tricky Triad," 5–6).

26. Meier, "Triad Trickery," 19.

27. Meier, "Triad Trickery," 13.

28. Meier, "Triad Trickery," 21.

29. Meier, "Triad Trickery," 24.

30. Morgan, "Logical Incompatibility," 1.

31. The distinction goes back to John Searle, *Speech Acts: An Essay in the Philosophy of Language* (Cambridge: Cambridge University Press, 1969), but it has had a life of its own in the philosophy of sport. For a recent overview, see William J. Morgan, *Sport and Moral Conflict* (Philadelphia: Temple University Press, 2020), 29–49.

32. Graham McFee, *Sport, Rules and Values: Philosophical Investigations into the Nature of Sport* (London: Routledge, 2004), 43.

33. Fred D'Agostino, "The Ethos of Games," in *Philosophic Inquiry in Sport*, 2nd ed., ed. W. J. Moran and K. V. Meier (Champaign, IL: Human Kinetics, 1995), 48–49.

34. Morgan, "Logical Incompatibility," 16.

35. Morgan, "Logical Incompatibility," 16.

36. Morgan, "Logical Incompatibility," 8.

37. World Anti-Doping Agency, *World Anti-Doping Code: 2015 with 2018 Amendments* (Montreal: WADA, 2018), 14.

38. Robert Simon, "Internalism and Internal Values in Sport," *Journal of the Philosophy of Sport* 27, no. 1 (2000): 7.

39. John S. Russell, "Are Rules All an Umpire Has to Work With?" *Journal of the Philosophy of Sport* 26, no. 1 (1999): 35.

40. Robert Butcher and Angela Schneider, "Fair Play as Respect for the Game," *Journal of the Philosophy of Sport* 25, no. 1 (1998): 1–22.

41. WADA, *Code*, 14.

42. Robert Simon, *Fair Play: Sports, Values, and Society* (Boulder, CO: Westview, 1991), 23. The fourth edition of the book is titled *Fair Play: The Ethics of Sport* (New York: Routledge, 2018).

43. Simon, "Theories of Sport," 97.

44. Fraleigh, *Right Actions*, 69.

45. Fraleigh, *Right Actions*, 71.

46. McFee, *Sport, Rules and Values*, 69.

Chapter 5

Sport and Social Conventions

Everyone has memories of magical moments in sport—those that galvanize or even create a kind of community. One of mine was at the team ski-jumping competition of the 2006 Torino Winter Olympic Games. It was a clear, cold night in Pragelato (which literally means "frozen field"), and my perch high up on a metal grandstand made it colder still. I was mixed in with fans from Norway, Japan, Austria, and many other countries, each of us decorated to support our favorite teams. As the skiers slid down the ramp and then leaped off into the sky, we cheered for our favorites and clapped politely for the others, pausing occasionally to sip hot chocolate or stamp our frozen feet.

Then, without warning, one jumper uncorked a great one—we all knew it from the moment he took off. A gasp of giddy excitement enveloped the whole arena as we watched him fly and wondered if he would ever land. When he did land, with a record jump, everyone—no matter who we were rooting for originally—shared in the thrill. Even his competitors seemed filled with joy by his feat, and they rushed over to congratulate him. We all felt like we had some part in his achievement, the athletes most of all but also the coaches, judges, and even the spectators perched in the stands. The moment was given meaning not just by its athleticism and beauty but also by its historical context—the stories of the athlete, his team, the sport itself, and the Olympic Games. As a former athlete, the feat brought back memories of my own (much more modest) triumphs in sport. *It is not the sponsorships, prizes, or medals that make sport great*, I thought; *it is the feeling of communal joy that we get at moments like these.*

My reflection, familiar enough to anyone who loves sport, illustrates the metaphysical conception of sport as a social phenomenon and the shared joy of its magical moments of achievement as an "internal good" that depends on the ideas of a given community—conventional ideas that can vary with time and place. Such conventionalist theories of sport differ from the essentialist theories discussed in the previous chapter by viewing sport as a social agreement among human beings—an agreement that might have been different and might well change. On their view, there is no universal, transcendent, ahistorical essence of sport independent of the various communities that have practiced it over the ages. Rather, sports are social conventions, norms of behavior within a community that could be otherwise—such as driving on the right (or left) side of the road.[1]

In denying that sports have essences, conventionalists do not suggest that they are somehow unimportant or that their rules and norms lack moral force. On the contrary, their claim is that essentialist theories of sport are too vague and imprecise to solve moral disputes. Conventionalists such as William Morgan are even prepared to concede that sports share common character- istics such as lusory goals or the pursuit of excellence. The problem, as he puts it, "is that asking objective, impartial standards of rational evaluation drawn from a general notion of athletic excellence to resolve conflicts over the nature and purpose of sport . . . is asking them to do something they are constitutionally unfit to do."[2] In other words, even if we could agree that the nature of sport is to cultivate excellence, we need a community to understand what that means.

SPORT AS A SOCIAL PRACTICE

Social practice theory, as Alasdair MacIntyre expounded in the early 1980s, forms part of a long line of conventionalist theories of sport. As Graham McFee points out, "Rule-following presupposes a rule-following community."[3] But there has been debate over exactly what kind of social entity sport is. Some view sport as a species of social contract akin to the seventeenth-century philosopher Thomas Hobbes's famed characterization of rationally self-interested humans voluntarily giving up a part of their liberty and subjecting themselves to laws for the greater good of peace and harmony.[4] John Rawls's twentieth-century version of the social contract includes notions of equality and fairness readily applicable to sport.[5] Other philosophers view sport as a more specific social relation—for example, Simon's theory of sport as a mutual quest for excellence through challenge.[6] MacIntyre's book, *After Virtue*, is not about sport per se, but he repeatedly uses games and sports as examples of social practices, which he defines generally as

> any coherent and complex form of socially established co-operative human activity through which goods internal to the form of activity are realized in the course of trying to achieve those standards of excellence which are appropri- ate to and partly definitive of that form of activity, with the result that human powers to achieve excellence, and human conceptions of the ends and goods involved, are systematically extended.[7]

We have already seen that sports and excellence were linked in ancient Greek thought and essentialist theory, so it comes as no surprise that this conventionalist theory should identify sport as an activity through which virtue might be cultivated. MacIntyre's theory goes beyond the axiom that sport builds character, however, by offering distinctions and insights useful to the critical assessment of how sports may succeed or fail to build character in a given community. The distinctions are between internal and external goods, as well as practices and institutions. The insights include the communal nature of sport and its need for moral traditions as well as some conception of a human *telos* to provide context for the virtues.

The overriding lesson of social practice theory applied to sport is that we acquire virtue through sport not so much by training and pursuing individual goals but, rather, by participating actively and thoughtfully in communities with histories, traditions, and shared standards of excellence. Because we participate in a variety of social practices in life, the virtues learned in sport can transfer to our participation in other sorts of practice communities and help us to resist the corrupting influence of institutions. Ultimately, social practices provide a flexible but consistent framework for living a coherent and meaningful life story.

COMMUNITIES AND VIRTUES

It is important in viewing sport as a social convention to remember the primacy of the community. Our modern tendency to privilege individual liberty over the common good is one of the things that such theories want to resist. A practice such as basketball is not an activity so much as a group of people. As MacIntyre explains, "To enter into a practice is to enter into a relationship not only with its contemporary practitioners but also with those who have preceded us in the practice, particularly those whose achievements extended the reach of the practice to its present point."[8] It is by understanding sports as communities and ourselves as responsible members of those communities that we can best acquire the virtues. Humility and trust, for example, are demanded of an athlete who must acknowledge the inadequacy of her own performance in comparison with the authoritative standards of her sport.

To improve, athletes typically work with coaches, thereby subordinating themselves in their relationship to other practitioners and subjecting themselves to a period of apprenticeship that demands respect, courage, and honesty. As MacIntyre explains, "Just so long as we share the standards and purposes characteristic of practices, we define our relationships to each other, whether we acknowledge it or not, by reference to standards of truthfulness and trust, so we define them too by reference to standards of justice and courage."⁹ Virtues in sport are cultivated not only by facing the artificial obstacles of the game itself but also by engaging in a community. Indeed, the ancient Greek idea of virtue (*aretē*) is always understood within a community—it derives from the recognition that humans are social animals. Our individual good cannot be separated from the good of our communities.

The teaching of this lesson of community interdependence is a common justification for the educational use of team sports, but individual sports also teach this lesson as long as they are understood as social practices. Peter J. Arnold uses MacIntyre's theory to defend the pedagogical value of sport in the *Journal of Moral Education*. Arnold characterizes sport as a valued social practice that teaches us through experience about the principle of equality and the duty of fair play. Sport, he says, demands that we commit to its internal goals and standards. "This entails acting in accordance with its rules and upholding its best customs, conventions and traditions. It involves exercising those virtues such as honesty, fairness, courage, determination and persistence which not only help characterise sport as a practice, but which are indispensable elements in allowing it to flourish."¹⁰

Sport's efficacy as education in community values is widely doubted, however. MacIntyre may be right that isolating oneself from practice communities is "to debar oneself from finding any good outside oneself,"¹¹ but it seems that people can and often do play sports without engaging meaningfully in sports communities.

Even within teams, individual athletes are often pitted against one another in winner-takes-all contests for starting positions that force them to focus on their personal interests to the exclusion of all others. In fact, individualistic and self-aggrandizing behavior seems more common among team-sport athletes. The game is not supposed to reward such behavior, but the market clearly does. If sports are to serve as education in community values, there must be an effort to manage them toward that end. Angela Schneider and Robert Butcher argue convincingly that athletes may rationally eschew the self-interested benefits of doping to gain the collective good of clean sport,¹² but how many athletes are even aware of such arguments, let alone able to act in accordance with them? "Perhaps," says W. Miller Brown, "we must acknowledge the predominantly individual character of sports and their goods."¹³ If the cultivation of virtue through sport depends upon it functioning as a community, the individualistic practice of sport may have no place in education.

INTERNAL VERSUS EXTERNAL GOODS

Although they disagree on whether the values of sport are absolute or relative, essentialists and conventionalists in the philosophy of sport largely agree that they are internal to it. This reflects the autotelic character of play and saves sport from being dependent for its value on some extraneous benefit. Suspicion that athletes' interest in wealth and honor somehow corrupts sport as a practice is found throughout sport history—especially during the nineteenth-century revival of the Olympic Games, which was motivated largely by values attached to the so-called amateur spirit. MacIntyre's distinction between goods internal and external to practices resonates particularly well in this context because it classifies money, prestige, and social status as *external* goods that can be achieved through any number of activities.

More valuable on MacIntyre's scheme are internal goods such as the joy I experienced witnessing the ski jumper's achievement at the Torino Olympics, or what the running community experienced when Roger Bannister achieved his four-minute mile. The notion of internal goods derives from Aristotle's claim that the enjoyment supervenes upon achievement in worthwhile activities.[14] MacIntyre adds that internal goods are practice specific, understandable only within the terms of a particular kind of practice, and recognizable only by those familiar with the practice—its particular history and challenges.[15] What is more, internal goods benefit the entire community, even though they are usually products of competition. External goods, by contrast, benefit the individual possessor to the exclusion of all others; prize money, medals, and even records are the property of individuals and teams, not entire communities.[16]

This distinction between internal and external goods therefore reflects the paradoxical nature of competition in which resistance to and even defeat of my opponent is a form of cooperation that serves to make us both stronger and better.[17]

Whereas external goods can be achieved solely through athletic skill, social virtues are required to realize internal goods. Going back to the four-minute-mile example, it is conceivable that Bannister cared only about the personal glory and pecuniary benefits he would reap from the feat. Some of his rivals, likewise, may have experienced the moment of Bannister's achievement with anger and disgust because the indivisible good of being the first four-minute miler was now lost to them. Experiencing internal goods requires social virtues such as justice, honesty, and courage—it's not just a matter of athletic skill.[18] Indeed, MacIntyre describes virtue as "an acquired human quality the possession and exercise of which tends to enable us to achieve those goods which are internal to practices and the lack of which effectively prevents us from achieving any such goods."[19] MacIntyre allows for great performances by practitioners who are "vicious and mean-spirited" but points out that they "necessarily rely on the virtues of others for the practices in which they engage to flourish and also deny themselves the experience of achieving those internal goods which may reward even not very good chess-players and violinists."[20] The bitter rival unable to appreciate the beauty of his competitor's performance deprives himself of the sport's internal goods because he lacks the requisite virtues. He can train, compete, and even win external goods, but he lacks the social virtues needed to gain access to a sport's internal, community-based goods.

The flip side of this connection between virtue and internal goods is the implication that focusing on external goods is harmful to both athletes and sport. In fact, persistent problems such as doping and other forms of cheating are frequently motivated by emphasis on external goods. As Schneider and Butcher explain, "If one practices a sport for the external rewards it brings, then provided that one can still gain those rewards, there is good reason to use any means to achieve them."[21]

An athlete who seeks internal goods, by contrast, will avoid unfair or efficient shortcuts (such as advantages gained through doping or special equipment) because she understands that they undermine the joy and satisfaction associated with, for example, a perfectly executed play. "There are good reasons, if one cares about one's sport," say Schneider and Butcher, "both to value victory and to value it only as the outcome of a fair and challenging process."[22] The argument is that the joys of achievement identified as internal goods in MacIntyre's scheme cannot be had by athletes who turn their back on the rest of the community. Doping and similar actions that seek a competitive advantage over others who eschew them may result in external reward,[23] but it undermines community trust and cohesion. If sports are understood as communities rather than sets of rules or individual pursuits, then emphasis on external goods harms the sport by harming the community.

Conventions are not essential, however, and social practice theory has also been used to argue *for* the acceptance of performance-enhancing drugs in sport. W. Miller Brown says that performance-enhancing drugs could increase an athlete's access to the internal goods of a sport, perhaps by allowing her to participate in sports competitively beyond the normal age of retirement. According to Brown, "The constraints of the practice, including the internalizing of the virtues, are compatible with the use of performance-enhancing drugs, novel and risky training regimes, and biomedical or surgical treatments or modifications of practitioners."[24] By banning drugs and other performance-enhancing technologies, he argues, we are cutting off individuals not just from the external goods associated with winning but also from internal goods that are acquired through skilled participation. Part of Brown's point is that the internal/external distinction of goods in sport is too harsh and that, in fact, goods present themselves in a kind of continuum between the two poles.[25]

Some goods are more internal; others, more external, but this distinction does not necessarily dictate their relative value. Brown explains that some external goods "conflict with the continued flourishing or development of the practice itself. Other external goods, such as entertainment, education, training, or protection of others, may not conflict with a practice's conduct but rather be direct consequences of its most capable performance."[26] Brown's argument does not suggest that athletes ought to cheat. His point, rather, is that some forms of doping might be part of a prudent pursuit of the goods valued by a sporting community and should therefore be permitted.

In short, the ontological distinction between internal and external goods does not, by itself, create the ethical distinction sport philosophers seem to be looking for. In the first place, certain goods classified as external to a sporting practice—such as health, recreation, and education—carry more social value than typical internal goods, such as the joy attending mastery of a difficult skill such as pole vaulting. In addition, certain of sports' apparent internal goods are of very dubious social value. I am thinking here of the thrill created in American football by the kinds of solid hits and high-speed tackles that make postgame highlight reels. Few football practitioners would deny that such tough defensive plays are among the internal goods of the game, but even fewer could justify their value or even their moral acceptability outside the game. MacIntyre seems to allow no room for external criticism of a practice's internal goods—even as he admits the possibility of "evil practices."[27]

Conventionalists criticize essentialist theories of sport for their inability to resolve moral disputes, but the kind of internalism that both metaphysical camps agree on seems to weaken sport's moral authority even further. If sporting communities are free to determine their own internal goods, and internal goods are all that really matter, what's to keep a sport such as American football from devolving into a despicable practice that kills most of its players?[28]

PRACTICES VERSUS INSTITUTIONS

MacIntyre's privileging of internal goods seems to be based upon their relation to social virtues. He notes that the very same virtues that provide access to internal goods can be obstacles to achieving external goods.[29] For example, when Luz Long helped his opponent, Jesse Owens, qualify for the long-jump finals in the 1936 Olympics, he exercised the social virtue of friendship and set the stage for a close and challenging competition, but he also reduced his own chances of victory. This paradox may seem to devalue virtues that reduce one's chances at victory, but it gains meaning in the distinction between practices, such as ski jumping, and institutions, such as the International Ski Federation, that oversee them. MacIntyre recognizes the necessity of institutions to the continued survival of practices, but he also warns that they threaten the well-being of those practices. "Institutions," MacIntyre points out, "are characteristically and necessarily concerned with what I have called external goods. They are involved in acquiring money and other material goods; they are structured in terms of power and status, and they distribute money, power, and status as rewards."[30]

The danger is that institutional values can take over within a practice, thereby eroding the practice's social virtues and internal goods and eventually leaving practitioners with no reason to participate but external goods. Sports, in this scenario, would be like dead-end jobs, activities done only for the money.

Sports are able to preserve their integrity only insofar as the virtues cultivated within the practice community and embodied by its members resist the corrupting power of institutions. Let us recall some of the social virtues required to appreciate an internal athletic good such as the gesture made by Olympic wrestler Rulon Gardner when he left his shoes on the mat after winning the bronze medal match at the 2004 Games in Athens.

First, we need to understand the history and traditions of the sport to even make sense of the gesture; then the sporting contest needs to have been conducted in accordance with certain virtues in order to imbue the gesture with value and meaning. Gardner was symbolically bidding a respectful farewell to his sport at the end of a successful and meaningful career. It was an emotional moment for those who watched, but that positive emotion depends ultimately on the virtues exercised both by the athlete and by his sport. Olympic wrestling needs the virtues of justice to motivate the fair running of the matches, truthfulness to ensure veracity of the results, and courage to face the risk of failure.

If these practice-sustaining virtues are overshadowed or replaced by an institution's characteristic emphasis on external goods, however, we end up with something more like made-for-television "Catch Wrestling" in which standards of fair competition and respect for tradition are sacrificed in favor of sensationalism and profit. As MacIntyre explains, "If in a particular society the pursuit of external goods were to become dominant, the concept of the virtues might suffer first attrition and then perhaps something near total effacement, although simulacra might abound."[31] One may witness the comic-book farewell of a popular professional wrestler, but it would be orchestrated by an institution such as World Wrestling Entertainment for the express purpose of maximizing its entertainment and merchandising value.

Institutions tend to threaten practices by privileging external goods and therefore undermining the virtues cultivated through the pursuit of internal goods. These virtues, in turn, encourage athletes to resist the corrupting influence of the institutions, perhaps by donating their time and money to help younger athletes. One benefit of seeing sport as a practice community is that it highlights individual practitioners' responsibility to their sport.

Virtue and excellence may be associated with sport (by essentialists and conventionalists alike), but they need to be distinguished from athletic skills. Unlike the technical abilities needed for success within a sport—such as leg speed in cycling or batting skill in cricket—virtues are dispositions that can be expressed in a variety of actions and activities. "Someone who genuinely possesses a virtue," says MacIntyre, "can be expected to manifest it in very different types of situation, many of them situations where the practice of a virtue cannot be expected to be effective in the way that we expect a professional skill to be."[32] A virtue such as courage, then, will be exercised not only when a soccer goalie faces a high-speed shot but also when he resists efforts by institutions to enlarge the goal so as to increase scoring and spectator appeal.

Practices, likewise, cannot be merely collections of people with shared sets of technical skills; rather, they need to be collections of people joined by shared values. As MacIntyre explains, "What is distinctive of a practice is in part the way in which conceptions of the relevant goods and ends which the technical skills serve—and every practice does require the exercise of technical skills—are transformed and enriched by these extensions of human powers and by that regard for its own internal goods which are partially definitive of each particular practice or type of practice."[33] It is the practitioners' dedication to the internal goods of their practice that enables them to resist the corrupting power of their institutions.

William J. Morgan sees in this antagonistic relationship between practices and institutions nothing less than the potential redemption of sport from corrupting influences such as capitalism: "While much of what is called sport these days is infected with the rational demeanor and ethic of the market, particularly the entertainment market, there is more to sport than is evident in its business side."[34] It takes practitioners to understand what this internal value is and to resist institutions' corrupting tendencies, not least by serving within those institutions as coaches, officials, organizers, and governing body members. The International Cycling Federation's declaration of the "primacy of man over machine" (a principle that bans innumerable technological efficiencies for bicycles) clearly reflects the perspective of practitioners over the interests of institutions and the industry that supports them. Most likely it is an example of virtuous practitioners resisting the corrupting power of institutions from within.

TELOS AND LIFE NARRATIVE

A final, often overlooked aspect of social practices is that they promote, in MacIntyre's words, "a certain kind of life."[35] This resonates with sport; one of the reasons we so appreciate achievements such as the four-minute mile or the prodigious ski jump is that we recognize them as products of a valued athletic lifestyle, characterized by virtues such as hard work and perseverance. Even in the heavily institutionalized and external goods–focused culture of contemporary sports, talk about virtues such as effort and discipline abounds. As the product of conventions, understandings of such virtues vary with social and historical contexts—but the practice may provide some reassuring continuity. Even when the *Chariots of Fire* ethos of natural aristocratic superiority caused athletes to train in secret or disguise their coaches, the connection between training and success was acknowledged among practitioners.

Today's popular culture likes to portray successful athletes as privileged playboys, but athletic achievement still depends, as it always has, on a particular way of life. In the documentary *Hoop Dreams*, a concerned mother explains the failure of her elder son, once a blue-chip basketball prospect, with a sigh: "Curtis's idea of being good," she says, "is that you don't have to follow the rules."[36] Whatever skills or virtues enabled Curtis to reach the athletic level he did failed to protect him from the temptations of success and also failed to transfer to other areas of his life. Why is this so often the case?

We have already observed that the athletic skills necessary to achieve a sport's external goods are not the same as the virtues nurtured and preserved by engagement in a practice. And just as skills such as dribbling and shooting a basketball are essentially useless off the court, virtues such as hard work and self-discipline are useless if a person is incapable of applying them outside sport. In fact, MacIntyre wouldn't call them virtues at all in this case. If a person really possesses the virtue of self-discipline, it will manifest itself in all aspects of her life because it will be understood as a feature of, in MacIntyre's words, "a social and moral life in terms of which it has to be defined and explained."[37] In other words, for athletic virtues to be authentic and not what MacIntyre calls "simulacra," they must manifest themselves within a unified and goal-directed life narrative.

The goal or *telos* here cannot be simply an athletic goal, even a big athletic goal such as winning an Olympic gold medal. It must, in MacIntyre's words, "transcend the limited goods of practices by constituting the good of a whole human life, the good of a human life conceived as a unity."[38] This unity, in turn, is characterized by a particular virtue: integrity, constancy, or singleness of purpose—a virtue that "cannot be specified at all except with reference to the wholeness of human life," according to MacIntyre.[39] This unified life may be different for different people at different times in different cultural contexts, but it will involve the same sorts of virtues. Indeed, it is plausible that the virtues of an ancient Olympic champion such as Milo of Kroton were not so very different from those of Olympic wrestling champions today because the activity itself has not changed dramatically. Virtues such as courage and justice can be expressed differently in different contexts and different activities, without changing fundamentally. Ultimately in social practice theory, virtues are what direct us toward a good life, understood as a kind of narrative to be written by each of us in our particular context.[40]

MacIntyre's conventionalist refusal to spell out a universal idea of virtue, relying instead on dynamically different practice communities, is appealing for its flexibility, but some remain frustrated by its apparent inconsistency. Graham McFee says that "MacIntyre's ideas cannot explain the normativity inherent in a practice but, instead, depend on it."[41] He allows that sport may teach us to follow rules but worries that following rules may be nothing more than habit. Sport should do more than train us to do an action. It should foster an understanding of why we do that action.[42] MacIntyre's social practice theory also demands such understanding. To fit MacIntyre's requirements for a valued social practice that cultivates virtues aimed at a unified, good life, sport must further promote an understanding of *why* we do sport as part of that life. Too often, this connection between sport, virtue, and life purpose is regarded as automatic or empty. Conventionalist theories of sport, and social practice theory in particular, provide a community-based framework for understanding and eventually fostering sport's ability to cultivate virtue, without resorting to a doctrine of transcendent ideals.

DISCUSSION QUESTIONS

1. Give an example of an internal good in your sport—a special moment that comes from achievement according to the sport's standards of excellence. Do these goods motivate you as much or more than external goods?
2. The logic and values of sport are sometimes at odds with the values of the institutions that govern them. Can you think of an example where a sports institution changed the rules for external reasons, such as money or popularity, harming the internal values of the sport?
3. Do you think team sports or individual sports are better for developing social and community virtues such as friendship and fairness?
4. If the virtues cultivated through sport are supposed to be expressed throughout a person's life, why do so many athletes get into trouble outside of sport?

NOTES

1. For an explanation of social conventions and how they apply to sport, see William J. Morgan, *Sport and Moral Conflict* (Philadelphia: Temple University Press, 2020), chap. 5.

2. Morgan, *Sport and Moral Conflict*, 105.

3. Graham McFee, *Sport, Rules and Values: Philosophical Investigations into the Nature of Sport* (London: Routledge, 2004), 74.

4. On sport as a social contract, see Heather L. Reid, *The Philosophical Athlete* (Durham, NC: Carolina Academic Press, 2002), 218–23; and Simon Eassom, "Games, Rules, and Contracts," in *Ethics and Sport*, ed. Mike McNamee and Jim Parry (London: E & FN Spon, 1998), 57–78.

5. John Rawls, *A Theory of Justice* (Cambridge, MA: Harvard University Press, 1971).

6. Robert Simon, *Fair Play: Sports, Values, and Society* (Boulder, CO: Westview, 1991), 23. The 4th edition of the book is titled *Fair Play: The Ethics of Sport* (New York: Routledge, 2018).

7. Alasdair MacIntyre, *After Virtue* (Notre Dame, IN: University of Notre Dame Press, 1981), 175.

8. MacIntyre, *After Virtue*, 181.

9. MacIntyre, *After Virtue*, 179.

10. Peter J. Arnold, "Sport and Moral Education," *Journal of Moral Education* 23, no. 1 (1994): 84.

11. MacIntyre, *After Virtue*, 240.

12. Angela Schneider and Robert Butcher, "Why Olympic Athletes Should Avoid the Use and Seek the Elimination of Performance-Enhancing Substances and Practices from the Olympic Games," *Journal of the Philosophy of Sport* 20–21 (1993–1994): 71.

13. W. M. Brown, "Practices and Prudence," *Journal of the Philosophy of Sport* 17, no. 1 (1990): 82.

14. MacIntyre, *After Virtue*, 184.

15. Says MacIntyre, "We call them internal [goods] for two reasons: first . . . because we can only specify them in terms of chess or some other game of that specific kind and by means of examples from such games . . . and secondly because they can only be identified and recognized by the experience of participating in the practice in question. Those who lack the relevant experience are incompetent thereby as judges of internal goods" (*After Virtue*, 177).

16. MacIntyre, *After Virtue*, 178.

17. For more on this paradox of competition, see Drew A. Hyland, "Competition and Friendship," *Journal of the Philosophy of Sport* 5, no. 1 (1978): 27–37; and Heather L. Reid, "Wrestling with Socrates," *Sport, Ethics and Philosophy* 4, no. 2 (2010): 157–69.

18. MacIntyre explains, "The kind of cooperation, the kind of recognition of authority and of achievement, the kind of respect for standards and the kind of risk-taking which are characteristically involved in practices demand for example

fairness in judging oneself and others . . . and willingness to trust the judgments of those whose achievement in the practice give them an authority to judge which presupposes fairness and truthfulness in those judgments, and from time to time the taking of self-endangering, reputation-endangering and even achievement-endangering risks" (*After Virtue*, 180).

19. MacIntyre, *After Virtue*, 178.

20. MacIntyre, *After Virtue*, 180.

21. Schneider and Butcher, "Why Olympic Athletes," 71.

22. Schneider and Butcher, "Why Olympic Athletes," 71.

23. Schneider and Butcher show that the competitive advantages gained by doping depend on others' compliance with a ban ("Why Olympic Athletes," 73).

24. Brown, "Practices and Prudence," 77.

25. Brown, "Practices and Prudence," 76.

26. Brown, "Practices and Prudence," 74.

27. This is pointed out by McFee, *Sport, Rules and Values*, 76.

28. This example is intentionally tantalizing. We will discuss the issue of violence in sport in chapter 10.

29. MacIntyre, *After Virtue*, 183.

30. MacIntyre, *After Virtue*, 181.

31. MacIntyre, *After Virtue*, 183.

32. MacIntyre, *After Virtue*, 191.

33. MacIntyre, *After Virtue*, 180.

34. William J. Morgan, *Leftist Theories of Sport: A Critique and Reconstruction* (Chicago: University of Illinois Press, 1994), 130.

35. MacIntyre brings this up in his description of the goods internal to painting. He says, "It is the painter's living out a greater or lesser part of his or her life as a painter that is the second kind of good internal to painting" (*After Virtue*, 177).

36. Emma Gates, quoted in *Hoop Dreams*, dir. Steve James, Kartemquin Films, 1994.

37. MacIntyre, *After Virtue*, 174.

38. MacIntyre, *After Virtue*, 189.

39. MacIntyre, *After Virtue*, 189.

40. MacIntyre encourages an aesthetic conception of this life: "The contrast, indeed the opposition between art and life, which is often in fact the premise rather than the conclusion of such theorists, provides a way of exempting art—including narrative—from its moral tasks . . . to think of a human life as a narrative unity is to think in a way alien to the dominant individualist and bureaucratic models of modern culture" (*After Virtue*, 211).

41. McFee, *Sport, Rules and Values*, 81.

42. McFee, *Sport, Rules and Values*, 81.

Chapter 6

Sport and Art

Not all metaphysical theories of sport are based on games and communities; many philosophers view sport rather as a form of art. In thinking about the relationship between sport and art, an image likely to come to mind is that of an ancient Greek athletic sculpture such as Myron's famous *Discus Thrower*. Such statues can seem so real as to be living, but at the same time their beauty derives from their *not* being alive—that is, that they are not imperfect human beings but, rather, representations of perfect ideal types. In fact, the *Discus Thrower* statues that we see today in the British Museum or Rome's Museo Nazionale are already representations of a representation of a representation. They are marble copies of the original bronze, long since lost, which was probably a "copy" of some nameless athletic model, who posed for the portrait of a famous Olympic victor at a particular moment in a particular competition, to be erected at Olympia or some other athletic sanctuary. Such statues were not meant to be realistic portraits of particular winners so much as generalized celebrations of an ideal cultural type.

In this way, the *Discus Thrower* represents something particular and at the same time expresses a general cultural ideal of beauty and goodness called *kalokagathia*. It is this intersection between the particular and the ideal that gives athletic art its power, and it is the mind of the spectator that brings those realms together. The interesting question, however, is not whether athletic statues and poetry are art. They are. It is whether sport itself can be art.

There are artistic sports. Some, such as artistic gymnastics, even carry the designation in their name. Many others—such as figure skating, ice dancing, diving, and synchronized swimming—employ aesthetic criteria or even "artistic merit" as standards of evaluation. R. Scott Kretchmar identifies these as "beautiful games" in which rules not only enable the game but the creation of art.[1] Further, sports are usually performed in venues specially designed or demarcated for spectatorship. And all sports—even rough games such as rugby—can be appreciated aesthetically by knowledgeable spectators in the right context. These parallels between sport and art, however, do not answer

81

the question of when and if sport can *be* art—a question further complicated by continuing debate over the definition, and even the definability, of both sport and art. Perhaps the best response is simply an exploration of the affinities between sport and art and, more precisely, sport's aesthetic nature.

What is the relationship between sport and beauty? What is the aesthetic value of athletics? Can spectators appreciate sport as art? Can athletes be artists, or even their own works of art? The question of whether sport is art may never be settled, but we can learn much about the metaphysical nature of sport by examining its relationships with art and the aesthetic.

SHARED ANCESTRY

Philosophical discussion about the relationship between sport and art grows out of sport's affinity with play. Friedrich von Schiller claimed in a nineteenth-century letter that beauty is the object of the play instinct.[2] Schiller located this play instinct at the intersection of the rational, ideal, or formal aspect of life and the aesthetic, real, material aspect: "There shall be a communion between the formal impulse and the material impulse—that is, there shall be a play instinct—because it is only the unity of reality with the form, of the accidental with the necessary, of the passive state with freedom, that the conception of humanity is completed."[3] Beauty, Schiller concluded, is produced through the playful unification of material and ideal. "The beautiful must not only be life and form, but a living form," he says.[4]

Of course, Schiller's location of beauty in play and the living form does not automatically turn sport (or even play) into art. More accurately, it identifies play as a common ontological ancestor of both sport and art, and it points to the importance of the human mind in the creation of beauty. Based on chapter 3, we might also observe that the play characteristics of being voluntary, extraordinary, autotelic, fun, and absorbing are frequently manifest in both art and sport. Such a "genetic" link based on play can account for the occasional resemblance between sport and art without implying their identity. It is sport's natural playfulness, explains Joseph Kupfer, that lends it so readily to aesthetic appreciation.[5]

Just as the seriousness of competitive sport creates problems for its categorization as play, however, it also seems to wreak havoc on sport's affinity with art. Karl Groos identifies the joy "rooted in playful experimentation and imitation" as a cause of full-fledged art.[6] The joy of sport seems rooted in different causes. Unlike art, sport is rarely made for the specific purpose of creating beauty, or even a significant aesthetic experience.[7] An Olympic figure skater may don a theatrical costume and execute a meticulously choreographed routine, but she is primarily pursuing points for the purpose of winning a competition and only coincidentally creating aesthetic value.

Not all definitions of art depend on the intentions of the artist, however. Essentialists look for something intrinsic to the work, whereas contextualists define art largely by its relation to other works of art.[8] There is also an anti-essentialist movement that rejects all efforts to define art in terms of any particular function. Clearly, if absolutely anything can be art, sport can also be art. But this trivial kind of identity doesn't tell us anything new or interesting about the nature of sport. For that, we need to ask philosophical questions about the similarities and differences between sport and art.

The affinity between sport and art is based on shared ancestry: both are descendants of play, and they share certain play characteristics that condition the spectator's aesthetic experience:

- First, they are both extraordinary—set apart from everyday life, often by explicit boundaries of space and time. Even when an ordinary object such as a soup can is presented as an artwork, it is made so precisely by removing it from its ordinary setting. This aesthetic transformation, which takes place in the mind of the beholder, depends on not just spectator pleasure but also particular kinds of knowledge and understanding.
- Second, both art and sport are autotelic—they are valued for their own sakes or as ends in themselves rather than as means to practical ends. Although both sport and art can be bought and sold for money, financial gain is not (or at least should not be) their primary purpose, and indeed the instrumental exploitation of both sport and art seem to diminish their aesthetic value. This reveals that both sport and art embody a moral dimension that informs their aesthetic value.
- Finally, this moral dimension raises questions about the roles of sport and art in education. Ancient Greek philosophers such as Plato saw a deep conceptual link between beauty and goodness, which was manifest in the educational ideal of *kalokagathia*. Modern thinker Karl Groos identifies the "moral elevation and profound insight into life" as factors that enable art to transcend the realm of "mere" play.[9] In this view, the link between sport and art goes beyond play and even aesthetics into the moral realm of intentions, ends, and finally social value. Where, then, does it start?

FRAMING: THE MIND OF THE BEHOLDER

Sport and art, observes Christopher Cordner, share the play characteristics of being "separated from the everyday world, whether by the frame around the canvas, or the touchline, the edge of the hockey rink, or the stage in the theatre."[10] These boundaries have a lot to do with aesthetic enjoyment, perhaps because they impose a rational limit on the otherwise free-flowing chaos of life. Aristotle claims that beauty depends on order,[11] and Nietzsche identifies the beauty of tragedy in the tension between Apollonian order and Dionysian chaos.[12]

Perhaps what boundaries do is act as a signal to adopt an aesthetic attitude to whatever they catch in their frame, as when a photographer chooses some section of a visual field to create an artistic image. Just as artwork is frequently concocted from everyday objects, images, sounds, and experiences, the raw human movements that make up sport also derive from common experience. It is the spatial and temporal frame circumscribing the object— the chalk lines on the field, the opening and closing whistles of a ball game, and the rising and falling of the curtain on the stage—that bring it out of the realm of the ordinary and offer it up as a package for aesthetic appreciation and enjoyment.

The framing of sport and art create what Marjorie Fisher calls "aesthetic situations"—interactions between spectators and artists (or artworks) that bring the best out of the performers by poising the audience to appreciate their work.[13] This can be seen in the architectural similarities of theaters and stadiums, or even in the way that museums invite spectators to interface with their artworks. An argument can be made that certain ordinary objects, such as Andy Warhol's famed Brillo Box, are made into art simply by being in a museum. It seems, rather, that the spectator makes that transformation by adopting an aesthetic attitude. As Arthur Danto said, "To see something as art requires something that the eye cannot descry—an atmosphere of artistic theory, a knowledge of the history of art: an artworld."[14] This is not to say that for sport to be art we simply need to put it in a museum. In fact, sporting events such as fencing tournaments are often performed in theaters built for the performing arts. What it does suggest is that the aesthetic value of sport, like art, depends at least partially on the attitude of the spectators and their willingness and ability to view the athletic performance aesthetically—as something set off from the ordinary.

The aesthetic framing of sport and art have been interpreted as a manipulation of time and space contrived specifically to raise awareness of freedom and possibility. Consider the moments leading up to the start of an athletic game or dramatic performance. We experience what Drew Hyland calls "the powerful thematizing, as opposed to the simple presence of the finitude of temporality and spatiality." This heightened awareness, in turn, challenges us to "turn that finitude into possibility."[15]

The passage from ordinary life to the extraordinary realm of the aesthetic can be as simple as blowing an opening whistle, or it might involve music, lighting, and rituals such as playing the national anthem. What is important to accomplish is a transformation of the "real world" with its stifling predictability and unrelenting inevitability into a "play world" characterized by possibility and opportunity—what philosophers sometimes call the "sweet tension" of uncertainty so characteristic of sport. The sense of possibility created by this framing might even transcend the game or performance. The opening ceremonies of the Olympic Games seek to create the mind-set that the historical anomaly of enduring world peace is somehow within our grasp.[16] By setting sport and art apart from the ordinary, we, in Jean-Paul Sartre's words, "strip the real of its reality,"[17] thereby carving out a mental space where we are open to possibility.

There does seem to be a conflict, however, between aesthetic values and athletic values. Danto's artworld is not the sports world, and even if one were to evaluate a sporting performance from within the artworld—perhaps by critically reviewing the drama of a game as if it were a tragedy—one would not thereby transform sport into art. The aesthetic value of the athletic maneuvers seems distinct from, and sometimes at odds with, their competitive purpose. Fans may delight in the spectacle of an American football player kicking out his toes as he runs away from a defender, but the player might simply be trying to avoid being tackled from behind. And if the player *is* performing a kind of dance for the audience, he is likely to be chastised in the sports world for "showboating" rather than focusing on the game. Some sports even have rules against athletes playing too much to the audience, and all sports by nature penalize athletes who fail to focus on the game.

Further, a sports fan interested primarily in the outcome of the game (or perhaps the outcome of his wager) may be insensitive to or even resentful of such artistic flair. We might say, because of this, that the fan lacks artistic sensitivity, but we would hardly say that she fails to appreciate sports.

What are we to say, then, about sports audiences who favor artistic considerations over athletic ones? The Olympic sport of ice dancing is famous for this. At the 1984 Sarajevo Winter Olympic Games, Christopher Dean and Jayne Torvill exploited loopholes in the competition rules to achieve such explicitly artistic goals as mesmerizing the audience, telling an archetypal story, and interpreting the music of Ravel's *Bolero*.[18] In Sarajevo, they won the favor of the crowd and a controversial gold medal. In the 1994 Lillehammer Games, the crowd awarded Torvill and Dean with a longer standing ovation than all other pairs, but the competition judges awarded them only a bronze medal. In this case, the purely aesthetic appreciation of their performance conflicted with competitive practicality as defined by the contest rules. Whatever the artistic value of Torvill and Dean's performance to the audience, its athletic worth was something different. Ice dancing may be both sport and art, but it does not follow that sport and art are the same thing.

On the other hand, sophisticated spectators of sport can find aesthetic value in a specifically competitive context. In this view, a highly experienced and knowledgeable spectator, such as an Olympic judge, is better suited to evaluate the aesthetic value of a performance than audience members who have never competed in and maybe rarely witness the sport. To be sure, the ability to recognize a beautifully executed, strategic play in team sports such as basketball requires a trained eye and a good understanding of the game. Further, experiencing the full emotional power of something like the decisive goal in the 1980 Olympic hockey semifinal between the United States and the Soviet Union depends on not only the competitive context of that game but also its relation to other famous events in the history of hockey and the Olympic Games.[19]

Similar claims can be made about art. For example, full appreciation of a Greek tragedy demands knowledge of history and mythology. Similarly, athletic aesthetics seem to demand sport-specific knowledge. In fact, knowledgeable spectators can take aesthetic pleasure in an efficient though not conventionally beautiful motion precisely because of its competitive value. Olympic champion Michael Johnson, for example, had an unusual but highly effective gait that some compared to the waddling of a duck. Casual spectators deemed it ugly, while true running aficionados found beauty in its genius and economy.

Athletic aesthetics may demand sport-specific knowledge, but it seems too strong to say that it simply reduces to competitive efficiency. As Lesley Wright explains, "We need to be more receptive to aesthetic possibilities, acknowledging that the aesthetic in sport is far ranging, involving an emotional response and not just the recognition of a technically efficient or functionally excellent performance."[20] Sport and art share the play characteristic of being set apart from ordinary life, and they both create aesthetic situations that bring artist (or artifact) and spectator together. Art is sometimes distinguished from sport on the basis of the intellectual engagement of the spectator. According to Karl Groos, this intellectual aspect is what elevates art beyond the merely aesthetic toward the "richer spiritual effect" that is "perceptible only to the higher senses."[21]

But intellectual engagement is a property of the spectator, not the object, and it is just as relevant to sport as it is to art. The content of the spectator's knowledge may be different in art and sport, but in both cases, beauty is truly in the mind of the beholder. It is not by applying artistic standards of beauty to sport that we appreciate it aesthetically; rather, it is by appreciating sport within an informed athletic framework that we imbue it with aesthetic and potentially artistic value.

ENDS AND MEANS

The second affinity that art and sport share is the play characteristic of autotelicity. As Robert Stecker says in his book *Aesthetics and the Philosophy
of Art*, "When we value something as aesthetically good, we value it for its
own sake or as an end rather than for something else it brings about or as a
means."[22] Sport, insofar as it is play, is likewise an end in itself. But some
thinkers such as David Best take the inseparability of means and ends to be
something that *distinguishes* art from sport. According to Best, "Where art, or
more generally the aesthetic is concerned, the distinction between means and
end is inapplicable."[23] What he means is that a beautiful touchdown and an
ugly one count the same in football, but a beautiful and ugly painting could
never have the same artistic worth. There is an end or purpose to sporting
movement (i.e., scoring points or winning games) that transcends the manner of achievement. Best admits that "aesthetic sports"—such as gymnastics,
diving, and figure skating—resemble the arts "in that their purpose cannot be
considered apart from the manner of achieving it."[24]

But he concludes that such sports still are not art because "the means never
quite reaches the ultimate of complete identification with the end which is
such an important distinguishing feature of the concept of art."[25] A poem, for
example, may be entered in a contest, but it would be absurd to say that what
mattered was whether the poem won and not how it was written. Winning
ugly, it seems, has no place in art contests.

On the other hand, the very existence of the phrase "winning ugly" suggests that athletes are at least aware of the aesthetic value of their performances. "A win is a win," they say. That's true of wins *generally speaking*.
But a *particular* win, it seems, may be ugly or beautiful—and beauty will add
to its worth. Terry Roberts claims, in fact, that Best's means-end distinction
between sport and art errs precisely in its equivocation between the general
and the particular. Roberts argues that Best is describing sports generally and
art particularly, and that when we consider both practices in the same way, the
means-end distinction disappears.

"Whether the aim, purpose, or meaning of a work of art can be identified
independently of the way it is accomplished is not a function of the nature of
the art work itself," says Roberts, "but rather it is a function of the way it is
described, particularly or generally."[26] For example, we can describe a soccer goal generally as putting the ball into the goal under certain conditions;
likewise, we can describe a song generally as putting musical notes in a certain order according to certain conditions. But if we discuss a particular goal
in a particular game or a particular song performed at a particular concert,
we will evaluate its aesthetic worth according to the manner in which it was

performed. The value of a sporting performance, like an artistic performance, transcends statistical evaluation.

As we saw in the previous section, competitive concerns inform the aesthetic value of sport, but only partially. Particular sport performances, even entire games or seasons, gain aesthetic value from the manner of their execution, their dramatic and historical context, and even the symbolic value projected on to them by spectators. To say that a symbolic sporting moment, such as Bob Beamon's record long jump in the 1968 Olympics, was nothing more than a leap of 29 feet, 2 1/2 inches (8.9 meters) would be an impoverished understanding of a rich and meaningful moment. As Terry Roberts says, "Just as we should not let the jaded interest of so-called 'typical' fans determine the place of scoring within the logic of sport, we would not let such generalized, and in that sense trivial, accounts determine the place of meaning within the arts."[27]

Sporting actions such as shooting a basketball may have an explicit purpose, such as scoring, but that purpose is internal to the game and, therefore, within the autotelic boundaries of play. Sport is not, like cars and telephones, something made purely to serve external ends.[28] Like art, it is an end in itself, and even the often-criticized goal of winning is nothing more than an internal part of the game.

Further, the instrumental use of art and sport seems independent from their autotelicity. The payment that a musician earns does not prevent his performance from being art; likewise, the buying and selling of an athletic performance does not (necessarily) prevent it from being sport. The fact that athletes or artists are paid does not imply that they perform solely for the money. Even if they are motivated to perform by the promise of earnings, the performance itself can still be autotelic. The presence of external motivations does not necessitate the absence of internal ones. People can and clearly do act out of complex motivations. As Christopher Cordner observes, "In both spheres an indefinitely wide range of motives is operative. An artist, like a sports player, may be moved by the desire to be the best in a given field, to make something perfect, to earn fame and fortune, to please an audience, or *épater le bourgeois*. Or he/she may just love painting or writing or running or baseball."[29]

Nothing prevents a professional musician from performing out of simultaneous desires for money, fame, beauty, social commentary, and sheer unadulterated joy. Likewise, nothing prevents a professional athlete from performing for the same complex of reasons. Professional basketball player Bill Bradley claims that he often played for the "pure pleasure" of it, sometimes forgetting the score, even in important games.[30]

What threatens aesthetic values is not so much the use of sport or art for external ends but, rather, its exploitation: the selling out of a practice's internal values in order to pursue external ends. It is one thing to be paid or patronized as an actor, musician, or artist and another thing to tailor one's art specifically to the interest of the market or the patron. The boxer who intentionally loses a match to gain gambling revenue is exploiting his sport because he sacrifices the internal demand that he try to win for the external goal of revenue. The boxer who receives a monetary prize for winning makes no such sacrifice. The boxer who "takes a dive" is further subject to moral condemnation; he has immorally exploited his sport by violating its internal requirements. His action is characterized as "an ugly thing to do," and he himself is likely to be disgusted by the prospect of performing it. The difference between use and exploitation is a moral one, and our reaction to it suggests that morality does have an effect on aesthetic value—in sport as well as art.

Stephen Mumford uses Diego Maradona's "hand of god" goal (which was later revealed to be an illegal handball) and Ben Johnson's steroid-fueled 100-meter race at the 1988 Seoul Olympics to illustrate the connection between moral and aesthetic value. However beautiful these things may have been to witness at the time, their beauty is diminished—and perhaps turned to disgust—by the discovery of their (im)moral context. Mumford compares these with Leni Riefenstahl's famous film *Olympia*, which was visually stunning and inaugurated a variety of creative cinematographic techniques but ultimately celebrated repugnant Nazi principles and supported their immoral regime. According to Mumford, the aesthetic value of the film, like the sports examples, is diminished by its moral context.[31] To some, the sport example will seem to involve more aesthetic diminishment than the art one. To others, neither example will seem aesthetically diminished by its moral context. But the difference will not depend on whether we make a moral distinction between ends and means so much as on whether we make a conceptual connection between beauty and morality.

ART AND SPORT TRANSCENDING PLAY

Karl Groos noted above that the moral connection is what elevates art (and sport) above the realm of mere play. One form of this elevation is just putting such practices into the service of social and humanistic ends, especially education. The ancient Greek use of sport for education pivoted on a strong conceptual connection between beauty and morality. *Kalokagathia*, which combines the ideals of beauty and goodness, was the driving force of not only Greek athletic art but also the gymnastic education that aimed to cultivate both simultaneously.

Plato's Academy is perhaps the most famous example of such gymnasia. In the context of Plato's philosophy, the ideal or "form" of the good is closely connected with that of beauty. In *Hippias Major*, for example, Plato says, "Then if beauty is the cause of goodness, the good comes into being through beauty. That is why we fervently pursue thinking and all other beautiful things—because their offspring, the good, is worthy of our zeal. Based on what we are discovering, the beautiful is a kind of father to the good."[32]

It is the understanding of these forms of goodness and beauty that both results in and is cultivated by performing beautiful bodily movements. Dancing, in particular, requires aesthetic as well as athletic sensibilities, and it employs such moral virtues as courage and self-control. By performing visually beautiful and controlled movements in Plato's Academy, students were prepared to perform morally beautiful and controlled actions in their civic lives.[33] Further, by imitating the feats of mythological heroes in athletic games, they came to understand heroic virtues.[34]

The roles of art and sport in education are less well defined today, but it seems at least possible that they might inform moral education. Immanuel Kant valued fine art because it seeks to engage our higher cognitive powers. An artist, according to Cordner, "seeks to produce something for contemplation."[35] Adds Best, "It is distinctive of any art form that its conventions allow for the possibility of the expression of a conception of life situations."[36] And though some find it difficult to imagine athletes designing their performances to express a particular conception of contemporary moral, social, and political problems,[37] sports can and often do inspire such contemplation among knowledgeable spectators.

In fact, athletics have been used to express conceptions of virtue and morality since their discernible origins in ancient Egypt and Mesopotamia, and the ancient Greek contests at the root of modern sport were explicitly tied to moral ideals.[38] Athletics always have and still do "enact or realize life-values," says Cordner, and this is a quality they share with art.[39]

Moreover, great artists and athletes attract us for the same reason: "The distinctiveness of their genius."[40] According to Teresa Lacerda and Stephen Mumford, genius adds aesthetic value to sport and art in a similar way: by opening our minds to new ideas.[41] Whether or not they intend it to be so, athletes' performances can be objects of intellectual contemplation and social criticism. Nadia Comaneci's "perfect 10" performance on the uneven parallel bars at the 1976 Olympic Games inspired people to contemplate the possibility of human perfection. Hassiba Boulmerka's performance at the 1992 Olympic Games inspired social commentary on attitudes toward females and female bodies in conservative Islamic countries.[42]

To say that these performances are not worthy of such contemplation because they were not intended by the athlete to be so is to call a great many objects of inspiration and contemplation unworthy. At the same time, to call them worthy of contemplation is to put them on a level with art without insisting that they are art. Art and sport share the ability to open our minds to possibility.[43] At the same time, intellectual contemplation of them engages the higher cognitive faculties capable of reflecting on such important conceptions as beauty and goodness.

For those who believe that beauty in sport is confined to the beauty of athletes' bodies, or perhaps the grace of their movement, it is worth recalling that Greece's ancient athletic stadiums and gymnasia (like ancient theaters) were located in notoriously beautiful natural environments. Aristophanes likens Plato's Academy to a paradise: "You shall descend to the Academy and run races beneath the sacred olives along with some modest compeer, crowned with white reeds, redolent of yew, and careless ease, of leaf-shedding white poplar, rejoicing in the season of spring, when the plane-tree whispers to the elm."[44]

The uncommon natural beauty of athletic settings such as Olympia, Nemea, and Delphi can be appreciated even today. What we have lost is the idea that immersion in beauty leads to an aesthetic appreciation of goodness and perhaps even the ability to develop aesthetic sensitivity as part of a good moral education—an education aimed at *kalokagathia*. The beauty of the ancient Greek athletic form represents such moral virtues as self-control, such religious virtues as humility, and such civic virtues as liberty. In this sense, the athlete's body is his or her own work of art. According to Fisher, "Athletes are artists both in so far as they perfect their own bodies but also the forms of their game."[45] Cordner identifies grace as "a total harmony of being," located in the person and not just her movement and ultimately linked to the moral realm.[46] What is more, athletic grace for Cordner is not just a matter of physical movement but also a manifestation of how the athletic aesthetic of grace is linked ultimately to the moral realm.

As in the Platonic idea of *kalokagathia*, one cannot strive for true beauty without also striving for goodness. Just as the birth of a child or the donation of organs is considered a morally beautiful act regardless of its visual repugnancy, virtue adds value to athletic victory and beauty to the athletic form. Though also present in art, the link between moral and aesthetic value is especially strong in sport.

All of this brings us back to our *Discus Thrower* and its enduring artistic value. The statue can be seen as the legitimate offspring of art and sport, two activities that are not identical but nevertheless share the common ancestor of play and manifest many of its genetic characteristics. They are metaphysically intermediate between the ideal and real, the formal and the material, and the universal and particular, and are therefore capable of expressing as well as representing beauty. They can both be appreciated aesthetically—simply as a form of pleasure or, when understood in their dramatic and historical contexts, as forms of symbolic meaning. They are both, at least ideally, auto-telic—in need of no justification beyond themselves. In fact, as Tim Elcombe concludes, sport may best be served by looking to art as an "ideal metaphor" to embody.[47] Although diving gives style points and swimming doesn't, beauty can and ought to be valued in both. And although both sport and art can be used for external ends, it is their intrinsic moral worth that informs their aesthetic value.

Finally, the educational value of sport and art demands the same engagement of higher cognitive powers needed to understand their moral dimension and to appreciate their aesthetic beauty. Not just performances but also the athletes themselves, can and ought to be appreciated as objects of intellectual and even ethical contemplation. This is, after all, the Hellenic heritage of modern sport and the genetic destiny it shares with art, as a legitimate and beautiful offspring of play.

DISCUSSION QUESTIONS

1. Compare your experience playing sports with your experience creating art. How are the experiences similar? How different?
2. Imagine a "beautiful play" in your favorite sport. How much of its beauty depends on an understanding of the competitive purpose of the game? Would a person unfamiliar with sport see the same beauty?
3. Does finding out that an athlete did something immoral diminish your aesthetic appreciation of her feat? For example, do Marion Jones's Olympic performances seem less beautiful because she later admitted to doping?
4. Moral goodness is said to make art and athletes more beautiful. Does this also go for romance? Is a person made more attractive by his moral qualities?

NOTES

1. R. Scott Kretchmar, "Beautiful Games," *Journal of the Philosophy of Sport* 16, no. 1 (1989): 42.
2. Friedrich von Schiller, "Letter XV," in *Essays and Letters*, vol. 8, trans. A. Lodge, E. B. Eastwick, and A. J. W. Morrison (London: Anthological Society, 1882). Reprinted in Ellen Gerber, ed., *Sport and the Body: A Philosophical Symposium* (Philadelphia: Lea & Febiger, 1974), 299.
3. Schiller, "Letter XV," 299.
4. Schiller, "Letter XV," 300.

5. Joseph Kupfer, "Sport: The Body Electric," in *Philosophic Inquiry in Sport*, 2nd ed., ed. W. Morgan and K. Meier (Champaign, IL: Human Kinetics, 1995), 391.

6. Karl Groos, "Play from the Aesthetic Standpoint," in *The Play of Man* (New York: Appleton, 1901). Reprinted in Gerber, *Sport and the Body*, 304.

7. According to Robert Stecker, the aesthetic conception defines art neatly as something made to create significant aesthetic value (or a significant aesthetic experience). *Aesthetics and the Philosophy of Art* (Lanham, MD: Rowman & Littlefield, 2005), 6.

8. Stecker, *Aesthetics*, 9.

9. Groos, "Play from the Aesthetic Standpoint," 303.

10. Christopher Cordner, "Differences between Sport and Art," in Morgan and Meier, *Philosophic Inquiry*, 427.

11. Aristotle, *Poetics*, trans. Malcom Heath (London: Penguin, 1997), 1450b.

12. Friedrich Nietzsche, *The Birth of Tragedy*, trans. Shaun Whiteside (London: Penguin, 1994).

13. Marjorie Fisher, "Sport as an Aesthetic Experience," in Gerber, *Sport and the Body*, 318.

14. Arthur Danto, "The Artworld," *Journal of Philosophy* 61 (1964): 580.

15. Drew A. Hyland, *Philosophy of Sport* (New York: Paragon, 1990), 121.

16. This is no coincidence; the Modern Games' founder, Pierre de Coubertin, saw an important parallel between the aesthetic power of sport and art. For an analysis, see Nicholas Attfield, "Coubertin's Music: Culture, Class, and the Failure of the Olympic Project," *InMedia* 6 (2017) online. DOI: https://doi.org/10.4000/inmedia.934.

17. Jean-Paul Sartre, *Being and Nothingness*, trans. Hazel E. Barnes (New York: Philosophical Library, 1956), 580.

18. Elizabeth A. Hanley, "A Perennial Dilemma: Artistic Sports in the Olympic Games" (unpublished manuscript, 2000), 5.

19. As Spencer K. Wertz points out, "The artistic merit or value of a particular sporting event is measured by whether that given game equals its moment, that is, whether or not it has lived up to its historical antecedents—its tradition" ("Representation and Expression in Sport and Art," *Journal of the Philosophy of Sport* 12 [1985]: 13).

20. Lesley Wright, "Aesthetic Implicitness in Sport and the Role of Aesthetic Concepts," *Journal of the Philosophy of Sport* 30, no. 1 (2003): 91.

21. Groos, "Play from the Aesthetic Standpoint," 302.

22. Stecker, *Aesthetics*, 4.

23. David Best, "The Aesthetic in Sport," in Morgan and Meier, *Philosophic Inquiry*, 379.

24. Best, "Aesthetic in Sport," 380.

25. Best, "Aesthetic in Sport," 381.

26. Terence J. Roberts, "Sport, Art, and Particularity: The Best Equivocation," in Morgan and Meier, *Philosophic Inquiry*, 418.

27. Roberts, "Sport, Art, and Particularity," 422.

28. Roberts, "Sport, Art, and Particularity," 419.

29. Cordner, "Differences between Sport and Art," 427.

30. Bill Bradley, *Values of the Game* (New York: Broadway Books, 1998), 5.

31. Stephen Mumford, *Watching Sport: Aesthetics, Ethics, and Emotion* (Abingdon, UK: Routledge, 2011), chap. 8.

32. Plato, *Hippias Major*, trans. Paul Woodruff (Indianapolis: Hackett, 1983), 297bc.

33. For more on Plato's theory of athletics in education, see Heather L. Reid, "Sport and Moral Education in Plato's *Republic,*" *Journal of the Philosophy of Sport* 34, no. 2 (2007): 160–75; and Heather L. Reid, "Plato's Gymnasium," *Sport, Ethics and Philosophy* 4, no. 2 (2010): 170–82.

34. This thesis is explained in Heather L. Reid, "Performing Virtue: Athletic *Mimēsis* in Platonic Education," in *Politics and Performance in Western Greece*, ed. H. Reid, D. Tanasi, and S. Kimbell (Sioux City: Parnassos Press, 2017), 265–77.

35. Cordner, "Differences between Sport and Art," 434.

36. Best, "Aesthetic in Sport," 385.

37. I do remember figure skater Katarina Witt explaining the music and choreography of her long program as a critique of the Balkan wars—but this is at best an exception that proves the general rule.

38. Heather L. Reid, *Athletics and Philosophy in the Ancient World: Contests of Virtue* (London: Routledge, 2011), 11–12.

39. Cordner, "Differences between Sport and Art," 429, 434.

40. Cordner, "Differences between Sport and Art," 427.

41. Teresa Lacerda and Stephen Mumford, "The Genius in Art and in Sport: A Contribution to the Investigation of Aesthetics of Sport," *Journal of the Philosophy of Sport* 37, no. 2 (2010): 182–93.

42. For a philosophical account of the significance of Boulmerka's performance, see William J. Morgan, "Multinational Sport and Literary Practices and Their Communities: The Moral Salience of Cultural Narratives," in *Ethics and Sport*, ed. Mike McNamee and Jim Parry (London: E & FN Spon, 1998), 184–204.

43. Drew Hyland suggests that athletes and artists both share the stance of play—that is, the stance of responsive openness: "What is a poet, if not one more open to the possibilities of words, of language, and more responsive to them? A painter's openness and responsiveness to light and to color astonishes us, as does the potter's to clay and form, the musician's to sound and rhythm, the dancer's to space, time, and the movement of the human body" (*Philosophy of Sport*, 118).

44. Aristophanes, "Clouds," in *The Comedies of Aristophanes*, trans. William James Hickie (London: Bohn, 1853), lines 1011–15.

45. Fisher, "Sport as an Aesthetic Experience," 320.

46. C. D. Cordner, "Grace and Functionality," in Morgan and Meier, *Philosophic Inquiry*, 412–13.

47. Tim L. Elcombe, "Sport, Aesthetic Experience, and Art as the Ideal Embodied Metaphor," *Journal of the Philosophy of Sport* 39, no. 2 (2012): 201–17.

Chapter 7

Mind and Body

The downhill skier's eyes are closed, and she seems completely detached from reality. The television camera zooms in close as she twists her body and curves her hands as she races down a course that exists only in her mind. What exactly is going on in this moment, and how does it relate to the metaphysics of sport? We might say simply that the skier's visualization technique is an invention of sport psychology—a way to habituate the mind to the challenge that lies ahead and a means of building confidence, overcoming fear, and improving physical performance.

But buried within our answer are metaphysical assumptions about the nature of the athlete and athletic performance that have far-reaching consequences for the practice of sport. Most notably, the language we use to describe the training technique breaks up the athlete into separate parts: a part that thinks, a part that feels, and a part that skis. With no more than a moment's reflection, however, we realize that all three parts must be involved in the skiing, otherwise why involve them all in training? It must be an accident of linguistic convention that we use terms such as "physical performance" and "physical education"—we know these things involve more than physical matter, more than the body, or do we?

The metaphysical nature of athletes, which is to say, the nature of persons, is infrequently discussed in the philosophy of sport literature. Our experience of ourselves as athletes, meanwhile, frequently seems at odds with traditional explanations of the nature of persons, which often differ significantly according to culture and even gender. The metaphysical question "What am I?" is intimately connected to the personal identity question "Who am I?" And the way that we approach and eventually answer these questions has profound implications not just for athletes' experiences in sport but also for such enduring issues as the role of sport in education, the impact of gender on sport participation, eating disorders, the use of drugs and genetic technologies, and even the experience of spectators.

In short, our metaphysical understanding of athletes has as big an influence on sporting practice as our metaphysical understanding of sport itself. At a minimum, we should seek to understand the variety of metaphysical conceptions of persons and their potential influence on the practice of sport. The purpose of this chapter is not to promote a particular metaphysical account but, rather, to inspire and enrich philosophical discussion and thereby to improve our understanding not just of athletes but also of sport as an enduring human practice.

Philosophical theories of persons in both Eastern and Western traditions usually center on the relationship between mind and body. Human experience, almost universally, takes note of these two aspects of personhood. How human beings understand them, however, is anything but universal. If we project the two concepts onto the dichotomy between material and nonmaterial existence, three possibilities emerge: both mind and body are nonmaterial (idealism), both are material (physicalism), or one is material while the other is nonmaterial (dualism).

The fourth possibility, that each has both material and nonmaterial aspects or qualities, is rarely discussed in the Western philosophical tradition but is assumed in the Eastern tradition; or, to be more precise, a strict dichotomy between material and nonmaterial existence does not condition the traditional Eastern view. A later Western approach called phenomenology leaves the dichotomy to one side, focusing rather on our experience as human beings in which we are always both mind and body or, to use the technical term, embodied. Because sport is a performative activity that integrates mind and body, it ultimately demands a holistic approach to the question of mind and body.

THE WESTERN DUALIST HERITAGE

Western philosophy debated the metaphysical nature of human beings almost from the start. There material nature of the body (*sōma*) was generally accepted, but opinions differed about the *psychē*—a word conventionally translated as mind or soul but understood also as the source of bodily appetites and movement. Some of the earliest philosophers, known collectively as the "pre-Socratics," were physicalists who denied the existence of nonmaterial things. Democritus, for example, theorized that everything was made of atoms (Greek for "uncuttables"), material particles assembled into objects that could be broken down and reformed into new entities like so many interchangeable Lego blocks. Early physicalists did not necessarily deny the existence of gods and minds. They simply understood those things to be particular configurations of matter.

Perhaps this was not such a stretch for them, given the anthropomorphic understanding of most ancient gods. The belief that gods and souls were immaterial proved more popular over time, however. Part of the appeal may have come from Pythagoras's theory that human souls were not only immaterial but also immortal and therefore capable of transmigrating from one body to another—even to other species.

At this early stage in Western philosophy, theories of mind-body dualism did not seem to denigrate sport. On the contrary, Pythagorean athletes were famously successful at the Olympic Games. They included the great runner Astylos, winner of three Olympic *stade* (200-meter sprint) races; and the imposing wrestler Milo, who prevailed at Olympia six times in a twenty-four-year span. Plato compliments Ikkos of Taranto, a Pythagorean runner and coach known for his chastity and self-discipline.[1] Plato appears to have embraced Pythagoras's understanding of mind-body dualism as well as his enthusiasm for athletics. In the *Republic*, gymnastics are advocated primarily as training for the soul and not for the body (410bc), and in the dialogue's concluding "Myth of Er," the soul of the athletic female Atalanta is depicted as choosing a male body for her next incarnation, because she is attracted by the honors afforded to champion athletes (620b).

In Plato's *Laws*, gymnastic education and athletic festivals are part and parcel of communitywide education, for males and females focused on *aretē*, something Plato believed to depend on the *psychē*.[2] And in real life, when Plato set up his school in a gymnasium called the Academy, there is no evidence that he discouraged or even deemphasized the athletic activities traditionally associated with that place.[3]

Unfortunately for sport, however, it was Plato's *Phaedo* that had the biggest influence on Western attitudes toward the mind and the body. *Phaedo* depicts Socrates just before his execution trying to console his distraught friends with the notion that his mind/soul (*psychē*) will endure and even prosper after death. He argues that the *psychē* must be immaterial, and therefore indestructible, because it is the organ that perceives perfect ideas—that is, the Platonic "forms"—which are themselves the unchanging immaterial prototypes of which all material things are imperfect copies.[4] In fact, Socrates argues, the mind/soul's affinity with the forms makes the body a distraction from or even impediment to understanding them. The body acts like a prison that the *psychē* must escape if truth is to be known (*Phaedo* 78b–84b).

This argument meshed well with the Western religious traditions of Judaism, Christianity, and Islam—all of which recommend spiritual and intellectual paths for coming to know God. The corollary idea that the body is a "prison," or at least a hindrance to spiritual and intellectual development, can be seen in the religious emphasis on the afterlife and in some religions' attempts to transcend and sometimes even denigrate the body.

It was the radical substance dualism of René Descartes, however, that had the biggest influence on modern Western ideas about the metaphysics of persons. It was not so much Descartes's distinction between body and mind that challenged sport—the Greeks had accepted dualism while promoting athletics. It was, rather, the identification of our human essence as *thinking* (understood narrowly as rational cognition) that challenged the importance of athletics. The Greek *psychē* had been a much richer and complex concept than Descartes's mind, not least because of its intimate connection to the body. This should not be a surprise. Descartes was a rationalist in search of one logically indubitable proposition when he arrived at his famous *cogito*: "I think, therefore I am."[5]

Because the information available to him about the external world, including his body, was always filtered through the senses, which were unreliable, Descartes concluded that knowledge was possible only through reason. He calculated that, as long as he was thinking, it must also be true that he exists. Because Descartes's theory identified thinking as the most—indeed, the only—certain thing about human existence, he declared us to be essentially "thinking things." It was a declaration different from Aristotle's classification of humans as "rational animals"; in that case, we are corporeal, distinguished from other animals by our capacity for reason. In Descartes's view, we are essentially incorporeal minds, and our bodies are just another doubtful feature of a world to which we lack certain access.

This dualistic legacy has profoundly affected the way we think and talk in the West about human beings generally and sport more specifically. Our minds are characterized as knowing subjects that move passive, corporeal bodies. Our bodies are compared to irrational animals or, worse, unthinking machines. Juvenal's Roman-era saying *"mens sana in corpore sano"* (sound mind in sound body) has been interpreted in modern times as a Hellenic approach to a balanced education, but Juvenal wasn't talking about sport or athletics at all—just mental and physical health.[6] The very idea that we need a balance between mental and physical education assumes that body and mind are educated separately—an idea that follows from a metaphysical understanding of the mind as essentially a thinking thing detached from the body, and by the understanding of physical movement as somehow independent from thinking.

THE CHALLENGE OF THE BODY

When Paul Weiss wrote the first major philosophical work dedicated to sport in 1969, he brought the Western dualistic heritage with him. The body, as he described it, presented "a challenge" to be overcome at least partially through

the medium of sport. Weiss begins by arguing that the body needs to be considered as much a part of the human being as the mind, but the very fact that
he needs to argue this point shows the force of the dualistic heritage. "Only
a man intoxicated with a Cartesian, or similar, idea that he is to be identified
with his mind will deny that he is a body too," says Weiss.[7] He goes on to
endorse the holistic philosophy of Maurice Merleau-Ponty (discussed below)
and to discredit physicalists with the quip "since they have at least mind
enough to think there is nothing more than a body, I have no mind to follow
them."[8] Weiss does not deny the primacy of intellectual activity in human life,
and (following Aristotle) he believes that the "full use" of either mind or body
precludes the "full use" of the other at any given time. Nevertheless, believing that both should be cultivated, he says, "A career devoted to one alone is
possible to only half a man."[9]

Weiss sees athletics as a way to unify mind and body. Sport and art require
controlled expression of the emotions, which he understands to be the inter-
mediaries between minds and bodies. He says these activities "offer excellent
agencies for unifying men" by "making it possible for minds and bodies to
be harmonized clearly and intensely."[10] Weiss explains the process using the
mathematical concept of a vector, a quantity having direction and magnitude.
He envisions the mind as providing a vector—that is, a future direction—for
the body. Through training, a "man uses his mind to dictate what his body is
to do," and the body slowly adapts to the desired vector, thereby "correcting
the disequilibrium between mind and body."[11]

Weiss's use of masculine pronouns here is not gender-neutral. He believes
that sports are more amenable to males because "the young woman's body
does not challenge her the way in which the young man's body challenges
him. She does not face it as something to be conquered, since she has already
conquered it in the course of her coming of age."[12] Weiss has been criticized
for writing a book about sport without having been an athlete (something he
admits at the outset of the book). We might add that he also lacks the experience of having been female. And, as we shall see, this lack of experience
could be one reason his philosophy of sport preserves such a strong dualism.
Nevertheless, Weiss turns the philosophical tide against the dismissal and
denigration of the body and grants it newfound importance in the understanding of human nature.

Forty years after Weiss's book, his dualistic theory of mind and body
in sport was revived and revised by Daniel Dombrowski in *Contemporary
Athletics and Ancient Greek Ideals*. Dombrowski rejects most of Weiss's
claims about women and athletics as defective. He compares them dialec-
tically with the views of philosophers such as Jane English, who do have
the relevant experience.[13] He then injects Weiss's semi-Cartesian dualism
with the ancient Greek concepts of *dunamis* (power) and hylomorphism to

transform Weiss's characterization of athletics as the pursuit of bodily excellence into a more holistic, but still dualist, idea of athletics simply as the pursuit of excellence (*aretē*). Not long afterward, Jesús Ilundáin-Agurruza wrote a book called *Holism and the Cultivation of Excellence in Sports and Performance: Skillful Striving*, which interprets excellence in sport and other performative activities in terms of mind-body integration.[14]

Weiss had theorized that athletics gave men the opportunity to become excellent in something they could actually master at a young age.[15] This set the stage for the pursuit of excellence in other activities later on. Dombrowski also recognizes this educational function as essential to sport's social value: "If we do not take it to be our main task to have athletes become excellent," he says, "we come to treat them as workers or appendages."[16] But if we understand human beings metaphysically as "bodyminds" (Ilundáin-Agurruza's term) or hylomorphs (Dombrowski's, from the Greek *hyle*, matter, and *morphē*, the form or structure given to matter by the mind) and we understand *aretē* (excellence) as a *dunamis* (power), we can value the cultivation of athletic excellence as education for virtues transferable to activities beyond sport. Dombrowski calls this process "dynamic hylomorphism"[17]; Ilundáin-Agurruza calls it "skillful striving." Dualism applied to sport, then, need not exclude the mind or denigrate the body, as some religious and Cartesian doctrines imply. In fact, the transfer of virtues cultivated in sport to nonathletic activities seems to require a close link between mind and body.

IDEALISM AND PHYSICALISM

Just as Cartesian dualism found its critics within the philosophy of sport, it was challenged within mainstream philosophy as well—first by the empiricists, who held (in opposition to rationalists such as Descartes) that all knowledge comes to us through the senses. Empiricists such as George Berkeley shared Descartes's concerns about our senses' ability to deceive and began to question the independent existence of matter itself. If a tree falls in the woods and no one is there to hear it, suggests Berkeley, not only does it not make a sound but also it might not even exist.[18]

Berkeley's theory that only ideas exist is called idealism, and it implies not only that people are essentially immaterial thinking things but also that people are deity-dependent—that is, they are ideas in the mind of god. Such strong idealism was embraced by relatively few, but the notion of human beings bereft of material existence led to a focus on immediate experience as the true source of identity. David Hume argued that we are nothing more than a "bundle of impressions" as if our existence amounted to a stack of mental photographs tied together with a temporal string.[19] Physical bodies seemed to have no role at all in the early modern philosophical debate about the nature of human beings.

If the discussion takes place among physicalists, however, human beings are understood as nothing more than bodies, or at least nothing more than physical matter. The term "physicalism" (as opposed to materialism) also betrays a link with the late nineteenth and early twentieth-century rise of physical sciences. Because such sciences are not equipped to measure immaterial entities, the motivation to deny those entities' existence was enhanced. Indeed, the ancient Greek and Roman Epicurean philosophers were also physicalists, and they devoted much of their studies to natural phenomena in order to liberate themselves from the fear and anxiety caused by mysterious beliefs about immaterial gods and other supernatural forces. Modern physicalists, in general, do not deny the existence of entities such as minds, thoughts, or emotions; they simply believe that such phenomena depend or "supervene" upon physical phenomena such as brains, firing neurons, and chemical reactions. As with dualism, nothing intrinsic to physicalism is incompatible with sport, but an accompanying attitude affects the way we view sport.

The attitude toward sport and humanity characteristic of physicalism is an emphasis on the body and a narrowly physiological approach to training. I once had a cycling coach who used to select athletes based on physical data such as watt generation and oxygen uptake; he wasn't interested in past racing results. Such body focus has its own philosophical tradition. In reaction to what he saw as religion's overemphasis on souls and the afterlife, Friedrich Nietzsche denigrates the "despisers of the body" and has his character Zarathustra declare, "Body am I and nothing else; and soul is only a word for something about the body."[20]

Physicalism within the realm of sport, however, is usually a response to scientific observation rather than religious doctrine. Empirical science has already learned so much about the structure and behavior of physical organisms that a purely physiological explanation for everything attributed to the human mind seems inevitable.

Attempts to reproduce human intelligence in computers, however, have revealed, as much as anything, how complex the human mind is. Thinking— narrowly understood as calculation, recall, and organization of ideas—is quite easily reproduced by machines. But our experiences of so-called *qualia*—things such as sound, color, or smells—are difficult to duplicate in machines, because machines lack consciousness. To be sure, a radio can decode music, an electronic sensor can recognize faces, and an alarm can be tripped by the presence of smoke, but these objects do not experience what we experience mentally in the presence of the same phenomena. This suggests that our minds are more than machines, or at least that human brains are importantly different from machines.

But what about our bodies? In comparison with human minds, our bodies seem relatively simple and predictable—maybe more so even than some modern electronic machines. Within sport there is a culture of treating one's body as a machine—sometimes even an expendable machine—one that can be repaired if broken and, once worn out, can be discarded. Athletes are described and often think of themselves in terms of numerical specifications: height, weight, body-fat percentage, squat kilograms, 40-meter time, VO^2 max, strength-to-weight ratio, and win-loss record. Training is approached scientifically, like the calculated tuning of a high-tech machine—efforts are measured and monitored with sophisticated sensors and then the numbers are crunched by computers to reveal every possible advantage.[21] Chemical and even genetic manipulation are not excluded; the body is a specimen, the site of an experiment, aimed at discovering and even transcending human capabilities.

In his book *Mortal Engines*, John Hoberman identifies the nineteenth-century development of ergometers, devices that quantify athletic performance, as the dawn of an era that would come to view athletes themselves as machines.[22] To be sure, that era has not yet come to a close. Indeed, robots now play soccer and other games—but can we say that they are athletes playing sports?

KINESTHETIC INTELLIGENCE

Paradoxically, physicalism's scientific orientation, when applied to sport, separates the body more radically from the mind even as it grants equal ontological status to both. That is to say, it not only regards movement as a self-contained function of the body but also views thinking as a self-contained function of the mind-brain that has little or nothing to do with the rest of the body. In fact, the dumb-jock myth—the belief that physical excellence excludes intellectual excellence—has thrived under physicalist hegemony.

Now that superior scientific brains can take charge of training and preparation, an athlete's own mind is allocated a diminished role in his or her performance. Even decisions of tactics and strategy within a contest are often radioed to the athletes from coaches on the sidelines. Of course, as long as athletes' minds are neglected in their training, the dumb-jock theory turns from a myth into a self-fulfilling prophecy.

At the same time, though, athletes' minds may find new ways to express themselves. Scientific and strategic thinking are not the only forms of human intelligence. As R. Scott Kretchmar points out in *Practical Philosophy of Sport*, intelligent qualities such as creativity, inventiveness, and insightfulness can be expressed in athletic performance.[23] There is no reason to think of rhetoric, mathematics, poetry, painting, and music as legitimate modes of expressing intelligence while excluding athletic movement. Knowing "that" can be distinguished from knowing "how" without diminishing the importance of the latter.[24] Ilundáin-Agurruza associates sports performance with a kind of gnostic wisdom that is "felt in the bodymind" rather than known in the brain.[25]

Maxine Sheets-Johnstone takes the connection between human bodies and intelligence even further. She claims that human rationality itself has its origin in the body's movement—that is, in kinesthetic ways of learning and knowing. In a special issue of the *Journal of the Philosophy of Sport*, Sheets-Johnstone uses the scientific approach of evolutionary biology to argue against the mind-body dichotomy at virtually every level.[26] She argues, first of all, that all human beings begin our lives in infancy by learning about our bodies and our world, or more specifically, how to move our bodies within our world. "Our first sense of ourselves," she says, "is as tactile-kinaesthetic bodies."[27]

Further, this is a universal experience for human beings that generates certain body-anchored common understandings that transcend cultural differences. What we call rationality—that quality Aristotle used to distinguish humans from other animals—turns out to be anchored in this kinesthetic making sense of the world that we undergo as infants. To deny this, Sheets-Johnstone concludes, is to be "so wedded to culture that we deny the common nature that binds us in a common humanity."[28] She concludes that reason, the characteristic so tightly identified with the human mind as to be its essence, originates in and depends upon a "bodily logos."[29]

Physicalism, then, while endorsing a more scientific approach to sport and granting ontological identity to mind and body, does little to heal the conceptual mind-body split. Even scientists must give up the assumption that minds and bodies are radically different in order to understand their cooperative role in human existence.

HOLISM AND EASTERN IDEALS

Regardless of the metaphysical makeup of the human mind and body, it is clear that the conceptual separation of the two has been the real source of problems for philosophy of sport—at least in the West. The Eastern philosophical tradition asserts no such essential separation between mind and body, or between subject and object.[30] The entire approach is more holistic—a focus on the connections between things rather than an analysis of their differences. In the words of the Chinese philosopher Zhuangzi, "Heaven and earth were born when I was born; the ten thousand things and I among them are but one thing."[31] In Eastern philosophy, knowledge of truth is often understood as a psychophysical awareness that transcends mere intellection; in this way, it connects the practical and theoretical, thereby healing any illusions of a mind-body split.[32] At the same time, Eastern philosophy does not take mind-body unity (or human-cosmos unity) to be given as metaphysical fact; rather, it regards these as an achievement—a form of wisdom that is, itself, cultivated and expressed through bodily movement. This achievement of mind-body unity is among the express purposes of martial arts training.

As with Greek, the Chinese terms for mind and body do not line up cleanly with the corresponding modern Western concepts. As Chung-Ying Cheng explains, the Chinese term *ti* represents human corporeality at its most basic level, but it understands the body in terms of systems, functions, and vital spirit rather than inert matter or substance. "It may be said that by virtue of the form of the physical body, *ti* realizes its living spirit and vitality, and by virtue of the living spirit and vitality, the physical body maintains its organic unity and organization."[33] Whereas Westerners tend to think of the body mechanically, in terms of muscles and levers, Easterners tend to focus on the internal flow of blood (*xue*) and energy (*qi*).[34]

The Chinese *xin* is usually translated as "heart-mind," not only because it is responsible for both cognitive and affective states but also because it is thought to be located in the middle of the body rather than in the head.[35] In addition, there is no clear Chinese counterpart to the Western faculty of reason that acquires pieces of truth through logic or apprehension. Knowledge is something closer to wisdom or understanding, an achievement that represents harmony both within oneself and with one's world. A wise person not only recognizes the interconnectedness of everything but also lives, acts, and moves accordingly. This achievement is called *de*—a kind of virtue very similar to the Greek *aretē*, and linked explicitly, like its Hellenic counterpart, with action and movement.

It is inconceivable from an Eastern point of view that human virtue (*de*) could exist without embodiment. As Cheng explains, "Virtue is not a matter of abstract understanding, but a matter of embodiment of a value in life practice and a matter of forming one's personality and spirit. It is in terms of the bodily and actual practice that knowledge can be said to be genuine."[36] As a result, the cultivation of *de* is fundamentally linked with physical action. In Confucianism, the performance of ritual (*li*) habituates body and mind together toward the proper orientation toward the world.[37]

Martial arts such as wushu, *chi-gong*, tai chi, and the more familiar karate and judo are traditionally directed toward the explicit goal of cultivating *de*, a process that includes not just disciplined movement but also the development of insight about the universe and one's connection to it (more on this in chapter 10).[38] Eastern thinkers often criticize Western sports, at least in their modern practice, for lacking any such effort. Charges Yasuo Yuasa, "Training in [Western] sports aims at developing the body's capacity, or more specifically, the motor capacity of the muscles in the four limbs, and does not include the spiritual meaning or training of the mind's capacity."[39] Is this a fair charge?

WESTERN SPORTS AND PHENOMENOLOGY

To be sure, metaphysical assumptions about the nature of athletes, particularly the mind-body relationship, condition how sports are practiced and interpreted. It is not a lockstep connection, however. Eastern martial arts can be—and often are—practiced according to the Western focus on physical domination and victory, rather than the Eastern emphasis on yielding and enlightenment. This philosophical contrast was illustrated by the popular *Karate Kid* movies, in which a traditionally trained youth is set against bullies who abuse martial arts techniques. In reality, athletes can—and often do—approach their Western sports with a holistic attitude toward mind and body. Indeed, the *experience* of sport, in its Eastern and Western forms, seems to lend itself to the holistic approach. American philosopher and former collegiate basketball player Drew Hyland is a good example. "As I move toward the basket, see my teammate cut, and throw him a pass," Hyland asks, "am I 'thinking' or 'physically acting'? The only sensible answer seems to be both, together, as one."[40] Another American basketball player, later a famous coach, has effectively applied the principles of Eastern philosophy to his sport. In *Sacred Hoops*, Phil Jackson identifies the secret of basketball success as "not thinking."[41]

One need not embrace Eastern philosophy in order to approach sport holistically. Hyland points to the holism embraced by the twentieth-century Western philosophical movement known as phenomenology. After Immanuel Kant identified as insurmountable the gulf between our experience of things (phenomena) and things as they are in themselves (noumena)—another distinction absent from Eastern philosophy—phenomenology responded by focusing only on phenomena. And in athletic experience, humans experience themselves as both mind and body.

The French philosopher Maurice Merleau-Ponty challenged Descartes's characterization of the "I" as a disembodied "thinking thing" by declaring, "I am my body." He explains that the "experience of one's own body runs counter to the reflective procedure which detaches subject and object from each other, and which gives us only the thought about the body, or the body as an idea, and not the experience of the body or the body in reality."[42] Hyland observes that this phenomenological holism better reflects the experience of skilled athletes than struggling beginners, concluding that "the lived body unity is a superior achievement, something for which we should strive as the explicit overcoming of the mind/body dualism which we often experience as alienating."[43] Athletics is the striving of whole persons to actualize their wholeness.

Another incongruity between athletic experience and the Cartesian heritage of mind-body separation is the notion that sports performance is a result of conscious cognitive calculation. The difference may be illustrated by contrasting the strict regimentation of a sport such as American football—where plays are carefully scripted, called, and executed—with the more intuitive flow of a game such as soccer, also a Western sport, but one with more universal appeal. Yuasa blames the calculating approach to sport on Western mind-body dualism and its assumption that training proceeds from mind to body. "Contrary to this order," he says, "the tradition of Eastern self-cultivation places importance on entering the mind from the body or form. That is, it attempts to train the mind by training the body."[44]

Yuasa admits that certain Western athletic values, such as perseverance in training, may have the effect of spiritual training, but only if we consciously embrace that objective and cease to view sport merely in terms of health and leisure.[45] Central to this change in attitude is an understanding that the human mind "is not simply consciousness nor is it constant and unchangeable, but rather it is that which is transformed through training the body."[46]

So, the metaphysical understanding of athletes, that is to say, of persons, especially in relation to the nature of their minds and bodies, is a crucial issue in the metaphysics of sport primarily because it affects our attitude toward sport and the people who practice it. The Western heritage of mind-body dualism drifted from a complex idea of hylomorphism toward a narrow understanding of the mind as purely rational and the body as mechanically physical. This attitude has had profound effects on sport, including the separation of mental and physical education, a disconnection between sport and spirituality, and an emphasis on the scientific production of performance that tends to view athletes as body-objects rather than persons. The paucity of sporting opportunities for females, the disabled, and even able but physically weaker or smaller males can be traced to this attitude, as can the myth of the dumb jock and athletes' obsession with their physical performance—a preoccupation that can lead to such ills as drug abuse and eating disorders.

I have heard it argued that traditional Eastern sports are free from all these problems because their philosophical heritage unites body and mind and links athletic training explicitly to the cultivation of spiritual virtue. We will explore this charge further in chapter 10. Globalization affects sport as well as economies, however, and neither Asian athletes nor traditional martial arts are immune from the problems of modern sport. It is much easier for individuals to change their philosophical orientations than entire cultures or practice communities. Individual athletes and coaches can adopt an attitude and approach to sport that rejects a strong Cartesian dualism and adopts a constructive holism. Metaphysical holism has roots in both Eastern and Western tradition and can be applied to Eastern and Western sports by both Eastern and Western athletes.

DISCUSSION QUESTIONS

1. Consider a runner who paces herself with a "rabbit" to achieve a faster time. Obviously, she *knows* the lap time she needs to run, and she is physically capable of doing it. So does the "rabbit" trick her body or her mind into running faster? What does the phenomenon of "rabbits" tell us about the relationship between an athlete's body and mind?
2. Find a video online of robots playing soccer or performing other athletic feats. Is it fair to call these robots "athletes"? Should we call what they are doing sport?
3. The "dumb-jock" myth is said to be a consequence of both dualism and physicalism. Do you think this myth still exists? Do you think the intellectual parts of sport (i.e., training theory, game strategy, and play calling) should be taken away from the athletes?
4. Based on your experiences with martial arts, or maybe just movies about them such as *The Karate Kid*, would you say that Western and Eastern sports have important differences in attitudes toward the body and mind?

NOTES

1. Plato mentions Ikkos in *Protagoras*, 316d, and *Laws*, 839e.
2. For analysis of sport in the *Laws*, especially as it applies to women, see Heather L. Reid, "Plato on Women in Sport," *Journal of the Philosophy of Sport* 47, no. 3 (2020), 344–61. DOI: 10.1080/00948705.2020.1811713.
3. For an overview of sport in Plato, see Heather L. Reid, Mark Ralkowski, and Coleen P. Zoller, eds., *Athletics, Gymnastics, and* Agon *in Plato* (Sioux City: Parnassos Press, 2020).
4. Aristotle more or less concurred with Plato's view, not because he endorsed the theory of the forms but, rather, because the mind/soul was an organ—unlike the eye or ear—that could perceive any kind of material or immaterial object. Aristotle, "De

Anima," in *Complete Works*, 2 vols., ed. Jonathan Barnes (Princeton, NJ: Princeton University Press, 1984), 429ab.

5. René Descartes, "Second Meditation," in *The Philosophical Writings of Descartes*, ed. J. Cottingham, R. Stoothoff, and D. Murdoch (Cambridge, UK: Cambridge University Press, 1985), 2:17–25. Note that "I think, therefore I exist" is a paraphrase of Descartes's main point in the Second Meditation; it is not an exact quotation. He uses the exact phrase in French, in *Discourse on Method*, chap. 4, and in Latin, in *Principles of Philosophy*, pt. 1, art. 7.

6. See David Young, "Mens Sana in Corpore Sano? Body and Mind in Greek Literature," *Proceedings of the North American Society for Sport History* (1998): 60–61.

7. Paul Weiss, *Sport: A Philosophic Inquiry* (Carbondale: Southern Illinois University Press, 1969), 37.

8. Weiss, *Sport*, 37.

9. Weiss, *Sport*, 38.

10. Weiss, *Sport*, 39.

11. Weiss, *Sport*, 41.

12. Weiss, *Sport*, 216–17.

13. Daniel Dombrowski, *Contemporary Athletics and Ancient Greek Ideals* (Chicago: University of Chicago Press, 2009), 57–60.

14. Jesús Ilundáin-Agurruza, *Holism and the Cultivation of Excellence in Sports and Performance: Skillful Striving* (London: Taylor and Francis, 2016).

15. Weiss, *Sport*, 99.

16. Dombrowski, *Contemporary Athletics*, 43.

17. Dombrowski, *Contemporary Athletics*, 126–31.

18. George Berkeley, *A Treatise Concerning the Principles of Human Knowledge* (Stilwell, KS: Digireads, [1734] 2006), §45.

19. David Hume, *A Treatise of Human Nature*, 2nd ed., ed. L. A. Selby-Bigge (Oxford, UK: Clarendon, 1978), 253.

20. Friedrich Nietzsche, "Thus Spoke Zarathustra," in *The Portable Nietzsche*, ed. Walter Kaufmann (New York: Viking, 1982), 146.

21. For a critique of this view of sport, see Heather L. Reid, "Why Olympia Matters for Modern Sport," *Journal of the Philosophy of Sport* 44, no. 2 (2017): 159–73. Reprinted in Reid, *Olympic Philosophy*, 415–32.

22. John Hoberman, *Mortal Engines: The Science of Performance and the Dehumanization of Sport* (New York: Free Press, 1992), 62–69.

23. R. Scott Kretchmar, *Practical Philosophy of Sport* (Champaign, IL: Human Kinetics, 1994), 74–77.

24. The distinction, traced to Gilbert Ryle, is examined in the context of sport by Gunnar Breivik, "Sporting Knowledge and the Problem of Knowing How," *Journal of the Philosophy of Sport* 41, no. 2 (2014): 143–62.

25. Ilundáin-Agurruza, *Holism*, 2.

26. Maxine Sheets-Johnstone, "Rationality and Caring: An Ontogenetic and Phylogenetic Perspective," *Journal of the Philosophy of Sport* 29, no. 2 (2002): 136.

27. Sheets-Johnstone, "Rationality and Caring," 138.

28. Sheets-Johnstone, "Rationality and Caring," 144.

29. Sheets-Johnstone, "Rationality and Caring," 145.

30. My comments about "Eastern philosophy" are, for the purpose of this book, discursive and generalized. I do not purport to take full account of this very rich and varied philosophical tradition. Rather, my aim is to provide an illuminating contrast to the Western ways of thinking with which most readers of this book are more likely to be familiar.

31. Zhuangzi, quoted in Arthur Waley, *Three Ways of Thought in Ancient China* (Stanford, CA: Stanford University Press, 2002), 9.

32. Thomas P. Kasulis, introduction, in Yasuo Yuasa, *The Body: Toward an Eastern Mind-Body Theory* (Albany: State University of New York Press, 1987), 2.

33. Chung-Ying Cheng, "On the Metaphysical Significance of *ti* (Body-Embodiment) in Chinese Philosophy: *benti* (Origin-Substance) and *ti-yong* (Substance and Function)," *Journal of Chinese Philosophy* 29, no. 2 (2002): 145.

34. Akio Inoue, "Critique of Modern Olympism: A Voice from the East," in *Sports: The East and the West*, ed. G. Pfister and L. Yueye (Sant Agustin, Germany: Academia Verlag, 1999), 165.

35. Waley, *Three Ways of Thought*, 44.

36. Cheng, "On the Metaphysical," 147.

37. Susan Brownell, *Training the Body for China* (Chicago: University of Chicago Press, 1995), 125.

38. Carl B. Becker, "Philosophical Perspectives on the Martial Arts in America," *Journal of the Philosophy of Sport* 19, no. 1 (1982): 19.

39. Yasuo Yuasa, *The Body, Self-Cultivation and Ki-Energy* (Albany: State University of New York Press, 1993), 32.

40. Drew A. Hyland, *Philosophy of Sport* (New York: Paragon, 1990), 96.

41. Phil Jackson, *Sacred Hoops: Spiritual Lessons of a Hardwood Warrior* (New York: Hyperion, 1995), 115.

42. Maurice Merleau-Ponty, *The Phenomenology of Perception*, trans. Colin Smith (London: Routledge and Kegan Paul, 1962), 198–99.

43. Hyland, *Philosophy of Sport*, 97.

44. Yuasa, *The Body*, 26.

45. Yuasa, *The Body*, 8.

46. Yuasa, *The Body*, 26.

PART III

Ethical Issues in Sport

Looking at sports today, a cynic might conclude that the phrase "sports ethics" must be an oxymoron. Ethics may be defined as the moral expectations of a civil society, but sport is often viewed as something separate from civil society—an escape from socially imposed restrictions that prevent us from expressing our authentic selves. Spectators cheer fights at hockey games, media outlets replay "highlights" of violent hits in American football, and soccer players intentionally deceive referees by strategically faking injury.

One gets the feeling that sports ethics, whatever they are, must somehow be separate from the moral conventions of society—some of the actions performed in a boxing match, for example, would be illegal if performed outside the ring in the very same place. Further, actions such as doping may be widespread and accepted within a particular sport's culture but lead nevertheless to civil prosecution, as the cases of Barry Bonds and Marion Jones have shown.

So, sports ethics is not identical to social ethics, but neither can it be completely independent. We might accept deception in baseball while condemning it in government, but that doesn't mean that there need be no moral agreement between sports and society. On the contrary, sports ethics can demand more universality than social ethics. The international nature of Olympic sports requires ethical standards that can apply across vast social and cultural differences. You simply cannot play a water polo game without some agreement as to how players ought and ought not to behave.

As we saw with the debate between essentialism and conventionalism in metaphysics, the study of sports ethics reflects a central tension: ethics are in some sense conditioned by individual social and cultural beliefs, but they also need some common ground from which to stage meaningful debate about the moral acceptability of individual behavior. If moral relativism is the case, and ethics simply collapses to each particular group's conventions—or perhaps

111

any individual's moral opinion—it is hard to see how a community might condemn even the most horrifying actions, such as murdering an opponent in order to win.

On the other hand, if sports ethics depends on a particular cultural ethos, say the nineteenth-century English gentleman's idea of amateurism, how can morality be anything other than a tool for cultural hegemony? Finally, does a community's acceptance of an action make it morally right? If doping becomes widespread and accepted among athletes in certain sports, is it therefore morally justified in those sports?

Our study of sports ethics is not designed to find definitive answers to these and other ethical questions surrounding sport. Its purpose is to develop skills in moral reasoning and to understand the diverse theories and principles used in that science. We will consider a variety of ethical issues in sport such as doping, cheating, violence, and commercialism, and we will use a variety of traditional ethical theories such as utilitarianism, deontology, virtue ethics, and even moral aesthetics.

But what will make our project specifically one of sports ethics is that we will be looking back to the metaphysical issues we discussed in the first section and trying to discern their moral implications for sport. We will contrast the metaphysical ideal of play with a win-at-all-costs attitude; we will consider the issue of cheating in light of the role that rules play in the construction of games; we will explore the connection between virtues and social practices while considering sport's apparent encouragement of vices such as deception and violence; and finally, we will examine the relationship between sport and art in light of ethical issues derived from the use of sports as commercial entertainment. Sports ethics are detached from neither social ethics nor mainstream moral theory and reasoning, but they are at least conditioned by the metaphysical nature of sport, and it is in this context that we shall explore them.

Chapter 8

Consequentialism and Play

Barry Bonds, by almost any measure, was one of the best athletes ever to play the game of baseball, but in 2011 he was convicted of perjury and obstruction of justice during the investigation of a company charged with trafficking performance-enhancing drugs. The charge that Bonds used steroids and human growth hormone was supported by eyewitness accounts and various other forms of physical and anecdotal evidence—including his seemingly superhuman performance. His criminal conviction, however, was not for using the drugs but rather for lying about it to a grand jury. The lying probably cannot be ethically defended, but what about the doping?

Does Bonds's case simply reflect a moral disconnect between sports ethics as represented by his actions within sport and social ethics as represented by the face he tried to present to the outside world? What if the steroids were administered to Bonds without his knowledge, as he claimed? What if the substances were only used therapeutically to help recover from injury and actually contributed to his health? What if steroid use was so widespread in the sport that Bonds was convinced that he had to dope just to be competitive? What if doping was encouraged at an institutional level to restore the spectator appeal of baseball and keep it from dying completely? How can we explore a sports ethics issue like doping in a way that takes account of social ethics but also accommodates the particular milieu of sport? One way is to evaluate Bonds's actions from a consequentialist point of view—that is, by looking at the *effects* Bonds's actions had on the community of baseball.

Let us explore Bonds's case using the mainstream ethical theory of utilitarianism along with sport-specific criteria derived from our early discussion about the relationship between sport and play. This discussion will focus on consequences rather than principles or virtues, because utilitarianism is a consequentialist ethical theory, and play, as we discovered in chapter 3, describes a desirable state of affairs that can be brought about by sport.

Utilitarianism is a moral theory that characterizes right action as that which produces the greatest good for the greatest number. Of course, debate is widespread about how to define and measure that good, as well as how to define the affected community. But let us bypass that debate for the purposes of our experiment by defining our community as the practice community of the sport of baseball and defining the good in terms of play character-istics—voluntariness, extraordinariness, autotelicity, absorption, and fun. This approach allows us to set aside the question of whether doping violates the deontological principle of fairness (to be discussed in the next chapter). Fairness is a question closely allied with rules, and in fact, steroids were not explicitly against the rules of Major League Baseball for at least part of the time that Bonds is supposed to have taken them.

What we are going to look at here is whether Bonds's use of steroids can be ethically defended because it produced more good than bad, or if it should be ethically condemned because it produced more bad than good, in terms of play characteristics within the sport of baseball.

It may seem as if we are stacking the deck against Bonds by using play characteristics as an ethical measure for his actions. A critic might object that we are talking about a professional athlete in serious pursuit of longstand-ing performance records and huge financial payoffs within what is properly called a business. Baseball is called a game, and games are rooted in play, but play can hardly be a valid criterion for judging the ethics of someone for whom sport is work. An equally strong criticism might be made, however, that such serious professionalism is precisely the cause of immorality in mod-ern sport. Just as Plato and Aristotle thought autotelic play to be more noble and important than work, or politics, or even war, so sport should strive to be as "playful" as possible in order to resist the corrupting influences of profes-sionalism. Many critics think the problem with sports today is that we take them too seriously, focus too much on winning, and pay too high a price for victory. Using play as a moral criterion can address that concern—but let's not beg the question by assuming that utilitarian play standards will condemn doping or even professionalism. In fact, the first characteristic of play, that it is voluntary and free, suggests that doping is just another thing that athletes should be free to do.

FREEDOM OR COERCION?

The first characteristic of play is that it is voluntary and free. Sport exhibits this characteristic because participation is always voluntary, and athletes often experience a sense of freedom while playing their sports. Freedom is likewise prized in utilitarian ethical theory. John Stuart Mill, one of the founding fathers of utilitarianism, wrote a famous essay called *On Liberty* that argues that the freedom of individuals, in terms of both thought and action, is one of the greatest goods that a community can provide. People need freedom to develop and thrive, and so do their communities. People whose lives are closely directed by rules and restrictions develop no greater faculty, says Mill, "than the ape-like one of imitation."[1] Those who are given freedom may make bad choices, acknowledges Mill, but "genius thrives in an atmosphere of freedom."[2] Thriving communities, according to Mill's utilitarianism, will maximize the liberty of their members. Thriving sports communities wishing to maximize their play characteristics should do likewise. Should that liberty include the permission to dope?

Some sport philosophers, such as W. Miller Brown, have argued that sport should allow doping, using Mill's conception of paternalism as support.[3] In *On Liberty*, Mill spells out the rare conditions under which paternalism—that is, the restriction of a person's liberty against their will—is permitted. He says, "The only purpose for which power can be rightfully exercised over any member of a civilized community, against his will, is to prevent harm to others."[4] Applied to the question of doping in sport, this so-called harm principle suggests that doping should not be prohibited for any reason other than to prevent harming others, and it is difficult to see how Bonds's taking steroids, the argument goes, harmed anyone else. Further, elaborate anti-doping mechanisms may cause more harm than they prevent.[5]

Mill does permit paternalism in the case of children or adults who are incapable of making informed choices about the risks and consequences of their actions. For that reason, Brown supports bans on drugs in youth and scholastic sports. But Bonds was an adult and a professional, with access to the best medical and athletic training advice. Even if he was motivated by greed and vanity, he was hardly an innocent child in need of protection from society. Brown concludes that those who advocate bans on drugs claim to be protecting sport's ability to promote values such as autonomy and self-reliance, but ironically, by banning drugs they actually deny those things to athletes.[6] It would seem, in Brown's view, that doping should be permitted to maximize the play characteristics of freedom and voluntary choice.

Returning to the relationship between play and freedom, however, we might recall another irony—or at least a paradox—from our earlier discussion of play. That is, that the freedom experienced in sport and play depends precisely on limitations and constraints. The play world is set apart from the ordinary world by boundaries of time and space. Sometimes these are formal and visible, as in the walls of a racquetball court and the specific time allotted to play a game. Sometimes they are imaginary, as when a child creates a make-believe house under the dining-room table.

These boundaries create a sense of freedom, not least by creating separation from the ordinary world beyond them. When I step into the racquetball court, I am, in a sense, stepping out of my workaday life with its obligations and demands. The boundaries carve out a space within which I feel free because I adopt a different attitude within them: a particular kind of stance toward the world. Drew Hyland, as we saw, calls this the "stance of play" and notes that both sport and art manipulate space and time precisely to raise our awareness of freedom and possibility.[7]

As Eleanor Metheny explains, the rules that are characteristic of sport perform a similar paradoxical function to boundaries of time and space:

> These rules [of sport] are paradoxical. They restrict in order to free. They impose restrictions on human behavior, and they limit human action; but within those restrictions they offer every man an opportunity to know the feeling of being wholly free to go all out—free to do his utmost—free to use himself fully in the performance of one self-chosen human action.[8]

So, if the sense of freedom and voluntariness characteristic of play depends not on the absence of external restrictions but, rather, on the presence of constraints such as rules and boundaries, then perhaps the imposition of rules banning doping ultimately creates a greater sense of freedom and voluntariness for the athletes. How could that be? Imagine that it becomes technically legal to use the small electric motors found in ebikes in cycling races. Many riders object to the practice and continue to race without the motors, but they find that they are quickly dropped from the pack. At that point, they feel forced to use an ebike or to abandon the sport because they cannot be competitive without it. In a similar way, if steroids are permitted in sport and they offer a significant competitive advantage, many athletes will feel as if they have no option but to use them. They won't feel as if they are exercising free choice; rather, they will feel coerced by the *lack* of regulation.

In one of the first philosophical articles about doping in sport, Warren Fraleigh argues that legalizing drugs would increase coercion on athletes to use them.[9] Former competitive powerlifter Mark Holowchak agrees and adds that such "coercive constraints" expose athletes to undue health risks.[10] Robert Simon questions whether "coercion" is too strong a term if we mean by it that athletes have no acceptable alternative—after all, sport participation is always voluntary.[11]

Empirical and anecdotal evidence suggests, however, that many athletes already feel coerced to choose between doping and sport. Verner Moller's interviews with elite athletes reveal that many of them regard doping as a necessary precondition for achieving the athletic goals they have already invested their lifetimes in pursuing. In the words of one athlete, "I have not [competed] for so many years just to stop now that I have reached a point when the dream can be lived out in reality."[12] Former U.S. Olympic Committee doctor Robert Voy confirms Moller's findings. "[I] know, after working elbow-to-elbow with elite-level athletes, that many drug users do not *want* to use drugs but feel they *have* to to stay even with everyone else."[13]

However, numerous athletes have quit their sports because of a wish not to dope. According to former track-and-field champion Katherine Hamilton, "There is an untold story about all the thousands [who] just drop out because they're just not willing to do the things to your body and to go down that road."[14] In the end, Major League Baseball's earlier refusal to ban and test for steroids arguably made athletes such as Bonds feel that they had less freedom of choice about whether to dope, not more. Permission, in this case, actually reduces freedom.

EXTRAORDINARY SERIOUSNESS

A second characteristic of play associated with sport is its extraordinariness: its distinction from ordinary life—in particular, work. This aspect is linked both to the boundaries discussed above and to the quality of autotelicity—that is, play being an end in itself instead of a means to some other end. A key idea here is that play as well as sport should not be taken too seriously. Paul Weiss says that play can be serious, "though not serious in the sense in which ordinary activities are."[15] He observes that "a child is at its best when it plays, [but] a mature man who plays is always less than what a man might be." Weiss thinks that a young man should play, but not all of the time, because there are "other, more useful or noble things he could do."[16] Randolph Feezell adds that play can have an internal seriousness, but it is not a serious matter "when contrasted to the world of work and human suffering."[17] One response to Bonds's case is to blame his doping on professionalism. Because playing baseball is his job, he is entitled to take it seriously and to use any means legally necessary to achieve his goals. Perhaps the ethical issue in this case is not so much doping as it is seriousness and professionalism.

The refrain is often heard that what modern sport needs is a return to amateurism, perhaps as depicted in the movie *Chariots of Fire*, especially by the fictional character of Lord Andrew Lindsay, a member of the English nobility with such an extraordinarily playful attitude toward sport that he is shown practicing hurdles with glasses of champagne balanced on them.[18] The word *amateurism* derives from the Latin root for love and is supposed to designate athletes who play sport for love rather than work. Amateurism was a big part of the early Olympic Movement, and Olympic athletes were subject to strict amateur regulations as recently as the 1980s. Some of the most famous Olympic athletes have run afoul of these regulations, including Jim Thorpe, Paavo Nurmi, and Bill Toomey. Advocates such as Avery Brundage refer to ancient Greek athletes in their defense of amateurism, but in fact ancient Greek athletes were not unpaid, and the idea of amateurism derives rather from Victorian England, where an effort was made to exclude the working classes from sport.[19] Over time, attitudes changed. In 1990, the word *amateur* was eliminated from the *Olympic Charter*, and amateur regulations in American collegiate sports have undergone criticism and legal challenges.[20]

What does all that mean for the ethics of sport and doping?

Perhaps the demise of amateurism and the rise of professionalism in sports—even at the scholastic level—mean that doping will inevitably increase. Voy identified the amount of money in international sports as one of the causes of doping problems during his tenure (the 1980s), but those were the latter days of amateur regulation. The money was not corrupting athletes, but promoters, by discouraging them from effectively testing for the drugs.[21] Among athletes, it is far from clear that professionalism increases the likelihood of doping. According to former International Olympic Committee (IOC) president Jacques Rogge, "The IOC's statistics and those in countries where the authorities perform tests at competitions or during training show that top level athletes, whether amateur or professional, dope less than the mainly amateur athletes at ordinary national level."[22]

What all this shows, however, is that classifying athletes according to whether or not they get paid does not automatically determine their attitude toward sport, much less their propensity to dope.

As with freedom, the play characteristic of extraordinariness is a matter of internal attitudes rather than external facts. In chapter 3, we learned that the experience of play as extraordinary was not only an attitude but also an attitude we freely choose.[23] This suggests, from an ethical point of view, that we are responsible for adopting that attitude or failing to do so. Can we say, therefore, that Bonds's doping was unethical because it represents his failure to adopt a properly playful attitude toward sport? Are seriousness and professionalism ethically improper attitudes for sport more generally?

Brown, who supports legalization of doping, believes that the use of drugs in sport is most often motivated by attitudes "characteristic of professionalism."[24] Robert Simon, likewise, compares employees at a firm who use stimulants to work longer hours while competing for promotions to athletes who take drugs.[25] Is the use of coffee or even dangerous prescription drugs for the purposes of advancing one's career importantly different from using performance-enhancing drugs in sport? Perhaps it is the serious, professional attitude that threatens sport's play characteristics—regardless of the level at which the attitude is adopted.

Again, however, this preliminary conclusion is revealed by closer scrutiny to be hasty. Returning to the characteristics of the extraordinary playful attitude discussed in chapter 3, we recall that Roochnik described it as "a full commitment of body and spirit to the activity."[26] Feezell added that the attitude expresses personal identity: "Far from being unimportant or frivolous, the free activity of play expresses some aspect of myself that I take to be 'real' or 'authentic.'"[27] But isn't an attitude in which we are fully committed to an activity that expresses our true identity characteristic of professionalism? Isn't the professional a person who pursues her career with heart and commitment because it represents *who she is*? Further, isn't she committed to her profession because she sees some intrinsic value in it apart from whatever extrinsic rewards she might gain from it? To be sure, professionals are, of course, paid for their work, but mere "jobs" are what people do "for the money." I would argue that a sincere professional attitude better expresses the relevant play characteristic. But would a sincere professional dope?

INTRINSIC VERSUS EXTRINSIC VALUES

Perhaps the problem is not professionalism as an attitude but, rather, that a professional attitude should be wasted on an unproductive, autotelic activity that lacks extrinsic value. Although Aristotle and Plato argued that autotelic activities such as play are nobler than productive tasks, Klaus Meier observes that, in cultures that value work, play is often regarded as "being aimless, wasteful, and not serious; a form of idleness, trifling, or sloth abhorrent to productive personality; or, perhaps, even as a morally unseemly enterprise characterized by profligate indulgence."[28] Perhaps Bonds's doping is morally reprehensible precisely because he took such risks and put such effort into an ultimately meaningless activity. Complaints about the exorbitant salaries paid to athletes such as Bonds for "playing a stupid game" abound in modern media. These salaries reflect the exchange value of major professional sports as media entertainment, but that is something different from the intrinsic or social value implied by autotelicity. Pornography also has entertainment value and is a big-money business, but that does not imply that it has intrinsic worth.

A further complaint, perhaps more relevant to the ethical point, is that sports such as professional baseball *may* have intrinsic worth (or, to use the social practice theory term, internal goods), but practitioners such as Bonds are focused only on extrinsic goods such as money and fame. Sigmund Loland describes this understanding of sport as "relativist" in that it considers the internal norms and values of sport only insofar as they serve to realize external goals. "Sport relativism," says Loland, "is an expression of pure instrumentalism."[29]

In this view of sport, doping is logical just so long as it results in the relevant external rewards. If Bonds viewed baseball this way, and his goal was primarily money and fame, his choice to dope was understandable, even successful. But what if he didn't care about external rewards so much as apparently internal goals, such as winning and setting records? He did achieve both the season-long and lifetime home-run records. Loland associates such goals with what he calls the "narrow view," under which "sport is linked to the exploration and transcendence of the limits of performance."[30] Again, given the records, Bonds's doping may be understandable here.[31]

Preferring what he calls a "wide theory" within which sport has meaning over and above mere performance, however, Loland himself rejects the relativistic and narrow views of sport.[32] He argues that sport's meaning not only is derived from its internal norms and values but also has a connection to deeper sociocultural and moral values. Doping is much more difficult to defend in a wide view of sport, because that view privileges community goods such as education over individual goals such as victory and profits. For doping to be justified on a wide view, it would have to have obvious social benefits over and above financial and entertainment value.

Loland's wide theory of sport seems consistent with Drew Hyland's account of the value of play. Hyland claims that play itself is "value neutral," but the *stance of play* may be valuable, depending on what we do while in that stance.[33] It is easy to see how qualities that make someone a good player, such as awareness, focus, courage, and perseverance, might also make him a good thief. What matters is that we put our play skills and activities in the service of valuable social goals. The ethics of Barry Bonds's doping, under this scheme, would depend upon the social benefits generated from it, and in his case, it is hard to imagine what those would be. The fact that Lance Armstrong doped in his pursuit of seven Tour de France victories needs to be weighed against the social benefit he provided by his inspiring cancer survivors as part of that campaign; indeed, the Livestrong organization has survived well beyond the disgraced cyclist's career.

From a conventional utilitarian standpoint, the calculation of social benefit makes sense. But whatever happened to the criterion of autotelicity? Isn't sport, insofar as it reflects the ideal of play, supposed to be valuable in and of itself? Wasn't the final point that it is absorbing and fun and does not need external justification? Our study of autotelicity showed that it was more an ideal than a reality and that people have complex motivations to play. Again, the key for play is a participant's particular attitude, his absorption in the activity, not the presence or absence of any additional goals.[34] To be absorbed by playing a sport and to be able to enjoy it completely are clearly intrinsic values. Athletes' experiences of "flow" or being in "the zone" might be the highest expression of playful absorption and enjoyment in sport. What we know about the zone is that it cannot be achieved on demand but, rather, results from a balance of skill and challenge.[35]

Enhancing one's performance with drugs, focusing on victory, and pursuing external goods do not produce more enjoyment in sport or more frequent experiences of the zone. If anything, they interfere with these play-like benefits. The autotelic value of sport, it turns out, depends on training and competing the old-fashioned way.

In this chapter we have explored the ethics of doping in sports by combining the consequentialist ethical theory of utilitarianism, which seeks the greatest good for the greatest number, with the sport-specific criteria of goodness provided by sport's metaphysical connection with play. Specifically, we looked at whether Barry Bonds's drug use could be ethically justified using the criteria of playful sports experiences such as freedom, extraordinariness, and autotelicity. What we found was that even though freedom might seem to be best served by the legalization of drugs in sport, in fact it is the rules and constraints characteristic of play that enable a sense of freedom in sport. Ironically, the permission to dope, on account of the concomitant harm linked with use of such drugs, seems to result in less freedom for athletes to do as they wish.

Using the criterion of play as extraordinary and set apart from life, we then explored whether seriousness and professionalism were at odds with the attitude of play. We found, instead, that if we understand professionalism as a commitment to and identification with a particular activity, it closely matches the attitude characteristic of play. It is the unprofessional exploitation of sport for extrinsic purposes such as wealth and fame—commonly known as instrumentalism—that seems to challenge the spirit of play and motivate the taking of steroids and other performance-enhancing substances.

Although sport can be viewed as a means to external ends or even as a way to discover the limits of human possibility, those conceptions challenge the intrinsic worth or autotelicity associated with play. Intrinsically valuable experiences such as fun and "flow" do not preclude external motivations— whether socially valuable, such as education, or socially damaging, such as greed—but external motives can interfere with our ability to experience these intrinsic goods in sport by pushing us toward unnecessarily risky behaviors such as taking steroids.

DISCUSSION QUESTIONS

1. It was argued that the ban on drugs in sport increases athletes' freedom. Enforcing the ban with drug tests and whereabouts reporting seems to restrict freedom, however. Does the "harm" caused by anti-doping measures outweigh the harm prevented by banning drugs?

2. How do you explain Jacques Rogge's claim that amateur athletes are more likely to dope than professionals? Is a more serious athlete more or less likely to dope than a less serious one?
3. If you were a coach and one of your athletes told you he wanted to take a drug that could guarantee victory, even if it would cause his death a short time later, what would be your reaction?
4. What are some of the social benefits of sport that might justify our taking it seriously according to the "wide theory"? Does doping negate any of these benefits? How?

NOTES

1. John Stuart Mill, *On Liberty* (Indianapolis: Hackett, 1978), 56.
2. Mill, *On Liberty*, 16.
3. W. M. Brown, "Paternalism, Drugs, and the Nature of Sports," *Journal of the Philosophy of Sport* 11, no. 1 (1985): 14–22.
4. Mill, *On Liberty*, 9.
5. This is the argument of Bengt Kayser and Barbara Broers, "Doping and Performance Enhancement: Harms and Harm Reduction," in *Routledge Handbook of Drugs and Sport*, ed. V. Moller et al. (London: Routledge, 2015), 363–76. Reprinted in Bengt Kayser, "Ethical Aspects of Doping and Anti-Doping: In Search of an Alternative Policy" (Doctoral thesis, KU Leuven, 2018), 89–115. Available online.
6. Brown, "Paternalism," 21.
7. Drew A. Hyland, *Philosophy of Sport* (New York: Paragon, 1990), 121.
8. Eleanor Metheny, "The Symbolic Power of Sport," presented to the Eastern District Association for Health, Physical Education and Recreation in Washington, DC, April 26, 1968. Reprinted in *Sport and the Body: A Philosophical Symposium*, ed. E. Gerber and W. J. Morgan (Philadelphia: Lea & Febiger, 1979), 235.
9. Warren P. Fraleigh, "Performance-Enhancing Drugs in Sport: The Ethical Issue," *Journal of the Philosophy of Sport* 11, no. 1 (1985): 26.
10. M. Andrew Holowchak, "'Aretism' and Pharmacological Ergogenic Aids in Sport: Taking a Shot at the Use of Steroids," *Journal of the Philosophy of Sport* 27, no. 1 (2000): 39.
11. Robert Simon, "Good Competition and Drug-Enhanced Performance," *Journal of the Philosophy of Sport* 11, no. 1 (1985): 9.
12. Anonymous cyclist, quoted in Verner Moller, "The Athlete's Viewpoint," in *The Ethics of Sports: A Reader*, ed. Mike McNamee (London: Routledge, 2010), 162.
13. Robert Voy, *Drugs, Sport, and Politics* (Champaign, IL: Human Kinetics, 1991), xv.
14. Hamilton, quoted in Tom Goldman, "Athlete's 'Nope to Dope' Became 'No to Sports,'" National Public Radio, 2011, http://www.npr.org/.
15. Paul Weiss, *Sport: A Philosophic Inquiry* (Carbondale: Southern Illinois University Press, 1969), 134.

16. Weiss, *Sport*, 140.

17. Randolph Feezell, *Sport, Play, and Ethical Reflection* (Urbana: University of Illinois Press, 2006), 13.

18. The character Lord Andrew Lindsay is fictional but based on Lord David Burghley, the sixth marquess of Exeter, who won the 400-meter hurdle race at the 1928 Olympic Games.

19. David C. Young, *A Brief History of the Olympic Games* (Malden, MA: Blackwell, 2004), 93–94. For a full account of Olympic amateurism, see David C. Young, *The Olympic Myth of Greek Amateur Athletics* (Chicago: Ares, 1984).

20. Taylor Branch, "The Shame of College Sports," *Atlantic Monthly*, October 2011, http:// www.theatlantic.com/.

21. Voy, *Drugs, Sport, and Politics*, 101.

22. Jacques Rogge, "An Apologia for Professionalism," *Olympic Review* 26, no. 4 (1995): 52.

23. David L. Roochnik, "Play and Sport," *Journal of the Philosophy of Sport* 2, no. 1 (1975): 41.

24. Brown, "Paternalism," 8.

25. Robert Simon, *Fair Play: The Ethics of Sport*, 2nd ed. (Boulder, CO: Westview, 2004), 77.

26. Roochnik, "Play and Sport," 41.

27. Feezell, *Sport, Play, and Ethical Reflection*, 25.

28. Klaus V. Meier, "An Affair of Flutes: An Appreciation of Play," *Journal of the Philosophy of Sport* 7, no. 1 (1980): 27.

29. Sigmund Loland, "The Ethics of Performance-Enhancing Technology in Sport," *Journal of the Philosophy of Sport* 36, no. 1 (2009): 156.

30. Loland, "Ethics of Performance," 157.

31. However, some take issue with the idea that drug-assisted sports performance is indeed the performance of "persons" to be tested in conventional models of sport. See Simon, "Good Competition," 9.

32. Loland, "Ethics of Performance," 158.

33. Drew A. Hyland, "The Stance of Play," *Journal of the Philosophy of Sport* 7, no. 1 (1980): 98.

34. Roochnik, "Play and Sport," 41.

35. Susan A. Jackson and Mihaly Csikszentmihalyi, *Flow in Sports* (Champaign, IL: Human Kinetics, 1999), 6.

Chapter 9

Deontology and Fair Play

At the 2011 World Fencing Championships in Catania, Italy, a top African fencer from Tunisia named Sarra Besbes mounted the platform to face Noam Mills of Israel, but the Tunisian didn't compete. Instead, she passively received the requisite number of touches, losing the round in such a way that caused Mills, the *winner*, to burst into tears.[1] Besbes was not the first athlete to refuse to compete with an Israeli—an Iranian refused to face an Israeli in the same tournament. But Besbes's case is different because she *did* enter the contest; she just refused to play the game and, therefore, lost intentionally. She didn't break any rules and was neither eliminated from the tournament nor sanctioned by the international or national governing body of her sport—in fact, it was the latter that asked her not to compete.[2] "I did my duty," Besbes said later in an interview, noting that she had remained passive rather than withdrawing in order to avoid sanction.[3]

Leaving aside the political issues underpinning this incident, what can we say about it from the perspective of sports ethics? The athlete didn't cheat, she broke no rules, she took no drugs, and she did not use violence or even foul language. Still, many would say that she failed to act ethically as an athlete, her behavior was not sporting, and it violated the principle of fair play. To understand why they might say these things, we need to examine the deontological principles that an essentialist view of sport implies.

Deontological ethical theories, such as that of Immanuel Kant, focus on moral laws or principles rather than the virtues of individual agents or the consequences of their actions. Kant's categorical imperative, "I ought never to act except in such a way that I can also will that my maxim should become a universal law,"[4] is presented as a moral duty discovered and legislated by reason. In the same way that Newton discovered laws of the physical universe (the phenomenal realm), Kant took himself to have discovered moral laws for practical concerns in the noumenal realm of thought. Applied to a case of cheating in sport, such as a fencer using an illegal foil to increase his chances of scoring, the categorical imperative would permit this only if he could rationally will that all others use the illegal equipment in the same way. But such a wish seems inherently irrational because any advantage gained by the special equipment would be wiped out if it were used universally. Further, because the equipment in question is barred by the rules of the sport, using it ethically would entail willing that everyone disregard the rules—a situation that, taken to its logical extreme, would eliminate sport altogether. What would fencing be if no one followed any of the rules?

As we saw in chapter 4, rules are central to the metaphysical nature of games, and they need to be obeyed just to make sport possible. But sports are also more than rules, which explains why we might be troubled by Sarra Besbes's action in the fencing tournament even though technically it broke no rules. Sports are conditioned by a certain spirit, commonly called *fair play*, which encourages or proscribes actions not specifically discussed in the rulebook. Metaphysical essentialists generally view fair play as a deontological principle (i.e., one derived from the essential nature of sport).

Following a legal philosophy called interpretivism, they compare the relationship between rules and fair play in sports to the relationship between civic laws and justice. Like justice, the deontological ethical principle(s) that govern sport are thought to be universal, unchanging, and discoverable through reason. They are also thought to be embedded in sport itself, so intrinsic to its nature that we couldn't make sense of sport without them. This approach to sports ethics is accordingly called "broad internalism." It is internal in the sense that the ethical principles it seeks are to be found within sport itself, and it is broad in the sense that it looks beyond the rules—in contrast to the narrow approach of formalism. When Sarra Besbes said that she "did her duty" by refusing to compete, she apparently was referring to a political duty. The question for broad internalists is, did she do her duty to sport?

In this chapter, we will combine the structure of deontological ethics with the metaphysical essentialism discussed in chapter 4 to explore the approach to sports ethics commonly called "broad internalism." We will do this by seeking moral guidance within the essential elements of sport as defined by Bernard Suits: the goal, the means, the rules, and the attitude. Might these elements carry normative implications for sport? If so, what would they be?

RULES AND THE LIMITS OF FORMALISM

Broad internalism emerged in sports ethics as a response to the limits of formalism, which equates moral permissibility with following the rules. As we saw in chapter 4, rules have obvious ethical import for games and sport. It makes no sense in Kantian terms to break the rules of the sport without willing that such rule breaking become a universal law. But might there be cases where certain kinds of rule breaking could be willed universally? The formalist approach to sports ethics, as we saw, holds the "logical incompatibility thesis," according to which players who intentionally violate rules fail to play the game. This position suggests that all intentional rule violations, however innocuous, are cheating.

To many, this position seems untenable. John Russell points out that inconsequential rule violations are left uncalled in many sports, and he even goes so far as to claim that basketball "cannot be played without constantly breaking rules."[5] Indeed, the foul to stop the clock in basketball is a paradigm example of the intentional rule violations that are accepted as a legitimate part of the game. Players who commit such fouls rarely try to conceal their actions and willingly accept the penalty. In these two details, strategic rules violations reflect Martin Luther King Jr.'s definition of morally justified civil disobedience.[6] But civil disobedience employs the intentional breaking of unjust laws to promote the higher principle of justice in society and the integrity of law more generally. That goal seems a bit loftier than trying to win a game, and it certainly is not the case that strategic fouls are committed to draw attention to and remove unjust rules. Nevertheless, the idea that all intentional violations of rules are cheating seems too strict.

At the same time, to define cheating only in terms of rule breaking may not be strict enough. Often, apparently immoral acts in sport are not technically illegal—as we observed with the fencing example at the opening of this chapter. At the 1984 Olympic Games in Los Angeles, the U.S. cycling team performed secret blood transfusions to improve riders' performance. The technique was very effective. The team won nine medals, including four gold. When it was later revealed that they had engaged in this practice, the medals were not stripped because—at that time—transfusions were undetectable in tests and not explicitly banned.[7]

The fact that such "legal" performance-enhancing techniques were nevertheless concealed by their perpetrators suggests an awareness of their immorality. But it might also just be strategic—an attempt to gain a legal advantage over competitors without their knowledge. All kinds of legal actions in sport are concealed from opponents. Teams often practice in secret and routinely conceal their communications during games—sometimes employing secret signs and signals. In most baseball and softball leagues, stealing signs is not prohibited by the rules as long as video technology is not employed. Still, the practice is morally controversial because many players and coaches believe that it interferes with the internal principles of the game.

A formalist response to cases in which apparently immoral actions are legal is simply to write rules against them. For a long time, the penalty in soccer for handling the ball or tackling an opponent near the goal was a penalty kick, but under these conditions it made strategic sense to commit the foul intentionally in order to prevent what would otherwise be a certain goal, as the chances of the penalty kick going in were lower. Recognizing this problem, FIFA changed the rule from a mere penalty kick to a red card, which ejects the offending player from the game and forces his team to play shorthanded. In this way, they eliminated the strategic motivation for the foul.

The idea of perfecting the rules has some appeal, but it also suggests that ethics in sport depends on more than rules. First, as Robert Simon points out, the very recognition that there is a problem with the rules entails some morally relevant sense of the game beyond the rules—but if games are nothing more than their rules, where do we get such a standard?[8] Second, as the ancient Chinese philosopher Laozi understood, moral behavior is difficult to legislate. On the contrary, the accumulation of rules and laws only decreases people's respect for them. As Laozi says, "The more prohibitions and rules, the poorer people become . . . the more elaborate the laws, the more they commit crimes."[9]

Professional European soccer's adoption of the video referee (VAR) system seems to bear out that thesis. Because the referee is incapable of monitoring the entire field at once, players were known to engage in all kinds of illicit behavior behind his back—often in full view of the television cameras. The attitude seemed to be that "it isn't cheating if you don't get caught"—a blatant rationalization for immorality. Further, actions such as Thierry Henry's intentional handball in a World Cup qualifying match are sometimes regarded with admiration. Said Henry of the incident, "I will be honest, it was a handball. But I'm not the ref. I played it, the ref allowed it. That's a question you should ask him."[10]

Even sports officials, however, are able to see that sports ethics involves more than just rules and penalization. In arguing that rules are not all that umpires have to work with, John Russell recalls a case in Major League Baseball where George Brett had a potentially game-winning two-run home-run disallowed because the pine-tar resin spread on the bottom of his bat for grip exceeded the maximum eighteen inches that the rules allowed.[11] It was recognized later that the excess pine-tar resin would have been, if anything, a disadvantage for the purposes of hitting a home run and that disallowing the hit on the basis of that technicality amounted, in effect, to putting the rules ahead of the game itself.

To the formalist way of thinking, that last statement is nonsensical because the game is nothing more than rules, but Russell and other broad internalists argue that there is something more: an intrinsic logic, perhaps best understood in terms of fair-play principles, that underlies and informs the rules of sport. Russell suggests that sports rules be interpreted according to these principles, which he enumerates as excellence, competitive balance, fair play, and the good conduct of games.[12] Whether or not this list accurately captures the deontological principle of fair play, we can recognize that there is such a thing and that it should be taken into account when making ethical decisions in sports. Rules are only part of the story.

RESPECT FOR THE GAME

Fair play in sport is often understood as an attitude, specifically an attitude of respect for the game itself. Suits argued that the "lusory attitude" was what made game playing possible, and Graham McFee claimed that what made rules function as rules was nothing other than people choosing to use them that way.[13] It should be no surprise that the aforementioned pine-tar incident was instigated by the opposing team's manager, Billy Martin, who requested after the home run was hit that Brett's bat be inspected. According to at least one account, Martin had noticed the pine-tar violation much earlier in the season but was waiting for a strategic moment to point it out.[14]

Such legalistic strategizing seems to involve a willful ignorance of the ethos, spirit, or unwritten rules of the sport, motivated by a narrow focus on winning. Renowned moral philosopher Peter Singer observes that partisanship appears to have trumped morality in pro soccer for both players and fans. "Fans don't seem to mind if members of their own team cheat successfully," he says; "they only object when the other side cheats. That is not an ethical attitude."[15]

So, what *is* an ethical attitude toward sport, given that sport itself depends in so many ways upon attitude?

Let us return again to Kant, whose categorical imperative prohibited me, in its first formulation, from making moral exceptions for myself, and in its third formulation obliged me to treat others never merely as means but always also as ends in themselves. In short, Kant's deontology demands an attitude of respect toward others and toward what he calls the "universal law." Applied to sport, and in particular to Suits's concept of the "lusory attitude," we might summarize an ethical attitude in sport as one of respect for the game. Suits claimed that the lusory attitude was that element of games that "unifies the other elements into a single formula,"[16] and he characterized it as an attitude directed at the process, rather than the goal, "since it willingly accepts rules that make achieving the goal harder."[17]

Respecting the game means, first of all, respecting the rules of that game, but it also requires us to respect the other essential elements of the game such as striving for victory and accepting the inefficiency of means. In short, we need to respect the *process* of playing the game. Further, it demands that we recognize other players' stakes in the game and our own role in facilitating their participation. Treating others as ends and not means when playing _quires us to recognize them as colleagues or co-strivers (this is the root meaning of the term "competitor"), rather than obstacles to be eliminated in pursuit of our own goals.

As Robert Butcher and Angela Schneider conclude in their account of fair play as respect for the game, "The athlete who respects the game wishes to play as well as possible against a worthy opponent playing as well as possible. This means that you allow your opponent every opportunity—as defined by the game—to play his or her best."[18] Although this attitude makes sense in terms of sports ethics, it may seem foreign to athletes who are more used to *denying* competitors the opportunity to play their best.

Psychological tactics such as "trash talking" or "sledging" are adopted precisely for the purpose of putting competitors "off their game." In American football, it is popular to "ice the kicker" by calling a time-out just as the opposing team attempts a field goal in order to interrupt a kicker's rhythm and give him time to doubt himself. Tennis players, too, have been known to stall or delay their play in order to interrupt the rhythm of opponents. These sorts of tactics are sometimes considered part of the game, and a player's ability to resist them may be counted among her athletic skills as long as they don't descend below the level of basic respect for persons, as some incidents of trash talking are known to do. But psychological resistance to insults hardly seems an essential sporting skill.

Worse are sports strategies that deny athletes the opportunity to test their skills. The strategy in baseball of intentionally walking batters by pitching the ball so far outside the strike zone that it is virtually impossible to hit appears to be one such practice. The rules provide for an advantage to be granted to the walked batter—but the practice circumvents the testing of both the hitter's and pitcher's skills as intended by the game. In cricket, a similar strategy of bowling underarm to batters is a way of preventing multiple runs—especially in situations where multiple runs might win the game. This practice is routinely jeered by spectators, as is stalling by kicking the ball back to the goalkeeper in soccer, or taking a knee to run out the clock in American football.

Graham McFee says that knowledgeable audiences are right to express their disapproval of what they recognize as inappropriate ways of playing a game. Following Suits, he calls such play "spoiling" because, even though it is technically permitted by the rules, it denies opponents the "possibility of playing the game according to its spirit."[19] On occasion it is an ally rather than an opponent whose opportunity to play is spoiled, as when cyclists are asked to sacrifice their own chances for victory by towing team leaders in their slipstream to the front of the pack, or when runners pursuing new record times are paced by "rabbits" who set a competitively untenable pace and then withdraw before the end of the race.[20] None of these actions is against the rules of sport, but they all, in some sense, fail to respect its spirit—even when they help athletes to win.

THE GOAL OF VICTORY

"Winning isn't everything," the saying goes; "it's the only thing." This quote, popularly attributed to the American football coach Vince Lombardi, summarizes either the true spirit of sports or the main thing that is wrong with sports—depending on where you stand. Any viable ethics of sport must take account of the role of winning, and if we ground ethics in metaphysics, the role of winning in games and sport is central. Suits places "the goal" at the top of his list of game characteristics, explaining it first as a general state of affairs that might be achievable outside a game (the *prelusory* goal), and then within the context of the game as the *lusory* goal, namely the state of affairs that constitutes winning the game. So, my goal in a swimming race is not simply to reach the far edge of the pool (a *prelusory* goal) but also to do so by swimming freestyle the length of the pool according to the other rules prescribed by the game, thereby winning the race (the *lusory* goal).

If we combine this metaphysical aspect of games with Kant's categorical imperative, we arrive at an ethical principle that suggests that everyone who plays games, including sports, ought to try to win, and further, they ought to *will* that everyone else who plays, including their opponents, tries to win, too. This approach to sport ethics, which emphasizes opponents' obligations to each other, is called contractualism.

Of course, we cannot logically say that everyone who plays games *ought* to win, because in all competitive games someone has to lose. Further, we must admit, as a matter of fact, that winning may not be the primary motivation or objective of many sports participants. As Warren Fraleigh explains, "The ends of achieving a specific state of affairs, of winning and of trying to win, are all necessary [but] it is not necessary that all participants adopt the end of winning as their personal intended end."[21] This means that, even if your primary purpose for playing a game of tennis is to improve your fitness or perhaps just to have fun, by agreeing to play the game you commit yourself to *contesting*: to using your own skills and challenging your opponent's skills in a genuine effort at victory.

If, on the other hand, I go with a friend to the tennis court purely for purposes of fitness and fun, and we just try to see how many times we can volley the ball without hitting it out of bounds, you can say that we are engaging in a worthwhile activity, maybe even playing a game, but we are not playing the game of tennis. So, aiming to win is one of the principles underpinning ethical sports participation, and Sarra Besbes broke this principle by standing passively in her match at the World Fencing Championships. Further, her opponent, was justifiably upset despite winning the match because she had been mistreated ethically.

Yet Noam Mills *won* the match and therefore achieved her goal, so why should she be upset? The victory for her must have lacked meaning because it did not represent what victory is supposed to represent, namely, demonstrated athletic superiority. Although it makes sense to say that all (or most) athletes hope to win by demonstrating athletic superiority, we cannot say that all (or most) athletes hope to win because their opponents provided no resistance. One thing most athletic games test is a competitor's ability to overcome her opponent's resistance. If that resistance is not provided, the test was not really carried out, and the victory therefore loses its value.

In fact, under many circumstances victory in an athletic contest fails to indicate athletic superiority. Nicholas Dixon lists bad refereeing, cheating, gamesmanship, bad luck, and even subpar performances by superior athletes or teams among common causes of such "hollow" victories.[22] His conclusion is that winning does not reliably indicate athletic superiority and, as Edwin Delattre had warned nearly twenty-five years earlier, we should not put so much emphasis on victory in sports: "To stress victory to the point of overlooking quality of performance is to impoverish our sense of success in competitive athletics."[23] So, in search of the intrinsic ethical principles that constitute fair play, a broad internalist looks beyond the rule-based definition of winning toward the ideal those rules are trying to capture.

A rich understanding of athletic success may also transcend physical performance to encompass moral virtues and consistency over time—the kind of excellence the ancient Greeks described as *aretē*. In the absence of virtues, the objective *value* of athletic victory, and especially the pride athletes take in it, is easily questioned. David Carr points out that taking pride in the discovery of a cure for disease seems more justified than pride in athletic achievements, the social value of which is much more difficult to justify.[24] It is when the virtues that (with imperfect reliability) lead to athletic victory are applied to more valuable social projects that athletics best defends its worth, especially as education. Said one American football coach recently, "I told the guys if I had one wish, it would be to put that scoreboard to death, because that really shouldn't be the standard. The standard should be excellence. I think it's a much better thing to live by than the scoreboard because that will help them more in life, as a dad, as a husband, as an employee and as a neighbor."[25]

We need not make the instrumentalist claim that the value of sport depends entirely on external benefits to affirm the idea that a conception of excellence internal to sport transcends the analytical definition of winning. Winning does matter in sport on the broad internalist account, but only insofar as it motivates the cultivation of noble qualities. So, striving to win, rather than winning itself, is a moral obligation for athletes—not only to themselves but also to their opponents—because the deontological principle of excellence depends on it.[26] Vince Lombardi got it right when he explained that what he meant was "winning isn't everything—but making the effort to win is."[27]

INEFFICENT MEANS

Late in 2009, FINA, the international swimming federation, banned the full-body hydrodynamic swimsuits that were threatening to turn their sport into a competition among manufacturers rather than athletes. In 2008, 105 world records were broken, 79 of them by swimmers wearing one particular brand of high-tech suit. At the Beijing Olympics alone, 94 percent of the gold medals were won by swimmers using the same suit.[28] Foremost in that group was Michael Phelps, but he eventually came to resent the suits and threatened to boycott the world championships the next year if they weren't banned. When they were banned, he expressed relief: "It's going to be cool come January 1 to be able to have all of us pretty much wearing the same suit . . . then we're going to be able to talk about swimming again, not suits."[29]

Since the hydrodynamic bodysuits began showing up in competitions in the early 1990s, they had caused improved times as well as controversy—not least because the early versions were custom-made for top stars and not available to everyone. As Sigmund Loland points out in discussing the ethics of performance-enhancing technologies, "A key principle to reach fair and valid outcomes seems to be that of *equality of opportunity to perform*."[30] With time, however, the suits became cheaper and more widely available. Makers even supplied free suits to Olympic swimmers who couldn't afford them. If everyone has equal access to a legal performance-enhancing technology, what could be the ethical problem? Further, why should a champion such as Michael Phelps, who was winning anyway, complain about it?

One explanation is that Phelps's complaint was sour grapes because his suit was no longer the fastest, and he had recently lost races to less-heralded competitors.[31] He wanted to win, and the object of the sport is to win by swimming faster, so he was just jealous that some competitors were swimming faster than he was. A better answer, however, is that he cares about his sport, and he recognizes the value of its *inefficiency*. Swimming in a pool is a notoriously inefficient way to move from one point to the next—most swimmers could run faster along the deck than they can swim in the water, and with less energy expended. But this inefficiency, according to Suits's account of games, is precisely what makes the activity a sport. "To play a game is to attempt to achieve a specific state of affairs, using only means permitted by the rules, *where the rules prohibit use of more efficient in favour of less efficient means*, and where the rules are accepted just because they make possible such activity" (emphasis mine).[32] Certain inefficiencies form part of the metaphysics of games and sports, and they imply deontological ethical principles that carry moral weight—principles focused on the ideal of cultivating excellence.

Sports equipment that improves the efficiency of achieving the lusory goal of a contest (i.e., that makes it easier to win) cannot be willed rationally to be a universal law according to Kant's categorical imperative because, again, if an athlete's objective is to win, he cannot rationally will that any advantage he gets from his equipment is also available to his competitors because it would cancel out that advantage. Once everyone has the hydrodynamic swimsuits, we still have the same sport, only the records are at risk because everyone gets to the finish line sooner.

But getting to the finish quickly is not, by itself, the objective of the sport of swimming. The point is to get to the finish as quickly as possible, given the inefficiencies imposed by the rules, and the job of the rule makers is to impose reasonable inefficiencies in a way that preserves the intrinsic values of that sport—especially the cultivation of excellence.[33] It might be unreasonable, for example, to make swimmers tie one hand behind their backs, or drag small boats through the water, simply for the sake of inefficiency. But it is not unreasonable, and indeed it might be imperative, to deny them such efficiencies as motors, flippers, or hydrodynamic bodysuits. Why? What's the difference?

The inefficiencies embedded in the rules of sport are not merely arbitrary; rather, they are designed to bring out through challenge certain excellences. The breaststroke, for example, is one of the slowest and least efficient competitive swimming strokes. For a time, swimmers found that they could win breaststroke races by remaining under water as long as possible and *avoiding* the traditional stroke. This was a skill, but not the skill to be tested in the race, so FINA changed the rules to limit the distance that can be swum underwater in those races.

Skills and virtues make up only part of an athletic performance. Access to good coaching, quality food, and facilities also contributes, as do equipment, weather, and even luck. But sport, by nature, seeks to reward the part of an athlete's performance that is under his or her control: a concept I call *athletic agency*.[34] In moral theory, an agent is one who intentionally causes a certain outcome and is, therefore, morally responsible for it and deserving of praise or blame. That winners in sport are routinely praised implies that they are morally responsible for their performance. So even though it may be impractical for *every* aspect of an athlete's performance to be under his control, the criteria for victory should emphasize athlete agency as much as possible.

The principle of athlete agency is linked to the principle of equal opportunity. What ethical sport ought to do, to use Loland's terms, is "eliminate or compensate for essential inequalities between persons that cannot be controlled or influenced by individuals in any significant way and for which individuals cannot be deemed responsible."[35] In basketball, for example, the uncontrollable inequality of height presents an advantage. But rule makers were able to compensate for that somewhat by giving extra value to shots made from a greater distance, thereby diminishing the importance of height in favor of shooting ability—a valued skill that can be influenced through training and practice. Efforts to make equipment and technology identical for all competitors, or at least to standardize it as much as possible, achieve a similar purpose.[36] Certainly there is room for equipment differences that help individuals to compensate for uncontrollable inequalities. Fiberglass vaulting poles, for example, made that sport more accessible to women and smaller athletes. But insofar as performance-enhancing technologies reinforce existing social inequalities—especially economic and technological advantages—they effectively reduce the principle of athlete agency and, therefore, should be banned.[37]

Fair play is sometimes understood as the application of moral principles to the realm of sport. Research suggests, however, that the structure of sport gave rise to the ideal of fair play, which then became part of social morality.[38] For broad internalists, fair play as an ethical principle originates in the metaphysics of sports and games, and for that reason it makes sense to see what the nature of sport can tell us about moral behavior within it.

We first saw that rules, by themselves, do not dictate the morality of a game, but deeper principles underpin them that should govern their application and interpretation. We learned that fair play is, at least partly, an attitude of respect toward the game and toward others that calls into question such common practices as intentional walks and running out the clock but also affirms the idea of playing one's best and valuing one's successes in sport. Winning is paradoxical, because it clearly is the end of an athletic contest, but we can't logically will everyone to win a game that only designates one victor. We can, however, rationally will that all competitors *strive* to win the game and, in this way, cultivate excellence. Striving to win, however, demands respect for the rules of the game and, more specifically, the skill-testing inefficiencies that the rules prescribe because it is those inefficiencies that make the activity a game capable of cultivating excellence. Finally, equality of opportunity and the agency of athletes must be preserved to justify the praise of winners integral to the nature of sport.

DISCUSSION QUESTIONS

1. Do you think there was anything morally wrong with Besbes's refusal to compete in a fencing match? If so, how might the fencing federation discourage such behavior in the future?
2. It was argued that attempts to interfere with an opponent's demonstration of skills (intentional walks or running out the clock) constitute a failure to respect the game. Can you make an argument for the opposing view—that such actions are consistent with respecting the game?
3. Use an example to illustrate the difference between the following versions of Lombardi's statement: "Winning isn't everything; it's the only thing" and "Winning isn't everything, but making the effort to win is."
4. Do you think there is a moral difference between an advantage gained through equipment, such as a hydrodynamic swimsuit, and an advantage gained through nature, such as height or talent? How do they relate to the concept of athlete agency?

NOTES

1. The incident was reported in several Italian newspapers, including Marco Ansaldo, "Immobile in pedana, tunisina boicatta Israele ai Mondiali," *La Stampa*, October 11, 2011, http://www3.lastampa.it/.

2. Ansaldo, "Immobile in pedana."

3. Besbes, quoted in Aymen Wafi, "Sarra Besbes: je m'en fiche . . . j'ai fait mon devoir," Koora.com, October 19, 2011, http://www.koora.com/.

4. Immanuel Kant, *Groundwork for the Metaphysic of Morals*, trans. H. J. Paton (New York: Harper and Row, 1948), 70.

5. John S. Russell, "Are Rules All an Umpire Has to Work With?" *Journal of the Philosophy of Sport* 25, no. 1 (1999): 39.

6. Martin Luther King Jr., *I Have a Dream: Writings and Speeches that Changed the World* (New York: HarperCollins, 1992), 90.

7. For a detailed account of the affair, see David F. Prouty, *In Spite of Us: My Education in the Big and Little Games of Amateur and Olympic Sports in the U.S.* (Brattleboro, VT: Velo-News, 1988), 121–71.

8. Robert Simon, *Fair Play: The Ethics of Sport*, 2nd ed. (Boulder, CO: Westview, 2004), 48.

9. Lao-Tzu, *Tao Te Ching*, trans. S. Addiss and S. Lombardo (Indianapolis: Hackett, 2003), 57.

10. Thierry Henry, quoted in Peter Singer, "Is It Okay to Cheat in Football?" Project Syndicate, June 26, 2010, accessed April 10, 2011, http://www.project-syndicate.org/.

11. Russell, "Are Rules All?" 30.

12. Russell, "Are Rules All?" 35–36.

13. Graham McFee, *Sport, Rules and Values: Philosophical Investigations into the Nature of Sport* (London: Routledge, 2004), 69.

14. Rick Weinberg, "Pine Tar Nullifies Home Run, So Brett Goes Ballistic," *ESPN*, 2009, accessed October 20, 2011, http://sports.espn.go.com/.

15. Singer, "Is It Okay?"

16. Suits, *Grasshopper*, 50.

17. Suits, *Grasshopper*, 17.

18. Robert Butcher and Angela Schneider, "Fair Play as Respect for the Game," *Journal of the Philosophy of Sport* 25, no. 1 (1998): 15.

19. Graham McFee, "Spoiling: An Indirect Reflection of Sport's Moral Imperative?" in *The Ethics of Sports: A Reader*, ed. Mike McNamee (London: Routledge, 2010), 146.

20. For a philosophical treatment of this practice, see Danny Rosenberg and Pam Sailors, "Racers, Pacers, Gender and Records: On the Meaning of Sport Competition and Competitors," *Sport, Ethics and Philosophy* 8, no. 2 (2014): 172–90, DOI: 10.1080/17511321.2014.933868.

21. Warren P. Fraleigh, "The Ends of the Sports Contest," in *Ethics of Sports*, McNamee, 107.

22. Nicholas Dixon, "On Winning and Athletic Superiority," *Journal of the Philosophy of Sport* 26, no. 1 (1999): 10.

23. Edwin J. Delattre, "Some Reflections on Success and Failure in Competitive Athletics," *Journal of the Philosophy of Sport* 2, no. 1 (1975): 138.

24. David Carr, "Where's the Merit If the Best Man Wins?" *Journal of the Philosophy of Sport* 26, no. 1 (1999): 2.

25. Dean Hood, quoted in Ryan Alves, "Real Life Lessons from the Gridiron," *Eastern Progress*, October 12, 2011, http://www.easternprogress.com/.

26. Indeed, this specific variety of broad internalism is sometimes called "mutualism," as epitomized by Robert Simon's definition of sport as a "mutually acceptable quest for excellence through challenge," *Fair Play*, 17 ff.

27. Lombardi, quoted in Gary M. Walton, *Beyond Winning: The Timeless Wisdom of Great Philosopher Coaches* (Champaign, IL: Leisure Press, 1992), xi.

28. British Broadcasting Service, "FINA Extends Swimsuit Regulations," *BBC Me Sport*, March 19, 2009, http://news.bbc.co.uk/.

29. Michael Phelps, quoted in Associated Press, "FINA Moves Up Bodysuit Ban," *ESPN Olympic Sports*, July 31, 2009, accessed October 20, 2011, http://sports.espn.go.com/.

30. Sigmund Loland, "Fairness in Sport: An Ideal and Its Consequences," in *Ethics of Sports*, McNamee, 117.

31. Associated Press, "FINA Moves Up Bodysuit Ban."

32. Bernard Suits, *The Grasshopper: Games, Life, and Utopia*, 2nd ed. (Peterborough, Ontario: Broadview, [1978] 2005), 54–55.

33. Recall Russell's words, quoted in chapter 4, that rules should be interpreted in such a manner that "the excellences embodied in achieving the lusory goal of the game are not undermined but are maintained and fostered." John S. Russell, "Are

Rules All an Umpire Has to Work With?" *Journal of the Philosophy of Sport* 25, no. 1 (1999): 39.

34. Heather L. Reid, "Athlete Agency and the Spirit of Olympic Sport," *Journal of Olympic Studies* 1, no. 1 (Spring 2020): 28.

35. Loland, "Fairness in Sport," 118.

36. Loland, "Fairness in Sport," 121.

37. Reid, "Athlete Agency," 32.

38. Claudia Pawlenka, "The Idea of Fairness: A General Ethical Concept or One Particular to Sports Ethics?" *Journal of the Philosophy of Sport* 32, no. 1 (2005): 57.

Chapter 10

Virtues and Vices

In the spring of 2011, the Japanese Sumo Wrestling Association made the extraordinary decision to cancel a grand tournament in the wake of a scandal. The problem was not violence, gambling, or associations with organized crime; rather, it was evidence in the form of cell-phone messages that revealed what had long been suspected: that sumo wrestlers were throwing matches to opponents who would otherwise finish with a losing record and therefore be demoted through the ranks. By Western sport scandal standards, this may seem mild. But the Japanese prime minister Naoto Kan called it "a very serious betrayal of the people," not least because sumo is the national sport, and it represents a traditional ideal of virtue.[1]

A serious effort is made in Japan to keep the sport of sumo morally pure and separate from the corrupting realities of modern life. Wrestlers live and train in so-called stables, are expected to show indifference toward victory, and conduct solemn religious rituals as part of their contests. Whereas the unscrupulous shenanigans of Western sports stars are so common as to be expected, immoral behavior in traditional Eastern sports, especially among the revered masters, is a serious affront. After all, the martial arts are traditionally valued as a means of cultivating virtue, and that value is often projected onto other athletic activities as well. In the East, champion athletes are also expected to be champions of virtue. In the West, by contrast, sports stars seem rather to be champions of vice. "The way to virtue in sport," argues Allan Bäck, "is to abandon [Western] sports—and perhaps to practice a martial art instead."[2]

The empirical data tracking sport and moral development in the West suggest that athletic competition not only fails to cultivate virtue but promotes vice.[3] Indeed, some view the scandals in Japanese sumo as evidence for how the trappings of Western-style sport can corrupt ancient athletic practices steeped in a tradition of moral purity. Traditionalists cite increasing money, media attention, and the influx of foreign wrestlers as causes of sumo's problems.[4] Purists, meanwhile, question sumo's status as a true martial art because of its emphasis on competition.[5] In fact, many were relieved when wushu, traditional Chinese martial arts, was denied status as an Olympic sport. The fear was that the Olympics, despite their ancient Greek athletic heritage, would ruin wushu's focus on the cultivation of virtue. "When Wushu tried to go Olympic," says champion Zhao Changjun, "somehow they lost the character of what Wushu really is."[6] In fact, the transformation of wushu into a competitive sport has coincided with a rise in corruption, including bribing judges and fixing matches.[7]

Despite all this, many philosophers continue to extol Western sport as a way of promoting virtue. So, which is it? Does competitive sport cultivate virtue, or does it promote vice? Is the contrast between East and West based on differences in the sport or in the culture? Does the promotion of virtue in sport depend on the community of practitioners or the surrounding society? Is virtue itself defined differently by different communities and in different sports?

The ethical question here is not just about people's behavior but also about whether and how the practice of sport and its supporting institutions facilitate and reward the cultivation of virtue or vice. The metaphysical theory of sport as a social convention discussed in chapter 5 tapped into the ancient theories of virtue ethics to be found both in Greek thinkers such as Plato and Aristotle and in the Chinese philosophers Laozi and Confucius. Virtue ethics focuses on the moral character of the person who acts rather than on his principles (as in Immanuel Kant's deontology) or the consequences of his action (as in John Stuart Mill's utilitarianism). Virtue, in both the Greek and Chinese traditions, is understood as the disposition or power to perform good actions, and virtue ethics generally involves extended discussion of how such dispositions are cultivated.[8] Aristotle identified training (*ethos*) as the source of character (*ēthos*), reflecting the traditional association between virtue (*aretē*) and athletic training in his culture.[9] Confucius, likewise, associated the cultivation of virtue with ritual practice.[10] Plato set up his Academy in a gymnasium, and Laozi's Daoism forms the foundation of several martial arts.

In modern times, Alasdair MacIntyre's social practice theory has revived virtue ethics, not least in its relation to sport. Perhaps if we combine traditional virtue ethics with the metaphysical understanding of sports as social practices, we will understand when and why sports and martial arts succeed or fail to promote virtue. From there, we may be able to identify ways to improve these practices.

To begin, let us recall that MacIntyre described a social practice as a cooperative activity that realizes internal goods through the pursuit and achievement of standards of excellence in that activity.[11] Practices generate practice communities, and by thoughtful participation in these communities social virtues such as honesty, justice, and courage are exercised and cultivated.[12] Eastern philosophy has long been lauded for its priority on community, but

Aristotle also emphasized the communal aspect of virtue ethics, famously categorizing human beings as "political animals"[13] and asserting that the purpose of communities is to facilitate virtuous action.[14] Participating in a practice community entails relationships with not only contemporary practitioners, such as teammates and opponents but also previous practitioners, such as coaches and historical champions, whose achievements have helped to establish the traditional standards of technical and ethical excellence for which practitioners strive.[15] Social practice theory is conventionalist in the sense that ethical standards are generated by these communities. It also burdens practitioners with great responsibility because our technical and ethical achievements form part of the standards for future generations.

A virtue-ethical approach entails that we *think* about practices such as sport as ethical, not merely technical, and that we take the end of our participation in them to be virtue. But if sports are social conventions, might they just as easily promote vice? Bäck claims that traditional martial arts promote virtue by nature, while the focus on winning Western sports makes them "hazardous to your moral health."[16] If virtue depends on community agreement, however, perhaps those communities can change the way they practice sport to better cultivate virtue. The debate, as William Morgan says, "is not whether sport involves the pursuit of excellence—on that general point they all concur—but rather what conception of athletic excellence and the mix of skills, attitudes, resolve, and the like that follow in its wake best capture its perfectionist character."[17]

In what follows, we will compare sports with martial arts in terms of their theoretical potential to produce MacIntyre's list of virtues—honesty, justice, courage, and integrity—in contrast to apparently vicious athletic phenomena such as deception, egoism, violence, and the failure to transfer athletic virtues beyond the field of play.

HONESTY VERSUS DECEPTION

Let us begin with the virtue of honesty or truthfulness. Confucius counts honesty among the five key virtues; Mengzi claimed that virtuous people are ashamed to have their reputation exceed their actual worth.[18] Aristotle, likewise, praised truthfulness (*apseudeia*) as a mean between the excess of boastfulness and the deficiency of self-deprecation with respect to a person's self-assessment, as well as his behavior and speech.[19] MacIntyre thinks honesty is essential to the relationships embedded within social practices; without it, we would not be able to achieve the relevant standards of excellence, and that renders the practice "pointless, except as a device for achieving external goods."[20]

If we think about the important relationships an athlete has in sports—with coaches, officials, and even opponents—we can see how honesty is important in each of them. In martial arts, the key relationship is with one's master, and honesty seems fundamental here. In a story in the book *Zen in the Art of Archery*, author Eugen Herrigel decides secretly to disregard his master's instructions to focus only on becoming selfless and instead works on aiming at the target. Not only does the master immediately recognize the deception and punish him for it, but Herrigel also discovers that his efforts at aiming were indeed counterproductive.[21]

Sport, likewise, generally rewards athletes who are honest with their coaches and punishes those who are not. In a basketball team, for example, a player who covers up her injury to try to get more playing time ultimately hurts the team's chances at victory, as does a self-deprecating player who defers to less-qualified teammates. Occasionally a coach might deceive a player in order to encourage him, for example, by telling a runner he's closer to the leaders than he is. In the earliest surviving manual that we have for athletic training, a coach even motivates an athlete with the false story that a woman he loved said he would be worthy of her only if he wins at Olympia.[22] But the coach-athlete relationship depends heavily on trust, and dishonesty almost always undermines trust. So at least as far as teammate and coaching relationships are concerned, the virtue of honesty seems to be rewarded by achievement in sports, as it is in martial arts.

The case of officials is a little different. The official's job, of course, is to enforce the rules (letter and spirit) of the game. Players who interfere with enforcement by using deception can be said, in effect, to be cheating. Traditional martial arts emphasize honor, have few rules, and have little need for officials.[23] Golf is similar in that players are expected to call penalties on themselves—a tradition that illustrates shared interest in a fairly played game.

In 2010, professional golfer Brian Davis called a two-stroke penalty on himself for a minor infraction that required a slow-motion replay to confirm. By doing so, he gave up his first PGA Tour victory and the million-plus-dollar prize that went with it.[24] Davis's action attracted attention because of the stakes involved, not because self-called penalties are rare. They are as common in golf as they are unthinkable in the professional soccer world discussed previously. This shows not that golf is nobler than soccer but, rather, that virtues and vices are cultivated in communities and, as Aristotle said, the whole community benefits from their exercise.

In fact, community standards can be changed by "moral entrepreneurs" such as Miroslav Klose, a German football player who scored a goal with his hand and told the referee, who canceled the goal. His action went viral on social media, and other players have imitated it in various leagues.[25] Insofar as a sports community values its standards of excellence, it wants those standards to be accurately measured. Some might be tempted to consider the strategic deception of referees among the skills to be tested by the game. But the mere strategic effectiveness of such antics does not transform them into game skills, and a community that condones them undermines its own practice. The sports community should do everything it can to discourage deceiving officials.

Deception of opponents, by contrast, seems to be part of most sports. Even Sun-Tzu, a philosophical father of the martial arts, endorses it. He declares that "all warfare is based on deception."[26] Deception in the form of feints and misleading cues is expected, condoned, and rewarded in almost all games, albeit within the limits established by the rules. It is acceptable in baseball, for example, to discourage a runner from stealing a base or taking off before the pitch is released by faking a throw to the baseman, who might then tag the runner out. But strict and complicated limits apply to this tactic.

Why is such deception allowed, and what is the reason for limiting it?[27] First, although deception is generally a vice, the ability to recognize it in others and to respond accordingly is certainly a skill worth having. This is also true in the martial arts. According to this line of reasoning, deception should be allowed and expected between opponents in sport because it enables players to cultivate the quality of not being easily deceived. One may even argue that deception could be used as a virtue under certain circumstances—as when I must deceive a would-be kidnapper about the presence of a child in my house in order to prevent the crime. In fact, Plato understood lying as a skill that could be put to either virtuous or vicious uses.[28] Deceiving competitors in sport may be valued in a practice community insofar as it cultivates useful skills, but it should be banned insofar as it interferes with other skills being tested. The balk rule in baseball, discussed earlier, seems designed to prevent the game of deception from overtaking the sport's fundamental skills of pitching and hitting.

In the end, the virtue of honesty in sport should be understood as Mengzi and Aristotle saw it—as a value for the accurate assessment of one's ability or worth. Insofar as sports and the martial arts seek to test the evolving skills of their participants, they fundamentally support this kind of honesty. By the same token, insofar as it interferes with the game—that is, the accurate assessment of relevant skills valued by the practice community—strategic deception needs to be discouraged by the reward structure of the game. This is not always easy to do, as the case of faking injuries in professional soccer attests—officials can't simply ignore such displays because the player may, in fact, need medical attention. Neither, however, should a player's ability to deceive the officials in this way be accepted by communities as a legitimate part of the sport. It is a strategic abuse of rules designed to protect players' safety.

Deception among players, on the other hand, is considered within some practice communities as a "legitimate" sports skill—especially insofar as it contributes to players' ability to avoid being deceived. It is an expected part of the competitive relationship that certain forms of deception, such as head fakes or feinted throws, will be used. But even though deception of coaches or officials, along with some surreptitious forms of opponent deception, such as faking injury, may increase one's chances at victory, these should be regarded as flaws in the game. Victories that come about through the cultivation of vice have no worth to the practice or to the practitioner, both of which should aim at the cultivation of virtue. As such they should not be valued or celebrated within the practice community, and as far as possible, they should be prohibited by the rules of the game.[29]

JUSTICE VERSUS ADVANTAGE

At the opening of Plato's *Republic*, the sophist Thrasymachus defines justice as "the advantage of the stronger."[30] It is a familiar characterization, supported by cynical observation of how the world often works. Today people express a similar idea with the comment "might makes right." Of course, Plato does not endorse this view—rather, he uses it as a provocative starting point from which to expound an essentialist theory of justice as the supreme virtue of city-states and individuals as well. When MacIntyre counts justice among the social virtues needed to experience the internal goods of a social practice, he, too, is thinking of a property of persons and communities.[31] Aristotle characterizes justice as the virtue that concerns our dealings with others, summarizing it as "treating equals equally and unequals unequally in proportion to their relevant differences."[32] This description jibes well with the common conventions of sport, which provide an equal opportunity for all participants and attempt to reward them according to merit. A just athlete might accordingly be one who respects competitors as equals and graciously recognizes the merit of the winner—that is, an athlete who displays "good sportsmanship."

But the reality of competitive attitudes in sport seems to better resemble Thrasymachus's definition: you use every advantage you can to win the game and prove your superiority over others. The very fact that athletes need to be exhorted to "be a good sport" reveals an apparent conflict between the natural emotions of competition and the moral expectations of justice, understood as the virtue of sportsmanship.

Perhaps the problem is competition itself. Most social practices, such as traditional martial arts, do not emphasize competition the way Western sports do. Perhaps the virtue of justice in sports runs counter to the competitive spirit, and sportsmanship is really just indifference toward competition. Maybe the good sport, like Confucius's gentleman, "never competes."[33] He may participate in a game of archery, but he is uninterested in the outcome. Traditional martial arts reflect this attitude by avoiding competition. Indeed, Bäck claims that if sports want to cultivate virtues such as justice, they need to leave competition behind.[34]

To some degree this contrast in attitudes toward competition seems to be cultural. The movie *Running Brave* tells the true story of Native American runner Billy Mills and his struggle to adapt to the ruthless competitiveness of college athletics. Growing up on the reservation, Mills would run just hard enough to win races, thereby avoiding the humiliation of his competitors by a wide victory margin. When he lets a fellow Indian runner catch up toward the end of a college race, however, his university coach scolds him despite the victory. "You gotta crush him, so he knows you're better!" the coach bellows.[35] Mills is at first put off by this attitude, but he eventually assimilates to the cutthroat style of collegiate sports and scores a surprising gold medal in the 1964 Olympic Games despite fierce opponents who jostle him to the edge of the track. The moral of the story is clear: real competitors give no quarter; nice guys finish last.

In the West, even children are taught to compete this way—sometimes to the point of running up the score against lesser opponents in a way that provokes humiliation and tears. High school basketball scores of 110–22 are commonly displayed on the Friday night sports roundup in the supposedly kind-and-gentle heartland state of Iowa. Philosophers debating the morality of this phenomenon point out, on the one hand, that the losers in such blowouts should not feel humiliated as long as they play to the best of their ability and,[36] on the other hand, that athletes who suffer from pretension may benefit from mild humiliation in sport.[37] Arguably, a just athlete simply wants accurate contest results. If a result is laughably lopsided, so be it. Sports, after all, are knowledge-seeking activities.[38] Knowledge that embarrasses people is still knowledge.

But surely the disposition to enjoy seeing competitors humiliated is not a virtuous one. Taking pleasure in another's suffering (schadenfreude) is, as Mike McNamee observes, "too active, too destructive of human sympathy, to be evidence of a love of justice."[39] A just athlete values justice generally, and not merely, like Thrasymachus, in terms of advantage. Blowouts are the result of unjust matchups—contests that fail to take fair account of the relative merits and compatibility of the competitors going in. Whatever accuracy the scores show in reflecting this disparity does not justify the contest's worth, and just athletes do not place much stock in such contests' results, even when the result is victory. It is not inconsistent with justice to make less than a full effort once victory is assured, or even to end clearly flawed contests early.[40]

In order for sport communities to promote the virtue of justice, they need not abandon competition completely. Rather, they need to emphasize *good* competition. The best contests, those that exercise the virtues and produce internal goods such as "flow," are almost always evenly matched.[41] Asian cultures prefer evenly matched contests, observes Bäck, noting that Thai boxers who dominate opponents are forced to retire for lack of bouts.[42] That claim seems to imply that Western sports and athletes generally prefer easy victories, those that do not challenge one's skills or, perhaps, are gained through an opponent's misfortune.[43] There certainly are such cases. I recall my father, a dedicated University of Southern California football fan, declaring at the beginning of one Rose Bowl, "I don't want it to be a good game. I don't want it to be close. I want a blowout!" It was an understandable emotion but not a sober reflection on sport—even though it did show that he at least *knew* what "a good game" was.

Further, his emotion was that of a fan, whose potential payoff is primarily pleasure, as opposed to the sport practitioner, who stands to learn and grow more from a closely fought game. It is easy to forget that an athlete's life is usually dominated by training rather than contests. They train not just for the end goal of victory; otherwise, they would only enter contests against much lesser opponents—a practice derided even in Western sports as "cherry-picking." Rather, they train to improve their competitive excellence, and they seek contests where that excellence will be justly tested. To say that competitive athletes only want to win is akin to saying that martial artists only want to fight. What they want is to possess the virtues associated with a just victory over a worthy opponent. This desire itself reflects the virtue of justice common in sports communities.

COURAGE VERSUS HUBRIS

Competition in sport has also been lauded for its ability to cultivate the virtue of courage. Because athletes necessarily face the risk of losing and often face the risk of physical harm, competition demands virtues such as courage, and in that way, they can serve as a means of Aristotelian-style virtue training. But there is a sense in which real-world risk is something quite different from sporting risk. You risk losing, but you only risk losing a game. You risk injury, but usually a trained medic is waiting on the sidelines to attend to your needs (risk and injury in sport will be discussed further in chapter 12). Unlike the potentially lethal fight that traditional martial artists train for but hope never to experience, modern athletes almost never face anyone trying to kill them.[44]

A serious question considers whether the courage cultivated within sport is, in fact, the same virtue needed in real life. Martial arts have a danger, in

Bäck's view, that is lacking in traditional sports and play.[45] They are designed to cultivate a kind of real-world courage appropriate for serious risks: a courage that does not promote violence and dominance over others but, rather, seeks to eliminate it. Bäck explains, "[A] martial art has the goal of dealing with violence by transforming the situation so that the violence and conflict with another completely disappear."[46] The image of the master martial artist is certainly not one of aggression and violence, and the Eastern philosophical principle of *yin*, or strength in yielding, can be appreciated even in Western sport. But is it true that the separate and playful nature of Western sports tranquilizes us about violence and prevents cultivation of the virtue of courage?

Part of this depends, of course, on what we mean by courage. MacIntyre does not seem to have had swordfights in mind when he counted courage among the virtues needed in social practices; rather, he mentions the need to "take self-endangering risks" and to "listen carefully to what we are told about our inadequacies."[47] Stating that it was not simply an absence of fear, because it may be virtuous to fear some things such as disgrace,[48] Aristotle identified courage as the mean between (over)confidence and fear.[49] This clarification reflects Plato's discussion of courage as wise endurance in the pursuit of noble goals,[50] or that quality of the spirited part of the soul that enables it to follow reason's lead.[51] In all these cases, courage relies heavily on intellectual discernment plus the ability—cultivated through practice—to follow through with rational decisions despite emotions such as fear.[52] In this sense, it reflects martial arts training's goal of liberation from the fear of death. But in the context of Zen Buddhism, that would be liberation from all *selfish* desires—including fame, fortune, and victory.[53] The goal is a state of *mushin* (no mind) that is characterized by a *lack* of self-regard and the *absence* of preoccupation about contest results.[54]

In discussing the value of dangerous sport from a Western perspective, by contrast, John Russell and Norman Fischer identify self-affirmation and self-possession as the primary benefits.[55] Does the contrast between Eastern selflessness and Western selfishness suggest that the "courage" cultivated in competitive sport communities is not a virtue at all?

In fact, on Aristotle's chart *hubris* or overconfidence would be the vice corresponding to courage. There does seem to be a connection between the more violent Western sports, such as boxing and football, and ego-puffing displays of bravado by athletes. Boxing is one of the world's oldest sports, predating even the Olympic Games, but it has struggled for legitimacy in the eyes of sport philosophers because its lusory goal, to use Bernard Suits's term, is the injury or disabling of one's opponent—that is, knocking him out so that he is unable to continue. If we define violence as the use of force with intent to harm, we can conclude that the sport of boxing condones violence. Traditional martial arts may also train practitioners to use force with the intent to harm but only in order to protect themselves or their communities in response to a violent attack, not just for sport or to win a game. Courage in the martial arts context concerns a real-life threat. But the courage required for boxing is bound up with the creation of an occasion for violence that has no good reason and is, therefore, morally unacceptable.[56] The ancient Greek vice of *hubris* involved excessive confidence or pride, especially in the willingness to violate socially accepted norms involving violence.[57] In effect, it represents the mistaken assumption that the normal rules don't apply to you. Because violence is generally prohibited in civil society, boxing's promotion of it can be seen to cultivate the vice of hubris rather than the virtue of courage.

It should be noted, however, that not all use of force in sport is violent and, in almost every other sport besides boxing, it is regulated in such a way as to *prevent* intentional harm or disabling of competitors. But the risks inherent in athletic competition do have the potential to cultivate the kind of wisdom-based courage that Plato and Aristotle described. The risk of losing, just for starters, fosters the humility foundational to Socrates's understanding of wisdom, as knowing that one doesn't know, as well as Laozi's enabling condition for greatness, namely, never considering oneself great.[58] It takes courage to confront one's fallibility by entering the contest, and it also takes courage to explore the limits of one's capabilities. Russell's defense of dangerous sports as a means of self-affirmation is based on their ability "to confront and push back the boundaries of the self by creating contexts in which some of the ordinary bounds of our lives can be challenged."[59] Russell may discount the idea that dangerous sports produce courage, but the benefits he sees in them seem to depend on courage.

What about the vice of hubris? Mike McNamee argues effectively that sports can go a long way to preventing it. He recounts a famous boxing match between Sugar Ray Leonard and Roberto Duran in which the former's technical superiority so embarrassed the latter that he conceded the match, although he was unhurt. According to McNamee, Duran's hubris, in the form of egotistical posturing and derisive rhetoric, set him up for this fall, which was deserved.[60] If indeed boxing promotes the vice of hubris by sanctioning violence, it is also capable of correcting that vice and promoting real courage. The difference depends on the values of the practice community.

INTEGRITY VERSUS ISOLATION

Even if a case can be made that sport cultivates or exercises virtues such as honesty, justice, and courage, these virtues have limited worth if they are confined just to sport. Many athletes, it seems, exhibit their virtues only in training and competition. I remember once watching one of my student-athletes at practice. Her behavior was exemplary: she arrived early, interacted constructively with her teammates, set an example of concentration and hard work in every drill, and asked good questions of the coaches that clarified everyone's understanding. She did all this despite suffering with the flu. At one point, she pulled out of a drill to vomit in a trash can and then returned and kept practicing.

In the classroom, by contrast, she was a different person from the gym. She would miss class for the slightest reason or arrive late and unprepared. Avoiding interaction with fellow students and the professor, she sat in the back and kept to herself. She almost never turned in an assignment on time, and even when she did, the work was sloppy and riddled with errors. Needless to say, her great success in sport was accompanied by constant academic struggle. What are we to say about cases like these? Where did my student's athletic virtues go? Are we to say that she selectively manifested her virtues in her sports practice community but chose not to exercise them elsewhere in her life? Or is she incapable of expressing them in other communities? Are athletic virtues isolated to sport?

If they are isolated to one activity, they're not genuine virtues at all. "Someone who genuinely possesses a virtue," says MacIntyre, "can be expected to manifest it in very different types of situation."[61] The virtues cultivated through martial arts do not suffer from isolation, according to Bäck, because martial arts itself is not isolated from the rest of one's life. It is a lifetime pursuit, undertaken deliberately as a path to spiritual enlightenment.[62] Because the sports arena is an artificial environment, Bäck continues, "excellence in the sport, even if attained, may thereby, for many people, be restricted to this artificial setting with its artificial rules."[63] Insofar as sport is play, set apart from the serious business of work and survival, Bäck concludes, "it is somewhat strange to talk of producing virtues for our whole life in a sport."[64]

In my student-athlete's case, it was more like sport was the serious part of her life, and school was just a necessary evil that made sport possible. Other student-athletes view sport as a necessary evil that makes college possible. Either way, there is a clear divide between their personalities as athletes and their personalities as students, and this divide affects the authenticity of their virtues. For MacIntyre, authentic virtues are understood as features of a "social and moral life in terms of which [they have] to be defined and explained."[65] They must "transcend the limited goods of practices by constituting the good of a whole human life, the good of a human life conceived as a unity." Conceiving of one's life in this way requires an additional virtue, which he describes as "integrity, constancy, or singleness of purpose."[66]

Although, as we have seen, sport is marked off from the rest of life by certain boundaries of space and time as well as attitudes and rituals, there's no reason it has to be *thought of* as something separate and isolated from an individual's life. Many aspects of human life are similarly framed. Religion and family come immediately to mind. But to say that the special sense we get when entering our church or our childhood home (or I daresay a martial arts dojo) makes these things somehow separate from our lives is nonsensical. These distinctive realms and activities combine to *make up* our lives. We are fundamentally the same person in all of them.

Different environments, activities, and communities call for different behaviors, and the challenges faced in a practice like psychology demand a slightly different set of virtues than the challenges faced in rock climbing. But people who fail to manifest basic virtues such as honesty or self-discipline in the different practices that call for them must be thinking differently about these activities. My student-athlete would probably say that sport *is* her life. She did not conceive of her life as a unity, which in MacIntyre's terms means that she did not have the additional virtue of integrity. What, however, if sport really *is her life*, and she shows integrity, constancy, and singleness of purpose *within* sport? This would be to make the erroneous assumption that one particular activity *could* constitute an entire life and, further, that excellence in one activity to the detriment of all others should be the end or *telos* of one's life. As Aristotle explains in *Nicomachean Ethics*, every activity aims at some good, and the final good or end is *eudaimonia*, a happiness or thriving that can only be understood in terms of a complete lifetime.[67]

It is, therefore, an error to think of one's life only in terms of a sport or to think of sport as something separate from one's life. Having the virtue of integrity means understanding one's life and all of its activities as aimed at a particular end. In effect, it requires us to integrate the various aspects of our lives into a coherent whole. Because happiness is the product of virtuous action, according to Aristotle,[68] we must select and engage in activities in such a way as to cultivate and exercise the virtues. This is precisely the reason that people engage in traditional martial arts, according to Bäck. But based on what we've seen so far, it can also be the reason that people engage in Western-style athletics as well. On a virtue-ethics scheme, the cultivation and exercise of virtue should be the reason for engaging in all sorts of activities and communities, not just sports or martial arts. Likewise, a person with MacIntyre's virtue of integrity will at least try to perform every action virtuously—even those that he doesn't particularly enjoy. We might think back to Albert Camus's Sisyphus, who found a way to voluntarily perform his eternal punishment of rolling a boulder up a hill, and therefore found happiness.[69] Having integrity means choosing to do everything with virtue because it is part of your life and who you are as a person.

The question remains whether sport rewards this kind of virtue, and the answer, regrettably, is that often it does not. This is less the fault of the activity than the communities and institutions that govern them. Student-athletes in particular are asked to perform simultaneously two very different practices, and yet the reward structure for athletic performance—for example, scholarships, playing time, and starting positions—is clearly tied to excellence, while the expectations for academics are minimized—a passing grade-point average and progress toward a degree. Many student-athletes exhibit virtue in both areas, but the reward system clearly favors isolation rather than integrity.

If the Japanese sumo scandal recounted at the start of the chapter reveals that even virtue-directed martial arts can be corrupted by Western-style athletic values, our subsequent discussion of virtue in sport suggests that Western-style sports communities might benefit from a virtue-directed approach. The most convincing aspect of Bäck's argument that traditional martial arts are more capable of cultivating virtue than is sport is that traditional martial arts, by his definition, are consciously undertaken for that purpose. Bäck claims that something about the practice itself, "the ritual, the formal exercises, the formal patterns (*kata*), the direct connection with ordinary life," accounts for the capacity of martial arts to produce virtue.[70] But these aspects are included (though, perhaps, deemphasized) when martial arts are "corrupted" by being made into sports. The issue from a virtue-ethics point of view is not so much the nature of the practice. Almost any practice with standards of excellence can be used to cultivate virtue, and almost any activity can be done virtuously. The issue is how we *think about* the practice, how we engage with the practice community, and how we integrate it into our lives.

In a book titled *Aretism: An Ancient Sports Philosophy for the Modern Sports World*, M. Andrew Holowchak and I argue that, in order for sport to be a good, it must be undertaken for the purpose of cultivating virtues that benefit not only the participant but also the greater community by producing more virtuous citizens.[71] In doing so, we follow contemporary philosophers of sport such as Fraleigh, Simon, Russell, and McNamee, as well as ancient virtue ethicists such as Plato, Aristotle, Laozi, and Confucius. Sport, as practiced in the modern world, does not reliably incentivize and reward the virtues, but then a virtuous person should not be motivated by external goods such as money and status. Indeed, both Western and Eastern virtue ethicists agree that the pursuit of fame and fortune *interferes* with the cultivation of virtue.[72]

Further, MacIntyre observes that the institutions that administer practices such as sport (i.e., the NCAA or FIFA) tend to be guided by external goods such as wealth, power, and status rather than the pursuit of virtue.[73] So the solution to the problem of virtue in sport is to be found within the minds of practitioners and the values of the practice community itself. The beauty of .

virtue as the real prize of athletic competition is that it benefits not just the victor but also the many communities of which she forms a part.

DISCUSSION QUESTIONS

1. Contrast self-called penalties in golf with the tendency in many sports to deceive officials. Do you think golfers would be less likely than other athletes to engage in deception outside of sports, such as understating income on one's tax return?
2. Have you ever been on a team that ran up the score against an inferior opponent? Have you ever been on the losing side of a blowout? How did your team react to the situation? Do you think that sports should have mercy rules to prevent the practice?
3. Several famous players have been excluded from the Baseball Hall of Fame because of vicious behavior outside of sport. Should character be a criterion for Halls of Fame, or only a player's athletic ability?
4. Why do you think that schools and colleges tend to encourage excellence in either athletics or academics but make it difficult to achieve both? How do you think they could change to promote a more integrated idea of virtue?

NOTES

1. Naoto Kan, quoted in Cable News Network, "Sumo 'Fixing' Scandal Rocks Japan," CNN International Edition, February 4, 2011, accessed October 21, 2011, http://edition.cnn.com/.

2. Allan Bäck, "The *Way* to Virtue in Sport," *Journal of the Philosophy of Sport* 36 (2009): 217.

3. Bäck, "The *Way*," 217. The empirical studies that Bäck cited are called into question by Mike McNamee, *Sports, Virtues and Vices: Morality Plays* (London: Routledge, 2008), chap. 4, for their methodologies and theoretical assumptions about the nature of morality.

4. Justin McCurry, "Sumo Threatened by Scandal and Crime," *Guardian*, July 4, 2010, accessed October 21, 2011, http://www.guardian.co.uk/.

5. A martial art, says Bäck, is a "method for enlightenment on the human condition through the ritualized practice of techniques designed to neutralize violence" ("The *Way*," 217).

6. Zhao, quoted in Gene Ching and Gigi Oh, "Where Wushu Went Wrong," *Kungfu Magazine*, November 3, 2006, accessed October 21, 2011, http://ezine.kungfumagazine.com/.

7. Anthony Kuhn, "Chinese Martial Art Form Sports Less Threatening Moves," *Los Angeles Times*, October 16, 1988, accessed October 21, 2011, http://articles.latimes.com/.

8. Heather L. Reid, "Athletic Virtue: Between East and West," *Sport, Ethics and Philosophy* 4, no. 1 (2010): 19, argues that the concepts of virtue in ancient Greek and Chinese philosophy, *aretē* and *de*, respectively, are both understood as forms of psychic power cultivated through training.

9. Aristotle, *Nicomachean Ethics*, 2nd ed., trans. Terence Irwin (Indianapolis: Hackett, 1999), 1103a15–18.

10. Confucius, *Analects*, trans. E. Slingerland (Indianapolis: Hackett, 2003), 1.12, 2.3, 9.10.

11. Alasdair MacIntyre, *After Virtue* (Notre Dame, IN: University of Notre Dame Press, 1981), 175; discussed in chap. 5.

12. MacIntyre, *After Virtue*, 180.

13. Aristotle, *Nicomachean Ethics*, 1097b9–1.

14. Aristotle, *Politics*, trans. C. D. C. Reeve (Indianapolis: Hackett, 1998), 1281a2–3.

15. MacIntyre, *After Virtue*, 181; McNamee, *Sports, Virtues*, 18.

16. Bäck, "The *Way*," 225.

17. William J. Morgan, *Sport and Moral Conflict: A Conventionalist Theory* (Philadelphia: Temple University Press, 2020), 105.

18. Confucius, *Analects*, 17.6; Mengzi, *Mencius*, trans. Irene Bloom (New York: Columbia University Press, 2009), 4B18. The honesty I have in mind here is not the Western idea of being forthright and telling the truth unbidden; that idea runs up against concern with "saving face" in Chinese culture. Rather, I am thinking about accurate self-assessment—much like Aristotelian *apseudeia.*

19. Aristotle, *Nicomachean Ethics*, 4.7.

20. MacIntyre, *After Virtue*, 191.

21. Eugen Herrigel, *Zen in the Art of Archery*, trans. R. F. C. Hull (New York: Vintage, 1999), 50–52.

22. Philostratus, *Gymnasticus*, trans. Jason König (Cambridge, MA: Harvard University Press, 2014), §22.

23. Bäck, "The *Way*," 218. The case, of course, is different with martial arts sports, which generally employ referees as well as multiple judges.

24. Jay Busbee, "Davis Calls Penalty on Himself, Gives Up Shot at First PGA Win," Yahoo Sports, April 18, 2010, accessed October 21, 2011, http://sports.yahoo.com/. It is worth noting that Davis did win more than half that amount for coming in second.

25. Nicky Bandini, "Napoli Hit the Summit after Cavani's Hat-Trick—and Klose's Mea Culpa," *The Guardian*, September 27, 2012. Video of the incident and the imitators is available on YouTube. Thanks to Rafael Mendoza for the example.

26. Sun Tzu, *The Art of War*, trans. Lionel Giles (Hong Kong: Forgotten Books, 2007), 1.18.

27. Deception has been the subject of recent debate in the philosophy of sport. See, for example, S. P. Morris, "Deception in Sports," *Journal of the Philosophy of Sport*

41, no. 2 (2014): 177–91; Adam G. Pfleegor and Danny Roesenberg, "Deception in Sport: A New Taxonomy of Intra-Lusory Guiles," *Journal of the Philosophy of Sport* 41, no. 2 (2014): 209–31; Steven Weimer, "Autonomous Authorization of Deception in Sport," *Journal of the Philosophy of Sport* 43, no. 2 (2016): 179–98; Leslie A. Howe, "Simulation, Seduction, and Bullshit: Cooperative and Destructive Misleading," *Journal of the Philosophy of Sport* 44, no. 3 (2017): 300–14.

28. Plato, *Hippias Minor*, in *Complete Works*, ed. John M. Cooper (Indianapolis: Hackett, 1997), 364c–70e.

29. M. Andrew Holowchak and Heather L. Reid, *Aretism: An Ancient Sports Philosophy for the Modern Sports World* (Lanham, MD: Lexington, 2011), 176.

30. Plato, *Republic*, trans. G. M. A. Grube (Indianapolis: Hackett, 1992), 338c.

31. He had such a hard time explaining exactly what justice is, however, that he devoted a separate book to the subject. Alasdair MacIntyre, *Whose Justice? Which Rationality?* (Notre Dame, IN: University of Notre Dame Press, 1989).

32. Aristotle, *Nicomachean Ethics*, 1130a8–10, V.3 1131a10–25.

33. Says Confucius, "The Master said, Gentlemen never compete. You will say that in archery they do so. But even then they bow and make way for one another when they are going up to the archery-ground, when they are coming down and at the subsequent drinking-bout. Thus even when competing, they still remain gentlemen." *The Analects of Confucius*, trans. Arthur Waley (New York: Vintage, 1989), 3.7.

34. Bäck, "The *Way*," 223.

35. Coach Bill Easton in *Running Brave*, dir. D. S. Everett and Donald Shebib, Englander Productions, 1984.

36. Nicholas Dixon, "Why Losing by a Wide Margin Is Not in Itself a Disgrace," *Journal of the Philosophy of Sport* 25, no. 1 (1998): 67.

37. Mike McNamee, "Hubris, Humility, and Humiliation: Vice and Virtue in Sporting Communities," *Journal of the Philosophy of Sport* 29, no. 1 (2002): 38.

38. This is the theory expounded in Heather L. Reid, "Sport, Philosophy, and the Quest for Knowledge," *Journal of the Philosophy of Sport* 36, no. 1 (2009): 40–49.

39. Mike McNamee, *Sports, Virtues*, 159.

40. Scholarly debate continues on the issue of blowouts. See, for example, Nicholas Dixon, "On Sportsmanship and 'Running Up the Score,'" *Journal of the Philosophy of Sport* 19, no. 1 (1992): 1–13; Jason Taylor and Christopher Johnson, "Virtuous Victory: Running up the Score and the Anti-Blowout Thesis," *Journal of the Philosophy of Sport* 41, no. 2 (2014): 247–66; Peter M. Hopsicker, "'Running' Up the Score? The Application of the Anti-Blowout Thesis in Footraces," *Journal of the Philosophy of Sport* 47, no. 2 (2020): 266–82.

41. Susan A. Jackson and Mihaly Csikszentmihalyi, *Flow in Sports* (Champaign, IL: Human Kinetics, 1999), 6.

42. Bäck, "The *Way*," 234 n. 1.

43. It is hard for me to believe that even traditional martial artists, when faced with a fight, never hope for a moment that the ground will give way under their opponent's feet. In fact, the serious stakes involved in martial arts fighting seem more conducive to the idea of survival by any means necessary than the "playful" context of Western sports.

44. Truth be told, nor do most modern martial artists. In fact, Western risk sports such as mountain climbing and scuba diving seem to present more danger than their Eastern counterparts these days. I am grateful to Jesús Ilundáin-Agurruza for this comment.

45. Bäck, "The *Way*," 230.

46. Bäck, "The *Way*," 230.

47. MacIntyre, *After Virtue*, 191.

48. Aristotle, *Nicomachean Ethics*, 3.6. Fearing appropriate things, further, excludes irrational fears of benign things such as mice.

49. Aristotle, *Nicomachean Ethics*, 1107a.

50. Plato, "Laches," in *Complete Works*, 196d and 192e ff.

51. Plato, *Republic*, 430b, 442c.

52. On the relationship between courage and knowledge in sport, see Jason M. Smith, "What Must I Know to Be Brave? Revisiting the Role of Knowledge in the Exercise of Courage in Sport," *Journal of the Philosophy of Sport* 44, no. 3 (2017): 374–87.

53. Winston King, *Zen and the Way of the Sword* (New York: Oxford University Press, 1993), 177.

54. For an analysis of *mushin* and other Eastern ideas in sport, see Jesús Ilundáin-Agurruza, "Everything Mysterious under the Moon—Social Practices and Situated Holism," *Sport, Ethics and Philosophy* 8, no. 4 (2014): 503–66, reprinted in Jesús Ilundáin-Agurruza, *Holism and the Cultivation of Excellence in Sports and Performance: Skillful Striving* (London: Routledge, 2018), chap. 10.

55. John Russell, "The Value of Dangerous Sports," *Journal of the Philosophy of Sport* 32, no. 1 (2005): 1–19; Norman Fischer, "Competitive Sport's Imitation of War: Imaging the Completeness of Virtue," *Journal of the Philosophy of Sport* 29, no. 1 (2002): 16–37.

56. Paul Davis, "Ethical Issues in Boxing," *Journal of the Philosophy of Sport* 20–21 (1993–1994): 56.

57. A prime example is Oedipus's killing of his father (whom he did not know) in a dispute over right of way at a road crossing.

58. Plato, *Apology*, trans. G. M. A. Grube (Indianapolis: Hackett, 1980), 22e; and Laozi, "Daodejing," in *Readings in Classical Chinese Philosophy*, 2nd ed., ed. P. Ivanhoe and B. Van Norden (Indianapolis: Hackett, 2001), 179, chap. 34.

59. Russell, "The Value of Dangerous Sports," 1.

60. McNamee, "Hubris, Humility, and Humiliation," 38–53.

61. MacIntyre, *After Virtue*, 191.

62. Bäck, "The *Way*," 218.

63. Bäck, "The *Way*," 221.

64. Bäck, "The *Way*," 222.

65. MacIntyre, *After Virtue*, 174.

66. MacIntyre, *After Virtue*, 189.

67. Aristotle, *Nicomachean Ethics*, 1094a, 1097b.

68. Aristotle, *Nicomachean Ethics*, 10.7.1.

69. Albert Camus, *The Myth of Sisyphus and Other Essays*, trans. Justin O'Brien (New York: Random House, 1955).

70. Bäck, "The *Way*," 228.

71. Holowchak and Reid, *Aretism*, 168–69.

72. Reid, "Athletic Virtue," 25.

73. MacIntyre, *After Virtue*, 181.

Chapter 11

Ethical Spectatorship

"Are you not entertained?" roars the fictional fighter Maximus, derisively addressing the crowd of Rome's Colosseum in the movie *Gladiator*. At least one real-life Roman spectator, the first-century philosopher Lucius Annaeus Seneca, very often was not entertained. What he saw at the Colosseum was stomach turning even by modern horror film standards: the live slaughter of exotic animals, the live slaughter of human beings by exotic animals, and even the live slaughter of human beings by other human beings. Our worries about violence in modern sport seem almost quaint by comparison. In fact, Seneca was known for his moral criticism of Roman spectacles even in ancient times. An inscription uncovered at Pompeii names him as "the only Roman writer to condemn the bloody games,"[1] and in letter 7, he warns against the corrupting effects of being a spectator at the arena:

> Nothing is as ruinous to the character as sitting away one's time at a show—for it is then, through the medium of entertainment, that vices creep into one with more than usual ease. What do you take me to mean? That I go home more selfish, more self-seeking and more self-indulgent? Yes, and what is more, a person crueler and less humane through having been in contact with human beings.[2]

As a Stoic philosopher, Seneca took virtue to be the highest good. Those concerned about virtue today might view his condemnation of the Roman arena as a warning about the morally corrosive potential of watching modern sports. Such warnings are not uncommon. Watching sports is blamed for a host of human ills, ranging from laziness to spousal abuse. On the other hand, sports' affinity with art, discussed in chapter 6, suggests that watching sports could be a source of social and moral edification. Whether or not you think that entertainment is among the purposes of sport, it is worth wondering when and under what conditions sports spectatorship is morally constructive—or destructive.

Our inquiry should start, as Seneca's does, with a critical attitude toward sport as entertainment, but it needn't necessarily finish with a negative conclusion. Seneca's oft-quoted condemnation, cited above, is counterbalanced by his expressions of admiration for gladiators as paragons of Stoic virtue. The events that the philosopher found aesthetically repugnant and morally hazardous were staged public executions, especially those in which condemned criminals were armed and set to kill one another without skill, honor, or any hope of survival. Worse than this sad spectacle, in Seneca's eyes, was the bloodthirsty bleating of the crowds screaming, not unlike modern sports fans: "Kill him! Flog him! Burn him!"[3]

The conduct of gladiators, in contrast, receives repeated praise from Seneca because they fight with valor in the face of death and are, by virtue of their enslavement, symbolically liberated from the vicious desires of mainstream society.[4] "The gladiator judges it ignominious to be set against an inferior," Seneca observes, "as he knows it is without glory to defeat one who can be defeated without danger."[5] After witnessing a barbarian plunge a knife into his own chest during a mock sea battle, Seneca calls the display "all the more striking because of the lesson men learn from it that dying is more honorable than killing."[6] Might modern sport be equally praised and condemned according to its moral effect on spectators?

It certainly has been. In 1977, Christopher Lasch lamented the "degradation" of modern American sport by the forces and values of the market, which understands sport as a form of entertainment.[7] Some thirty years later, William Morgan describes sport as a kind of moral wasteland in which winning trumps fair play; an assertive egoism triumphs over mutual moral respect; an anything-goes-as-long-as-I-don't-get caught attitude prevails over expressions of good will toward others; and a pervasive mistrust poisons most interactions and relations in sports, undercutting any sense of solidarity—of community—within them.[8]

On the positive side, Mike McNamee likens modern sport to medieval morality plays, which were performed to educate the illiterate about the value of virtue and the dangers of vice.[9] Graham McFee thinks that sport functions as a moral laboratory, in which virtues and vices are challenged and tested in artificial contests with relatively low stakes as preparation for more serious moral challenges outside the game.[10] And Stephen Mumford, using an aesthetic ethics, describes sports as "contests of virtue" in which spectators observe real-life struggles between virtue and vice and draw meaningful moral lessons from the spectacle.[11]

The possibility that watching sport may be morally beneficial, however, does not imply that it always is. In this chapter, we will explore the ethics of spectatorship, assessing its potential dangers and possible benefits. Is the partisan desire that your team wins at any cost morally defensible? Do sports' previously discussed affinities with art demand the disinterested appreciation of purists? Does knowledge of the game—or experience playing it—enhance a spectator's appreciation of it? Is it morally acceptable to cheer the skillful performance of an immoral athlete?

PARTISANS VERSUS PURISTS

Critics of sport spectatorship like to observe that the term "fan" derives from "fanatic"—a word that implies irrational and even dangerous passion. Those who praise the entertainment value of sport likewise point to its ability to elicit passion as a positive rather than a negative feature. People such as my nephew, who found himself seated among rowdy Oakland Raiders fans, dressed as marauders and painted head-to-toe in team colors, can tell you such passion is daunting. He was wearing the jersey of the opposing American football team—a lonely drop of green amid a sea of silver and black. There were sideways glances and muffled whispers, but nothing more than that. One face-painted fan even congratulated him for his team's victory after the game. Maybe he was just lucky. Violence among fans from opposing teams is not uncommon and sometimes is deadly. Such incidents are universally condemned, however, and are rare in comparison with the widespread phenomenon of passionate but harmless partisan fans. Some take their devotion as a point of pride, believing that their support helps the team to win. Loyal fandom can even be the object of praise. But to what extent is it morally defensible? When do "rabid" fans become as worrisome as rabid dogs?

In the philosophy of sport, debate about the ethics of spectatorship is rooted in the distinction between partisan and purist fans. Nicholas Dixon established the distinction in 2001, identifying partisans as fans who passionately support their favorite team and long for its success, whereas purists are impartial lovers of the game itself who appreciate displays of athletic excellence without allegiance to any particular team.[12] He went on to praise the virtues of partisanship, especially loyalty, but was met with skepticism and criticism from others concerned with its moral dangers. The critics argue that partisan fans overemphasize victory, wanting their team to win at any cost and for any reason—including cheating, poor officiating, opponents' misfortune and more. Partisan fans have been known to harass officials, taunt opposing players, and attack opposing fans. The virtues of loyalty and commitment are easily transformed by partisan passion into the vices of bias and hatred. And even if partisans behave themselves, critics say, their support of one team over the other is usually arbitrary—based on some contingency such as place of birth or residence, rather than the athletic virtues that sport is supposed to celebrate. In short, critics say that partisanship clouds our moral appreciation of sport—of the kinds of intrinsic virtues and values we studied in previous chapters.

Purists, by contrast, are fans of the game itself rather than any particular team. They are able to appreciate the beauty of an excellent performance or closely fought contest aesthetically without their pleasure depending on which team the athlete plays for or who wins. Purist spectators are morally superior to partisan ones, the argument goes, because they are able to understand and appreciate the true beauty and value of sport without having their experience of it obfuscated by unruly partisan passions.

However, in the same way that sport is not an art or science—even though it has affinities with both—watching sport is not the same as appreciating art or conducting experiments. Even those philosophers who praise purism in sports spectatorship acknowledge the value of moderate partisanship. To the extent that spectators sincerely identify with athletes, they must sincerely care about the outcome of the contest. Does rooting for the protagonist in a novel or play destroy our aesthetic appreciation of it? Ethical spectatorship is not so much about eliminating partisanship as it is about promoting aesthetic appreciation of sport based on an understanding of its values.

BOUNDARIES AND FRAMING

The problems with partisan spectatorship are almost always caused by a failure to recognize boundaries. Fans who contemplate suicide because their team lost, or those who ignore public-safety protocols to celebrate a win, are not only taking sport "too seriously," but they are carrying their passions beyond the reasonable boundaries of sport. We observed in chapter 6 that art and sport share the common play characteristic of being separate from ordinary life. This separation is marked by physical boundaries such as a tennis court's outline, and rituals such as the postgame handshake, but it occurs in the mind of the spectator. The boundaries and rituals signal to spectators (and to athletes) to adopt a particular attitude—to create a mental frame that focuses our attention on what we see within it and diminishes our awareness of the outside world. In theater, the transition is called a "suspension of disbelief." Indeed, the beginning of a basketball game is not unlike the opening of a play, where the curtain opens up and invites us to focus on and engage emotionally with what happens within that particular frame of space and time.

Although relaxation and entertainment are part of what we expect from watching sport, a true aesthetic attitude is one of *heightened* awareness. As Lasch observes, "[Games] obliterate awareness of everyday reality, but they do this not by diminishing awareness but by raising it to a new intensity of concentration."[13] This intensity of spectator concentration is powerful enough to be felt by the athletes, who often thrive on it to the point of performing at a higher level. Their reaction is in contrast to most workaday tasks, such as teaching and gardening, where external observation might be dreaded and associated with poorer performance. Auto-repair technicians jokingly state that their fee is double if a customer wants to watch.

What seems different from this sport and the performing arts is that spectators expect to witness excellence. The players feed off this expectation and are moved to live up to it. During the pandemic lockdown of 2020, when spectators were banned from arenas, some athletes found it more difficult to perform. Further, because the expected excellence of athletes has a moral connection, the spectator's act of framing can encourage ethical behavior. Both athletes and fans prefer their team to win deservedly—immoral behavior reflects negatively on both.

So, one thing that gives sport and art aesthetic value is spectators' willingness to see them as extraordinary—to frame them off as spaces within which special things are expected to happen or even where the *un*expected is expected to happen. Indeed, the space of art and sport, as we observed earlier, is characterized especially by the senses of freedom and possibility. This not only makes art and sport welcome escapes from the stifling predictability of the "real world," but it also reinforces a community's value for freedom and possibility—inspired not least by their ability to enable greatness. It is uncontroversial that the quality of genius is valued, and in comparing the concept of genius in art and sport, Teresa Lacerda and Stephen Mumford note its association with the aesthetic values of creativity and originality, which depend, in turn, upon an atmosphere of freedom and possibility.[14]

If we understand sport in Bernard Suits's terms as "a voluntary effort to overcome unnecessary obstacles,"[15] the sporting genius or virtuoso can be understood as one who "can find new ways of overcoming . . . obstacles or can respond to their unpredictability through their creative acts."[16] The ethical spectator, then, simultaneously frames sport as something separate from the ordinary world and elevates expectations of excellence by reaffirming such values as freedom and possibility within that frame.[17] Lasch observes that one of play's virtues is "its capacity to dramatize reality and to offer a convincing representation of the community's values."[18] In sport, likewise, an appreciation of freedom and the chances for excellence that it creates demand a certain kind of knowledge.

The ability to engage higher intellectual powers was a criterion expected by some to separate art from sport, but as I argued in chapter 6, sport is just as capable as art of engaging those powers if approached with the appropriate background knowledge. Even to see—much less appreciate—a brilliant play in basketball, a spectator needs a good understanding of the game. Because many modern sports spectators played popular games such as football and basketball in their youth, such knowledge is not uncommon. But as the audience of spectators expands in response to mass marketing and especially to the rise of television, there emerges a need to "dumb things down." Morgan says that television "cannot but help to lower the level of understanding of fans"[19]; Lasch observes that "as spectators become less knowledgeable about the games they watch, they become sensation minded and bloodthirsty."[20] Both critics point as evidence to the increased tolerance of fighting in professional hockey as it expanded into warm-weather markets where spectators lacked experience playing the game. A similar correlation may be identified between the low rates of sports participation among ancient Romans (especially in contrast with the ancient Greeks) and the lurid violence of their spectacles.[21]

The worry here is not so much about violence per se—which appears in a variety of cultures and epochs, including our own—but, rather, that violence appeals to raw emotions rather than understanding. That was also the basis for Plato's criticism of poetry and drama. By disengaging reason, he thought, we might disengage our ability to distinguish between art and reality.[22]

All of this brings us back to the question of boundaries and framing: distinguishing sport from ordinary life and having the knowledge to appreciate the human excellences displayed within that frame. If the aesthetic appreciation of sport is to function as a mode of moral education, it must involve the affirmation of common values, such as freedom, and it must also identify their link with excellence. This requires knowledgeable spectators who can distinguish aesthetically between performances that affirm those values and those that do not. Indeed, the role of the spectator in ancient Greece was precisely to witness and affirm that the victory was awarded on merit to the person who earned it[23]; that is, to affirm that the game was fair, a concept that, in many languages, carries both aesthetic and ethical connotations. Discerning fairness requires understanding the game and, to use the language of social practice theory, an appreciation of its "internal goods," which is most available to current and former practitioners.[24] Reducing sport spectatorship to the dubious entertainment value associated with violence, sex, or greed not only removes it from the aesthetic sphere of engaging the higher intellect, but also fails to separate sport from ordinary life as a place where excellence is expected. The aesthetic framing of sport, in the end, is a moral responsibility, and spectators' failure to understand and expect excellence of athletes is ultimately a moral failure.

AUTOTELICITY VERSUS INSTRUMENTALISM

Purist spectators like to claim that their disinterest in who wins enables them to fully appreciate sport. Partisans, by contrast, are so emotionally invested in their team's success that the game functions merely as a means to the end of personal gratification or perhaps winning a bet. Viewing sport as a means to an end rather than an end in itself constitutes a failure to frame it properly as something autotelic. Autotelicity was another of sport's important affinities with art, and indeed the value and experience of beauty seem antithetical to instrumentalism. Aristotle makes clear that what is *kalon* (good or noble) is done for its own sake.[25]

As we observed in chapter 6, however, scholars such as David Best take the intrinsic instrumentality of sport—that is, the need to play for the end of victory—as the key thing that *distinguishes* art from sport; in art, the ends and means are indistinguishable.[26] If orientation toward victory is fundamental to sport, then ethical spectatorship would seem to demand partisanship—or at least some interest in the outcome. The key question for ethical spectatorship of sport seems to be about balance: when do instrumental interests in winning, profit, or self-promotion begin to cancel out the aesthetic value of sport?

Beauty matters in sport. Although deliberately playing to the crowd is discouraged and sometimes penalized, performing an action with grace and style is generally valued. "Winning ugly" is never as good as winning beautifully. Not all sports award style points, but style still counts. Cesar Torres illustrates this point with the South American debate over soccer-playing styles, where "art football" is often preferred to "results football."[27] Soccer's nickname, of course, is "the beautiful game," and Torres argues, based on the rules and various critical interpretations of quality play, that its beauty is associated with "forward looking or creative" offense and virtuosity rather than defense and conservative, negative play—even when the latter favors victory.[28] It is no coincidence that these qualities were associated with the aesthetic values of freedom and possibility, as well as the ethical value of excellence. A good sport spectator acknowledges such values and can appreciate them even while he roots for his favorite team. Being able to recognize beauty and virtuosity, even in the play of a rival, is characteristic of a fan who understands sport itself.

If interest in victory need not disrupt sport's aesthetic autotelicity, however, what about the quest for profits? The ethical-aesthetic values of freedom, possibility, creativity, and even genius are not reliably supported by the market. Lasch observes that the managerial apparatus of businesses works to reduce or even eliminate the risk and uncertainty at the center of sport's aesthetic value.

When sports can no longer be played with appropriate abandon, they lose the capacity to raise the spirits of the players and the spectators, to transport them into a higher realm of existence. Prudence, caution, and calculation, so prominent in everyday life but so inimical to the spirit of games, come to shape sports as they shape everything else.[29]

The vision of sport as a business whose purpose is to generate profit is instrumentalist in a way that partisanship is not because the final goods in question are, to use Alasdair MacIntyre's term, external to the game. To play a sport to win is still fundamentally to play a sport, and rooting for an athlete or team to win is congruent with that. But play a sport or root for a team solely for the purpose of earning money brings the potential of selling out a sport's internal values—as a boxer or sumo wrestler does when he throws a fight for gambling interests.

In fact, gambling illustrates an extreme form of spectator instrumentalism—one in which interest is detached not only from the quality of play but sometimes even from victory. Gambling spectators' interest is limited strictly to the outcome of their bets. Upon visiting a Keirin bicycle racetrack in Japan, I was overwhelmed by the spectators' lack of engagement with the sport they were betting on. Everyone was scribbling on paper and staring at screens displaying the odds—almost no one was watching the actual races. These spectators were not framing the sport as a place to affirm values such as freedom. Playful possibility was transformed into idle chance. Excellence had no more to do with the spectators' expectations than it would if they were feeding slot machines.

Gambling spectators' disengagement with sport may be a symptom of the market-driven self-centeredness that Morgan identifies as the central problem with modern sport. Following Lasch, he calls it "a thorough going narcissism . . . whose self-serving ways leave little if any room for others in sports or for the larger good of these practices themselves."[30] One might counter that a certain self-centeredness or individuality is part of sport's beauty: Dick Fosbury's unorthodox high-jump technique or Julius Erving's above-the-rim basketball play are examples that come to mind. Indeed, Víctor Durà-Vilà identifies such originality as having both aesthetic and ethical value: "[A] philosophy of football that promotes an aesthetically satisfying way of playing will, in turn, encourage the positive values of creativity, skill, technique, vision over discipline, improvisation over dullness, and individuality over uniformity."[31] But this is not the kind of individualism that Morgan has in mind. "The problem," he says, "is the kind of hyper-individualism to which markets give rise, wreaking havoc on sports because they turn them into crass exercises of self-promotion and self-assertion."[32]

Instrumental individualism does not care for the goods of the game or even so much for victory; it is, rather, an attitude of doing whatever it takes to increase one's market value. In many cases, this entails not so much athletic or moral excellence but, rather, a flamboyant, obnoxious, or "bad boy" personality that appeals even to fans who know little about the game. Spectators' tendency to frame sports as nothing more than businesses, adds Morgan, contributes to our "abysmally low moral expectations" of them.[33] Spectators' acceptance of instrumentalism in sports is as morally problematic as the instrumentalism itself.

THE MORAL DIMENSION

It may be tempting to believe that the so-called moral degradation of sport has nothing to do with spectatorship and, more generally, that morality has nothing to do with aesthetics. Could we seriously blame moviegoers for depictions of moral depravity they passively witness on the silver screen? Probably not. But we should beware of making what Marcia Eaton calls the "separatist mistake," namely, the assumption that aesthetics and morality are separate.[34] As Torres explains, "Separating the aesthetic from the moral threatens the unitary aspect of experience and valuation in art, sport, and beyond."[35] Certainly, sport seems a particularly clear example of the connection between morality and aesthetics. Mumford argues that moral considerations inevitably intrude on the aesthetic appreciation of sport: ethically bad features detracting from its aesthetic value and ethically good features adding to it.[36] He points as evidence to our awareness of Ben Johnson's steroid abuse detracting from the aesthetic enjoyment of his 100-meter sprint victory in the Seoul Olympics.

It is characteristic of sport that we want to know not just who won but also whether they *deserved* to win. The detection and punishment of cheaters is (at least presented as) a priority, and even immoral actions that have nothing to do with sport can tarnish an athlete's image and detract from his or her results. Swimmer Michael Phelps's eight gold medals at the Beijing Olympics were tarnished in many fans' eyes after he was photographed using illegal recreational drugs at a party. Revelations of golfer Tiger Woods's marital infidelities not only stained his image but also seemed to affect his game.[37]

Such moral scrutiny of athletes is evidence of a lingering conceptual connection between athletic and moral excellence. I say *lingering* because, as we saw in chapter 1, the link between athleticism and virtue goes at least as far back as the ancient Greek ideal of *kalokagathia*, a word that unites beauty and goodness and was explicitly associated with athletics and gymnasium life. The beauty of the Greek athletic form represented such moral virtues as self-control, such religious virtues as humility, and such civic virtues as liberty. In other words, it affirmed important community values. Just as an athlete's beautiful body produces beautiful actions, so moral virtue on Aristotle's account is the capacity to produce virtuous actions, which are not only beautiful in themselves but also are performed for the sake of beauty.[38]

Unfortunately, an ethical aesthetic such as *kalokagathia* is probably *not* the motivation for the media's moral scrutiny of athletes in the modern world. As Morgan observes, sports commentators in the print and media "have long given up the mantle of moral criticism in favor of what can best be described as shrill carping: part of what some call the *outrage industry*."[39] In other words, rather than upholding high moral expectations for sport across the board—especially on the playing field—the media capitalizes on moral scandals that draw in viewers and bring in revenue. It's not unlike the gambler who bets that a team will lose. She is not interested in a quality game or in the values that underpin it; she is interested only in her personal profits. If the media could make as much money playing up moral virtue as they do in sensationalizing vice, they might contribute to the cause of ethical aesthetics. Likewise, if commentators educated audiences on the nuances of the games—praising, for example, good team play rather than individualistic sensationalism—aesthetic appreciation of virtue in sports might be more widespread.

It all comes back to the spectators, however, and their ability to appreciate the moral aspects of the game, which is based on their understanding of sport as a vehicle for promoting virtue and foundational values. Athletics, like art, in Christopher Cordner's words, "enact or realize life-values."[40] This ability is the foundation of art's value as moral education. It is said that art "shows" rather than "tells" us the morally relevant features of the world, by presenting us with complicated particular situations. Literature and drama in particular are thought to be a useful part of ethical education because they exercise our capacities for making good moral judgments.[41]

Sport may be better than art in this respect, because the contest of virtues acted out on a playing field is neither scripted nor contrived toward a particular outcome. Mumford suggests that spectators view sport not as a struggle between individuals for victory or a prize but, rather, as a battle between virtues—both athletic virtues such as height or skill and moral virtues such as courage and self-control.[42] This approach would allow us to appreciate more than simple outcomes in our spectatorship of sport. It may even allow sport to function as a "moral laboratory" through which we can reflect on the moral incidents we see in a relatively harmless and inconsequential environment.[43]

Not only that, but moderate partisanship forces spectators to control their own competitive passions and challenges them to keep sport in perspective. Connecting ethics and aesthetics in sport may be key to its potential as a form of moral education for spectators.

"But I just want to *enjoy* watching sports," a fan may rejoin. The requirements that spectators frame sport properly, appreciate its autotelic elements, and adopt a morally critical eye might seem antithetical to the purely aesthetic enjoyment of sport. Pleasure, not morality, might seem to be a spectator's proper goal, and a morally critical attitude toward sport may seem as if it will rob all the pleasure from a spectator's experience.

This is not the case, however, as it is obvious that knowledge of the game enables a spectator to engage more closely with the action and ultimately to enjoy it more. Many sports, such as baseball, golf, curling, and cricket, have almost no spectator appeal to those unfamiliar with those games. Further, having played a particular game increases spectators' aesthetic appreciation because they understand and value the sport's internal goods.

Finally, a lingering link between virtue and athletics affects our aesthetic experience of sport. People are much more likely to overlook the moral unscrupulousness of a musician, artist, or author than they are that of an athlete. Aesthetics and ethics are not independent in sport, and if Plato is right about beauty's ontological connection with the good,[44] we should not try to separate aesthetics and morality at all.

What we should try to do as spectators is to treat sport more like art—that is, to have high moral expectations for it and to try to learn from its moral lessons. There is, after all, an authenticity to the drama of sport that art and literature as mere representations of reality cannot claim. Returning to the example of ancient Rome, spectacles including public executions, exotic animal hunts, reenacted sea battles, and gladiatorial death matches were staged by political leaders to manipulate the populace. They were designed to demonstrate the state's intolerance of criminals, the scope of its empire, the strength of its military, and the authority of its rule—those great gladiatorial fighters, after all, executed their opponents only upon the highest official's explicit command.

By adopting a morally critical approach, however, Seneca was able to appreciate and find inspiration in the virtue of gladiators and other "lowly" performers without being sucked into the propaganda of the promoters or pushed by partisan passion beyond the reasonable boundaries of sport. He did this, first, by framing the contests with an expectation of extraordinary virtue; second, by understanding the symbolic connection between the gladiator's predicament and the challenges of everyday life; and, third, by exercising the moral discernment needed to find beauty in displays of virtue and to express revulsion and disgust at gratuitous violence among unskilled fighters. In the end, the ability to appreciate sport ethically and aesthetically should result in spectators taking more pleasure in it and perhaps even in modern sport becoming more worthy of admiration. Any fan's most powerful weapon is the off button on his TV's remote control.

DISCUSSION QUESTIONS

1. Do you know any fans who are so partisan that it clouds their appreciation of sport? Does an impartial, purist approach enhance our experience as spectators or detract from it?
2. Ugly athlete behavior, such as fighting in hockey, is caused partly by lack of knowledge and low moral expectations among spectators. How might audiences be educated to better appreciate games such as hockey and to have higher moral expectations of athletes?
3. Do you think it is fair for the sporting press to subject athletes to moral scrutiny outside the game? Can you think of an example where such scrutiny crossed the line and became part of the sensationalist "outrage industry" rather than legitimate journalism?
4. Recently, a fan was ejected from a basketball game for loudly criticizing officials' calls from his seat behind the scorer's table. What does his ejection say about the sport's moral expectations of spectators? Do you think it was fair?

NOTES

1. Corpus Inscriptionum Latinarum 4.4418, quoted in Allison Futrell, ed., *The Roman Games* (Malden, MA: Blackwell, 2006), 240n55.
2. Lucius Annaeus Seneca, *Letters from a Stoic (Epistulae Morales ad Lucilium)*, trans. R. Campbell (London: Penguin, 1969), 7.2–3.
3. Seneca, *Letters*, 7.5.
4. This point is argued in detail in Heather L. Reid, "Seneca's Gladiators," in *Athletics and Philosophy in the Ancient World: Contests of Virtue* (London: Routledge, 2011), 90–98.
5. Seneca, "On Providence," 3.4, in Futrell, *Roman Games*, 95.
6. Seneca, "Letters," 70.20–27, in Futrell, *Roman Games*, 148.
7. Christopher Lasch, "The Degradation of Sport," *New York Review of Books* 24, no. 7 (1977), reprinted in *The Ethics of Sports: A Reader*, ed. Mike McNamee (London: Routledge, 2010): 369–81.
8. William Morgan, *Why Sports Morally Matter* (Abingdon, UK: Routledge, 2006), 26.
9. Mike McNamee, *Sports, Virtues and Vices: Morality Plays* (London: Routledge, 2008), introduction.

10. Graham McFee, *Sport, Rules and Values: Philosophical Investigations into the Nature of Sport* (London: Routledge, 2004), chap. 8.

11. Stephen Mumford, *Watching Sport: Aesthetics, Ethics, and Emotion* (Abingdon, UK: Routledge, 2011), chap. 10.

12. Nicholas Dixon, "The Ethics of Supporting Sports Teams," *Journal of Applied Philosophy* 18, no. 2 (2001): 149–58. Following critiques from John Russell, Stephen Mumford, and Randolph Feezell, Dixon moderated his defense of partisanship in Nicholas Dixon, "In Praise of Partisanship," *Journal of the Philosophy of Sport* 43, no. 2 (2016): 233–49.

13. Lasch, "Degradation of Sport," 369.

14. Teresa Lacerda and Stephen Mumford, "The Genius in Art and in Sport: A Contribution to the Investigation of Aesthetics of Sport," *Journal of the Philosophy of Sport* 37, no. 2 (2010): 182.

15. Bernard Suits, *The Grasshopper: Games, Life, and Utopia*, 2nd ed. (Peterborough, Ontario: Broadview, [1978] 2005), 55.

16. Lacerda and Mumford, "Genius in Art," 187.

17. Marcia Muelder Eaton claims that aesthetic appeal is generally tied up with cultural values and traditions. *Merit, Aesthetic and Ethical* (New York: Oxford University Press, 2001), 13.

18. Lasch, "Degradation of Sport," 380.

19. Morgan, *Why Sports*, 30.

20. Lasch, "Degradation of Sport," 381.

21. This is too simplistic an explanation, in my view; for a more detailed account, see Heather L. Reid, "Was the Roman Gladiator an Athlete?" *Journal of the Philosophy of Sport* 33, no. 1 (2006): 37–49; and "The Epicurean Spectator," *Sport, Ethics and Philosophy* 4, no. 2 (2010): 195–203, reprinted in *Athletics and Philosophy*, 81–89.

22. Plato, *Republic*, trans. G. M. A. Grube (Indianapolis: Hackett, 1992), 569b–608e.

23. Heather L. Reid, "Olympia: Running towards Truth," *Sport, Ethics and Philosophy* 4, no. 2 (2010): 136–45.

24. According to Cesar Torres, aesthetic values in sport are properly derived from its internal goods. Cesar Torres, "Furthering Interpretivism's Integrity: Bringing Together Ethics and Aesthetics," presidential address to the International Association for the Philosophy of Sport, Rochester, New York, September 2011, 21.

25. Aristotle, *Nicomachean Ethics*, 2nd ed., trans. Terence Irwin (Indianapolis: Hackett, 1999), 1120a24.

26. David Best, "The Aesthetic in Sport," in *Philosophic Inquiry in Sport*, 2nd ed., ed. W. Morgan and K. Meier (Champaign, IL: Human Kinetics, 1995), 379.

27. Torres, "Furthering Interpretivism's Integrity," 9–10.

28. Torres, "Furthering Interpretivism's Integrity," 20.

29. Lasch, "Degradation of Sport," 380.

30. Morgan, *Why Sports*, 25.

31. Víctor Durà-Vilà, "Why Playing Beautifully Is Morally Better," in *Soccer and Philosophy: Beautiful Thoughts on the Beautiful Game*, ed. T. Richards (Chicago: Open Court, 2010), 146.

32. Morgan, *Why Sports*, 31.

33. Morgan, *Why Sports*, 25.

34. Eaton, *Merit*, 57.

35. Torres, "Furthering Interpretivism's Integrity," 10.

36. Mumford, *Watching Sport*, 61.

37. The Phelps and Woods examples should be distinguished from the Maradona and Johnson examples in that the relevant ethical breaches were external to sport.

38. Aristotle, *Nicomachean Ethics*, 1120a. For more on the link between Aristotle's view of ethics and aesthetics applied to sport, see Heather L. Reid, "Athletic Virtue and Aesthetic Values in Aristotle's Ethics," *Journal of the Philosophy of Sport* 47, no. 1 (2020): 63–74; and "Aristotle on the Beauty of Fair Play," *Estetica: Studi e Ricerche* 11, no. 1 (2021): 201–10.

39. Morgan, *Why Sports*, 32.

40. Christopher Cordner, "Differences between Sport and Art," in Morgan and Meier, *Philosophic Inquiry in Sport*, 429, 434.

41. Jeffry Dean, "Aesthetics and Ethics: The State of the Art," *Aesthetics Online*, 2002, accessed November 1, 2011, http://aesthetics-online.org/.

42. Mumford, *Watching Sport*, 81–82.

43. McFee, *Sport, Rules*, 137.

44. Plato, *Two Comic Dialogues: Ion and Hippias Major*, trans. Paul Woodruff (Indianapolis: Hackett, 1983), 297bc.

PART IV

Sport and Education

A philosopher walks into a gymnasium, frustrated with his regular students' unwillingness to learn, and is impressed by the masterful ball-playing skills of a certain young athlete. The youth seems poor and disadvantaged but clearly has the capacity to learn complex skills, so the philosopher comes up with a scheme to educate him. He offers to support the youth's athletic training if he agrees to take lessons with the philosopher for a certain period every day. The athlete, eager for the financial support, takes up the philosopher's offer and begins his daily studies, earning a tidy sum for each lesson properly learned.

After a time, the philosopher notices that the athlete's motivation to study has shifted from the money to intellectual honor, and so he cleverly announces that he will no longer be able to pay the student for completing the lessons. The athlete offers to continue studying for free. But the philosopher laments that the lessons are causing him to forgo more practical work and says he needs to end them so that he can find a regular job. The student, having developed a great passion for his studies, balks at this idea and offers to turn around and pay the philosopher for the lessons.

This is not the plot of a modern made-for-TV movie; it is the ancient origin of the ongoing saga that mixes sport and academics in education for youth. The gymnasium was in Samos, Greece; the year was around 535 BCE; the lessons were in geometry; and the philosopher's name was Pythagoras.[1] The student's name apparently was Pythagoras as well, and it is said that he migrated with his soon-to-be-famous teacher to the Greek colony of Kroton in southern Italy where they again went to the gymnasium to recruit students, and eventually founded what may be the first academic-athletic institution in history.

Even before Pythagoras's arrival, Kroton was famous for its athletes. In the Olympic Games of 576 BCE, its citizens took the top seven places in the prestigious *stadion* race, inspiring the saying that "the last of the Krotoniates was the first among all other Greeks."[2] Perhaps he was attracted to the city, as he had been with the student, for its athletic virtues. In any case, Pythagoras's school may be counted among the causes of Kroton's continued athletic dominance. He was specifically linked with the city's most famous athlete, the wrestler Milo, who is said to have married his daughter.[3] Graduates of the Pythagorean school excelled in nonathletic endeavors as well, especially medicine, mathematics, music, and politics.

When Plato traveled to Italy shortly after Socrates's death, he was greatly influenced by the Pythagoreans, and it is likely that he got the idea to found his school in the Academy gymnasium after visiting one of their schools there.[4] Indeed, Plato is the philosopher we most associate with the educational use of sport. His *Republic* declares gymnastics to be a tool for educating the soul,[5] and the *Laws* prescribes gymnastic education and games for both genders and all ages.[6] I believe that Plato saw philosophy itself as a reflection of athletic struggle.[7] He uses athletic metaphors constantly and depicts Socrates as competing with and defeating rival sophistic educators. Plato may even have inspired his less athletic student, Aristotle, to see ethical virtues reflected in the beauty of the pentathlete's body.[8] The final goal of ancient Greek athletic-academic education was always *aretē* (virtue, excellence), a disposition expected to lead to success in any activity or profession.

Somewhere along the line, however, this holistic idea of education fragmented. Academics, though taking its name from Plato's gymnasium, became precisely those educational activities that take place *outside* the gymnasium. Sport and other performance activities that took place within the schools came to be known as "physical education"—a name that reflects the troublesome mind-body split discussed in chapter 7. The idea of sport as education for virtue, which we discussed in chapter 10, became more of a slogan than an intentional pedagogy. Especially at the youth level, coaches, parents, and schools propound the theory that sports builds character, but empirical studies of moral development in athletes suggest that it fails in practice.

The grand American experiment of intercollegiate athletics seems to promote sport more for its market value than its intrinsic educational value. At a cultural level, the function of sports heroes as role models for youth carries on from ancient times. Here, as in schools and universities, however, the educational value of sport is neither intrinsic nor automatic. Pythagoras made his athlete into a scholar; Plato made his athletes into civic leaders. Perhaps the most important practical question for philosophers of sport is what can be done to make sport a more effective educational tool.

1. The story is recounted in Iamblichus, *The Pythagorean Life*, trans. Thomas Taylor (London: Watkins, 1818), chap. 5.

2. Strabo, *The Geography of Strabo*, ed. H. L. Jones (Cambridge, MA: Harvard University Press, 1924), 6.1.12.

3. Stephen G. Miller calculates that 28 percent of the Olympic victors in the gymnic (i.e., nonequestrian) events between 588 and 488 BCE were from Kroton. Milo won six Olympic wrestling titles between 540 and 520 BCE; Pythagoras arrived in Kroton around 530 BCE. *Ancient Greek Athletics* (New Haven, CT: Yale University Press, 2004), 217.

4. The story of Plato's visits to Italy is recounted in *Letters III* and *VII.*

5. Plato, *Republic*, trans. G. M. A. Grube (Indianapolis: Hackett, 1992), 410bc.

6. Plato, *Laws*, trans. Trevor Saunders (London: Penguin, 1970), 805cd, 833cd.

7. Heather L. Reid, "Wrestling with Socrates," *Sport, Ethics and Philosophy* 4, no. 2 (2010): 157–69.

8. Heather L. Reid, "Aristotle's Pentathlete," *Sport, Ethics and Philosophy* 4, no. 2 (2010): 183–94.

Chapter 12

Sport in Schools

Like most Americans and many around the world, I was introduced to sport at school. At the elementary level in 1970s California, we had a regular recess period where we went outside to play freely. In junior high school we had a physical education (PE) class, separated by sex, for which we changed into gym clothes, lined up on hash marks, did a series of calisthenics including jumping jacks and burpees, then played games such as basketball or softball. We also had extracurricular sports teams. I played on almost all of them and received embroidered patches for my participation, which I proudly sewed onto a special jacket.

In high school, physical education was not required for those who participated in sports. I not only played "school sports," such as soccer, but I was also in the unofficial "club sport" of cycling. My free public school had the equipment and facilities for all of these sports, except cycling, but I had a part-time job that enabled me to buy a secondhand bike. I had no particular goal in all of this. For women at that time, athletic scholarships were rare, and professional sports almost nonexistent. Youth sports were simply a fun, healthy thing to do; they didn't seem to me to have a particular purpose or goal.

If I ask myself today what I *learned* from those experiences, however, I have to conclude that they had a huge impact on my education and development. And I don't just mean my physical development; I mean my character development: my personal and social virtues and values. Indeed, the most memorable lesson from my school sports experience had nothing to do with sport.

It was a sunny day in gym class when our teacher announced that girls who wished to would now be allowed to join the boys' PE class. I could tell from her body language and tone of voice that she was not recommending the change. Nevertheless, two other girls and I stood up on our hash marks and crossed the field to join the boys. We were eager for the challenge, to test ourselves athletically and to participate in the rigorous games of soccer and basketball that we had watched the boys play. They had a system where you could wear different colored shorts (gold was the highest) based on your performance in various tests, such as running, agility, sit-ups, and pull-ups. At that age, there wasn't a huge difference in performance between us and the boys, except for upper-body strength. I could do almost everything at the gold or silver level, but I couldn't do the requisite number of pull-ups. It didn't really matter, though; I enjoyed the challenge. I even played on the boys' soccer team in high school because we didn't have a girls' team, and the law protected my right to play.

My experience in school sports taught me to deal with personal limitations, to value equality of opportunity, and to enjoy the process of achievement. I think it had at least as big an impact as my study of history or math. What is more, I don't think my experience is unusual. Sports and physical education remain in schools because people like me remember them as beneficial—even if we struggle to explain how and why.

Some value sport and PE in schools as a way to promote bodily health; others see it as a way to counterbalance or provide a release from the serious business of academics. Still others see it as serious business—as preparation for success in a competitive society, or maybe in professional sports. Criticism of scholastic sport comes from every angle: some think it doesn't warrant its share of the budget or risk of injury; others think it is too important to be left up to the schools. In reality, physical education is a highly developed academic field, which includes the study of philosophy. What philosophy of sport can contribute to the effectiveness of sport in the schools centers mainly on its function as moral education.

PHYSICAL EDUCATION VERSUS CHARACTER EDUCATION

Although the idea that "sport builds character" is a popular argument for its existence in schools, the very term "physical education" suggests that its object is bodily health. As we saw in chapter 7, the most profound contrast in the use of sport as education between Ancient Greece and the modern West is a different way of looking at the relationship between mind and body. Although most ancient Greeks were dualists—that is, they believed in the separation of mind and body—and they prized the soul (*psychē*) over the body, they understood human movement to originate in the *psychē*. Hence, athletic training was understood as a kind of spiritual training, and the beauty it produced in well-trained bodies was understood as a reflection of virtue or good character (*aretē*). As we saw in chapter 10, the Greek idea was not much different from many Eastern philosophical perspectives, which avoid clear distinctions between mind and body and understand the movement involved in martial arts training specifically as a method of spiritual development.

The Greek system, however, was expressly competitive and rule governed. In Plato's *Republic*, it is stipulated that children's games be strictly governed by rules, so that they may grow up to be law-abiding adults,[1] and athletic competition is used in education to select students with the qualities, such as resoluteness and endurance, necessary for higher-level studies.[2] Plato's assumption, like Pythagoras before him, is that students who show character in the pursuit of athletic excellence have the potential to excel in academics and civic leadership.

Nowadays, by contrast, the prevailing assumption is that athletic excellence is a sign of low academic potential. Many people believe that an inverse relationship exists between athleticism and intelligence, a phenomenon popularly known as the "dumb-jock myth" (also discussed in chapter 7). Any correlation between low academic and high athletic performance among students is most likely explained by social factors, such as opportunities for advancement and reward.

The metaphysical roots of this belief, however, begin with Cartesian dualism, which not only posits the separation of mind and body but also asserts thinking to be our essential function. There is a problem with metaphysical physicalism—the belief that nonphysical minds and souls don't exist and that human beings can be understood in entirely material terms. This view is inspired and endorsed by empirical science, which tends to limit its studies to phenomena that can be observed. The problem here is not so much philosophical as cultural, in that this culture tends to view athletes in terms of their bodies and to leave the thinking part of their training up to others—especially scientists. A narrowly physiological approach to training is typical here, and it predictably infects even school sports. The focus is on physical parameters such as height and weight, number of sit-ups or pull-ups performed, or the amount of weight lifted in a bench press; moral development is disregarded.

Rather than reinforcing the mind-body split, sport in schools should act intentionally to heal it by aiming sports and "physical education" toward character development. Even Eastern philosophy does not regard mind-body unity as metaphysical fact. Rather, as we saw in chapter 7, it regards such unity as an achievement—a form of wisdom that is, itself, cultivated and expressed through bodily movement. Some educators recognize an overemphasis on the intellectual in modern schools, but most have come to accept uncritically education as a purely intellectual endeavor. It is undeniable, however, that human beings have both minds and bodies and that bodily movement involves the mind,

For instance, Paul Weiss thought athletic training could "correct disequilibrium between mind and body" by teaching us to carry out our ideas in action. Jim Parry notes that the experience of moral concepts such as trust are mediated through the body in sport, thereby transcending mere theoretical understanding. When we learn trust through participation in team sports, he says, "responsibility begins to emerge from the physical awareness of the other and the needs and concerns of the other in the context of risk."[4] Pierre de Coubertin believed that moral character was primarily formed in the body. In sport, he said, "the muscles are made to do the work of a moral educator."[5] Moral virtue is explicitly an embodied concept; it is performed and not merely understood.[6] Indeed, a plethora of subjects, including music and other performing arts, are taught using a holistic approach that combines physical practice with intellectual training. Sport's tendency to separate itself from the intellectual cannot help but hamper its educational potential.

SPORT LOGIC VERSUS CHARACTER LOGIC

The solution to the problem of an overly narrow approach to sport in education is not as simple as dropping the term "physical education" in favor of something like "kinesiology," which rightly emphasizes movement (*kinēsis* in Greek), rather than bodies. Nor should PE classes be replaced with competitive sports. Physical education programs are grounded in serious research, and PE teachers are usually better trained as educators than coaches are. The right move is to direct all types of movement activities toward character development—and to assess them accordingly. Youth sport functions best as moral education when moral education is its intentional goal. As things stand, the evidence for sport as a form of moral education is almost entirely anecdotal.

Perhaps the most famous testimonial comes from the existentialist philosopher Albert Camus, who once remarked that the context in which he really learned about ethics was that of sport.[7] Some evidence from social science, meanwhile, suggests the contrary: that sport does more harm than good to moral character.[8] Such findings are attributed by some to an overemphasis on competition, which they view as intrinsically immoral. Others point to the presence of money and the high-stakes game of college recruiting, which can affect children as early as junior high school. Even from a philosophical point of view, the question is complex. For one thing, there are rival ethical theories, some of which might endorse traits conducive to competitive success, whereas others might condemn them. As David Carr points out, "One man's cooperation may be another's herd instinct."[9] Further, the moral value of things such as courage and self-discipline seem to depend on the nature and purpose of the activity. A courageous, disciplined thief, for example, is not a public good. In short, there are places where sport-logic and character-logic diverge.

The oldest and most obvious of these is what the Greeks called the *technē-aretē* (skill-virtue) distinction. Plato argued that the moral value of a skill depends on the ends it serves, and learning to discern proper ends is distinct from learning skills. For example, the value of a skill such as lying depends on whether you are using it to steal someone's savings or to protect someone from a would-be torturer. In sport, technical skills combined with competitive virtues such as courage and self-discipline lead to victory and often reward. But the skills of most sports, such as shooting a ball into a goal using only one's feet, have little value independent of the sport.[10]

Youths devote most of their time in sport to learning and practicing such skills, which are essential to competitive success. The *technē-aretē* distinction means that we cannot take athletic success as evidence of moral virtue, however, because the win may depend more on technical skill than good character. As MacIntyre points out, moral virtues may hinder success in some practices. In basketball, for example, victory sometimes depends partially upon the strategic breaking of rules (i.e., fouling to stop the clock). In many sports, further, the morally questionable practice of deception is intentionally cultivated and rewarded. An athlete who refuses to engage in such practices because she values transparency or rule adherence for moral reasons might find herself at a competitive disadvantage. As sport-philosopher John Russell points out, the inherently partisan nature of competitive sport (i.e., its inherent focus on winning) can hinder its educational potential, especially among the youth.[11]

Sport's emphasis on skills and success need not be eliminated to promote its potential as moral education, however. For one thing, the development of skills requires virtues in itself, and the desire for success motivates the exercise of those virtues. Youth, especially, require the experience of competitive failure to motivate the cultivation of performance virtues. The refrain is common across various sports: "It was not until I lost that I realized I needed to train seriously." Indeed, Russell identifies performance virtues such as "resilience, persistence, patience, hardiness and grit" as a category of dispositions to be cultivated in sport, especially at the youth level.[12]

Ilundáin-Agurruza's conception of "skillful striving" takes the link between skill development and virtue cultivation even farther—interpreting the pursuit of excellence as a lifestyle expressed in performance.[13] The important thing is to put the competitive spirit evoked by sport into the service of character development, to prioritize the character logic of virtue over the simple sport logic of victory. It is instructive to note that the suggested use of athletic contests to reveal potentially gifted students and philosophers in Plato's *Republic* does not specify that the *winners* of the contests were those selected for advancement. It suggests rather that athletes' performances in the contest reveal important facts about their character—including the lack of interest in fame and fortune as opposed to virtue.[14] Sport logic and character logic align when the emphasis is virtue as opposed to victory.

RISK AND DANGER

Competition is important to sport's educational potential because it introduces the kind of moderate risk that is necessary to cultivate virtue. Fundamental is the risk of failure, essential to any activity that selects winners and losers. Success and self-esteem are rightly promoted in education, but so is the possibility of failure. Unlike underperformance and failure in academic subjects, falling short of expectations within the field of sport is experienced in a way that encourages a sense of personal responsibility. For one thing, the failure is publicly visible, as in losing a race or dropping a pass—sometimes it is witnessed by spectators or posted on the internet for anyone to see. Characteristically, such failures are followed by encouragement from coaches and teammates, who have failed publicly themselves.

Anyone who doubts the connection between the risk of failure and motivation to virtuously develop skills should spend fifteen minutes at a skateboard park. It is legitimate to ask, however, especially in the context of children and youth sports, how much risk is needed to develop moral character. The vision of skillful achievement witnessed at the skateboard park will be accompanied by visions of scraped knees and elbows, perhaps even broken bones or head trauma. When it seems as though the risk of failure can be had in other performance activities such as music or drama, we should seriously ask whether the added risks of sport can be defended in terms of character education.

How much risk is needed to build character? The question is not a new one. In Plato's *Republic*, students are exposed to "labors, pains, and competitions" to test their souls "more thoroughly than gold is tested by fire" (413cd), and exposing children to warfare is said to be "worth the danger" as long as reasonable precautions are taken (467cd). In the more pragmatic *Laws*, danger is to be provided by war games that employ missiles hazardous enough to "inspire fear" and thereby "to reveal the brave man and coward" (830e).[15] It is further specified that deaths occurring as a result of these games should be considered involuntary because "even if a few people die, others who are just as good will be produced to replace them, whereas if fear dies (so to speak), [we'll] not be able to find in all these activities a yardstick to separate the good performers from the bad—and that would be a bigger disaster for the state than the others" (831a).

Such ideas by themselves may inspire fear in modern parents and teachers; clearly, Plato's social and historical context is very different from our own. The basic point, however, stands. To cultivate a virtue such as courage, which depends on dealing intelligently with an emotion such as fear, students need to engage in activities dangerous enough to authentically conjure that emotion.

Of course, *lack* of fear in dangerous situations is just as big a problem as excessive fear. For Aristotle, virtues occupy a "golden mean," between excesses such as cowardice and rashness.[16] Courage is an appropriate, rational response to pain and fear—it is not the absence of pain and fear. What is more, it demands an accurate recognition of risk. The irrational fear caused by roller coasters and video games cannot cultivate courage the way a rational fear of injury can. Having survived a roller-coaster ride or ten thousand crashes on a virtual motorbike is not nearly as educative as having survived the pain of exhaustion or a sprained ankle. As Irena Martínková and Jim Parry point out, children and youth need to be taught risk recognition, risk assessment, risk management, and risk avoidance.[17]

These skills do not appear magically upon exposing students to danger, but they can be cultivated through adventurous and outdoor pursuits that promote self-reliance, confidence, teamwork, and task completion—without compromising safety. As Aristotle observed, not only does the courageous person recognize danger, but she stands firm against it because she also recognizes that a good or noble end is to be served by doing so.[18] Likewise, the noble cause of character education justifies and limits the danger inherent in sport for youth.

This "commonsense view" that risky sports should be tolerated in children's education just enough to develop basic virtues is challenged by John Russell, who argues that the choices of children (and adults acting on their behalf) to engage in dangerous activities "should frequently be respected, even if the risks of such activities are greater than necessary to promote the developmental goods sought by the common sense view—and thus represent unnecessary threats to the goods that the common sense view aims at securing."[19] Russell's argument hinges on the value of "self-affirmation" attained in dangerous sports by "creating special contexts in which one could test oneself at the limits of one's being."[20]

The pursuit of self-affirmation aims beyond basic virtues to the higher goal of human flourishing by "pressing individual boundaries and thus defining new self-understandings and conceptions of the self."[21] Because the goods of such experiences are best available to children, Russell concludes, "preventing participation in dangerous sports until adult competence is established . . . denies access to important, time-limited opportunities for self-affirmation."[22] Of course, such activities should be limited to those at which the child has a reasonable chance of succeeding and avoiding serious injury, but Russell says that even caring parents may push a child to take certain risks, such as skiing down a more difficult slope, in cases where they judge the child's skills to be adequate. In short, taking risks is an important part of moral education for children, and sport provides a relatively safe and controlled environment in which to experience this.

MORAL EDUCATION IS EXPERIENTIAL EDUCATION

To say that sport and physical education in schools should be directed toward moral education is not to say that these activities alone will suffice. The point is, rather, that virtue and morality are learned much like athletic skills are: through experience and practice. Aristotle recognized this and pointed out that *ethos*, the word for practice, training, or habituation in Greek, is deeply connected with *ēthos*, the word for moral character from which we derive the term ethics.[23] The memorization and even the understanding of moral principles such as the Golden Rule have little effect on moral behavior in comparison with a student's personal experience. Moral behavior is less a product of remembering to "treat others as you want to be treated" and more the result of being treated ethically by others—especially institutions and authority figures such as teachers and coaches.

Perhaps one of biggest strengths of Russell's argument for allowing children to engage in dangerous sport is the idea of respecting their choices. A child who feels respected is more likely to respect others. Likewise, students who are respected by their parents, coaches, and teachers as persons with multiple concerns and commitments are more likely to respect others in the same way. Too often children are challenged to choose between family, sport, and study—even within the schools.

By combining such commitments and not forcing a choice between them, schools best serve their students, especially in terms of moral education. Sport has a great *advantage* over classroom-based methods of learning ethics because, in sport, moral concepts and dilemmas are experienced firsthand. Those aforementioned studies that point to sport's failure as moral education missed the point insofar as they tested knowledge of principles or levels of moral understanding, rather than moral behavior.[24] Sport in schools allows children the chance to work with moral concepts such as fairness in practice, to test the concepts themselves, to confront others who fail to act on them, and even to reckon with one's own failure to act on them—all in a relatively contained and controlled environment.

This is why Graham McFee calls sport a *moral laboratory*, arguing that even abstract moral rules, such as "thou shall not kill," must be made sense of in concrete contexts.[25] In sport, we learn not only rules, but more important, how to be governed by rules, and, most important, how to behave in accordance with the moral principles, such as fairness, that underpin those rules.[26] The ideas of fair play and the level playing field are not sports specific; rather, they are real moral concepts that are best learned through experience; sport, understood as a moral laboratory, offers the opportunity to do that.

The problem is that this opportunity tends either to be taken for granted as something automatic, or ignored entirely. PE teachers sometimes receive training in character education, but they are rarely considered to be moral educators. Coaches in youth sports aren't even considered to be teachers—yet they are probably the most effective moral educators (for better or worse) that students have. As Carr points out, coaches' function as moral educators derives from their particular relationship with young people, and their effectiveness at this function depends almost entirely on their individual willingness to see their jobs "in the context of wider concerns about how to live and what to value in life."[27]

Parry proposes that sports and physical education activities in schools be seen intentionally as "practices which act as a context for the development of human excellences and virtues and the cultivation of those qualities of character which dispose one to act virtuously."[28] Such a proposal surely has implications for the training and treatment of coaches and physical educators, as well as the actual practice of sports in the schools. As McFee explains, "In teaching the rules of a game (for example, cricket), a teacher sensitive to [moral] principles might inculcate those principles too. . . . Thus, the model is of abstract principles learned from (and in) concrete instances in sport, then applied to concrete moral situations."[29]

Sports and physical education in schools should strive to improve not just bodily health and athletic skills but also moral character in children. Its goal should be not just winning games but also playing them fairly—and discussing whether certain actions are fair rather than passively leaving those decisions to others. Indeed, philosophical reflection on and discussion of one's sporting experience could be an important part of this process.

Students in my philosophy of sport course begin by writing about their most meaningful experience in sports, and the vast majority of these essays discuss school sports. Many discuss losing and injuries—especially the rehabilitation of injuries. Being disabused of feelings of false invincibility combined with the discovery that hope and persistence really can bring them to a better place is a big life lesson for many young athletes. Recognition of sport's potential as moral education in the schools is only the first step toward realizing it.

DISCUSSION QUESTIONS

1. What did you learn from your experience in sports as a child? Does it make sense to distinguish mental from physical benefits in these activities?
2. Have you ever learned a (positive or negative) moral lesson through sport? What were the factors that led you to reflect on the experience? Did it change your later behavior?
3. Have you ever learned from the experience of risk or injury in sport? Can similar lessons or virtues be cultivated through e-sports?
4. If coaches were considered, above all, moral educators, how might the current system of education and evaluation change?

NOTES

1. Plato, *Republic*, 424e.
2. For example, Plato, *Republic*, 502d–3e. For a full account, see Heather L. Reid, "Sport and Moral Education in Plato's *Republic*," *Journal of the Philosophy of Sport* 34, no. 2 (2007): 166–69.
3. Paul Weiss, *Sport: A Philosophic Inquiry* (Carbondale: Southern Illinois University Press, 1969), 41.
4. Jim Parry, "Sport, Ethos and Education," in *The Ethics of Sports: A Reader*, ed. Mike McNamee (London: Routledge, 2010), 319.
5. Pierre de Coubertin, "The Olympic Games of 1896," in *The Olympic Idea: Pierre de Coubertin—Discourses and Essays*, ed. Carl-Diem Institut (Stuttgart, Germany: Olympisher Sportverlag, 1966), 10–14.
6. Chung-Ying Cheng, "On the Metaphysical Significance of *ti* (Body-Embodiment) in Chinese Philosophy: *benti* (Origin-Substance) and *ti-yong* (Substance and Function)," *Journal of Chinese Philosophy* 29, no. 2 (2002): 147.
7. Albert Camus, "The Wager of Our Generation," in *Resistance, Rebellion, and Death*, trans. Justin O'Brien (New York: Vintage, 1960), 242.
8. In reviewing more than forty years of social scientific research on the subject, Jennifer Beller and Sharon Stoll say that "a constant was found: Sport does not appear to develop character no matter how defined." Sharon K. Stoll and Jennifer M. Beller, "Do Sports Build Character?" in *Sports in School: The Future of an Institution*, ed. John Gerdy (New York: Columbia University Press, 2000), 20.
9. David Carr, "What Moral Educational Significance Has Physical Education?" in McNamee, *Ethics of Sports*, 308.
10. This is especially true of dangerous sports, according to John S. Russell, "The Value of Dangerous Sport," *Journal of the Philosophy of Sport* 32, no. 1 (2005): 1–19.
11. John S. Russell, "Robert L. Simon on Sport, Values, and Education," *Journal of the Philosophy of Sport* 43, no. 1 (2016): 54.

12. Russell, "Simon on Sport," 53. For Russell's general account of performance virtues, see "Resilience," *Journal of the Philosophy of Sport* 42, no. 2 (2015): 159–83.

13. Jesús Ilundáin-Agurruza, *Holism and the Cultivation of Excellence in Sports and Performance: Skillful Striving* (London: Taylor and Francis, 2016), 1.

14. Plato, *Republic*, 502d–503a.

15. Plato, *Laws*, trans. Trevor J. Saunders (London: Penguin, 1970).

16. Aristotle, *Nicomachean Ethics*, 2nd ed., trans. Terence Irwin (Indianapolis: Hackett, 1999), 1106a.

17. Irena Martínková and Jim Parry, "Safe Danger—On the Experience of Challenge, Adventure and Risk in Education," *Sport, Ethics and Philosophy* 11, no. 1 (2017): 75–91, DOI: 10.1080/17511321.2017.1292308.

18. Aristotle, *Nicomachean Ethics*, 1115b.

19. J. S. Russell, "Children and Dangerous Sport and Recreation," *Journal of the Philosophy of Sport* 34, no. 2 (2007): 176–193.

20. Russell, "Children and Dangerous Sport," 181.

21. Russell, "Children and Dangerous Sport," 181.

22. Russell, "Children and Dangerous Sport," 187.

23. Aristotle, *Nicomachean Ethics*, 1103a.

24. Carwyn Jones, "Character, Virtue, and Physical Education," *European Physical Education Review* 11, no. 2 (2005): 140–42; Robert Simon, "Does Athletics Undermine Academics? Examining Some Issues," *Journal of Intercollegiate Sport* 1, no. 1 (2008): 48.

25. Graham McFee, *Sport, Rules and Values: Philosophical Investigations into the Nature of Sport* (London: Routledge, 2004): 140–42.

26. McFee, *Sport, Rules*, 145.

27. Carr, "What Moral?" 313.

28. Parry, "Sport, Ethos and Education," 324.

29. McFee, *Sport, Rules*, 140.

Chapter 13

Collegiate Sports

In 2021 the Supreme Court of the United States decided a case brought by a group of college athletes against the National Collegiate Athletics Association (NCAA), the governing body for collegiate sport. The students argued that the NCAA's limit on the educational benefits they could receive was unfair. The NCAA countered that allowing schools to offer such things as computers, academic awards, paid internships, and scholarships for postgraduate study would compromise the distinctively amateur nature of college sports. This would blur the line between college and professional sports, disenchanting its fans.

The court sided with the students, effectively denying the NCAA's claim that college sport was exceptional and holding them to the same antitrust regulations that govern businesses. Commentators interpreted the decision in terms of the larger debate about whether college athletes, some of whom generate vast amounts of revenue, should be paid. But the facts of this particular case highlight important philosophical questions that are too often overlooked: what are the educational benefits of college sport supposed to be, and what is wrong with professionalism?[1]

Though the physical education and youth sport programs discussed in chapter 12 are fairly common worldwide, the phenomenon of college sports is concentrated in the United States. Nevertheless, it constitutes perhaps the grandest modern experiment in combining sport and education—one that involves athletes from all over the world. As in the ancient Greek gymnasium, modern student-athletes are expected to harmonize their academic and athletic pursuits of excellence. And, as Pythagoras tempted an athlete to study with financial rewards in ancient times,[2] modern colleges and universities offer scholarships that can cover the full cost of attendance, including room and board—something fellow students may pay upwards of $100,000 to receive.

The institutions use sport to attract students, to engage alumni, and to raise money. At some schools, specifically those with high-profile football and basketball programs, athletic departments generate huge revenues. Much of that money goes to finance other sports, some goes to support academic programs, and in some cases multiple millions go to pay a single coach's salary. The athletes themselves are not paid. Amid ongoing scandals involving recruiting, academic fraud, and criminal misbehavior in college sport, the question of athlete pay is the hottest topic of debate. Discussion of college sport's social and educational benefits, by contrast, is rare—even among the faculty of these very same institutions.

Perhaps this is because many believe that the educational benefits of sport are obvious and don't need defending; they uncritically adopt the "sports builds character" slogan discussed in the last chapter. Even those who doubt the educational benefit of sport itself generally recognize that athletic scholarships provide opportunities to earn a college degree for many students who otherwise would be unable to attend.

Almost no one argues that the intensity and pressure of competing at a very high (dare I say professional) level is good for students, however. Defenders of the educational value of intercollegiate sport, including the philosophers Robert Simon and Drew Hyland, generally limit their praise to smaller, non-scholarship programs and prescribe a variety of reforms such as restrictions on season length and travel time to keep athletics from dominating students' lives. Hyland, who played college basketball at Princeton, encourages institutions to treat athletics as a part of the educational program, rather than a business. Indeed, the professional nature of college sport is generally seen as an impediment to its educational value—not least by the NCAA itself. Despite charging more than a $1 billion for the rights to the March Madness basketball tournament,[3] the NCAA presents itself as a nonprofit defender of the amateur character of college sport.

Those who defend the professional aspects of college sport generally regard it as separate from the educational mission of the institution. For them, intercollegiate athletics is a multibillion-dollar industry that legitimately benefits institutions of higher education and, by rights, it should also benefit the athletes whose "labor" generates that revenue. Most agree that the scholarship is an important form of compensation, but many worry that its value is compromised by the taxing demands of elite-level sport. Training, team meetings, travel, and games take up so much time that many student-athletes struggle to sustain the level of study needed to earn a degree in the time that their scholarships allot. They find themselves forced to choose between excellence in athletics *or* academics—and because their academic funding usually depends on athletic performance, it's no surprise that they feel pressure to privilege the former. Student-athletes are sometimes dissuaded from pursuing difficult majors, and even if they were to complete, for example, a premedical degree, the cost to attend medical school would not be covered by their athletic scholarship.

The *NCAA v. Alston* decision may change that, but it won't resolve the contest between athletics and academics in young people's lives. Neither will future court decisions about endorsements and salaries. The philosophical debate about just compensation for college athletics is not about money; it is about ends, excellence, ethics, and—lest we forget—education.

PROFESSIONAL VERSUS AMATEUR

In the Alston case the NCAA argued that its limits on athlete compensation were needed to preserve the "amateur" nature of college sports, which widens consumer choice by providing a product distinct from professional sports.[4] They did not even attempt to deny the commercial nature of college sport, even as they argued that college athletes must not be professionals. The Supreme Court noted that the NCAA's conception of amateurism has changed steadily over the years and quoted the lower court's finding that the NCAA "nowhere define[s] the nature of the amateurism they claim consumers insist upon."[5]

On the face of it, and in most dictionary definitions, the term "amateur" refers to anyone who engages in an activity without being paid. It can also refer to someone who is incompetent or inept. That second meaning hardly applies to college athletes, who perform close to, often at, and sometimes above a professional level. What keeps them from being professionals according to the dictionary definition is that sport is not their "main paid occupation." Despite the fact that many student-athletes receive valuable compensation and devote most of their time and effort to their sport, the NCAA wants to preserve the idea that they are students first. We can expect this idea of amateurism to be defended in college sport, even as the restrictions on athlete compensation are lifted.

Amateurism in sport is not an idea confined to American colleges. As we saw in chapters 2 and 8, it has a prominent role in the history of the Olympic Games—especially their revival around the turn of the twentieth century, a period commensurate with the emergence of college sports in the United States. The idea of amateurism in those days was bound up with distinctions of social class, specifically a working versus a leisure class, and based on the ancient Greek belief that doing something for its own sake was always more noble than doing it for any external reward. We have seen this idea of "autotelicity" emerge in sport's metaphysical links with play (chapter 3) and art (chapter 6). It is also characteristic of *kalokagathia* (beautiful goodness), an elevated moral status associated with both aristocracy and athletics.[6]

The so-called Crown Games, in which the prize was nothing more than a wreath of olive or laurel, were accordingly *more* prestigious than "money games" offering valuable prizes. The ancient Greek athletes upon whom the modern ideal of amateurism was based were certainly not amateur in the sense of being unpaid, nor did most of them have some separate occupation during their athletic careers. The point was that they engaged in sport as an end in itself rather than a means to some external end and thereby expressed their closeness to the gods—who have no needs and therefore do everything autotelically. Amateurism in this ancient context was not about payment or skill level but, rather, about attitudes and intentions. The word itself derives from the Latin word for love and expresses the idea of doing sport for "the love of the game."

The real question is why doing something for love, for its own sake, and as an end in itself excludes the possibility of payment. The fact than an athlete receives a valuable prize or even a salary does not prove that he or she is motivated by those things to play the sport. In fact, current usage of the term "professional" better describes the attitude expected of an amateur.

Whereas we generally use the term "job" to describe something we do strictly "for the money," we reserve the term "profession" for activities placed at the center of our identities and our lives. Professions generally demand specialized education and long apprenticeships, and when people enter into a profession such as law, or medicine, or academia, they become part of a group of highly trained specialists who seek to preserve the quality of their activity by holding each other to high standards. Professionals are paid (often handsomely) for their work, but in contrast with mere "jobs," that payment is not the only—or even the central—end of their work. Indeed, lawyers working pro bono or doctors volunteering to treat children in a war zone do not cease to be professionals when they work without pay. If anything, such actions are considered *more* professional than their compensated work and in some industries are referred to as "professional courtesies" or "professional obligations."

It is no secret that the goal of most college and university students is to become a professional rather than simply to do jobs. They go to college to receive the education necessary, not only the knowledge specific to their profession, but also the generalized skills and dispositions appropriate for someone who aims to achieve excellence in their field. In fact, the term "liberal arts"—often used derisively to describe subjects in the arts and humanities lacking any specific link to a profession—probably derives from the ideal of a "liberal professional" who can freely offer his or her expert services to clients independent of any corporation or institution. The term is still used in Europe to classify lawyers, accountants, psychologists, architects, and other professionals who work for themselves. It is astonishing, given that learning to be professional is central to the enterprise of higher education, that the NCAA insists on amateurism in athletics. Embedded in the idea that college athletes must remain amateur because they are students first seems to be a pernicious assumption that one cannot be a student of sport.

THE EPISTEMOLOGY OF EXCELLENCE

It would be a mistake to defend college sports as a training program for professional athletes, even though many student-athletes attend college with precisely that goal in mind. Even in the powerhouse programs, the chances of success are just too low. If any other preprofessional program at the university had similarly low placement rate, it would be scrapped. Sport on college campuses needs to defend its educational value for the vast majority of student-athletes who, to paraphrase an NCAA advertisement, plan to "go pro" in something other than sport.

Comparing sport with academic programs in performing arts such as music, dance, and drama, former NCAA president Myles Brand argued that the development of "physical skills" justifies the presence of athletics in universities.[7] No draconian rules prevent students of these subjects from earning money for their performances. Brand says the opinion that performing arts are appropriate subjects for earning college credit though sports are not probably has its origins in social elitism. Philosophers of sport may add to that the metaphysical belief that mind and body are distinct and should be educated separately. Sports are deemed unworthy of college credit precisely because they are too physical.

The joke that "he went to college but majored in football" only works because sport is seen as separate, even a distraction from intellectual education. Majors in the performing arts are accepted in part because they incorporate the academic study of theory, history, and other traditional subjects. Perhaps football could be a legitimate major if it, too, included courses in sport philosophy, physiology, and psychology. But the educational value of performance itself needs to be acknowledged and understood. Sports and performing arts at the collegiate level demand more than "physical skill." Like learning to speak a foreign language, they demand regular practice, persistence in the face of failure, and interactive public performance.[8] Indeed, almost every profession, from law to medicine to accounting demands not only specialized knowledge and highly developed skills but the ability to transform those things into a service for the client. In other words, professionalism is performance—excellent performance—and activities such as sport, dance, drama, and music teach us how to achieve it.

Characteristically, performance demands the *integration* of mind and body. It defies the epistemological distinction between knowing how and knowing that. It is, in contrast with many educational activities, essentially holistic. Sport philosopher Jesús Ilundáin-Agurruza has investigated the cultivation of excellence in performance, a process he calls "skillful striving." He notes that in athletics, martial and performing arts, "latent skills flourish and weaknesses can be made assets by nurturing intellectual, physical, emotional, and social abilities through disciplined movement, purposeful reflection, and emotional control."[9] The process involves moving and acting as what he calls "holistic, integrative bodyminds," and it brings together more than the body and the mind. The pursuit of performative excellence connects skills with virtues and ethics with aesthetics and because doing your best is moral, skill is beautiful, virtues improve skills, and skill is community based.[10] Of course, doing the best you can at sport, to the extent that your skills become beautiful, takes the kind of commitment we associate with professionalism.

Another thing we associate with professionalism is community—specifically professional guilds and organizations such as the American Bar Association, which work to preserve the quality and integrity of the practice. Ilundáin-Agurruza emphasizes the communal nature of skillful striving, maintaining that "laudable character is built on discipline, responsibility, and a social framework that provides personal paradigms and standards of excellence."[11]

Similar claims about "practice communities" are made by Alasdair MacIntyre, whose social practice theory provides the modern framework for linking sport with virtue cultivation—as we learned in chapters 5 and 10. What we have in elite sports communities, including college teams, are what might be termed a "performance community," in which the pursuit of excellence in a common practice is pursued by a group of like-minded practitioners. It doesn't matter whether the sport is team or individual—the bonding between members of a track team is just as great as players on a basketball team. Performance communities can even include competitors from other schools, and athletes from different sports. The common denominator, the basis for mutual understanding, is the commitment to excellence. And because excellence can be achieved at a relatively young age, sport is a fruitful arena in which to develop performance virtues—to develop the pursuit of excellence as a way of life.

ETHICS AND EXPLOITATION

This performance-based argument for the educational value of elite sport may justify a young adult's athletic commitments, but does it justify athletic professionalism at universities? Elsewhere in the world, it is not uncommon for university students also to be professional athletes. Italy's national soccer team has several, including the star of its 2021 UEFA cup team, Matteo Pessina, who is pursuing a degree in economics at a prestigious university. "I have always thought that [studying] helps in playing soccer," he says.[12] Of course, no law prevents professional athletes in America from also enrolling in college. Few do because the demands of pro sports are hard to reconcile with serious study during the brief period of youth traditionally devoted to both. In other words, the dilemma for young elite athletes who want to study is pretty much the same whether they play professionally or in college. In order to defend its place on campus, college sport must articulate not only its athlete compensation practices but also benefits of keeping elite sport and elite education under a single roof, so to speak.

The ethical worries revolve around the concept of exploitation—that is, one party benefitting disproportionately or unfairly from their relationship with another. The economic benefits of college sport for the NCAA and its member institutions are obvious and easily quantified. Many less tangible benefits include school spirit, reputation, and engagement with alumni. Although some argue that colleges and universities themselves are economically exploited by professional sports franchises who use them to train their players,[13] most claim that student-athletes are the ones exploited by the business model of college sport. In a concurring opinion on the Alston case, Justice Kavanaugh characterizes the relationship between institutions and athletes as one between business and labor.

"The bottom line," he says, "is that the NCAA and its member colleges are suppressing the pay of student athletes who collectively generate billions of dollars in revenues for colleges."[14] He goes on to compare student-athletes to skilled workers such as cooks and camera crews, as well as college-educated professionals such as nurses, lawyers, and journalists. Is this how we should think about student-athletes—as labor whose wages have been suppressed by price-fixing agreements in the NCAA?

The NCAA no longer argues that college sport is not a business. As its former president Myles Brand points out, however, it is not the same kind of business as professional sport. "Neither higher education, of which college sports is only a small part, nor intercollegiate athletics is truly capitalistic," Brand explains. "They do not generate revenue to make a profit; they generate revenue to fulfill a purpose, to meet the mission of higher education."[15]

In other words, the revenue generated by the business of college sports needs to serve the goals of the colleges themselves: education. And because the "workers" in this business of college sport are also students, it makes sense for colleges and universities to compensate them in terms of education—as they do. Remember that the Alston case struck down limits on education-related benefits for student-athletes. Other cases have struck down restrictions on what student-athletes can earn from outside sources, for example, by selling the rights to their name, image, and likeness. The question is not *whether* college athletes should be compensated but, rather, how they should be compensated, by whom, and to what extent.[16]

The danger, as Drew Hyland points out, is that thinking about college sport as nothing more than a business has "allowed us, no, led us, to forget what we recognized once to our credit, that athletics is a powerful educational force."[17] Colleges and universities could begin by treating athletics as an educational program, articulating its benefits, offering college credit for it, and assessing it accordingly. In particular, they might explore its potential as a form of moral education. Robert Simon has shown how athletic values can harmonize and reinforce academic values: "Participation in competitive athletics can require intellectual honesty and a concern for truth, including accuracy about one's own values and talents, in ways parallel to academic inquiry."[18]

Hyland echoes Simon's reference to self-knowledge but adds to the list of educational benefits from sport the experience of "deep, passionate commitment" and sensitivity to social issues such as racism.[19] Combining Ilundáin-Agurruza's account of skillful striving and MacIntyre's idea of social practice communities, we have also identified elite athletics as a training ground for the virtues of performance useful for achieving excellence in myriad professions that college graduates pursue.

If student-athletes better understood the educational value of their sports experience, they might not feel exploited by their colleges. Student-athletes are sometimes criticized for seeking to be paid, but most students are financially motivated to attend college. A college education is understood and even promoted as a means to the end of increased lifetime earnings. We can hardly blame young people in this environment for failing to see the intrinsic benefits of education. Further, when colleges use sport as a means to financial rather than educational ends, they perpetuate the pernicious idea that money is what really counts in higher education. Universities teach ethics most effectively, it turns out, through their ethical treatment (or mistreatment) of students.[20] When they treat student-athletes as means to financial ends, they are teaching them to treat others as means to ends, too—no matter how often Immanuel Kant's moral injunction against this behavior is repeated in the classroom. Likewise, when universities exploit athletes under the guise of amateurism, they are teaching everyone that such exploitation is morally permissible.[21]

Sport has great potential to serve the educational mission of colleges and universities, but its abuse is equally effective at undermining them. No question, college sport generates revenue, and athletes should be fairly compensated. But the question is about what constitutes appropriate compensation, and it should not be assumed that monetary value is the only valid measure of it. The ideal of amateurism focuses on means and ends, privileging things done for their intrinsic value as ends in themselves. Engaging in the pursuit of excellence through elite-level sport, further, has the potential to generate performance virtues important for professionals.

In terms of attitude, amateurism and professionalism turn out to be more similar than different. Fairness isn't always a question of finance. And we shouldn't assume that money is what student-athletes really want. "It's never been and never will be about money," blue-chip basketball prospect Jalen Duren said about the college recruiting process. "I just want to get better, and I love the game too much to cheat it that way."[22] No more "amateur" approach to college sport can be imagined—whether or not he gets paid.

DISCUSSION QUESTIONS

1. In terms of educational benefit, do you think sports at small colleges that do not offer athletic scholarships are better than in big-time college programs? Why or why not? *Not better, opportunities, etc*

2. Would it be OK to "major in football" if college sports programs were more like music, theater, and dance majors that combine performance with theoretical and technical study? Should sports participation receive college credit at all? *arts vs. football would have same struggles*

3. Describe the educational benefits of being part of a college sports team (whether the sport is team or individual). How might they apply to a future profession?

4. What is the crucial difference between a college athlete and a professional athlete? Is it a matter of internal attitude or external compensation?

— age diff. and authority between coach
— ex. Lebron

salary
- job
pay based on
• performance

NOTES

1. For a fuller discussion of this issue, see Heather L. Reid, "Amateurism, Professionalism and the Value of College Sports," *Journal of Intercollegiate Sport* 14, no. 3 (2021): 67–79, https://doi.org/10.17161/jis.v14i3.15676, from which some of the material in this chapter is taken.

2. The story was recounted at the start of chapter 12.

3. *National Collegiate Athletic Assn. v. Alston*, 594 U.S., Justice Gorsuch, opinion of the court (2021), 7.

4. *NCAA v. Alston*, opinion, 10.

5. *NCAA v. Alston*, opinion, 10–11.

6. *Kalokagathia* was discussed in chaps. 1, 6, and 11. Aristotle links it explicitly with autotelicity in *Eudemian Ethics*, 1248b34-35. For an analysis, see Heather L.

Reid, "Athletic Virtue and Aesthetic Values in Aristotle's Ethics," *Journal of the Philosophy of Sport* 47, no. 1 (2020): 63–74.

7. Myles Brand, "The Role and Value of Intercollegiate Athletics in Universities," *Journal of the Philosophy of Sport* 33, no. 1 (2006): 20.

8. Foreign language is, in fact, declining in popularity as a graduation requirement and more generally as a subject on American campuses; the need for constant practice for success might be one reason for this.

9. Jesús Ilundáin-Agurruza, *Holism and the Cultivation of Excellence in Sports and Performance: Skillful Striving* (London: Routledge, 2016), 3.

10. Jesús Ilundáin-Agurruza, "A Different Way to Play: Holistic Sporting Experiences," in *Philosophy: Sports*, ed. R. Scott Kretchmar (New York: MacMillan, 2017), 331.

11. Ilundáin-Agurruza, *Holism*, 1.

12. Enrico Currò, "Matteo Pessina, lo studente goleador che voleva smettere," *La Reppublica*, June 29, 2021. My translation.

13. J. Angelo Corlett, "Economic Exploitation in Intercollegiate Athletics," *Sport, Ethics and Philosophy* 7, no. 3 (2013): 295–312.

14. *National Collegiate Athletic Assn. v. Alston*, 594 U.S., Justice Kavanaugh, concurring, (2021), 4.

15. Myles Brand, "Pay for Play Is Fine—But Not in College Sports," *Huffington Post*, August 20, 2008.

16. Phillip Zema, "Should Student-Athletes Be Paid?" *Sport, Ethics and Philosophy* 13, no. 2 (2019): 198–212, argues that colleges and universities are not obligated to compensate athletes beyond tuition, room, and board, but student-athletes should be free to receive external compensation.

17. Drew A. Hyland, "*Paidia* and *Paideia*: The Educational Power of Athletics," *Journal of Intercollegiate Sport* 1, no. 1 (2008): 70.

18. Robert Simon, *Fair Play: The Ethics of Sport*, 2nd ed. (Boulder, CO: Westview, 2004), 167.

19. Hyland, "*Paidia* and *Paideia*," 67.

20. Derek Bok, "Can Higher Education Foster Higher Morals?" in *Social and Personal Ethics*, ed. W. H. Shaw, 501 (Belmont, CA: Wadsworth, 1996).

21. The question of whether collegiate athletes are financially exploited is currently making its way through the courts; for an analysis of the question, see Taylor Branch, "The Shame of College Sports," *Atlantic Monthly*, October 2011, http://www.theatlantic.com/.

22. Jalen Duren quoted in Billy Witz, "The Dynamics of College Sports Are Changing," *International New York Times*, June 28, 2021.

PART V

Sport and Social Epistemology

From an essentialist perspective, race, class, sex, gender, and disability are irrelevant to sport. Even when characteristics associated with these social categories impact sports performance (i.e., when wealth is an advantage or being female is a disadvantage), they are not integral to a sport's constitutive rules. From a conventionalist perspective, by contrast, sport is embedded in social and historical contexts that affect how it is practiced. As women and people with disabilities become more integrated into society, classifications and adaptations are made for them in sport to preserve its internal goods and promote the cultivation of relevant virtues.

Both essentialists and conventionalists attribute social value to athletic excellence and compare its distribution of honor favorably with that of society. They often point to instances where sport has challenged and even subverted social hierarchies—the most famous example being Jesse Owens's performance at the 1936 Berlin Olympic Games, which challenged Nazi assumptions about racial superiority.[1] These competing perspectives on sport's relationship with society indicate its epistemological power. Jesse Owens's performance did not change sport or society; it changed the *beliefs* people have about social groups.

Epistemology is the branch of philosophy that deals with knowledge and belief. One of the first things it teaches is to distinguish between our personal beliefs—that is, the way things seem to us—and shared ideas such as knowledge or truth. Beliefs make progress toward truth and knowledge through processes of justification that demand social engagement.

In chapter 1, I characterized sport itself as a knowledge-seeking process because it starts with a question, accepts the fallibility of existing beliefs, and sets up a rational and transparent process for justifying answers—namely the contest. Because social ills such as racism, sexism, and ableism are based on beliefs about superiority and value, sport's relationship with them can be interpreted partly in epistemological terms. Sport, in other words, has the power to change people's minds about the value of people from various social groups, but it can also be used to reinforce conventional beliefs. The questions from the perspective of social epistemology[2] are about how beliefs are formed and justified within and among groups.

Racism, sexism, and ableism are usually based on presumptions about superiority, whereas assignments of value in sport—at least ideally—result from excellence demonstrated in fair and open contests. If a contest is not fair and open, however, the beliefs it generates may do more social harm than good. It must also be recognized that people of different backgrounds have different perspectives, sometimes called competing narratives, that need to be incorporated into the belief justification process. The best ideas resonate within a diversity of narratives, not just the perspective of the most powerful.

The issue of sport's relationship with society is complicated by the fact that it often assigns social value to people based on athletic performance. As we have seen, many consider the virtues that contribute to athletic performance to have value beyond sport, and they take the pursuit of excellence in sport to be a great way to cultivate such qualities. But socially irrelevant factors such as height, oxygen uptake, and hormone levels also affect athletic performance. Though sport may attempt to control or compensate for such factors in order to emphasize the socially valuable ones, at best it can do so imperfectly. In practice, sport tends to reward those already privileged in society—arguably because they created it to validate their strengths and continue to rig it in their own favor. Perhaps we should dissociate social value from athletic excellence altogether—as many spectators have done.

Much of mainstream society sees sport as a source of entertainment and revenue, nothing more. Within the sporting community, however, it seems inevitable that value will be attributed to athletic excellence, and hierarchies will be established according to it. Given that athletes (as well as coaches and officials) from different races, classes, sexes, and abilities are members of that community, sport has a special responsibility to make sure that its internal goods are fairly available to all of them. Only then can it hope to promote the external good of more justified social beliefs.

NOTES

1. Conventionalist William J. Morgan discusses the case of Algerian runner Hassiba Boulmerka in "Multinational Sport and Literary Practices and Their Communities: The Moral Salience of Cultural Narratives," in *Ethics and Sport*, ed. Mike McNamee and Jim Parry (London: E & FN Spon, 1998), 184–204.

2. Social epistemology deals with the pursuit of knowledge and truth between and within social groups. For an overview, see Alvin Goldman and Cailin O'Connor, "Social Epistemology," in *The Stanford Encyclopedia of Philosophy*, Winter 2021, ed. Edward N. Zalta, https://plato.stanford.edu/archives/win2021/entries/epistemology -social/.

Chapter 14

Sport, Race, and Class

The name of the backwater industrial college was Carlisle, but the inscription on the commemorative football reads "1911: Indians 18, Harvard 15."

Carlisle was a school for Native Americans, and its upset of Harvard couldn't help but have overtones about race and social class. The victory was due largely to Carlisle's star player—a mixed-race athlete from humble origins by the name of Jim Thorpe, who would go on to dominate the next year's Olympic Games. In Stockholm, Thorpe triumphed in both the pentathlon and decathlon, winning eight of the fifteen individual events. The Swedish king, Gustav V, famously declared Thorpe the greatest athlete in the world, and the champion was welcomed home to the United States with a ticker-tape parade.

But apparently not everyone was pleased by his victories. Late in 1913 some newspapers revealed that Thorpe—like many college athletes at the time—had been paid to play baseball over a couple of summers, which violated Amateur Athletic Union (AAU) rules. Although the official protest period had long since expired, AAU officials retroactively withdrew Thorpe's amateur status, and his Olympic medals and titles were stripped.

There is little doubt that racism and social elitism rather than sincere concern for the purity of sport motivated at least part of the condemnation. One of Thorpe's Olympic teammates, Avery Brundage, became a zealous promoter of the Olympic amateurism movement, which was eventually exposed as an effort to exclude the lower classes—and, not coincidentally, certain racial groups—from athletic competition. This kind of social bias was not new to sport. Ancient athletics had been used from the start by royalty and aristocrats to validate their supposed genetic superiority, and participation in the ancient Olympic Games was reportedly limited to free Greek males. The religiously motivated desire to determine the worthiest victor pushed back against such restrictions, however, and as diversity increased in ancient Greece, especially under the Roman Empire, the pool of athletes became similarly diverse.[1] Sport has involved social discrimination from its very origin, but at the same time it has resisted racism and classism.

201

Sociologists, who tend to see sport as a reflection of society, have had much more to say about race and class than philosophers, who tend to focus on the internal nature and value of sport independent of—or at least distinguishable from—external social realities. Broad internalists and social practice theorists alike have argued that sport's commitment to equality of opportunity contributes educationally and practically to equality in society, but critics contend that its exaltation of winners undermines that cause. Within sport, racial and economic discrimination appears to have faded over time. Racial segregation in American sports died off in the 1950s, and South Africa's apartheid resulted in its exclusion from the Olympic Games starting in 1964. John Carlos and Tommie Smith used the 1968 Olympic medal stand to protest racial injustice, and in 1983 Jim Thorpe's Olympic medals and titles were reinstated.

Today, people of every race and economic background compete at the highest levels of sport. Excluding athletes from competition based on the color of their skin or the depth of their pockets is all but unthinkable. It is not clear whether the change derives from the essence of sport, as internalists contend, or a change of belief among the members of sporting communities, as social practice theorists would have it. It is not even clear whether all the change has been for the better.

Racial and economic discrimination remain persistent problems in society, and it is worth asking whether sport contributes to those problems, and how, in any case, it can contribute to a solution. The resistance to racist thinking supposedly embedded in the nature or practice of sport has clearly failed to eradicate it in society or even within the sports community. Collective beliefs about race and class continue to affect sport at every level, from youth and school sports to professional and international competitions. Overtly racist incidents in professional soccer led FIFA to form a Task Force Against Racism and Discrimination in 2013. After the killing of George Floyd, a black high school and college athlete, by a white police officer in 2020, athletes around the world began "taking a knee" before sporting contests to draw attention to racial inequality—often to a chorus of boos from the crowd. Race and class may be irrelevant to the basic epistemology of sport, but they cannot be ignored by philosophers or practitioners of sport.

RACISM AND THE ORIGIN OF SPORT

Some say that race was not even a concept in the ancient world,[2] but if we define racism as a belief in superiority based on ancestry, we find it at the very origin of sport. As we saw in chapter 1, mythological heroes such as Heracles, whose *athla* (labors) make him the primordial athlete, were placed near the top of the social hierarchy, just below the gods and above all other mortals. Heroes' athleticism demonstrated their extraordinary *aretē*, which was initially believed to result not from talent or training but divine ancestry. Accordingly, the ancient Greek aristocracy (a term that means "rule of the best") understood their social status as a matter of entitlement based on genetic proximity to gods and heroes. Because athleticism was taken to be a sign of this proximity, it had been used to demonstrate and defend elevated social positions as far back as the third millennium BCE. The real or imagined athletic feats of ancient kings such as Gilgamesh, Shulgi, and the pharaohs of Egypt were publicly celebrated to impress and reassure subjects.[3] The very fact that these subjects needed assurance, however, shows that belief in genetic entitlement to social status did not rise to the epistemic level of knowledge. There apparently were doubts about whether aristocrats really were descended from gods, really did perform such extraordinary athletic feats, and really were, therefore, worthy to lead.

The emergence of competitive sport and the Olympic Games around the eighth century BCE only fed such doubts. The perceived link between athleticism and aristocracy persisted, but a religiously motivated interest in relatively fair and open competition also challenged it. The logic of religious sacrifice demanded that worshippers offer their best to a god who is not easily fooled. Excluding anyone from the competition that selects a symbolic sacrifice risks leaving the worthiest candidate on the sidelines. The common religious interest in an open and accurate selection of victors pushed elites to compete with their social inferiors, and the results (predictably) eroded belief in the aristocrats' natural superiority. Sport not only called into question the legitimacy of existing social hierarchies in ancient Greece, but people began using it to defend or improve their social status. The idea that *aretē* might be a matter of training rather than birth began to take hold.

Aristocrats tried to preserve the illusion of their natural superiority by importing their social privileges into athletic competition. They hired coaches and devoted their copious leisure time to training, but the most effective method was the introduction of equestrian events in which success depended primarily upon wealth, and the victory crowns went to the owners. The Olympic victory of a chariot that the Spartan princess Kyniska sponsored has been touted as a triumph of feminism in a male-only milieu, but it was interpreted by some ancient authors as evidence that Olympic victory depended on affluence rather than *aretē*.[4] Spending money on the Games was thought praiseworthy, but since wealth itself was not considered evidence of virtue or aristocracy, a "bought" victory held little social value.[5] In fact, an aristocrat's closeness to the gods—who have no practical needs—was expected to be accompanied by disinterest in money. This is why "money games" that offered valuable prizes were much *less* prestigious than "crown" games such as the Olympics where victors earned nothing more than a wreath of sacred vegetation.[6]

The crowns won by lower-class athletes in non-equestrian events, meanwhile, changed collective beliefs about the link between aristocracy and social value so much that it led, by some accounts, to the invention of democracy.[7] Sport in the ancient world was thus transformed from a means of reinforcing "racist" ideas about natural aristocracy to a method for promoting democracy by its truth-seeking logic. Because the religious context created a common community interest in finding the worthiest victor, serious efforts were made to construct a fair contest and to open up access.[8]

This phenomenon offered the opportunity to demonstrate their virtue even to those who were not believed to have it; indeed, the glory associated with Olympic victory motivated some cities to recruit and support lower-class athletes.[9] By Roman times, the upper classes had essentially withdrawn from competitive sport, not least to avoid doubts about the justice of their social entitlement.[10] But Roman sports continued to function as a means of proving social worth—especially for gladiators who could earn freedom from slavery by demonstrating their virtue in the arena.[11] Not only were gladiators considered *infamia*—a status below even the lowest social class—they were often racially or ethnically distinct from the Roman elite. So, the proto-historical link between athleticism, virtue, and aristocracy seems to have benefited athletes more than "aristocrats." Can we say the same today?

RACE AND THE EPISTEMOLOGY OF SPORT

To say that some Roman gladiators were "racially distinct" is not to affirm that "race," understood as a biological category, was an issue in the ancient world.[12] In fact, the belief that humanity could be divided into discrete racial groups based on physical traits didn't emerge until the Middle Ages and wasn't connected with ideas about deterministic biology until modern times.[13]

Today, race is generally viewed by scholars as a socially constructed identity rather than a biological category.[14] As such, it fails as a valid classificatory concept—inside of sport or out. The "racism" we observed in ancient athletics was based not on physical characteristics but, rather, on ethnicity and socioeconomic status. Something similar may be said of issues surrounding race in sport today—that they turn more on questions of culture and social justice than real or perceived physical differences. In this sense, race is external to sport—a social perception irrelevant to the logic and values of athletic contest. On the other hand, the very concept of discrimination—of designating some people as more worthy than others based on their athletic performance—is baked into its epistemology.

The logic of the sporting contest is simple: equality of opportunity and reward according to merit—where merit is determined by demonstrated athletic excellence without regard for social categories such as race and class. Even if some sports-relevant biological trait, such as the predominance of fast-twitch muscle fibers, could be correlated with skin color or other characteristics associated with race, it remains irrelevant because sport picks winners based on what individual athletes or teams do in the contest, not who they are considered to be in society. Exclusion of athletes for social reasons undermines the epistemological validity of the contest result.

As we saw in chapter 9, the value of winning and the merit of the victor depend logically on as many people as possible having an equal opportunity to compete. Denying anyone the opportunity, for whatever reason—including the presumption that they will lose—introduces the possibility of error. Obviously, it is impractical to open athletic contests to everyone in the world, but the epistemology of sport impels practitioners at least to examine the reasons for exclusion and to be on guard against social narratives and constructions of power corrupting the contest system.

Despite its incompatibility with sport logic and values, philosophers recognize that discrimination based on race and class seems to persist in practice. We can observe, for example, that athletes of color and from disadvantaged backgrounds are "overrepresented" (that is, they participate at a higher percentage than they account for in the general population) in sports such as football and basketball, where facilities, coaching, and equipment are provided free by communities or public schools.

Likewise, socially disadvantaged groups are underrepresented in sports requiring expensive equipment and private facilities such as golf and figure skating. Such disparities are not necessarily caused by the actions of racist individuals or even discriminatory policies; rather, they reveal the permeability of the barrier that separates sport and society. Social advantages linked with race and especially wealth carry over into sport—often in the form of expensive equipment or facilities—and undermine sport's epistemological commitment to inclusion and equality of opportunity.

It may also be true that sport's epistemological commitment to equal opportunity is the problem. Pointing out that equality in sport serves the strong by legitimizing their victories, rather than the weak as it does in political systems, Rasmus Bysted Møller and Verner Møller argue that the logic and values of sport assist rather than resist the forces of racism. "No evidence suggests that judging people according to their ability will help overcome racism," they write. "On the contrary, ideas about differences in abilities among different races and ethnicities has been part of racist thinking and the success of black athletes has done nothing to remedy this to the benefit of the black community."[15]

The link between virtue and victory that broad internalists and social practice theorists tout for its ability to liberate sports practitioners from false beliefs about racial superiority may foster the kind of hierarchical thinking that perpetuates racism inside and outside of sport. "Equating moral worth with excellence," argue Møller and Møller, "implies a fascist contempt for the genetically and socially weak and unsuccessful."[16] Is sport's epistemological indifference to race and class undermined by its commitment to competition? Does the educational effect of practicing sport resist the forces of racism, or does it enhance them?

SPORT AND THE EPISTEMOLOGY OF RACISM

Philosophers who argue that sport promotes racial equality usually point as evidence to people of color who have achieved athletic success. For people of African descent especially, but for marginalized groups worldwide, sport in the modern world appears to provide a relatively unobstructed opportunity for achieving and demonstrating individual excellence—even as lingering prejudice and stereotypes impede more conventional paths to success. In the United States, where blacks still lag behind whites in such things as graduation rates and income, their athletic success is outstanding. Despite accounting for only about 12 percent of the general population, African American players constitute more than a third of college and well over half of professional football and basketball players.[17]

Ironically, segregation in American sports was originally justified by the belief that blacks were physically inferior and *not good enough* to play with whites.[18] Now the prevailing perception is that whites are athletically disadvantaged compared with blacks. Professional basketball player Bill Russell's career spanned the transformation. He was the only black player on his team as a rookie in 1957, and then as the coach of the Seattle Supersonics he had only two white players on the team. "In basketball, it took only twenty years to go from the outhouse to the in-crowd," Russell says.[19] By some accounts, black athletic success even paved the way for the election of President Barack Obama by opening up American minds to what blacks were capable of doing.[20]

Sport's epistemological impact on racism includes dispelling unjustified beliefs about racial superiority and rewarding practitioners for judging themselves and their competitors on the evidence of performance rather than prevailing social perceptions or stereotypes. Individuals often learn to overcome racist beliefs—about superiority as well as inferiority—by participating in integrated sports. Observing that athletes are among the only students to socialize and eat together in mixed-race groups on campus, Drew Hyland questioned the basketball team at his college about the issue of voluntary segregation among other students on campus. The players explained that their commitment to the team enabled them to "put the question of race in its place." Hyland suggested to the team that they try to share their insight with the rest of the campus, and he reports that they "have come to understand that they should not, ethically cannot, regard their successful experience of integrated community as simply that they are 'the lucky few,' that instead the gift they had been granted conferred on them a *responsibility* to distribute that gift as best they could more widely."[21] This step is important because the beliefs and attitudes fostered by participation in racially integrated sport are not always shared by spectators and society at large. In the minds of many, black athletic success has led not to belief in racial equality but, rather, to a competing narrative of inborn athletic superiority accompanied by intellectual inferiority.[22]

In effect, this racialized version of the "dumb-jock" myth discussed in chapter 7 preserves the social privilege of those who fail athletically by negating the ancient connection between victory and virtue. It attributes athletic success to natural talent or brute strength rather than recognized virtues such as hard work and intelligence, thereby demoting the perceived social value of sport from the level of art, religion, and education to that of mere entertainment. This narrative prevails even in college sports where the free or discounted education offered to standout athletes was intended to provide a means for poor or socially marginalized youth to move up the social ladder.

Instead, the value of college degrees that athletes earn in every racial category is diminished—not just because the commitment that sport demands can undermine the quality of their academic experience, but more commonly because the achievement of excellence in sport is perceived as being at best disconnected and at worst incompatible with the achievement of excellence in society. Once victory is no longer taken to be a sign of virtue, the value of those who achieve it is reduced accordingly to the entertainment or revenue they can produce—a conclusion that devalues all but the most spectacular sports.

Conventional wisdom, it seems, easily trumps evidence when it comes to sport's ability to promote racial equality. The revised stereotype of black athletic superiority not only deprives individuals of credit for the virtues (athletic or otherwise) that lead to their success, but it creates the unwarranted expectation that African American youth will be successful in sport and should focus on it rather than academic or even artistic pursuits.

At the same time, it erects a psychological barrier for athletes from other racial groups who may avoid sports such as sprinting or basketball because they believe themselves to be naturally inferior. Such beliefs are challenged by counter-examples such as Christophe Lemaitre, the first white sprinter to break the symbolic ten-second barrier in the 100 meters. Lemaitre thinks psychological barriers may be holding back other white sprinters and hopes that his performances can "make the statement that it has nothing to do with the color of your skin and is just a question of work and desire and ambition."[23] But the very existence of counter-examples like Lemaitre depends, in the first place, on equal opportunities and fair competition—not just in sport but also society. It is for this reason that athletes, as Hyland said of his basketball players, have a special responsibility to promote the lessons of equality beyond the realm of sport.

TAKING A KNEE: SPORT AND SOCIAL ACTIVISM

The fact that sport's competitive logic permits exceptional individuals such as Serena Williams and Tiger Woods to become celebrities does not mean that it can eradicate racism—not within sport and certainly not in society at large. Becoming rich and famous as the result of athletic excellence is not the same as being accepted into the upper echelons of society, and even if it were, the celebration of a few athletic elites does little to address the suffering of racial minorities who do not happen to have what it takes to achieve athletic stardom—which is to say, almost all of them. The current situation in the United States, which is certainly not unique, handily illustrates the point that Møller and Møller make about equality in sport serving only the elite while leaving the larger social problem of racial inequality behind. The ability of sport to have a positive impact on racism in society depends largely on its heroes leveraging their fame to benefit the many who are left behind. Even athletes who, for one reason or another, have not suffered personally from the ravages of social discrimination bear a responsibility to promote equality of opportunity and diversity in society because they have benefited from them in sport.

With this general idea in mind, the American football player Colin Kaepernick knelt rather than stood as the national anthem was played before a preseason game in 2016. He was not protesting a personal grievance, or even racism in sport, but, rather, the injustices that African Americans and other people of color suffer, in particular police brutality. "To me, this is bigger than football and it would be selfish on my part to look the other way," said Kaepernick.[24] The fact that sport had provided him—and other people of color—with wealth and notoriety did not absolve him of the responsibility to fight for social justice.

It is telling that the backlash against Kaepernick's protests criticized him in various ways for failing to appreciate his own position of privilege. He was accused of being ungrateful for his salary and of ruining the entertainment value of sport by dragging politics onto the field. He was said to be unpatriotic and disrespectful of the flag and the armed forces. After President Trump echoed this sentiment, adding that NFL owners should fire such protestors, however, athletes all the way down to high school began taking a knee in solidarity.[25] After seeing the video of George Floyd's murder in 2020, even Kaepernick's opponents understood why he had protested. The act of taking a knee spread to European football, as mentioned above, but Kaepernick himself was excluded from the NFL. A television commercial where he says "Believe in something. Even if it means sacrificing everything," won an Emmy Award.[26] Belief, as we have seen, is the real battlefield when it comes to fighting racism through sport.

Colin Kaepernick was not the first and will not be the last star athlete to engage in social activism. The idea that athletes should benefit their communities traces back to Heracles's *athla* and the religious belief that Olympic victories brought concrete rewards from the gods.[27] In the modern world, athletes across the globe have long engaged in community service projects and established foundations to support those less privileged. The leveraging of athletes' political power to change minds in the service of racial equality got its start in the 1960s.

In the fiftieth anniversary edition of his book, *The Revolt of the Black Athlete*, Harry Edwards identifies four separate waves of black athlete activism.[28] The first wave struggled for legitimacy, the second for access, and the third wave was led by elite athletes who used their notoriety to draw attention to the suffering of the many. The iconic image from this movement shows the African American Olympic medalists John Carlos and Tommie Smith protesting poverty and inequality from the award podium at the 1968 Games with bare feet and gloved fists in a black power salute. Kaepernick is part of a fourth wave of athlete activism that is harnessing the power of social media to achieve social change by changing social beliefs.

Human beings are natural organisms that defy orderly biological classification, yet we believe in social categories and allow our judgments to be swayed by stereotypes. Sports, by contrast, are artificial creations designed to choose winners fairly and transparently through the epistemological process of contest. Historically, sport has functioned both to reinforce and to challenge collective beliefs about social hierarchy. The logic of competition demands equality of opportunity, but it also celebrates the superiority of victors. When those victors come from racial and economic backgrounds not expected to succeed, they help to erode unjustified beliefs about the natural superiority of one race over another. On the other hand, those who believe themselves superior are capable of concocting new narratives that deprive successful athletes and sport itself of the perceived social worth that they have historically enjoyed. Sport's ability to combat racism and classism depends not just on the success of athletes of color and the experience of integrated competition;

it also demands that those within the sports community strive to improve the beliefs of those outside of it.

DISCUSSION QUESTIONS

1. Ancient aristocrats tried to defend their social status by introducing athletic events where wealth gave them a better chance at victory. Does wealth provide an advantage in some sports even today?
2. If scientific studies proved that biological differences between whites and blacks can affect athletic performance, would separate athletic classes for the races be justified according to the logic of sport?
3. Do college sports dispel or reinforce beliefs about racial superiority among athletes and spectators? Do they help underprivileged students to climb the social ladder?
4. Because sports can provide fame and fortune to only a few athletes of color, do those stars have a moral obligation to help combat racism in society at large?

NOTES

1. Sofie Remijsen, "Only Greeks at the Olympics? Reconsidering the Rule against Non-Greeks at 'Panhellenic' Games," *Classica et Mediavalia* (2019): 67, argues that the whole concept of Greek identity was flexible and negotiated partly via participation in the Games.

2. See, for example, Frank M. Snowden Jr., *Blacks in Antiquity: Ethiopians in the Greco-Roman Experience* (Cambridge, MA: Harvard University Press, 1970).

3. For a detailed account, see Heather L. Reid, "Athletic Heroes," *Sport, Ethics and Philosophy* 4, no. 2 (2010): 125–35. On the ancient relationship between sport and aristocracy in relation to the practice of athletic nudity, see Heather L. Reid and Georgios Mouratidis, "Naked Virtue: Ancient Athletic Nudity and the Olympic Ethos of *Aretē*," *Olympika* 29 (2020): 29–55.

4. The accounts are in Xenophon, *Agesilaus* 9.6, and Plutarch, *Ages* 20.1, both in *Arete: Greek Sports from Ancient Sources*, ed. Stephen G. Miller (Berkeley: University of California Press, 1991). The motivations and extent of female exclusion at the ancient Olympic Games is the subject of scholarly debate; for a good overview, see John Mouratidis, "Heracles at Olympia and the Exclusion of Women from the Ancient Olympic Games," *Journal of Sport History* 11, no. 3 (1984): 41–55; and Thomas F. Scanlon, *Eros and Greek Athletics* (New York: Oxford University Press, 2002), esp. chaps. 4–7.

5. According to Pausanias, *Description of Greece*, trans. William H. S. Jones and Henry Ormerod (Cambridge, MA: Harvard University Press, 1918), 5.21.7, statues

set up at Olympia to punish cheaters had sayings to this effect, including "the contest at Olympia is one of *aretē* and not of wealth."

6. The modern Olympic amateurism rules that tormented Jim Thorpe and many others were often defended as a reflection of athletics in ancient Greece. In fact, ancient Greek athletes were never amateurs in the modern sense of deriving their income from something other than sport. Starting with Milo of Croton in the 6th century BCE, many ancient athletes dedicated their lives to and derived their living from sport. See Jean-Manuel Roubineau, *Milon de Crotone: ou l'invention du sport* (Paris: Presses Universitaires de France, 2016).

7. These arguments are made in detail in Heather L. Reid, *Athletics and Philosophy in the Ancient World: Contests of Virtue* (London: Routledge, 2011), chaps. 1–3. The democracy thesis was originally proposed by Stephen G. Miller, "Naked Democracy," in *Polis and Politics*, ed. P. Flensted-Jensen and T. H. Nielsen (Copenhagen: Festschrift, 2000), 277–96. See also Paul Christesen, *Sport and Democracy in the Ancient and Modern Worlds* (Cambridge: Cambridge University Press, 2012).

8. Heather L. Reid, "Olympia: Running towards Truth," *Sport, Ethics and Philosophy* 4, no. 2 (2010): 136–45.

9. For details, see Mark Golden, *Greek Sport and Social Status* (Austin: University of Texas Press, 2008).

10. See, for example, Donald G. Kyle, *Sport and Spectacle in the Ancient World* (London: Blackwell, 2007).

11. Heather L. Reid, "Was the Roman Gladiator an Athlete?" *Journal of the Philosophy of Sport* 33, no. 1 (2006): 43.

12. We know from artistic and written sources that people with the physical characteristics (skin color, hair texture, eye shape, etc.) now associated with race were present in Greek and Roman sports, and that they were sometimes excluded or allowed only limited roles in sport. But the rationale for this was social status or ethnicity rather than race. For details, see James R. Coates and Bettina Kratzmueller, "Being the 'Others'?—Blacks in Blood Games," in *Sport and Violence*, ed. J. Aquesolo (Seville: Universidad Pablo de Olavide, 2006).

13. Michael James and Adam Burgos, "Race," in *The Stanford Encyclopedia of Philosophy*, ed. Edward N. Zalta, 2020, https://plato.stanford.edu/archives/sum2020/entries/race.

14. See, for example, Koffi N. Maglo, "The Case against Biological Realism about Race: From Darwin to the Post-Genomic Era," *Perspectives on Science* 19, no. 4 (2011): 361–90.

15. Rasmus Bysted Møller and Verner Møller, "Philosophy, Race, and Sport" in *Routledge Handbook of Sport, Race and Ethnicity*, ed. John Nauright and David K. Wiggins (New York: Routledge, 2017).

16. Møller and Møller, "Philosophy, Race, and Sport."

17. The Institute for Diversity and Ethics in Sport, *Racial and Gender Report Card*, 2021, accessed February 8, 2022, https://www.tidesport.org/racial-gender-report-card.

18. John Hoberman, *Darwin's Athletes: How Sport Has Damaged Black America and Preserved the Myth of Race* (Boston: Houghton Mifflin, 1997), 99–114.

19. Bill Russell, *Second Wind: The Memoirs of an Opinionated Man* (New York: Random House, 1979), 188.

20. For example, Jim Litke, "Black Athletes Eased Obama's Presidential Path," *NBC Sports*, November 5, 2008, accessed November 21, 2011, http://nbcsports.msnbc.com/.

21. Drew Hyland, "*Paidia* and *Paideia*: The Educational Power of Athletics," *Journal of Intercollegiate Sport* 1, no. 1 (2008): 69.

22. Hoberman, *Darwin's Athletes*, 146.

23. Christophe Lemaitre, quoted in Christopher Clarey, "A French Revolution in the Fast Lanes," *International Herald Tribune*, November 18, 2011, Kindle edition.

24. Kaepernick quoted in Steve Wyche, "Colin Kaepernick Explains Why He Sat during National Anthem," *NFL.com*, August 27, 2016.

25. Megan Garber, "They Took a Knee," *The Atlantic*, September 24, 2017.

26. Ryan Parker and Kimberly Nordyke, "Nike's Polarizing Colin Kaepernick Ad Wins Emmy for Best Commercial," *Hollywood Reporter*, September 15, 2019.

27. See Heather L. Reid, "Olympic Sacrifice: A Modern Look at an Ancient Tradition," *Philosophy: Royal Institute of Philosophy Supplement* 73 (2013): 1–13.

28. Harry Edwards, *The Revolt of the Black Athlete* (Champaign-Urbana: University of Illinois Press, 2017).

Chapter 15

Sport, Sex, and Gender

At the 1992 Olympic Games in Barcelona, Spain, Shan Zhang was on a roll. The Chinese skeet shooter hit all 150 targets in the qualification round, then set a new Olympic record and equaled the world record in the semifinals with a perfect score of 200. In the final round of six shooters, Zhang missed two targets but still finished first. A photograph of the gold medalist hoisted aloft by the silver and bronze medal winners beautifully illustrates the Olympic ideal of friendship and equality—not just because of the athletes' joyful expressions, but especially because Zhang is a woman and the second- and third-place athletes are men.

"At that time, I was no longer me," Zhang reflected later, "[I was] just like a machine running freely according to its preset program." Unfortunately, "the machine" never got a chance to equal her feat. At the next Olympic Games in Atlanta skeet shooting was open to men only. Unable to defend her title, the dismayed Olympic champion retired from the sport. When a separate women's event was added to the Sydney 2000 program, she started training again, but didn't make the final. In 2004, she didn't even make the Olympic team. Zhang never stopped shooting, though; she loves the sport too much. "If there is an old lady on the skeet range," she said, "it must be me."[1]

It is tempting to think that Shan Zhang's Olympic victory and the challenge it posed to male egos motivated the subsequent exclusion of women from open competition.[2] It is also possible that a spirit of inclusiveness allowed women into the sport initially, then once there were enough of them, the ideal of fairness motivated a separate category and set of medals. According to this narrative, the failure to include a women's class in Zhang's event at the 1996 Games was a travesty of administration corrected by the following Olympics rather than a malicious attempt to exclude her because of her sex. Whichever narrative is correct, the case brings up the philosophical question of why we have women's categories at all in sport. Rationales typically point to biological differences that supposedly give one group a competitive advantage and are justified with reference to fair play as equalizing opportunities for athletes

213

who otherwise would be unable to compete. Shan Zhang's story shows that such justifications need at least to be questioned.

The most interesting philosophical question about girls and women in sport is not whether or why they should participate—they should, and they have participated since ancient times for the same reasons boys and men do, and perhaps a couple of special ones. The more interesting questions are whether sports should ever be segregated by sex, how qualification for the woman's class should be determined, and to what degree socially defined aspects of gender—including cultural and religious expectations about dress and behavior—should be allowed to impact sport.

I have phrased these questions ethically by using the verb "should" so we can explore them according to the three ethical standards introduced earlier in the book: deontology, consequentialism, and virtue. But we will also be considering the issues epistemologically—in terms of beliefs generated and justified by each practice—from the perspectives of the athletes themselves, their practice communities, and society at large. Examining each question from different perspectives will produce diverging and even conflicting answers. So, our goal will not be to arrive at or defend simple solutions, but to better understand the complexity of the issue so that informed decisions in specific contexts can be made with sensitivity.

SHOULD SPORT BE SEGREGATED BY SEX?

Contrary to popular belief, female athletes have existed since the origin of sports. Ancient Greek mythology even had the athletic heroine Atalanta, mentioned in chapter 1, whose name means "equal weight" and who is depicted competing on equal terms and consistently defeating men. In practice, sports in the ancient world were segregated by sex, probably because they derive from rites of passage connected to gender roles.[3] Social assumptions about masculinity and femininity also impact modern sport, but sex segregation, like other classifications, is justified as an effort to improve competition by isolating variables for which athletes are not responsible.

As Sigmund Loland explains, "Competitors ought to be differentiated in classes only in cases in which inequalities in person-dependent matters that they cannot influence in any significant way and for which they cannot be held responsible have systematic and significant influence on athletic performance."[4] This explains things such as weight classes in wrestling and age classes in swimming, but are sex classes really justified by the ideals of sport? Leaving aside for a moment the thorny question of what exactly qualifies a person to compete in the women's class, and assuming that women and girls have the same right to play as men and boys, we will explore the issue of sex segregation from the perspectives of fair play, practical impact, and community values.

In chapter 9, we recognized the ideal of fair play in sport as something that demanded an attitude of respect for others and for the game itself, the logic of which can be summarized as equality of opportunity and reward according to (demonstrated) merit. Does sex segregation reflect this ideal by treating women as equals and rewarding them according to merit? As philosopher Jane English pointed out back in the 1970s, the whole idea of a women's class suggests inferiority and the need for protection.[5] Eileen McDonagh and Laura Pappano put it even more strongly, arguing that sex segregation in sport sets up an abled/disabled binary that designates men as superior and strong, and women as weak and inferior.[6] It does not go unnoticed that many sports and teams use "women" to designate a subcategory: there is "soccer" and "women's soccer"; *Real Madrid* and *Real Madrid Femenil*.[7] As our discussion of race and class in the previous chapter showed, it is difficult for sport to ignore social categories if they are preimposed onto its epistemological structure. If, as the civil rights struggle showed, separate cannot be equal when it comes to public services,[8] how can sex segregation contribute to equality in sport? Doesn't the principle of equality demand the elimination of all classifications?

Before we answer that ethical question, let me take a moment to consider its epistemological dimension by remembering my grandfather. He was a fire chief back in the day and believed that women could not be firefighters until he watched me race through a hailstorm at the Tour of Denver bicycle race. After that, he changed his belief to "women cannot be firefighters except for Heather." The memory makes me laugh, but it also makes a good point about how we justify our beliefs about sex and gender.

It goes without saying that such decisions should not be based on stereotypes, but neither can you rely on personal experience. The fact that you have never participated in an integrated contest or met a woman capable of competing fairly with men does not mean such things are impossible. Even if biology and performance tests show that men, on average, are much more adapted or likely to succeed in a sport, this does not, by itself, justify the exclusion of women. What about the exceptional ones? Sport rewards not the average but the outlier—the swimmer with freakishly large feet, the cross-country skier with exceptionally large lungs.

Another thing we should think about is "reward according to merit." If merit consists purely in athletic performance, open competition may deny the possibility of meaningful participation to all kinds of people who lack the requisite "raw materials" through no fault of their own. If, on the other hand, merit is understood in terms of virtues such as courage, striving, and resilience, then the "natural" inequalities correlated with sex should be compensated for somehow.

As we saw in chapter 4, the internal goods that constitute sport's greatest rewards depend on challenge and close competition. Depriving an athlete, on the basis of sex, from the benefits and rewards intrinsic to sport can hardly be fair—even if it is done in the name of fairness. "The ideal of sex equality as sexual assimilation (sex blindness) seems inappropriate to the realm of sports," argues Robert Simon. "The operative principle should be equal concern and respect for all participants, and this may sometimes justify differences in actual treatment."[9] Sometimes the principle of equal opportunity demands that we compensate for relevant inequalities.

Sometimes is not the same as always, though, and as Pam R. Sailors points out, any answer to the question of sex segregation in sport "should include consideration of whether we are discussing an individual sport or a team sport, whether the sport involves direct or indirect competition, whether we are discussing contact or non-contact sports, and whether the level of completion is amateur or professional."[10] Part of the problem with classification by sex is that it imposes a sweeping binary that is based, at least partly, on presumptions about what women and men can do rather than on evidence.[11]

In this way sex categories differ from weight classes, which make more precise distinctions based on a criterion that demonstrably affects the competitive balance in sports such as wrestling, boxing, and martial arts. Rowing also offers a lightweight division in an effort to make competition more equitable, though lightweight rowers remain eligible to compete in the open class. A similar model exists for sex classes in some sports: individual women may compete in the men's class, though men are barred from competing in the women's class. This solution preserves the principle of equal opportunity for exceptional females and gives them access to an appropriate challenge, but does playing with the men really benefit them more than being stars in a separate women's league? Does it benefit women's sports as a whole?

Whether or not it makes sense in principle, the consequences of sex segregation in sport also need to be considered. If the result of integration would be a drastic reduction in opportunities for women to participate competitively, their access to the internal goods of sport would be drastically reduced in comparison with men. Based on their statistics, very few of today's female gold medalists would have had a chance at Olympic victory had their competitions not been restricted to women. Heroes such as Serena Williams and Jessica Ennis-Hill would probably be also-rans in integrated elite competition. "The recognition of sex differences in sports," says Simon, "frees women from traditional restrictions and makes it possible for them to engage in highly competitive forms of athletics in a variety of major, traditionally male, sports."[12] Angela Schneider agrees: "In a society where men's interests and strengths dominate . . . excluding women from elite sport (on whatever grounds) would have the morally disastrous consequences of further restricting the realm of what is possible for women."[13]

Looking at the issue today, when women's sport is practiced professionally and females are among the most widely recognized Olympic champions in some countries, it is hard to argue from a consequentialist perspective that the elimination of women's categories would constitute the greater good for athletes, sport, or society at large. On the other hand, we don't really know what the consequences of integration would be because with a few exceptions such as equestrian and motor sports, athletic competition is segregated by sex.

Aside from principles and consequences, the impact of sex segregation on sporting social practices—specifically, their ability to cultivate virtue, as we studied in chapter 10—needs to be considered. What is the epistemological impact of segregation on practitioners, especially in light of the enduring link between virtue and athleticism? Does the fact that they must compete in a separate category suggest to females that they are not only athletically but also morally inferior? How can women be expected to compete equally with men in academia, business, government, and the military if they aren't allowed to compete together in sport? Plato's *Republic* proposed the integration of males and females in gymnastic education precisely because he envisioned full access to citizenship for women, including military service and government.[14]

Integrated sports—especially in youth competition where sex-based performance differences are smaller—teach boys and girls not only that they can compete but also that they can work together as a team. Even when the level or type of competition consistently favors one sex over the other (i.e., in rugby or long-distance swimming), male and female athletes can still train together, compete on mixed teams, and cultivate virtue as members of a single practice community. That was the model I experienced in cycling at the U.S. Olympic Training Center, and it is a model used by several sports in high school and college settings.

The question of whether sport should be segregated by sex does not admit an "always or never" answer. Not only should we consider different perspectives, the nature and purpose of particular events can yield different answers. The current approach of the IOC and NCAA is to let individual sports decide on the condition that they respect such principles as safety, fairness, and inclusion.[15] Even in sports where sex differences seem negligible, like equestrian and shooting, integration does not, by itself, amount to equal respect or opportunities for men and women.[16]

Segregation, meanwhile, may provide females the opportunity to reap sport's internal goods and even to be recognized as stars, but it also perpetuates a myth of inferiority and prevents them from eroding it in open competition. Alternatives that preserve a protected class for women while allowing those capable to compete with men may seem to solve the dilemma, but they also risk depriving women's sport of its superstars. The principles of fairness and inclusion need to be balanced, and practical consequences in specific contexts, including the educational impact on practitioners and the epistemological impact on collective beliefs, all need to be considered when imposing a sex binary on sport.

HOW SHOULD SEX ELIGIBILITY BE DETERMINED?

One big appeal of integrated sport is that it would eliminate the need to define and test athletes' eligibility for the women's category, thereby settling controversies over intersex, transgender, and other nonbinary athletes.[17] In principle, sex segregation is based on biological differences outside of a person's control that affect sports performance significantly enough to justify separate categories. It is for this reason that I have been using the term "sex," which traditionally refers to physical phenomena (i.e., chromosomes, reproductive glands, genitalia, and hormones), rather than "gender," which includes social and cultural factors.

As it turns out, however, the biological concept of sex is not so clearly delineated as many assume, nor is it easily separated from the social concept of gender. This means that the differences between men and women that affect sports performance (i.e., the fact that men, on average, have more muscle mass than women) may partly result from gender expectations that lead to boys doing more physical activity than girls.[18] As a result, some philosophers say that sex and gender cannot be meaningfully distinguished.[19] This is a problem for sport, which is supposed to *resist* social considerations in its selection of winners—a process directly affected by competition categories.

In contrast with classification criteria such as age and weight, determination of an athlete's sex is not as easy as it may seem. It usually appears on birth certificates, but unlike the date, sex assignment is a judgment call that may result in individuals with intersex characteristics such as internal testes being designated as female. Historically, this has led to questions about and even challenges to certain athletes' eligibility to compete as women based not on their birth certificates but, rather, on their appearance. It should be obvious to us by now that feminine appearance is not relevant to sports performance, yet the first sex verification tests were visual inspections in which athletes paraded naked before judges or had their genitalia examined and verified by doctors.[20]

Genitalia are the main thing used to determine sex at birth, but they are no more relevant to sports performance than appearance is. In any case, early sex testing was disrespectful and discriminatory because it was never required of men and sometimes only of those women whose appearance caused suspicion.[21] Eventually sex verification tests were done in a laboratory, first by testing chromosomes (which, again, are not reliably connected to sports performance), and eventually by testing hormone ratios, especially testosterone levels, which are widely believed to directly affect performance and are controlled in an antidoping context for men as well as women.[22] This apparently biological and sport-specific criterion has its own problems, however.

Not only is the impact of testosterone on athletic performance not well understood,[23] several athletes who were designated female at birth and raised as girls and women nevertheless have failed the testosterone test. Privacy laws prevent us from knowing who most of them are, but some have self-identified as part of lawsuits aimed at restoring their eligibility.[24] The most famous is Caster Semenya, a South African runner whose performance and appearance inaugurated new debate about sex verification in 2009. She was subjected to a physical examination, the details of which remain private, but reportedly revealed that she had intersex characteristics including a naturally high level of endogenous (internally generated) testosterone. After legal wrangling that went all the way to the Court for the Arbitration for Sport, Semenya returned to competition with a softer appearance and slower times that made many suspect that she had agreed to take hormone suppressants to remain eligible.[25]

Taking medically unnecessary drugs in order to compete in the women's class raises a host of ethical questions for sport. For one thing, it reprises Claudio Tamburrini and Torbjörn Tännsjö's suggestion that women be allowed to use performance-enhancing technologies to compete on equal terms with men and have a fair chance at the rewards in men's sports.[26] It also implies that Semenya has done something wrong, akin to cheating or doping, by competing in women's middle-distance events. Assuming that Semenya was given the choice of competing with the men or suppressing her natural hormones, the case further introduces the idea that sex can be chosen medically. If this is the case, then what is to prevent male athletes from suppressing their natural hormones in order to compete in the women's class?

This last hypothetical resembles the situation of transgender athletes, but it trivializes the situation to believe that any athlete's main motive for transitioning is to reap the lesser benefits of women's sport by exploiting the unfair advantage of having been a man. The sports question has nothing to do with an athlete's motives for wanting to compete in the women's category and everything to do with respecting the justification for that category, which is based on competitive advantages outside one's control. As self-identification becomes an accepted means of determining gender in society, groups such as Athlete Ally and the Canadian Centre for Ethics in Sport argue that it should also be sufficient in sport. Critics of self-declaration policies, meanwhile, imagine male athletes self-identifying as women in order to cherry-pick women's events.[27] What they don't imagine, but seems equally plausible, is women self-identifying as males—especially at the junior level—to gain access to the better facilities and coaching usually offered to boys and men. In its "Framework on Fairness, Inclusion and Non-Discrimination on the Basis of Gender Identity and Sex Variations" released in the fall of 2021, the IOC states that "athletes should be allowed to compete in the category that best aligns with their self-determined gender identity," provided they meet the eligibility criteria established by each sport to guarantee "fairness."[28]

The IOC's new policy supersedes the blanket requirement that transgender athletes in all sports maintain the same levels of testosterone required of cisgender women for at least twelve months before competition, and it allows the governing bodies of individual sports to set their own eligibility criteria for women's events. The only condition is that certain principles are respected, namely inclusion, prevention of harm, nondiscrimination, fairness, no presumption of advantage, evidence-based approach, primacy of health and bodily autonomy, stakeholder-centered approach, right to privacy, and periodic review.[29]

The framework states that eligibility criteria must not require athletes to undergo physical exams or pressure them to undergo medically unnecessary treatment.[30] But it also stipulates that they should be prevented from "claiming a gender identity different from the one consistently and persistently used" for the purpose of sport, and that no athlete should have a "disproportionate competitive advantage" over other athletes in their category, namely one that "exceeds other advantages that exist at elite-level competition."[31] Here, they must have in mind the physical and psychological variations within sex categories that affect performance but are considered acceptable. This is not exactly the deontological idea of fairness we have identified, but the attempt to emphasize sports-relevant biological factors rather than socially determined ideas of gender is clear from the Framework's rejection of any presumption of advantage based on physical appearance or transgender status, accompanied by its epistemological insistence that restrictions be based on "robust, peer-reviewed research" specific to the event in question.[32] The consequences of the framework remain to be seen.[33]

THE IMPACT OF GENDER ON SPORT

Whether or not sports are categorized by sex, and whether or not eligibility for such a category can be defined in purely biological terms, social ideas about gender have an impact on sport. The philosophical question is what impact gender expectations *should* have and to what degree sport *should* try to resist them. The question is important, as it was in the case of race and class, because sport may be an effective tool for combating unjustified beliefs and social oppression. Simone de Beauvoir identified it as such all the way back in 1949 when she observed in *The Second Sex* that society turns girls' bodies against them at adolescence with expectations about appropriate clothing and activities that demand passivity. This weakens them not only physically but also psychologically; "Not to have confidence in one's body," she says, "is to lose confidence in oneself."[34] De Beauvoir suggested that active participation in sport could counteract the social objectification of women,[35] and later feminist philosophers have developed that idea.[36]

There is not widespread agreement on *how* sport should fight the oppression of women, however. Jane English says that sport should change to reward feminine virtues such as flexibility and cooperation rather than strength and aggression.[37] Others argue that sport should minimize gender difference, emphasizing equality and integration.[38]

A huge step for women in sport was made in the 1970s when Title IX, an American law banning sex discrimination in education programs, was applied to sport. I was in high school at the time and experienced the change firsthand; suddenly girls were allowed to participate in the boys' PE and sports programs. I played soccer on the boys' team (because there was no girls' team) and experienced not only the greater speed and aggression of the male players, but also a special kind of team bonding after kids from another school ridiculed us for having a girl on the team.

Not everyone's experience with Title IX has been positive, though. The concern that gender expectations prevent boys and men from competing all-out against girls and women continues to have an impact. A top-ranked wrestler gave up a good shot at a state title in the 2010 Iowa high school championships by forfeiting to a much lower-ranked girl in the first round. His father explained it in gender terms: "Wrestling is a combat sport and they're out there and it gets violent at times, and my son doesn't believe that girls should be engaged in that way."[39] The failure to look beyond gender can go both ways. Boys who have sued successfully under Title IX to play field hockey on the girls' team (because it is not a boys' sport in the USA) have been forced to wear skirts[40]; it is hard not to see this as a gender-based attempt to discourage or even shame them.

As a matter of fact, dress regulations may be the aspect of sport where gender has its most visible impact. Beach volleyball attracts a lot of attention (and criticism) because women usually play in very skimpy bikinis whereas the men wear tank tops and baggy shorts.[41] Some see sexual objectification in this, though the rules stipulate only that "shorts or a bathing suit" must be worn.[42] Since beach volleyball became an Olympic sport, shirts and head coverings—including the full-body suit and hijab that the Egyptian athlete Doaa Elghobashy wore at the 2016 Games in Rio—have been permitted.[43] The cultural and religious expectations of Muslim women, in particular, have been an issue for international sport. Even when full-body uniforms are permitted, they can hinder performance. Head coverings were banned for safety reasons from soccer, a rule that sidelined women's teams from some Muslim countries until sports-specific hijabs were developed and FIFA decided to allow religious headgear (for men as well as women).[44]

Some view Muslim dress requirements as oppression of women, but respecting a person should include respecting their religion.[45] It may not be realistic in practice for sport to ignore gender expectations, but it is worth asking how big a concession it should make. Beach volleyball Olympian Kerri Walsh Jennings says she wears a bikini to optimize performance, not to be sexy.[46] Should she be required to wear a full-body suit to level the playing field? Should uniform requirements ever be different for men and women? In swimming, where hydrodynamic materials make full-body coverings a competitive advantage, the size of men's suits is restricted compared to women—does that mean they have an unfair advantage when it comes to comparing times?

The very question of whether athletes' uniforms make them look sexy brings in another officially irrelevant aspect of gender that sport cannot ignore, namely sexuality and especially heteronormativity.[47] Sport sometimes seems more conservative than society on this issue. Professional athletes in high-profile men's sports such as American football and European soccer are reluctant to come out as gay.[48] Same-sex couples can marry in countries all over the world, but a figure skating pair must consist of one man and one woman in which the man performs specific moves (such as lifting the woman) and the woman performs others (such as spinning with her head close to the ice while her partner supports her weight in a "death spiral").[49] Though men, on average, are stronger and heavier than women, there is no sporting reason beyond those rules that the athletes performing those roles must be male or female.

On the other hand, pairs figure skating, introduced at the 1908 Olympics, may be the oldest sport in which men and women compete together equally as a team. Figure skating as a sport, meanwhile, seems to be one of the least homophobic. Indeed, the costumes and artistry of some male figure skaters have pushed the boundaries of masculinity enough to effect social change with respect to gender and sexuality—not unlike Jackie Robinson effected social change with respect to race.

All of this goes to show that sport's capacity to surprise us—to reveal aspects of humanity overlooked by presumptions—is the key to its social power. Unless people who aren't expected to thrive in sport—not just "typical" women, but also atypical men—are given that opportunity, sport cannot fully celebrate humanity. It is true, on average, that men are stronger, faster, and more aggressive than women, but sport is not designed to indicate group averages. Rather, it is designed to reward the extraordinary performances of individuals and teams who, almost by definition, are anything other than average. This means that averages, whether social or scientific, shouldn't be used to exclude people from sport. It also means that we shouldn't think only about elite men and women competing against each other in sports such as swimming and soccer when we think about sex and gender in sport.

Fairness may be achieved without segregation in sports such as shooting and car racing, whereas sports such as gymnastics may alter events (i.e., rings versus balance beam) to accommodate different abilities. At the same time, contrived differences in competition conditions (i.e., race length, ball size, shotput weight) should be based on evidence rather than presumption and aim at inclusion and opportunity for both sexes—the same principles apply to eligibility criteria for women's categories in different sports. Even when sex segregation and other distinctions are justified at the elite level, they should be seriously questioned in youth and master's sports, as well as recreational leagues. Mixed-gender events, in which women and men compete together as teams, are an increasingly popular approach to diversity that respects competitive difference.[50] Finally, there's no reason to exclude women from sport in positions where athletic performance is irrelevant. They are and should be welcomed as coaches, officials, trainers, managers, and entrepreneurs. Sport philosophy teaches us that women are good for sport and so is fair play; sport philosophers should think of creative ways to accommodate both of them.

DISCUSSION QUESTIONS

1. Have you participated in sports or particular contests that were not segregated by sex? How did that experience differ from sex-segregated sport?
2. If you had an athletic daughter, and athletes could freely choose their sex category, would you encourage her to compete with the boys? Why or why not?
3. Can you identify an aspect of your sport that is impacted by socially defined gender expectations (including heteronormativity)? Would the sport be harmed by eliminating it?
4. Think of a creative way to promote sex integration in your sport while preserving the principle of competitive fairness. What would be the social advantages and disadvantages?

NOTES

1. For the quotes and Zhang's biography, see International Olympic Committee, "Zhang Shan: The Only Female Shooter to Win Gold in a Mixed Competition," *Olympic.org*, July 5, 2020, accessed January 13, 2022, https://olympics.com/en/news /zhang-shan-the-only-female-shooter-to-win-gold-in-a-mixed-competition. For more on gender equity in the Olympics and the photo of Zhang with her fellow medalists, see Kevin Helliker and Matthew Futterman, "At the Rio Olympics, Women Athletes Bump against a Gold Ceiling," *Wall Street Journal*, August 5, 2016, accessed January 13, 2022, https://www.wsj.com/articles/at-the-rio-olympics-women-athletes-bump -against-a-gold-ceiling-1470425132.

2. A similar charge has been made with respect to women's ski jumping. See Jason Laurendeau and Carly Adams, "'Jumping Like a Girl': Discursive Silences, Exclusionary Practices and the Controversy over Women's Ski Jumping," *Sport in Society* 13, no. 3 (2010): 435; John Gleaves, "Too Fit to Fly: How Female Nordic Ski Jumping Challenges the IOC's Approach to Gender Equality," in *Rethinking Matters Olympic: Investigations into the SocioCultural Study of the Modern Olympic Movement*, ed. International Center for Olympic Studies (London: University of Western Ontario, 2010), 278–88; and Gertrud Pfister, "Sportification, Power, and Control: Ski-Jumping as a Case Study," *Junctures* 8 (2007): 51–66.

3. For a philosophical overview of women in ancient athletics, see Heather Reid, "Heroic *Parthenoi* and the Virtues of Independence: A Feminine Philosophical Perspective on the Origins of Women's Sport," *Sport, Ethics and Philosophy* 14, no. 4 (2020): 511–24.

4. Sigmund Loland, *Fair Play in Sport: A Moral Norm System* (New York: Routledge, 2001), 60.

5. Jane English, "Sex Equality in Sports," *Philosophy and Public Affairs* 7 (1978): 269–77.

6. Eileen McDonagh and Laura Pappano, *Playing with the Boys: Why Separate Is Not Equal in Sports* (New York: Oxford University Press, 2008), 23.

7. The Olympic Games, in contrast with the norm, tend to use "men's" as well as "women's" when designating events. Thanks to Rafael Mendoza for this example.

8. Racial segregation in the United States became illegal after the Supreme Court decided that a "separate but equal" policy did not constitute equal protection under the law, in a case called *Brown v. Board of Education.*

9. Robert Simon, *Fair Play: The Ethics of Sport* (Boulder, CO: Westview, 2004), 136.

10. Pam R. Sailors, "Off the Beaten Path: Should Women Compete against Men?" *Sport in Society Cultures, Commerce, Media, Politics* 19, nos. 8–9 (2016): 1125–37, reprinted in *Sex Integration in Sport and Physical Culture*, ed. Alex Channon, Katherine Dashper, Thomas Fletcher, and Robert J. Lake (London: Routledge, 2018).

11. Angela Schneider, "Girls Will Be Girls, in a League of Their Own—The Rules for Women's Sport as a Protected Category in the Olympic Games and the Question of 'Doping Down,'" *Sport Ethics and Philosophy* 14, no. 4 (2020): 481, points

out that "from a philosophical perspective, it would seem that one can be logically opposed to heteronormality and a gender binary, but still see a biological sex binary."

12. Simon, *Fair Play*, 118.

13. Angela J. Schneider, "On the Definition of 'Woman' in the Sport Context," in *Values in Sport*, ed. T. Tännsjö and C. Tamburrini (London: Routledge, 2000), 137.

14. Heather L. Reid, "Plato on Women in Sport," *Journal of the Philosophy of Sport* 47, no. 3 (2020): 344–61.

15. The "IOC Framework on Fairness, Inclusion and Non-Discrimination on the Basis of Gender Identity and Sex Variations" will be discussed in the next section. The NCAA's policies can be found at ncaa.org.

16. Several case studies are included in Channon et al., *Sex Integration in Sport.* See especially Janet S. Fink, Nicole M. LaVoi, and Kristine E. Newhall, "Challenging the Gender Binary? Male Basketball Practice Players' Views of Female Athletes and Women's Sport," *Sport in Society: Cultures, Commerce, Media, Politics* 19, nos. 8–9 (October–November 2016): 1316–31.

17. Terms for these categories can be disputed. By "intersex" I mean people with differences of sexual development that result in natural sex characteristics, including testosterone levels, outside the norm. By "transgender" I mean individuals whose assigned sex at birth is different than the gender with which they identify.

18. Anne Fausto-Sterling, *Myths of Gender: Biological Theories about Women and Men* (New York: Basic Books, 1993), 218.

19. For the sake of clarity I use these terms traditionally, but I recognize that sex distinctions are neither clear-cut nor uncontaminated by social factors. For an overview of the philosophical debate, see Mari Mikkola, "Feminist Perspectives on Sex and Gender," in *The Stanford Encyclopedia of Philosophy*, Spring 2022, ed. Edward N. Zalta, https://plato.stanford.edu/archives/spr2022/entries/feminism-gender/.

20. For an overview of sex testing and gender verification in sport, see Seema Patel, *Inclusion and Exclusion in Competitive Sport* (New York: Routledge, 2015), chap. 2.

21. On the ethics of "target testing" for sex, see Pam R. Sailors, Sarah J. Teetzel, and Charlene Weaving, "The Complexities of Sport, Gender, and Drug Testing," *American Journal of Bioethics* 12, no. 7 (July 2012): 24.

22. Sailors, Teetzel, and Weaving "The Complexities," 24, point out that combining antidoping regulations with sex testing is ethically problematic.

23. As Rebecca Jordan-Young and Krystyna Karkazis argue in *Testosterone: An Unauthorized Biography* (Cambridge, MA: Harvard University Press, 2019), many of our beliefs about testosterone remain assumptions that a growing body of research literature does not support. See also K. Karkazis and M. Carpenter, "Impossible Choices: The Inherent Harms of Regulating Women's Testosterone in Sport," *Bioethical Inquiry*, 15 (2018): 579–87; and K. Karkazis, R. Jordan-Young, G. Davis, and S. Camporesi, "Out of Bounds? A Critique of the New Policies on Hyperandrogenism in Elite Female Athletes," *American Journal of Bioethics* 12, no. 7 (2012): 3–16.

24. For an overview, see Patel, *Inclusion*, chap. 5.

25. The details of Semenya's case are covered in Mizuho Takemura, "Gender Verification Issues in Women's Competitive Sports: An Ethical Critique of the IAAF DSD Regulation," *Sport, Ethics and Philosophy* 14, no. 4 (2020): 449–60.

26. Claudio Tamburrini and Torbjörn Tännsjö, "The Genetic Design of a New Amazon," in *Genetic Technology and Sport: Ethical Questions*, ed. C. Tamburrini and T. Tännsjö (New York: Routledge, 2005), 181–98.

27. Sarah Teetzel, "Transgender Eligibility Policies in Sport: Science, Ethics, and Evidence," in *Reflecting on Modern Sport in Ancient Olympia: Proceedings of the 2016 Meeting of the International Association for the Philosophy of Sport at the International Olympic Academy*, ed. Heather L. Reid and Eric Moore (Siracusa: Parnassos Press, 2015), 164, calls this the "elephant in the room" during discussions of trans athletes' eligibility.

28. International Olympic Committee, "IOC Framework on Fairness, Inclusion and Non-Discrimination on the Basis of Gender Identity and Sex Variations" (Lausanne: IOC, 2021), https://stillmed.olympics.com/media/Documents/News/2021/11/IOC-Framework-Fairness-Inclusion-Non-discrimination-2021.pdf, 3.

29. IOC, "Framework on Fairness," 3–5.

30. IOC, "Framework on Fairness," 5.

31. IOC, "Framework on Fairness," 4.

32. IOC, "Framework on Fairness," 4.

33. According to a position paper from the sports medicine community criticizing the IOC Framework, its consequences might include "(1) exclusion of transgender or DSD athletes on the grounds of performance advantage or (2) self-identification that all but equates to no eligibility rules." See F. Pigozzi, X. Bigard, J. Steinacker, et al. "Joint Position Statement of the International Federation of Sports Medicine (FIMS) and European Federation of Sports Medicine Associations (EFSMA) on the IOC Framework on Fairness, Inclusion and Nondiscrimination Based on Gender Identity and Sex Variations," *BMJ Open Sport & Exercise Medicine* (2022): 3.

34. Simone de Beauvoir, *The Second Sex*, trans. H. M. Parshley (New York: Knopf, 1952), 310.

35. Beauvoir, *Second Sex*, 311–12.

36. For example, Iris Marion Young, *On Female Body Experience: "Throwing like a Girl" and Other Essays* (New York: Oxford University Press, 2005). For an overview, see Pam R. Sailors, "Feminist Philosophical Approaches to Sport," in *Routledge Encyclopedia of Sport Studies*, ed. V. Girginov (New York: Routledge, forthcoming).

37. English, "Sex Equality," 287.

38. Iris Marion Young, "The Exclusion of Women from Sport: Conceptual and Existential Dimensions in Philosophy of Sport," *Philosophy in Context* 9 (1979): 44–53, reprinted in *Philosophical Perspectives on Gender in Sport and Physical Activity*, ed. Paul Davis and Charlene Weaving (New York: Routledge, 2009).

39. Jamie Northrup, quoted in Barbara Pinto and Olivia Katrandjian, "Wrestler Joel Northrup Forfeits to Female Opponent in Iowa State Championships," *ABC News*, February 18, 2011, accessed November 21, 2011, http://abcnews.go.com/.

40. For an overview of the issue, see Adam S. Darowski, "For Kenny, Who Wanted to Play Women's Field Hockey," *Duke Journal of Gender Law & Policy* 12, no. 153 (2005): 154–77.

41. See, for example, Pam R. Sailors, Sarah Teetzel, and Charlene Weaving, "No Net Gain: A Critique of Media Representations of Women's Olympic Beach Volleyball," *Feminist Media Studies* 12, no. 3 (2012): 468–72.

42. FIVB, *Official Beach Volleyball Rules 2021–2024*, 16.

43. See Laura Walters, "Evolution of Women's Beach Volleyball Uniforms," *Stuff*, August 8, 2016, accessed January 27, 2022, https://www.stuff.co.nz/sport/olympics/82926043/evolution-of-womens-beach-volleyball-uniforms.

44. For a philosophical discussion of the issue, see Douglas McLaughlin and Cesar Torres, "A Veil of Separation: Intersubjectivity, Olympism, and FIFA's Hijab Saga," *International Journal of Applied Philosophy* 28, no. 2 (2014): 353–72.

45. For a recent opinion piece on the issue, see Shireen Ahmed, "Proposed French Law Banning Hijab in Sport Is Heinous and Harmful," *CBC Sports*, January 25, 2022, accessed January 29, 2022, https://www.cbc.ca/sports/opinion-shireen-ahmed-france-ban-hijab-1.6325820.

46. Jennings, quoted in Walters, "Evolution."

47. See Charlene Weaving, "Unraveling the Ideological Concept of the Female Athlete: A Connection between Sex and Sport," in *Philosophical Perspectives on Gender in Sport and Physical Activity*, ed. Paul Davis and Charlene Weaving (New York: Routledge, 2009).

48. For an analysis, see Eric Anderson, "Openly Gay Athletes: Contesting Hegemonic Masculinity in a Homophobic Environment," *Gender & Society* 16, no. 6 (2002): 860–77.

49. International Skating Union, *Special Regulations & Technical Rules Single & Pair Skating and Ice Dance 2021*, rules 300 and 619.

50. Many of these events got their start in the Youth Olympic Games and are now included at the elite level. At the Tokyo 2020 Games, there were mixed gender sports in archery, athletics, badminton, equestrian, judo, sailing, shooting, swimming, table tennis, tennis, and triathlon. Beijing 2022 featured mixed events in skiing, figure skating, curling, snowboarding, freestyle skiing, short-track speed skating, luge, and ski jumping. My husband noted in the mixed curling that women were often commanding while men did the sweeping.

Chapter 16

Sport, Disability, and the Paralympic Games

Blake Leeper is an athlete who defies categorization. An African American born without lower legs in Kingston, Tennessee, Leeper grew up playing sports on standard prostheses that sometimes fell off when he moved too quickly. In 2009, he got his first pair of blades—the high-tech J-shaped prostheses made especially for sprinters—and discovered just how fast he could be. Three years later he won a silver medal in the 400 meters at the Paralympic Games in London, finishing just behind Oscar Pistorius, the original "blade runner," who had become the first amputee runner to compete in the Olympic Games a few weeks earlier.

Leeper, too, hoped to transcend the category of Paralympian. In 2017, he broke Pistorius's record in the 400 meters and ran fast enough at the 2019 USA Track and Field Championships to be a serious contender for the 2020 Olympic team, at least as part of the 4x400 relay. Leeper's spectacular performances didn't make believers out of everyone, however. Despite Pistorius's previous participation in the Olympics, World Athletics Federation (IAAF) officials put the burden on Leeper to prove that his prostheses did not give him an unfair advantage over nondisabled athletes.[1]

"Anybody that faces a disability, to actually look them in the face and say they have an advantage is just crazy to me," said Leeper. "I guarantee if that's the case, you'll see a lot more people amputating their legs and coming and trying to qualify for the U.S. trials."[2] Leeper underwent tests to produce scientific evidence that his prostheses did not constitute an advantage, but his request for qualification was denied by the Court for Arbitration in Sport (CAS) based on a recently changed Paralympic rule that limits how tall athletes can stand on their prostheses. An expert testified that, based on their studies, Leeper would be significantly shorter on natural legs than he is on his racing prostheses. Leeper's lawyer, Jeffrey Kessler, countered not only that changing to shorter prostheses would constitute an undue burden because it would force him essentially to relearn how to run, but also that the study itself was racist because it failed to include any black subjects. "Guess what? Some African-Americans have longer legs," Kessler concluded.[3] The IAAF maintained that it was aware of no studies that prove African Americans have significantly different body dimensions, and the case was decided in their favor.

In 2022, a study was published demonstrating that running prostheses provide no competitive advantage compared to biological legs over 400 meters,[4] but it came too late for Leeper's Olympic dream. Kessler, who has also represented Oscar Pistorius and Caster Semenya, says these exclusions are not really about evidence anyway; rather, the IAAF is defending an outdated understanding of what athletes should look like.[5]

Sebastian Coe, head of the IAAF, points out, "Accessibility and fair competition are not always compatible, and when they aren't, fair competition has to be the overriding principle."[6] Nobody contends that Leeper and other athletes with disabilities have the right to compete in sports, but the question is—as it was in the case of sex—about categorization. In considering the topic of disability in sport, we need to ask once again about the ethics and epistemology of segregation, eligibility, and compensation. As Leeper's case shows, categories in sport are as much about belief, knowledge, and perception as they are about principles such as fairness. As philosophers, we need to question our own assumptions and perspectives on disability, following the challenge Blake Leeper poses to those who believe he has an unfair advantage to "Walk a mile in my legs."[7]

THE EPISTEMOLOGY OF SEGREGATION

Understanding that situations look different to different people is an important skill for educated people. We can learn to understand others' perspectives with the help of art, literature, philosophy, and just listening. The most important thing, however, is never to assume that our own point of view is better, more correct, or "the way things really are" just because it is ours. Recalling that race is now rejected as a legitimate basis for segregation in sport, and sex segregation is questioned, though still the most common norm, we need to ask why almost no one questions disability as a basis for segregation in sport.

What is it about the people with disabilities that motivates their exclusion from mainstream sports?

One of arguments against sex segregation in sport discussed in chapter 15 was that it sets up an abled/disabled binary in which men represent the able norm and women their disabled inferiors.[8] In fact, the actual abled/disabled binary in sports raises similar epistemological concerns. By labeling people with physical impairments as "disabled," we imply that they fall short of some norm or ideal of "ability." Likewise, by excluding people with disabilities from mainstream sports and keeping events such as the Special Olympics, Deaflympics, and Paralympics separate, we seem to imply that they fall short of "real athletes" or "real sport"—especially the Olympic Games.

However much practical sense it makes to keep disability sports separate, we need to consider the educational message it sends about the "place" of people with disabilities in society and in schools themselves.[9] In particular, we need to ask ourselves whether segregation serves to protect the interests of disabled people or, rather, the belief of nondisabled people in their own superiority.

In chapter 14, we identified belief in superiority based on ancestry as racism; the analogous belief in superiority based on ability is called ableism. This attitude not only deems certain abilities essential while ignoring or diminishing others, but it designates those who lack such abilities as inferior.[10] Historically, this way of thinking can be traced to the "medical model" of disability, which interpreted a person's impairment as a deficiency with respect to the norm of healthy functioning—like an injury or illness that needs to be cured.

Because it is not uncommon in a medical setting to confuse facts and values, what is normal becomes what is good or desirable and, vice versa, what deviates from the norm is undesirable or bad.[11] The medical model is reflected in the history of disability sport, which has its roots in competitions organized at Stoke Mandeville in the United Kingdom as therapy for World War II veterans recovering from spinal injuries.[12] Sports are still recognized as a valuable form of psychological as well as physical therapy, but the Paralympic Games in particular have steadily distanced themselves from that model, focusing instead on media-friendly competition for elite athletes who happen to be disabled.[13] Nevertheless, as Gregor Wolbring points out, vestiges of the medical model remain because to qualify for the Paralympics "one has to define oneself as impaired within a medical classification . . . and prove that one cannot equitably compete against normative Olympic athletes."[14]

In modern disability studies, the medical model that equates disability with deficiency has largely been displaced by a social model that locates the problem not in a person's impairment but, rather, in society's failure to adapt to it.[15] It recognizes, as Leslie Pickering Francis says, "that there are many

possible world designs, only some of which result in disabilities for individuals with impairments."[16] From a policy perspective, the social model trans-
forms disability from a health issue to a human rights concern and has led to
laws and initiatives worldwide aimed at addressing the economic and social
deprivations that people with impairments encounter.[17] The social model
primarily demands a major change in the way we look at and understand
people with disabilities.[18] Some argue that we should abandon terms such as
"disability" in favor of "different ability"[19]; others draw on gender theory to
argue that we should drop the whole abled/disabled binary.[20]

Complete integration is also the vision that some have for sport—or at least
a set of games for those who use high-tech prostheses and those who don't.[21]
Already the Paralympic Games have been combined with the Olympic Games
for purposes of bidding and hosting. The main insight that the social model
of disability provided, however, is that we should integrate by rethinking the
environment. The social problem, in other words, is not too many people in
wheelchairs but rather too few curb cuts, ramps, and elevators. Applied to
sport, this model suggests not that wheelchair athletes are tragically deficient
and unable to do sporting events such as the Boston Marathon but, rather, that
the course should be set up to accommodate them.

Of course, wheelchair athletes cover the marathon course about thirty
minutes faster than runners do, so we may need a separate class to protect
them. The runners, I mean, or more accurately, to protect the ableist illusion
that nondisabled people are superior. Or is their separate category justified
by the fact that the wheelchair athletes are using vehicles, similar to bicycles,
which makes it a different kind of race? Then why are athletes without disabilities usually barred from entering wheelchair races?[22] Perhaps we should
view wheelchairs as a kind of prosthesis that provides an unfair advantage?
This was the reason for disqualifying Leeper, but it raises questions about
the deeper motivations for keeping para-athletes separated. "There seems to
be a fear that running on prosthetics might become faster than 'normal' running," say Ivo van Hilvoorde and Laurens Landerweerd.[23] We may argue that
the prostheses aren't natural, but all runners have high-tech artificial things
attached to their limbs called shoes, and athletes in mainstream sports use
equipment such as vaulting poles and golf clubs all the time.

What about amputees who exceed the performance of nonamputees without the aid of prostheses? Amputee wrestlers such as Anthony Robles, Rohan
Murphy, Kyle Maynard, and Zion Clark have been successful in the mainstream version of their sport, perhaps because the weight classes and emphasis on core strength in wrestling make their lack of limbs a slight advantage.
Amputee weight lifters, likewise, regularly outperform "normal" athletes in
weight-classified events such as the bench-press.[24] Should these athletes be
segregated from "normal" competitors? How is their extraordinary physical

situation different from that of a basketball player who is uncommonly tall or a gymnast who is uncommonly light? What does "normality" have to do with sport, anyway? When it comes to the question of segregating sports for the disabled from mainstream sports, we have to ask ourselves if it is not just an excuse to exclude those who are different, or worse, an effort to preserve some ableist illusion of social superiority.

CLASSIFICATION AND FAIRNESS

Even if, philosophically speaking, socially constructed ideas of normality and disability need to be questioned in the context of sport, and even if, in principle, there may be no reason for segregation, practically speaking, classification is central to events such as the Paralympic Games. The International Paralympic Committee's justification for classification is to ensure that "sporting excellence determines which athlete or team is ultimately victorious" by minimizing the impact of the impairment and thereby supporting the Paralympic Movement's vision "to enable Para-Athletes to achieve sporting excellence and inspire and excite the world." This is "not only important for elite sport," they hasten to add, "but also is essential for promoting grassroots participation in Para-sports by people with an Impairment."[25]

Again, we meet the paradox of classification encountered in chapter 15: excluding anyone from a contest goes against the logic of sport because the person who merits the victory could theoretically be among those excluded. But by controlling for relevant inequalities outside of an athlete's control, more athletes have a chance at success and, in particular, the internal goods of sport that depend on challenge and close competition. Let us recall Loland's criteria for an inequality to justify a separate classification in sport: it must exert a significant impact on performance, exert a systematic impact in most if not all competitions, and be outside of competitor impact and control.[26] In other words, we use categories to limit the benefits gained through the "natural lottery" such as sex, age, height, and weight, so athletic virtues such as fitness, skill, and strategy may be the deciding factors in sport.

Classification is crucial for disability sport because impairments that affect performance differ drastically among individuals. If you grouped all athletes with disabilities together or only used traditional categories (i.e., sex, weight, age), then the contest results would mostly reflect the relative severity of the competitors' impairments rather than their athletic virtues.[27] However, "There is no medical categorization of disabilities that fits smoothly and logically into the context of sport," say Ivo van Hilvoorde and Laurens Landerweerd. "What is considered a disability in 'regular life' may even become an advantage in the context of elite sports."[28] An athlete's eligibility and classification are therefore decided by a panel of classifiers who have both medical and sport-specific expertise.[29] For Paralympic athletes, there are ten impairment types, and within each type classes are formed depending on the degree of limitation in that particular sporting activity.[30] A huge number of classifications have been invented, and while contests routinely combine athletes from different classifications, a single event such as the 100 meters will award many sets of medals. For the 100-meter sprint at the 2020 Tokyo Paralympic Games, there were sixteen classifications for men and thirteen for women—most of which ran multiple heats.

The need for effective classifications poses a practical challenge for organizers, who want contests to be fair but also entertaining to watch. As Carwyn Jones and David Howe put it, they need to "strike a balance between creating enough classes to allow reasonably fair contests without having so many that sports contests are reduced to idiosyncratic comparisons of minute differences in physical function."[31] Spectators may not have the patience to watch a dozen iterations of the same event with only a few competitors each, but athletes will lose interest in participating in contests where they don't have a chance.

Women and athletes with high support needs are the hardest hit by the organizers' dilemma,[32] and that becomes a kind of catch-22 because it is hard to promote inclusion in sport when sport is not as meaningful as it should be for lack of numbers. Winning athletes can be discouraged by the classification system, too, because success in one group may cause them to be moved to another, more difficult one.[33] Some elite Paralympians, as we mentioned, are capable of competing in the Olympic Games, but a question arises whether compensation can or should be made for their disability. If categorization is justified in terms of isolating involuntary variables in order to emphasize athletic excellence, then why can't compensation be allowed for the same reason?

COMPENSATION AND HANDICAPS

"Handicap" is no longer an acceptable term to describe disability, but the idea of a handicap in sport still applies. Handicapping in sport refers to compensation given to disadvantaged competitors in the interest of closer competition. In horse racing, the faster animals are made to carry more weight. In golf, a numerical handicap is calculated into each player's score. In races, slower competitors may be allowed a head start. Maybe while playing basketball in the driveway, your dad kept one hand behind his back. Handicapping on the playground is in the spirit of fun, but handicapping in contests is motivated by fairness and is sometimes referred to as "leveling the playing field."

Because these advantages are given in compensation for inequalities outside the athlete's control, they differ from the advantages gained by performance-enhancing technologies designed to "tip the playing field" in a particular athlete's favor. Using the concept of athlete agency discussed in chapter 9, we might say that compensation is justified when it increases athlete agency but unfair when it reduces it. Is it possible that technology can compensate for athletes' disabilities, thereby making integration possible?

The short answer is that it can and it is, though not without controversy. And we don't need to resort to drastic scenarios like Tamburrini and Tännsjö did when they suggested that genetic engineering be used to allow women to compete equally with men[34]; a simple golf cart will do. In the 1990s a top golfer named Casey Martin sued the Professional Golf Association (PGA) under the Americans with Disabilities Act over its rule requiring players to walk the course. Martin has a recognized disability that makes it painful and even dangerous for him to walk, so he was allowed to use a cart at the college level. The PGA refused his request, claiming that the rule change would be "an unacceptable intrusion on the integrity of golf."[35] They did not deny that Martin needed the accommodation but argued that walking the course was fundamental to the game of golf, and using the cart would give him an unfair advantage. The case went all the way to the United States Supreme Court, which ruled that walking was not essential to the game of golf and that using a cart does not fundamentally alter its nature.[36]

In effect, the Martin case tested the question raised by the "social model" of how much the sporting environment should change to accommodate athletes with disabilities. The court's answer was that sports are not required "to change their basic nature, character or purpose insofar as that purpose is rational, rather than a pretext for discrimination."[37]

Casey Martin did not represent a huge challenge to the fundamental nature of golf because carts are used by a majority of "normal" golfers, even required on some courses for logistical reasons. It probably also helped that Martin's disability wasn't visible—he looked like a normal golfer, too. The case of Oscar Pistorius, the aforementioned "blade runner" who eventually competed with nondisabled athletes in the 2008 Olympic Games, posed a much greater challenge to the "nature of the sport." Pistorius argued that the IAAF was ignoring its Olympic commitment to nondiscrimination and violating his human rights by barring him from competing on an equal basis with nondisabled athletes.[38]

This time, however, the argument that Pistorius had an unfair advantage was bolstered not only by the fact that he looked different from the other runners, but also by scientific evidence that compared his prostheses favorably with natural legs. The technology designed to compensate for disability seemed to cross the threshold of equality into the realm of unfair performance enhancement. This was different than wheelchairs or golf carts because Pistorius was competing in the same class and category as runners on natural legs, and the technology in question directly impacted his athletic performance. "Artificial legs that outperform normal legs," explains Wolbring, "are a different story altogether for they literally move beyond what a legged culture defines as normal."[39]

Suddenly, a sports world largely enamored with performance technology saw it as a threat. Nontherapeutic performance-enhancing technologies had long been an issue of contention, but enhancements designed to compensate for impairments were widely accepted. Stars such as Tiger Woods underwent LASIK surgery to improve his vision beyond 20/20, so-called Tommy John surgery is common among baseball pitchers, and the percentage of athletes with permission to use asthma drugs outpaces the occurrence of the disease in the general population.[40] Why are therapeutic enhancements for disabled athletes thought of differently? Is it ableism or the fear that sports such as sprinting may be "taken over" by athletes with high-tech prostheses? The possibility that such devices may provide an unfair advantage is acknowledged even by disabled athletes. After losing to Brazilian Alan Oliveira in the 200 meters at the 2012 Paralympic Games, Pistorius claimed that the length of Oliveira's blades gave him an unfair advantage, even though they were legal.[41] This might have led to the rule change that rendered Blake Leeper's blades too long to compete in the 2020 Olympics, but at least this debate about inclusion is based on justifiable reasoning and scientific evidence rather than subjective presumptions or conventional wisdom.

SOCIAL ACTIVISM

As Blake Leeper waits for the evidence on his prostheses to work through the legal system, he has turned his attention—like many Paralympians do—to the larger issues of disability. Restoring his Olympic eligibility will affect relatively few athletes—not least because the expense of training and equipment is too great for most of the world, but also because the spectacle of an athlete with disabilities competing in the Games—as inspiring and exciting as it may be—does not, by itself, do much to improve the lives of disabled people worldwide. The social and psychological benefits of sport can be transformational for people with disabilities, offering a completely new way to define themselves and their goals. Says Rohan Murphy, "I always viewed my disability before I started to wrestle as a negative, but once I started to wrestle, it became a positive."[42] The social model of disability that has opened doors for people such as Murphy in sport, however, depends on a larger acceptance in and adaptation of society. The fact observed in chapter 14 that the benefits sport provides to an exceptional few athletes of color do not resolve the social problem of racism that applies to people with disabilities, too. In fact, many athletes with disabilities engage in activism after retirement to challenge the discrimination they find outside of sport, and they are encouraging active athletes to join them.[43]

Most commonly, athletes engage in activism by using their visibility to build awareness. Paralympians have spoken publicly against discrimination, campaigned for disability rights, and used social media to highlight inequality.[44] The increasingly popular spectacle of disability sport in general and the Paralympic Games in particular seems to be fulfilling the IPC's vision to "inspire and excite the world." Some even say that the Paralympic Games better fulfill the ideals of sport that the Olympic Games do. John Russell, for example, argues that providing opportunities for people with disabilities to engage in athletic striving "reflects respect for the dignity of those athletes as fellow striving human beings."[45] On the other hand, media coverage of disability sport has been criticized for not respecting these athletes' dignity either by objectifying them sexually[46] or by playing up the "tragedy" of their disability in what amounts to "inspiration porn" aimed at nondisabled viewers.[47]

No matter how fast Paralympians can run, social integration of people with disabilities is a slow process that demands the changing of minds and not just laws, urban landscapes, and sporting rules. In fact, the culture and architecture of gymnasiums and fitness clubs are changing very slowly despite the growing popularity of disability sport. Hoping to change that, Blake Leeper recently led an open-air spinning class in New York's Times Square. "People of all abilities were spinning alongside each other," he said, "and it was a really powerful experience to look out at the crowd and see right in front of my eyes what inclusion and representation can—and should—look like in fitness classes."[48]

DISCUSSION QUESTIONS

1. Does the existence of separate sports events for disabled people perpetuate the idea that non-disabled people are socially superior?
2. Examine your favorite sport from the perspectives of the "medical model" and the "social model" of disability. How might the sport change to become more accessible to those with disabilities?
3. Should amputee wrestlers be forced to compete in higher weight classes to compensate for the advantage gained by their missing limbs? Does the same go for powerlifters in events like the bench press?

4. Is there an ethical difference between the use of technology to compensate for disability, i.e., prostheses, and its use by non-disabled athletes to enhance performance?

NOTES

1. For an overview of Leeper's story, see Matthew Futterman, "Another Double Amputee's Fight for the Olympics Is Dealt a Major Setback," *New York Times*, October 27, 2020.

2. Blake Leeper quoted in OlympicTalk, "Blake Leeper, Olympic Hopeful Double Amputee, Has Prosthetics Ruled Ineligible," *NBC Sports*, February 27, 2020, accessed February 1, 2022, https://olympics.nbcsports.com/2020/02/27/blake-leeper-double-amputee-prosthetic-legs-ineligible/.

3. Jeffrey Kessler quoted in Futterman, "Another Double Amputee's Fight."

4. Owen N. Beck, Paolo Taboga, and Alena M. Grabowski, "Sprinting with Prosthetic Versus Biological Legs: Insight from Experimental Data," *Royal Society Open Science* 9, no. 1 (2022), DOI: 10.1098/rsos.211799.

5. Futterman, "Another Double Amputee's Fight."

6. Coe quoted in Matthew Futterman, "Track and Field Aimed for Inclusion. Instead It Sidelined Star Athletes," *New York Times*, July 30, 2021.

7. Blake Leeper quoted in OlympicTalk, "Blake Leeper, Olympic Hopeful."

8. Eileen McDonagh and Laura Pappano, *Playing with the Boys: Why Separate Is Not Equal in Sports* (New York: Oxford University Press, 2008), 23.

9. Stanislav Pinter, Tjasa Filipcic, Ales Solar, and Maja Smrdu, "Integrating Children with Physical Impairments into Sports Activities: A 'Golden Sun' for All Children?" *Journal of the Philosophy of Sport* 32, no. 2 (2005): 147.

10. See, for example, Gregor Wolbring, "Paralympians Outperforming Olympians: An Increasing Challenge for Olympism and the Paralympic and Olympic Movement," *Sport, Ethics and Philosophy* 6, no. 2 (2012): 251–66. Reprinted in *Olympic Ethics and Philosophy*, ed. Mike McNamee and Jim Parry (New York: Routledge, 2013).

11. Ejgil Jespersen and Mike McNamee, "Introduction," *Ethics, Dis/Ability and Sports* (New York: Routledge, 2009).

12. Jespersen and McNamee, "Introduction."

13. See Carwyn Jones and P. David Howe, "The Conceptual Boundaries of Sport for the Disabled: Classification and Athletic Performance," *Journal of the Philosophy of Sport* 32, no. 2 (2005): 133–46. Ian Brittain, *The Paralympic Games Explained*, 2nd ed. (New York: Routledge, 2016) also comments on the Paralympics' move away from therapeutic uses.

14. Wolbring, "Paralympians Outperforming Olympians."

15. Jespersen and McNamee, "Introduction."

16. Leslie Pickering Francis, "Competitive Sports, Disability, and Problems of Justice in Sports," *Journal of the Philosophy of Sport* 32, no. 2 (2005): 127–32.

17. Colin Barnes, "Understanding the Social Model of Disability: Past, Present and Future," in *The Routledge Handbook of Disability Studies*, 2nd ed., ed. Nick Watson and Simo Vehmas (New York: Routledge, 2019), chap. 2.

18. Brittain, *The Paralympic Games Explained*, chap. 4.

19. Jespersen and McNamee, "Introduction."

20. Margrit Shildrick, "Critical Disability Studies: Rethinking the Conventions for the Age of Postmodernity," in *The Routledge Handbook of Disability Studies*, 2nd ed., ed. Nick Watson and Simo Vehmas (New York: Routledge, 2019), chap. 3.

21. Wolbring, "Paralympians Outperforming Olympians."

22. Wolbring, "Paralympians Outperforming Olympians," notes that nondisabled athletes are not allowed to compete in wheelchairs, which are considered medical devices rather than athletic equipment.

23. Hilvoorde and Landerweerd, "Disability or Extraordinary Talent?" 238.

24. At the beginning of the current millennium, Paralympians held outright powerlifting world records in four weight classes. For example, in the able-bodied 60-kilogram weight class, the world record holder lifts 190 kilograms; Paralympic athlete Mathana Metwaly Ibrahim from Egypt holds the world record at 202.50 kilograms in the same weight class. International Paralympic Committee, "Powerlifting on an Upswing," Paralympian Online, 2000, accessed November 21, 2011, http://www.paralympic.org/.

25. International Paralympic Committee, *IPC Athlete Classification Code*, November 2015 (Bonn: IPC, 2015), 3.

26. Sigmund Loland, "Classification in Sport: A Question of Fairness," *European Journal of Sport Science* 21, no. 11 (2021): 1477–84.

27. A similar point is made by Jones and Howe, "The Conceptual Boundaries of Sport," 137.

28. Ivo van Hilvoorde and Laurens Landerweerd, "Disability or Extraordinary Talent?" in *The Ethics of Sports*, ed. Mike McNamee (London: Routledge, 2010), 232.

29. Brittain, *The Paralympic Games Explained,* chap. 4.

30. International Paralympic Committee, *IPC Athlete Classification Code*, November 2015 (Bonn: IPC, 2015), 3.

31. Jones and Howe, "Conceptual Boundaries," 142.

32. Brittain, *The Paralympic Games Explained*, chap. 4.

33. Loland, "Classification in Sport," 1477–84.

34. Claudio Tamburrini and Torbjörn Tännsjö, "The Genetic Design of a New Amazon," in *Genetic Technology and Sport: Ethical Questions*, ed. C. Tamburrini and T. Tännsjö (New York: Routledge, 2005), 181–98.

35. PGA Tour Commissioner Tom Finchem quoted in Seema Patel, *Inclusion and Exclusion in Competitive Sport* (New York: Routledge, 2015), chap. 6.

36. Patel, *Inclusion and Exclusion*, chap. 6, provides an excellent legal summary of the case.

37. Patel, *Inclusion and Exclusion*, chap. 6.

38. Details of Pistorius's case are also covered in Patel, *Inclusion and Exclusion*, chap. 6.

39. "Paralympians Outperforming Olympians."

40. See, for example, Macallan Penberthy, "Rio Olympics' Special Guest: Asthma," *Foundation for Biomedical Research*, August 2, 2016, https://fbresearch .org/rio-olympics-special-guest-asthma/.

41. Patel, *Inclusion and Exclusion*, chap. 6.

42. Murphy, quoted in Steven Schnee and Astrid Rodrigues, "The Amputee Wrestler: Rohan Murphy Can Take You Down," *ABC Sports*, December 9, 2010, accessed November 21, 2011, http://abcnews.go.com/.

43. B. Smith, A. Bundon, and M. Best, "Disability Sport and Activist Identities: A Qualitative Study of Narratives of Activism among Elite Athletes with Impairment," *Psychology of Sport and Exercise* 26 (2016): 139–48.

44. Smith, Bundon, and Best, "Disability Sport and Activist Idenities."

45. John S. Russell, "Striving, Entropy, and Meaning," *Journal of the Philosophy of Sport* 47, no. 3 (2020): 419–37, 428.

46. Charlene Weaving and Jessica Samson, "The Naked Truth: Disability, Sexual Objectification, and the ESPN Body Issue," *Journal of the Philosophy of Sport* 45, no. 1 (2018): 83–100.

47. Jan Grue, "The Problem with Inspiration Porn: A Tentative Definition and a Provisional Critique," *Disability and Society* 31 (2016): 838–49.

48. Blake Leeper quoted in Vicki Salemi, "Shining a Spotlight on National Disability Employment Awareness Month," *Forbes*, October 29, 2021.

PART VI

Sport and Politics

At the 2022 Winter Olympic Games in Beijing, China, an eighteen-year-old freestyle skier named Eileen Gu caused a political firestorm by refusing to be "political." Born and raised in the United States by her Chinese immigrant mother, she spent summers in China with family and became as nimble in Mandarin as she is on her skis. Reversing the usual athlete's path of changing nations to improve their own chance of success, Gu decided in 2019 to compete for China rather than the United States because she thought she could inspire more young girls to take up sport that way.

Her choice drew questions and criticism, but what really aggravated people was her refusal to choose sides. "I feel just as American as Chinese," explained Gu when repeatedly pressed on the question. "My mission is to foster a connection between countries and not a divisive force."[1] Part of a new social media-savvy generation, Gu was aware of the power that her notoriety provided, and she was determined to use it for the greater good.

Some interpreted Gu's choice as a political statement, an endorsement of Chinese government policies and a betrayal of the United States. "You've got to pick a side because you're either American or you're Chinese, and they are two very different countries," said the American politician Nikki Haley. "Every athlete needs to know when they put their flag on, you're standing for freedom or you're standing for human rights abuses. There is no in-between."[2] Haley made Gu's switch from Team USA to Team China sound tantamount to a turncoat soldier going to fight for the enemy in the midst of a war.

Sport has, indeed, been described as "war minus the shooting,"[3] but is it politically similar? Are athletes wearing a national team uniform expected to carry out the commands of their government—or even to agree with their government's political positions? If competing for a national team does not amount to endorsing a government, then what exactly does it mean? How can athletes and sports organizations claim to be politically neutral when they have political goals? What, in short, is the proper relationship between sport and politics?

There is a lot of talk about keeping sport separate from politics, but the boundary between them is inevitably blurred. It helps to distinguish between politics understood in terms of parties, policies, and governments, and politics understood in terms of social missions such as Gu's and global visions such as the International Olympic Committee's goal of "promoting a peaceful society concerned with the preservation of human dignity."[4]

But we also have to recognize that sport and politics are closely linked. Sport is not war, but it does involve competition that produces winners and losers, and it takes place in a social context that can draw political inferences or even make political points from that process. Athletes are not soldiers, but they do represent nations (as well as sponsors), and they have their own political views. Further, sports communities share internal values derived from their common practice that transcend traditional political boundaries such as race, nationality, or social class.

When the IOC talks about political neutrality, it is trying to avoid the instrumentalization of sport and athletes by governments to serve their own political ends. When members talk about promoting peace, they take themselves to be globalizing the internal goods of sport, but they are using sport to serve political—not to mention financial—ends. In order to avoid the political instrumentalization of sport, we must first understand that the relationship between sport and politics is "both/and" rather than "either/or." The philosophical question is how to make the relationship healthy.

Eileen Gu may be finding a way. She, too, defies traditional distinctions, rejecting the "either/or" division and modeling a healthy "both/and." She is Chinese and American; white and Asian; a cover model and a model student; an athlete and an activist; a teenager and an entrepreneur. Despite, or perhaps because of this, she is a social media superstar in the United States and China alike, attracting lucrative endorsements from international brands. Does she have to identify as communist or capitalist? Democratic or authoritarian? One thing we can say for sure is that she is an Olympic athlete, a medalist in three events.

Does she have to side with any nation's government? Can her politics be her own? Can they be athletic politics—even Olympic politics? She certainly makes them sound that way. "It's not about nationality," says Gu, "it's about bringing people together. It's about sharing culture. It's about learning from each other and forging friendships."[5] If Eileen Gu is being politically exploited by anyone, it seems to be the Olympic spirit itself.[6]

In the following chapters we explore the relationship between sport and politics, first by looking at the relationship between sport and governmental politics, then by examining the "internal" politics of international sport in the age of globalization.

NOTES

1. Eileen Gu quoted in Alastair Talbot, "Former UN Ambassador Nikki Haley Slams US-Born Skier Eileen Gu Who Opted to Ski for China in Beijing Olympics," *Daily Mail*, February 16, 2022, https://www.dailymail.co.uk/news/article-10517867/ .html. Gu's insistence that her choice was not political does not negate the fact that China does and has used sport politically—see Victor D. Cha, *Beyond the Final Score: The Politics of Sport in Asia* (New York: Columbia University Press, 2009).

2. Haley quoted in Talbot, "Former UN Ambassador."

3. The expression is attributed to George Orwell. According to Peter J. Beck, "'War Minus the Shooting': George Orwell on International Sport and the Olympics," *Sport in History* 33, no. 1 (2013): 72–94, it was inspired by the author's recognition of sport's political power; in particular as a tool of nationalism.

4. International Olympic Committee, *Olympic Charter* (Lausanne: IOC, 2021), 8.

5. Gu quoted in Nectar Gan, "China's Eileen Gu Wins Gold in Freeski Halfpipe to Make Olympic History," *CNN*, February 18, 2022, https://edition.cnn.com/2022/02 /18/sport/eileen-gu-halfpipe-gold-olympics-intl-hnk-spt/index.html.

6. It is interesting to note that Eileen Gu participated in the Youth Olympic Games, where participants were educated about Olympic ideals.

Chapter 17

Sport and Political Ideologies

We have encountered the concept of instrumentalism—using sport as a means to external ends—repeatedly in this book. The most notorious example of instrumentalizing sport to serve political goals has to be the 1936 Olympic Games in Berlin, Germany—referred to these days as the "Nazi Olympics." Videos from these Games juxtapose images of Hitler and swastika-adorned pageantry with those of a smiling African American sprinter named Jesse Owens. It was the year of the first Olympic torch relay—a spectacle that symbolically connected ancient Greece with Nazi Germany. These Games were also the subject of Leni Riefenstahl's film *Olympia*, famed for its aesthetic grandeur and groundbreaking sports photography techniques, yet condemned as political propaganda.

We can look back at these images and choose the interpretation we like: the dark foreshadowing of a twisted regime's evil ambition, or the triumph of pure athletic achievement over racist propaganda. One of the International Olympic Committee's (IOC) favorite images is that of Owens with friend and rival Luz Long of Germany, who generously helped his opponent to avoid fouling out of the long-jump qualifications. The story is meant to show how sport can succeed where politics fails.[1]

But in a way, the IOC's telling of this (true) story of athletic friendship is just as political as the (false) story that Hitler refused to shake Jesse Owens's hand. The stories simply support different political ideals. The Olympic Movement may strive to keep itself free from political influence,[2] and former IOC president Avery Brundage may have declared that "sport transcends all political and racial situations,"[3] but sport is, always has been, and perhaps always will be at some level political. As we saw in chapter 1, athletic rituals and displays were put to political use as far back as the third millennium BCE. The ancient Romans were masters in the political use of sport—gladiator fights (*munera*), exotic beast hunts (*venationes*), and staged naval battles (*naumachia*) demonstrated to the masses the strength and scope of the empire as well as the emperor's ability to rule it while keeping them safe.[4] Imperial triumphs served purposes—such as the public exhibition of virtue and justice—analogous to those of traditional Greek sport. Meanwhile, the wildly popular chariot races allowed a diverse population to root for four color-coded teams and symbolically gathered all of Rome into one universe with the emperor at its center.[5]

To say that sport has a political dimension is not necessarily to condemn it. An identifiable link between sport and democracy goes back to ancient Greece, and a connection between sport and fascism may have endured beyond the Nazis' Games. During the Cold War, sport was used to demonstrate the validity of communism. More recently, sport has been linked with the ideals and processes of capitalism. Whatever political ideal sport gets linked with, however, it also seems to contain its own political power—a power borne of its playful, gratuitous, noninstrumental nature. As our study of sports metaphysics showed, sport's value derives ultimately from its *lack* of external purpose—its autotelicity. It is this sport-specific value that *resists* political instrumentalization.

There's no question that the 1936 Olympics were of great political value to the Nazi Party. Through sport, the Germans outperformed the previously dominant Americans, suggesting to the world that authoritarianism was better than democracy.[6] But sport also enabled Jesse Owens to refute Nazi race theories and to temper national rivalry through his friendship with Luz Long. As historian Richard Mandell observes, "The portrayal of the Berlin Olympics to the world as a nonpolitical festival was itself a political act, as well as a lie."[7] Portraying sport as nonpolitical would equally be a lie, but that is not to say that sport lacks political power of its own.

SPORT AND DEMOCRACY

Perhaps the first political ideal said to be derived from sport is democracy. Ancient Greek athletics predated the birth of democracy by centuries, and many of the foundational ideas of democracy appeared in sport long before they became ideals of governance. Archaeologist Stephen Miller argues that the concept of *isonomia*, equality before the law, is a creation of sport and constitutes its most important contribution to society.[8] To this we may add freedom from tyranny, rule of law, equal treatment, and public scrutiny to the list of characteristics common in both ancient sport and democracy.[9]

The inclusion and success of nonaristocrats in ancient Greek athletic competition, as we discussed earlier, eroded the belief that excellence and worthiness to lead were a matter of noble birth. Insofar as democracy is understood as rule of the people, by the people, and for the people, it depends upon the once revolutionary idea that common people are capable of leadership.

Because sport was one of the only arenas in which relative commoners could demonstrate their *aretē* (virtue) in competition with aristocrats, it provided a place for democratic ideas to take root. In modern times, sport still provides an opportunity for lower classes to demonstrate publicly their worth. Indeed, in his 1989 presidential address to the International Association for the Philosophy of Sport, Peter Arnold argued that sport was an ideal means for teaching democratic values.[10]

Freedom is usually the first democratic value to be associated with sport, and it is connected specifically with the idea that sports participation is always voluntary and never forced. Miller marvels at the willingness of freeborn, possibly noble men to subject themselves voluntarily to the rules of sport and risk being flogged in public if they transgressed them.[11] Because public flogging was a punishment otherwise associated exclusively with slaves and animals, participation in sport effectively entailed the renunciation of certain privileges associated with social status. In ancient Rome, citizens and even senators who wanted to compete as gladiators had to formally renounce their civil rights by swearing to be "burned by fire, bound in chains, to be beaten, to die by the sword."[12]

Lest all this make democracy sound like some swashbuckling adventure, the point is that the freedom within both sport and democracy depends upon participants' willingness to give up some portion of their liberty by subjecting themselves to the rules of the game. As Arnold puts it, "In so far as sport demands of its participants freedom with responsibility and involves benefits as well as burdens, it is in accord with the democratic process."[13] It is the public's voluntary acceptance of and adherence to law that makes democracy possible, not least by subjecting everyone equally to punishment under those laws.

So, the freedom in democracy isn't just pure freedom, as in the absence of constraints (i.e., negative freedom). It is also freedom from imposed tyranny by means of voluntary subjection to the law (positive freedom). Likewise in sport, it is the athletes' understanding of and voluntary subjection to contest rules that make the freedom experienced within the game possible. Importantly, this voluntary subjection is undertaken collectively—that is, we agree to follow rules or laws on the understanding that everyone else will follow the rules, too. As Arnold explains, "When an individual voluntarily chooses to enter a sport he or she can be regarded as tacitly accepting an agreement with others to participate in a way that the rules lay down."[14]

Further, neither political leaders nor elite athletes can expect to be "above the law" in sport or democracy. In fact, the rule of law in sport is often enforced indirectly by the spectators. In general, they are aware of the rules, and if an official fails to call some transgression, the crowd is expected to protest. These days, slow-motion replays are often displayed on giant video screens in the arenas, making it easier for spectators to see infractions. This creates the kind of collective responsibility and collective authority expected in a democracy.[15] So freedom in sport and democracy depend on voluntary subjection to rules that depend for their enforcement on officials empowered and scrutinized by the public. Democracy is a community effort for which each member bears responsibility.

Equality in sport and democracy is likewise bound up with rules or law. In the ancient context, where social equality was all but unknown, athletes were equal before the absolute standards of sport, such as distance, speed, and strength, as measured by the performances of other competitors rather than the subjective interpretation of any human being.[16] We can compare it with the difference between winning a race and winning a job. The interview process in the latter depends upon the subjective judgment of one or more powerful officials, and the reasons for their choice are seldom obvious and almost never made public. Candidates rarely even know who their competitors are. A running race, by contrast, takes place out in the open where everyone can see the process and judge its fairness for themselves.

Democratic elections, likewise, should be transparent processes that depend not on special judges but, rather, objective results. Doubt about the results, whether or not merited, challenges the legitimacy of the government as recent controversies over presidential elections in the United States have shown. Equality in democracy is expressed in equality of opportunity. It must allow for reward according to merit. Said the ancient Greek statesman Pericles in describing Athenian democracy, "But while the law secures equal justice to all alike in their private disputes, the claim of excellence (*aretē*) is also recognized; and when a citizen is in any way distinguished he is preferred to the public service, not as a matter of privilege, but as the reward of merit."[17] Sport, too, treats competitors equally as a precondition for rewarding worthy victors.

"Democracy," says Arnold, "is based on the belief that each human being is of value."[18] Sport also strives to value each of its participants, although like democracy, many worthy participants have been excluded historically because of their sex, race, class, or disability. On the other hand, sport seems to have taught us something about the value of democratic ideals: freedom in the form of voluntary participation, equality before the law, and collective responsibility for the enforcement of the law. Democratic thinking is community based, as were athletics in ancient Greece as they performed their religious function of propitiating powerful gods. In the nudity of ancient athletes, Miller sees the roots of democratic equality—once we take our clothes off, social differences are harder to spot.[19] And once we witness the excellence of our fellow competitors, the pretense of hierarchies is harder to sustain. It is our willingness to subject ourselves equally to the law that makes sport and democracy function as just systems of governance. As Arnold observes, sport teaches athletes not only to abide by common rules but also to "understand that it is only by following them that the aspirations and interests of others as well as themselves . . . can be realized."[20] Democracy values not only individuals but also the community as a whole.

SPORT AND AUTHORITARIANISM

Given the historical and conceptual connections between sport and democracy, it may be surprising that the Nazis found the Olympic Games to be an effective means for promoting fascism. Whereas democracy prizes individual freedom, authoritarian regimes promote nationalistic devotion. Whereas democracy is based on equality before the law, authoritarianism seeks to control the many. Whereas democracy is based on universal human value, fascism posits the superiority of a particular race or nation and seeks to eliminate those who weaken or degrade the state. According to philosopher Torbjörn Tännsjö, contempt for weakness is the core of fascist ideology, and it is also intrinsic in competitive sport.[21]

In his view, sport, and especially our admiration for athletic victors, is more closely aligned with the ideals of fascism than democracy. Tännsjö gives ideological and pragmatic justifications for this claim. It is simply a matter of fact that team sports have been used by authoritarian leaders to create a chauvinist zeal in their own populations, which favors the formation of totalitarian governments, the oppression of minorities, and military expansion.[22] The Nazis are an obvious example here, but it would be naive to think that sport's authoritarian potential died along with their regime. Even democratic governments and educational institutions openly use sport to promote community spirit and garner popular support for their projects. Could all those rabid sports fans who paint their faces in team colors and chant against opposing teams be a fascist force in modern sport?

On the face of it, sport's ability to generate community spirit in schools, cities, states, and even nations seems like a positive force. It is sobering, however, to read the words of Joseph Goebbels, Adolf Hitler's minister of propaganda and one of history's most notorious anti-Semites. Said Goebbels on April 23, 1933, "German sport has only one task: to strengthen the character of the German people, imbuing it with the fighting spirit and steadfast camaraderie necessary in the struggle for its existence."[23] In fact, Baron Pierre de Coubertin had been motivated by similar concerns to revive the Olympic Games. He saw it as a chance to strengthen French youth and prevent further military defeat.[24]

Perhaps the positive or negative value of sport's spirit-building power depends upon the end goals of the relevant community. Endemic in any nationalistic or community-spirit promotion, however, is the risk of denigrating outsiders. The Nazi promotion of a pure Aryan race excluded not only Jews but also blacks and homosexuals. Attempts were made, with varying success, to ban Jews from the German team and blacks from the 1936 Games more generally. It was claimed by one Nazi newspaper that the ancient Greeks would "turn in their graves" if blacks were allowed to compete.[25] As we observed in the previous section, racial exclusion from sport seems to be a thing of the past, but exclusions and marginalization based on criteria such as sex and disability endure. The point is that team and nationalistic spirit can have an ugly side. Tännsjö cautions that "there is only a small step from being a soccer hooligan to joining a fascist organization modeled on the Hitler Jugend."[26]

Nationalism becomes an especially dangerous force when it is used to manipulate individuals to act against their own interests for the benefit of very abstract and perhaps merely symbolic values. When American gymnast Kerri Strug vaulted and landed on an injured ankle at great personal risk in the team competition at the 1996 Olympic Games, she was lauded as a national hero. But it is not at all clear how her sacrifice benefited the nation. It did not even benefit the team, which would have won the gold medal even without her final vault. An athlete who risks injury for the sake of his team seems to reflect the value of a soldier who risks injury and even death for the sake of his country. But in the soldier's case, especially when the battle is for the defense of one's own homeland, personal and national interests may be aligned.

The athlete's case is not so clear. Instead, praise of this kind of athletic devotion may be seen as a way to train youth to sacrifice their interests for the state and to blindly obey its commands. According to Tännsjö, "This kind of sacrifice is the rule rather than the exception when a nationalistic ideology gets a firm hold on the members of a nation—in particular if the nation in question does not face the least *threat* from any other nation."[27] The *Olympic Charter* states clearly that the competition is between athletes and not countries,[28] but the ideology of athletes competing for the benefit of their national teams is such a part of international sport that it is hard to imagine sport without it.

For his part, Tännsjö believes that nationalism in sport is dying and will soon be overtaken by corporate identifications. In fact, athletes are often torn between commitments to their professional and national teams. Meanwhile, teams that represent cities and state universities routinely include athletes from outside the area—often from outside the country. It is common for teams such as English football's Manchester City not to have a single player who was born in that city. Many national teams include players recruited from other countries and fast-tracked to citizenship.

This phenomenon does not eliminate sport's fascistic tendencies, however. According to Tännsjö, it makes them worse, because it shows that our admiration for sports heroes springs not from nationalism but from contempt for weakness, the idea at the very core of Nazism.[29] Fascism, like sport, celebrates youth and strength (not to mention masculinity). It encourages us to imagine those who are stronger as superior, not merely in terms of athletics, but in general as well. As we saw in the chapter on disability, the strong are also considered morally superior on this view. Because such an attitude leads to neglect and even contempt for those who are weaker, Tännsjö argues that we have a moral obligation to resist it—indeed, to resist sport altogether.[30] If the fascistic danger of sport really derives from sport's selection and celebration of winners, it seems that the danger cannot be removed without changing sport fundamentally.

But is sport really intrinsically fascist? Philosophers Claudio Tamburrini and M. Andrew Holowchak resist Tännsjö's argument. Tamburrini replies, first of all, that nations, at least in the sporting context, are not abstract symbols but, rather, groups of people.[31] On that view, Kerri Strug was risking injury not for the benefit of some hollow abstraction but, rather, for the real emotional benefit of a group of real people who were watching and perhaps receiving valuable inspiration from her display of courage. Likewise, Eileen Gu was not endorsing the Chinese government but, rather, inspiring the Chinese people. Further, says Tamburrini, it is an overstatement to characterize the public's attitude toward losers as one of scorn or contempt.[32]

Finally, it is too narrow in Tamburrini's view to interpret our admiration for athletic excellence as simply based on strength.[33] Holowchak takes this last point a step further, pointing out that Nazi ideals of strength certainly surpass athletic superiority. "At the core of Nazism are brutality, single-purpose focus, and a crush-at-all-costs attitude," says Holowchak. "With strength comes desert: Because one is 'better' (i.e., outperforms others) at some physical task, one is thereby 'better' (i.e., morally superior) and deserving of more of the good things in life (whereas losers deserve contempt)."[34] But this kind of attitude is certainly not entailed by sport, Holowchak argues, adding that it constitutes a violation of Immanuel Kant's ethical imperative to treat others as ends and never as means.[35] Whatever authoritarian tendencies it may have, sport can undermine them by keeping winning in perspective and showing respect for nonwinners. That sincere end-of-the-game handshake may be politically more important than it first appears.

SPORT AND COMMUNISM

In the second half of the twentieth century, international sport was more often associated with communism. At first glance, it seems odd that competitive sport should be embraced by a political system that focuses on cooperation and sharing. The philosophical founder of communism, Karl Marx, said almost nothing about sport. He, along with his more practical successor, Vladimir Lenin, envisaged physical education and sport as a routine part of school and of working life—a vision not dissimilar from that of most societies around the world.[36] In 1920, Lenin declared, "The physical culture of the younger generation is an essential element in the overall system of communist upbringing of young people, aimed at creating harmoniously developed human beings, creative citizens of communist society."[37]

If anything was radical about the early communist view of sport, it was that they expected all members of the society, including women, to partake. The goals of communist sport were originally modest. It was not until the 1940s that competitive sport was envisioned as a kind of propaganda for communist ideals. Said N. N. Romanov, head of the Soviet Sport Committee in 1947, "Sport [is] a mass, popular movement with the goal of establishing the capacity of Soviet athletes to struggle for national and world records for the glory of our homeland."[38]

As we have seen, by this time it was not particularly original to use sport as political propaganda. What was odd about communists doing it was the apparent conflict between athletic values and their own political ideals. On the other hand, sport's ability to level class differences and to discount social differences goes well with communist goals. Perhaps the most notable impact of communism in sport was nearly equal training and funding for men and women, which effectively gave communist women an advantage over female athletes from countries where resources were distributed disproportionately to men.

Anthropologist Susan Brownell notes that in China equal athletic opportunities for women appeared around 1955 (nearly twenty years before the passage of Title IX gender equity legislation in the United States), and the results were immediate: only two years later, a Chinese woman bettered the high-jump world record.[39] East German and Soviet women also had great success in international sports during the Cold War era. It is plausible, moreover, that funding and attention for women's sports in the rest of the world was motivated at least partly by an effort to keep up with communist women's success. In fact, Lenin himself had envisioned sports as a tool of female emancipation, calling it an "urgent task to draw working women into sport."[40]

But not every marginalized group benefited from the communist approach to sport. Communist countries largely rejected disability sports, which may betray their interest in propaganda at the expense of political ideals. Huge government resources were committed not so much to increasing lifelong participation for the masses but, rather, to the early selection, development, and performance of elite athletes. Those elite athletes, whose success was supposed to prove the superiority of the communist way of life, in fact lived lives radically different and largely separate from the common people. Resentment was accordingly expressed at the special privileges given to athletes, and much of the populace came to perceive athletics as nothing more than a diversion from the harsh reality of life in a communist system.[41]

The unbridled zeal to "prove" communism's superiority through sport eventually led in East Germany to experimentation with performance-enhancing drugs on athletes as young as fourteen years of age, often without their knowledge or consent.[42] In these cases, sport not only fails to demonstrate the superiority of a regime's ideals but also runs counter to them and undermines the legitimacy of both the government and the political system it is trying to promote.

SPORT AND CAPITALISM

Since the fall of communism in Eastern Europe, sport has been more closely aligned with its opposing political ideal: capitalism. Countries such as China, without a history of capitalism, may even be promoting sport as a way to teach their citizens the values they will need to compete in a global market. Philosopher Ann E. Cudd argues that widespread use of athletic metaphors such as "a level playing field" in capitalistic discourse betrays important similarities between sport and capitalism—some of which should be taken more seriously. "Skills associated with good athletes such as strategic decision making and team play," she observes, "are valued in business executives, managers, and investors."[43]

Capitalism, in opposition to communism, allows private ownership of the means of production as a way to create markets for almost everything, including labor. Cudd notes that both sport and capitalism are voluntary, rule governed, and competitively challenging.[44] She also warns that both sport and capitalism exhibit a competitive culture that can "breed a psychology of intensity, greed, and egotism."[45] Although competition, or at least play, is thought to have intrinsic value in sport, Cudd believes that competition in capitalism is valued only for its results.[46] Such instrumentalism is a cause for concern.

As in sport, competition in capitalism needs to be directed toward noble goals. Just as lopsided victories fail to achieve the internal goods of sport, a capitalistic competition that results in one party having control of most or all the wealth would fail to achieve the internal goods of capitalism by unbalancing and then effectively terminating market action. So, winning is not and cannot be everything in any enlightened view of sport or capitalism. Cudd prefers a model of competition more reflective of Robert Simon's ideal of a "mutual quest for excellence"[47]—that is, a model of economic competition that is at the same time a form of cooperative interaction that has the effect of increasing the overall level of welfare in the society.[48]

In sport, the model evokes a noble rivalry between two or more athletes who inspire each other as well as other athletes in their sport to achieve at higher levels. The tennis rivalry between Chris Evert and Martina Navratilova is a good example. Not only did these two women push each other to ever higher levels of play but also they brought the quality and visibility of women's professional tennis to unprecedented levels, thereby benefiting the larger community. One might compare this with the business rivalry between computer giants Apple and Microsoft; it has resulted not only in great success for the rivals but also in better products for the industry and all of the consumers who use them.

As in sport, however, healthy competition depends on the existence of a level playing field and a willingness to play by the rules. A successful capitalist economy, Cudd argues, depends on a balance between firms, consumers, and workers, which in turn depends on fair competition.[49] The understanding of competition as the alienated and unbridled pursuit of victory is harmful both to sport and to capitalism, not least because it ignores the importance of cooperation and respect within healthy competition.[50]

Unfortunately, according to many commentators, an unhealthy and sometimes brutish win-at-all-costs attitude prevails in both sport and capitalism today—to the point where one seems inseparable from the other. Competitive sport in education is sometimes justified as a way of preparing youth for the cutthroat world of business, but this may amount more to a rationalization of people's brutish impulses than an explanation of sport's educational value.[51] If Cudd is right about the need for a model of cooperative pursuit of excellence in capitalism, however, sport may indeed be good preparation—but only as long as the principles of fair play are emphasized, rather than the end goal of victory.

In *Leftist Theories of Sport: A Critique and Reconstruction*, William Morgan rejects as too simple those theories that equate the logic and ethos of capitalism with the logic and ethos of sport.[52] Morgan is hardly apologizing for capitalism here—as we have already seen, he is harshly critical of it. In *Why Sports Morally Matter*, Morgan identifies "capitalism run amok" as our greatest social threat.[53] "The result," he says, "is that sports are treated more as means than ends, as pursuits with a value to be instrumentally calculated in the same fashion as any other commodity: by the money they fetch."[54] This hyper-instrumentalist capitalism is equally damaging to American business in Morgan's view.

However, sports are importantly *unlike* business, *unlike* capitalism, and even *unlike* politics in that they are fundamentally noninstrumental, gratuitous ends in themselves. Moreover, to really experience what makes sport great, you need to practice it under those gratuitous conditions.[55] From the outside, it may be hard to see sport as anything other than a capitalistic endeavor. Why does it exist, if not to make money? But from the inside, as a participant, and even from the perspective of an experienced and informed spectator, sport's unique and intrinsic value can be appreciated.

The point here is not that sport cannot be used as a means to market ends. It certainly has been instrumentalized this way in the modern world. The point, rather, is that it contains within itself the power to *resist* such instrumentalization. Morgan uses Alasdair MacIntyre's notion of a social practice (detailed in chapter 5) to distinguish between production and culture. Sport's status as a social and cultural practice means that it is more than just another means of production. Specifically, Morgan identifies sport's gratuitous logic—its contrivance of unnecessary obstacles—as the feature that most distinguishes it from everyday life and gives it its emancipatory potential, even while it is harnessed to capitalist goals.[56]

That is to say, sport has the power, by virtue of its noninstrumental character, to liberate us from the pervasive instrumentalism of capitalist society. Just as MacIntyre identified the power of social practices to resist the instrumental logic of the very institutions that govern them, Morgan identifies the power of sport to resist capitalistic forces.[57] More generally, sport's intrinsic gratuity may empower it to resist all kinds of exploitation—including political exploitation by any regime or ideologue.

The resistance is not automatic, however. Sport practitioners, as we discussed in chapter 10, must first of all *choose* to view sport as something more than merely a means to external ends. This would seem to require a change of culture, especially when athletes themselves are exploited by their sponsors and teams as means to institutional or financial ends. Morgan argues that sport, like religion and academia, should be kept separate from forces such as capitalism in order to protect its integrity.[58] Sports should be managed by communities of practitioners, past as well as present, who derive their authority from a shared understanding of the sport itself rather than wealth or bureaucratic power.[59]

This is not such a far-fetched prospect, especially in Olympic sports governed by international federations. The key is that those who manage sport recognize its intrinsic value and resist its instrumentalist abuse. The relationship between sport and political ideals—whether democracy, authoritarianism, communism, or capitalism—is too often one of exploitation and even abuse. But sport has a politics of its own that resists such exploitation. Jesse Owens's athletic triumph at the 1936 Berlin Olympic Games was not a triumph of democracy over fascism—after all, he faced serious discrimination in his home country. Nor does Eileen Gu's stardom in the 2022 Beijing Winter Games amount to an endorsement of Chinese government policies. Instead, these phenomena represent triumphant expressions of the intrinsic values of sport over instrumentalist political forces.

DISCUSSION QUESTIONS

1. Give a specific example from sport that illustrates the following features of democracy: voluntary participation, equality before the law, and collective responsibility for the enforcement of the law.
2. When athletes such as Kerri Strug take great personal risks for their national teams, do you view them as victims of fascist exploitation (i.e., sacrificing their rational self-interest for the good of the state) or as courageous leaders inspiring their communities? Does it matter whether the athlete is from a democratic country?
3. When an athlete represents a national team, does it imply an endorsement of that country's government policies? What about when an athlete represents a particular sponsor?
4. Point-shaving scandals in which athletes manipulate scores or even lose games in exchange for payment go at least as far back as the famous "Black Sox" scandal surrounding baseball's 1919 World Series. Does the phenomenon of point-shaving show that sport and capitalism are at odds? Why or why not?

NOTES

1. International Olympic Committee, "The New Exhibition at the Olympic Museum on the Theme of Hope," *Olympic.org*, March 28, 2011, accessed November 25, 2011, http:// www.olympic.org/.

2. According to the *Olympic Charter*, International Olympic Committee members swear to act independently of commercial and political interests (31); national Olympic committees are commanded to keep themselves free from political pressures (61); and political demonstrations (94) or speeches by politicians (99) are forbidden in Olympic venues.

3. Brundage, quoted in Richard Mandell, *The Nazi Olympics* (Champaign: University of Illinois Press, 1987), 289.

4. Heather L. Reid, "The Epicurean Spectator," *Sport, Ethics and Philosophy* 4, no. 2 (2010): 196.

5. The Roman writer Cassiodorus compares the Circus Maximus as a whole to a model of the universe. The twelve gates represent the signs of the zodiac, two-horse chariots are imitations of the moon, and four-horse chariots, the sun. The attendants who announce the heats play the role of the morning star, forerunner of the sun. The race's seven goals stand in for the days of the week, and the twenty-four heats represent the hours in a day. The turning posts signify the limits of east and west being orbited by the planetlike racing chariots. The dolphin sculpture at the center of the track represents the sea, and the Egyptian obelisks that mark the turns honor the sun and moon. "Variae," 3.51, in *The Roman Games*, ed. Alison Futrell (Malden, MA: Blackwell, 2006), 74.

6. Mandell, *Nazi Olympics*, 205.

7. Mandell, *Nazi Olympics*, xvii.

8. Stephen G. Miller, *Ancient Greek Athletics* (New Haven, CT: Yale University Press, 2004), 233.

9. Heather L. Reid, "Boxing with Tyrants," *Sport, Ethics and Philosophy* 4, no. 2 (2010): 146.

10. Peter J. Arnold, "Democracy, Education and Sport," *Journal of the Philosophy of Sport* 16 (1989): 100–110.

11. Miller, *Ancient Greek Athletics*, 233.

12. Donald G. Kyle, *Spectacles of Death in Ancient Rome* (New York: Routledge, 1998), 87.

13. Arnold, "Democracy, Education and Sport," 107.

14. Arnold, "Democracy, Education and Sport," 107.

15. Reid, "Boxing with Tyrants," 149.

16. Stephen G. Miller, "Naked Democracy," in *Polis and Politics*, ed. P. Flensted-Jensen and T. H. Nielsen (Copenhagen: Festschrift, 2000), 279. For more on the meaning of nudity in ancient sport and its relevance to modern antidoping policies, see Heather L. Reid and Georgios Mouratidis, "Naked Virtue: Ancient Athletic Nudity and the Olympic Ethos of *Aretē*," *Olympika* 29 (2020): 29–55.

17. Pericles, quoted in Thucydides, *History of the Peloponnesian War*, trans. B. Jowett (Oxford, UK: Clarendon, 1900), 2.37.1.

18. Arnold, "Democracy, Education and Sport," 101.

19. Miller, "Naked Democracy," 283.

20. Arnold, "Democracy, Education and Sport," 107.

21. Torbjörn Tännsjö, "Is Our Admiration of Sports Heroes Fascistoid?" *Journal of the Philosophy of Sport* 25, no. 1 (1998): 23.

22. Tännsjö, "Admiration of Sports Heroes," 23.

23. Goebbels, quoted in American Israeli Cooperative Enterprise, "The Nazi Olympics," Jewish Virtual Library, 2001, accessed November 25, 2011, http://www.jewishvirtuallibrary.org/.

24. Alfred Erich Senn, *Power, Politics and the Olympic Games* (Champaign, IL: Human Kinetics, 1999), 20.

25. The main Nazi newspaper, *Volkischer Beobachter*, quoted in Hugh Murray, "Review of Hoberman's *The Olympic Crisis*," *Journal of Sport History* 16, no. 1 (1989): 106.

26. Tännsjö, "Admiration of Sports Heroes," 25.

27. Tännsjö, "Admiration of Sports Heroes," 25.

28. International Olympic Committee, *Olympic Charter*, 18.

29. Tännsjö, "Admiration of Sports Heroes," 26.

30. Tännsjö, "Admiration of Sports Heroes," 28.

31. Claudio Tamburrini, "Sport, Fascism and the Market," *Journal of the Philosophy of Sport* 25, no. 1 (1998): 37.

32. Tamburrini, "Sport, Fascism and the Market," 39.

33. Tamburrini, "Sport, Fascism and the Market," 43.

34. M. Andrew Holowchak, "Fascistoid Heroism Revisited: A Deontological Twist in a Recent Debate," *Journal of the Philosophy of Sport* 32, no. 2 (2005): 104.

35. Holowchak, "Fascistoid Heroism Revisited," 102.

36. James Riordan, *Sport, Politics, and Communism* (Manchester, UK: Manchester University Press, 1991), 25.

37. Vladimir Lenin, quoted in Riordan, *Sport, Politics, and Communism*, 25.

38. Romanov, quoted in Robert Edelman, *Serious Fun: A History of Spectator Sports in the USSR* (New York: Oxford University Press, 1993), 122.

39. Susan Brownell, *Training the Body for China* (Chicago: University of Chicago Press, 1995), 26.

40. Lenin, quoted in Riordan, *Sport, Politics, and Communism*, 26.

41. Riordan, *Sport, Politics, and Communism*, 3.

42. W. Franke and B. Berendonk, "Hormonal Doping and Androgenization of Athletes: A Secret Program of the German Democratic Republic Government," *Clinical Chemistry* 43, no. 7 (1997): 1262–79. The story is also told in Steven Ungerleider, *Faust's Gold* (New York: St. Martin's, 2001).

43. Ann E. Cudd, "Sporting Metaphors: Competition and the Ethos of Capitalism," *Journal of the Philosophy of Sport* 34, no. 1 (2007): 52.

44. Cudd, "Sporting Metaphors," 56.

45. Cudd, "Sporting Metaphors," 58.

46. Cudd, "Sporting Metaphors," 60.

47. Robert Simon, *Fair Play: Sports, Values, and Society* (Boulder, CO: Westview, 1991), 23.

48. Cudd, "Sporting Metaphors," 62.

49. Cudd, "Sporting Metaphors," 62.

50. Cudd, "Sporting Metaphors," 66.

51. M. Andrew Holowchak and Heather L. Reid, *Aretism: An Ancient Sports Philosophy for the Modern Sports World* (Lanham, MD: Lexington, 2011), 193.

52. William J. Morgan, *Leftist Theories of Sport: A Critique and Reconstruction* (Champaign: University of Illinois Press, 1994), 29.

53. William J. Morgan, *Why Sports Morally Matter* (Abingdon, UK: Routledge, 2006), 7. Morgan also attributes obsession with winning to capitalism in *Sport and Moral Conflict* (Philadelphia: Temple University Press, 2020), 21.

54. Morgan, *Why Sports Morally Matter*, 26.

55. Morgan, *Why Sports Morally Matter*, 107.

56. Morgan, *Why Sports Morally Matter*, 45.

57. Morgan, *Why Sports Morally Matter*, 130.

58. Morgan, *Why Sports Morally Matter*, 204.

59. Morgan, *Why Sports Morally Matter*, 234.

Chapter 18

Internationalism, Globalization, and Peace

The ideal expression of harmoniously globalized sport may be the closing ceremony of the Olympic Games. Instead of marching into the stadium as orderly, uniformed regiments lined up behind their countries' flags, the athletes abandon national ranks and burst into the stadium in a colorful, cacophonous, joyful swarm. Gymnasts perch on the shoulders of weightlifters; victors offer an up-close look at their newly won medals; and Korean swimmers pose to have their pictures taken with American basketball stars. It is a welcome image of a peacefully globalized world, but it wasn't part of the original Olympic plan. Rather, it was the suggestion of a seventeen-year-old local boy named John Ian Wing during the 1956 Melbourne Games. "The march I have in mind is different than the one during the Opening Ceremony and will make these games even greater," stated Wing in a letter to Games officials. "During the march there will only be 1 NATION. War, politics and nationality will be all forgotten, what more could anybody want, if the whole world could be made as one nation."[1]

In fact, the world in 1956 and even athletes' behavior at the Games had been characterized less by harmony and more by simmering political tension and bitter national rivalry. Infamously, a violent water polo match between Russia and Hungary had to be canceled because of fighting that tinged the pool water with blood. Sport may seek to promote international harmony, but the reality often falls far short of the ideal.

The relationship between sport and globalization is simultaneously ancient, modern, and futuristic. It derives from the phenomenon of the ancient Olympic Games, the religious purpose of which had the (probably unintended) effect of pacifying and unifying diverse and often warring tribes in the ancient Mediterranean. It is replicated in the philosophical underpinnings of the modern Olympic Games, which were inspired by the ideals of the European enlightenment. And it is futuristic in that international and especially

Olympic sport functions as a kind of trailblazer for the political future of a globalized world. The term "globalization" refers primarily to "fundamental changes in the spatial and temporal contours of social existence."[2] For some time, advances in travel and communication technology have been "shrinking the world" and increasing contact between people despite geographical and cultural distance. Olympic-style sport has long been at the forefront of this process. Increased intercultural contact through trade and shipping even had a hand in the development of the ancient Olympic Games,[3] and developments in telegraph and train technology helped to motivate the first modern Olympic Games in 1896.[4] In recent years, we have experienced an acceleration of the globalization process, and predictably, international sport and the Olympic Games in particular seem to have embraced the phenomenon.

Spectators in every corner of the world can experience and discuss sporting events live through television and social media. More than three billion people watched the 2020 Tokyo Olympics.[5] Relatively cheap and increasingly quick transportation makes it easier for athletes to compete with competitors from different cultures and backgrounds long before they arrive at the Olympic Games. It has also made professional sports an exportable product. America's National Football League plays annually in Europe. The Tour de France routinely starts in foreign countries. Formula One car racing, once a strictly European affair, loads its cars and equipment on planes and flies off to compete at tracks as far flung as Bahrain, India, and Malaysia. Even when leagues don't travel, their athletes do. European football, American basketball, and even Japanese sumo include athletes from outside the geographical region, often from the other side of the globe. Indeed, sport may involve more interaction among culturally diverse people than any other human activity. In that sense, it can teach us something about globalization—but the lesson isn't always positive. What can we learn about globalization from sport, and how can sport's values be protected from its dangers?

GLOBALIZATION: THE REALITY

For all its potential benefits, globalization brings with it some serious problems, not least of which is its tendency to benefit the wealthy and powerful, who in turn often try to impose their cultural paradigm upon the rest of the world. As far back as 1950, the philosopher Martin Heidegger worried that the removal of distance between people, rather than increasing possibilities for richer interaction, would homogenize our differences into one bland experiential mass.[6] What would the Olympic Games be if the cultural diversity of the athletes was eliminated and the only difference that remained was the color of their uniforms? The philosophical vision behind the Olympic Games is cosmopolitan, based on a vision of global community. Its stated goal is "to place sport at the service of the harmonious development of humankind, with a view to promoting a peaceful society concerned with the preservation of human dignity."[7]

In practice, however, the global playing field of sport seems tilted toward the West and toward wealth. It is a mechanism well adapted for reinforcing existing power structures and promulgating the cultural values of the elite. The Olympic Movement, like most of international sport, is dominated by Western cultures, especially North America, Great Britain, and Western Europe. This is seen not only in the selection of host cities (including Tokyo 2020, the Summer Games have ventured just four times outside the West) but also in the cultural origin of the Olympic sports and, perhaps most visibly, in the ethnic makeup and political ideals of the International Olympic Committee (IOC) itself. The situation is changing quickly, however, not least because sport is more politically powerful in Asia than in the West.[8] Beijing is the first city to host both the Winter and Summer Olympic Games, very plausibly because they enhance China's profile on the global stage.

The Olympic Movement is sometimes accused of being Eurocentric, despite its universalistic ideals. This is not to say that the International Olympic Committee self-consciously privileges Europe or the West but, rather, that its perspective is conditioned by a European heritage and set of assumptions that are not always shared by the rest of the world. Indeed, the very *understanding* of what universalism is differs around the world. In the philosophical heritage of Europe, for example, following figures such as René Descartes and Immanuel Kant, there is a one-size-fits-all understanding of universal truth. Even complex ethical concepts are thought reducible to purely rational formulas that can be communicated to and applied by everyone.[9]

The philosophical heritage of China and most of Asia, by contrast, tends to think of universal truth as something inexpressible and able to accommodate multiple diverse expressions.[10] The problem is not that the world contains different and sometimes incompatible viewpoints. The problem is failing to acknowledge this. In the current era of globalization, where the wealthier and more powerful countries of North America and Europe tend to dominate economics and politics, it is easy for the West to think of its own heritage and values as the universal standard.

This phenomenon can be especially frustrating as it extends to political ideals. The political controversy surrounding the Games' return to Beijing in the winter of 2022 shows that sport cannot completely transcend politics. In the West, liberal democracy—in particular the rule of law—is often seen as the only acceptable form of government. Jim Parry observes that Western liberals who insist on individual autonomy (i.e., autonomy-based liberalism) cannot tolerate illiberal cultures (i.e., those who do not allow individual autonomy). Rights-based liberalism, by contrast, "protects all cultures that provide their members with a decent environment and life chances."[11] Even so, it is hard to know the appropriate limits of tolerance across cultural boundaries. Democratic politics presuppose feelings of trust, commitment, and belonging that are hard to find at an international level.[12]

At the same time, it can be difficult to sort out how much of one's resistance to foreign politics is merely cultural and how much is moral. Many believe morality itself is conditioned by cultural differences or that ethics is completely relative. But uncritical acceptance of all cultures (however abhorrent their practices) is not politically responsible. Parry sees it as a kind of concealed ethnocentrism. "It is not true that to respect other cultures is to abstain from criticizing them," he explains. "Rather relativism is a kind of disrespect—failing to apply to others (denying to others) the standards of justification and argument we apply to ourselves."[13] Tolerance of cultural difference, then, is only respectful up to a point. A community with no moral standards is not a community at all. What we need is a community that respects cultural difference while upholding some mutually acceptable standards of morality.

Sport may provide a model for this insofar as it promotes general principles of justice such as equal opportunity and fair play while making room for diverse styles of play. But even as individual athletic contests offer level playing fields and common starting lines, equal opportunity is far from reality in the global village. Huge economic disparities between countries and within countries challenge the ideals of distributive justice. National teams are far from equal in terms of facilities, coaching, medical support, and even funding for travel. The IOC commission on Olympic solidarity tries to overcome these international disparities by distributing a portion of the Games' television revenue to the national Olympic committees most in need, but the demand is huge, and the resources are limited.[14]

The euphoric spectacle of the Olympic Games should not lull us into thinking that global athletic competition is really fair. The tables that rank countries according to medals won, for example, embody none of the principles of fairness expected in sport. The teams do not have the same number of athletes, and they do not compete in all the same events. Further, Olympic medal table rankings correlate more reliably with gross domestic product (an indicator of size and wealth) than with any other variable.[15] Countries may proudly outperform their predicted rankings, and athletes from relatively small and poor countries, such as Jamaica, may come to dominate competitors from larger and wealthier neighbors—but this neither rectifies nor justifies globalization's tendency to favor those who, to use a popular sports metaphor, were "born on third base but thought they hit a triple."

It is also worth remembering, from a cultural point of view, that the traditions and ideals of the West, particularly Europe and the United States, continue to dominate Olympic sport. The image of women in skimpy bikinis playing beach volleyball in a stadium as a mixed crowd of males and females looks on may seem emblematic of a laid-back California attitude toward sports. In many cultures, however, such a spectacle is at best immodest and at worst grounds for serious punishment. It may be tempting to declare that such cultures repress women, deny human liberty, and need to rise to the standards of the international community. But there is a real risk that such sentiments are ultimately cultural hegemony—the imposition of the values of the dominant class upon all others.

Cultural hegemonists, further, need to be careful of what they wish for because the dominance of one particular culture—no matter how rich and valid it is—may cause the demise of other local cultures and of cultural diversity in general. It is hard to imagine *any* single culture being so great that no other cultures are needed or desired. I really love Italian cuisine, but I would never wish that all other cuisines should disappear, leaving me with only one choice. Just as we value a variety of culinary styles and traditions, we may value variety in other cultural products such as art, music, literature, and even sport.

MULTICULTURALISM: THE METHOD

Multiculturalism is a response to the phenomenon of globalization that emphasizes the appreciation of cultural diversity and seeks to preserve it, even while working toward common principles such as justice and fairness. Sport provides some good examples of this. In World Cup soccer, for example, teams from around the globe play according to a common set of rules while exhibiting a variety of culturally specific styles. As we saw in chapter 11, aesthetic rather than pragmatic values are often demonstrated in the play of teams from South America. Meanwhile, teams from Northern Europe are expected to play more conservatively and defensively. Part of the beauty of the tournament comes from the diversity of playing styles, and it would be a shame if pressure to win dictated a single successful style of play.

Globalization, like sport, carries this risk of homogenization not least because it diminishes the isolation of communities. Words and images from outside a community inevitably arrive inside, while words and images from inside a community inevitably make their way outside. The development of social media has accelerated this phenomenon and helped to attract international attention to previously ignored oppression in countries around the world. Sports, however, are also communities in themselves—practice communities—as we learned in chapter 5, and that means they can value diversity within their community even as its boundaries remain porous. In other words, the soccer community can value and preserve diverse styles of play even while promoting one common game.

It is important to distinguish between strangeness and difference. Declaring something strange is not just to say that it is different but also to express an emotional reaction of puzzlement or even repulsion. Valuing diversity, by contrast, involves expressing a reaction of acceptance and curiosity toward new and different ways. Within sport this means, first of all, the acceptance of multiple interpretations of a game. Let the South Americans play "beautiful" soccer while the Northern Europeans play conservative soccer, and try to ensure that diverse styles are encouraged by the rules. Let us not call one style of soccer strange—even if it turns out to lead to fewer victories. Let us try to appreciate the different values and objectives that different people bring to the game.

Multiculturalism may also mean temporarily setting aside intercultural debates to make athletic interaction possible. For example, some people regard the Muslim requirement of head coverings for women as a form of unjust oppression. The Iranian women's soccer team was forced to forfeit a qualifying match and give up its chance of competing in the 2012 Olympics because they insisted on wearing head scarves, which go against the international soccer federation's rules.[16] It is certain that the wearing of head scarves is not a violation of human rights, and the rule prohibiting them is not fundamental to the game of soccer. Why not make an exception to the rule, or rewrite it in such a way that allows Muslim women to play soccer and observe their religious beliefs? If the motivation for the rule is safety, work to develop a safe head scarf. A multicultural sporting community that values diversity must make an effort to encourage it.

The Olympic Movement seems to value cultural diversity, but it must not become so narrow in its interpretation of its own ideals that they become an obstacle. Jim Parry maintains that the *concept* of Olympism, understood at a high level of generality, may admit of diverse interpretations or *conceptions* that bring the concept to life in particular contexts.[17] Multiculturalism in the Olympic Movement must be a concerted effort. Not only should athletes, officials, and IOC members represent a variety of cultural backgrounds and perspectives but the program of sports itself should show more cultural variety. Judo and tae kwon do are the only two sports on the current Olympic program with a non-Western origin, and even they had to be adapted to a Western-style scoring system that chooses clear winners and losers.

New sports are considered for the Olympic program based on such criteria as history and tradition, universality, and popularity. This system seems to set the cart before the horse in multicultural terms because sports tend to become popular and universal *after* they are accepted into the Olympics. Parry suggests a compensatory policy according to which one popular sport from each continent would be included in the official program.[18] This would combat globalization's tendency to homogenize sport while serving the Olympic Movement's cultural education goals. It is a multicultural solution to one of globalization's problems.

SUSTAINABILITY: THE COMMON CAUSE

One thing that underpinned the ancient Olympic Games' success at unifying and pacifying diverse Hellenic tribes was the idea that they were working toward a common cause. In their case, the cause was religious. As we saw in chapter 1, the ancient games were a form of worship designed to propitiate common gods and, therefore, receive such collective benefits as abundant harvests and healing from illness. This worthwhile religious purpose inspired a ban on attacking worshippers in transit to the site, known as the *ekecheiria*. In some years, the *ekecheiria* was extended to a temporary suspension of military hostilities.[19] Even when wars continued, however, delegations from the tribes could meet safely at Olympia, and for that reason it was a good place to negotiate peace treaties.

In fact, all kinds of intellectuals and politicians met and debated common issues at the ancient Olympic Games. Many of the most famous orations dealt precisely with Panhellenic unity and the importance of working together rather than against one another.[20] An Olympic Truce is still called every four years, and the United Nations passes a resolution endorsing it, but its success in stopping wars is—at best—limited. The Olympic Games would benefit from a common global project akin to the religious cause that united the ancient Greeks. The issue of environmental sustainability seems perfect, and indeed, it has been adopted by the movement as a third objective alongside sport and culture.

Sustainable development can be defined as a strategy that "meets the needs of the present without compromising the ability of future generations to meet their own needs."[21] Given the global effect of environmental degradation, sustainability requires a global response. In the words of William Scheuerman, "A dogmatic insistence on the sanctity of national sovereignty risks constituting a cynical fig leaf for irresponsible activities whose impact extends well beyond the borders of those countries most directly responsible."[22] Common ground among nations, including some agreement about the nature of moral responsibility, must be found if the world is to find an effective solution to its environmental challenges.

A system of liberal democracy confined to nation-states is not well placed to deal with this problem. Indeed, continued environmental degradation potentially erodes democracy by undermining its legitimacy and perceived effectiveness.[23] This may seem an issue far removed from sport and Olympism, but after the United Nations, the Olympic Games may provide one of the best forums for international discussion and debate. The IOC's Sustainability and Legacy Commission seeks to make the Olympic Games a model of eco-responsibility, not least by including environmental concerns as part of the process for selecting host cities and subjecting the Games to scrutiny from nongovernmental organizations (NGOs) and the media.[24]

Of course, modeling is a form of education, and the practice of sport can itself better model an ideal of sustainability. Observing that the Olympic motto *citius, altius, fortius* (faster, higher, stronger) suggests unlimited growth in human performance, despite the limited nature of human bio-motor abilities, Sigmund Loland sees a reflection of the ecological crisis, which is caused by the pursuit of unlimited growth of wealth and population on a planet with limited natural resources.[25] Sports that focus on absolute records, such as the 100-meter dash, the 50-meter freestyle swim, or the kilometer time trial in cycling, are the least sustainable because they are the least complex. They try to replicate identical testing conditions and leave pure performance as the only variable. It is no coincidence that these sports also have an increased incidence of drug use and other performance-enhancing techniques. Sports such as basketball, where a variety of skills and techniques are demanded, are more sustainable.

Loland sees a solution to this problem in increasing the diversity and complexity of less sustainable sports.[26] For example, why not vary the surface and other external conditions that sprinters face? Why not test the swimmers not only in pools but also in open water? Rather than ranking athletes by single-record performances, why not keep track of their consistency over a season under different conditions? Rethinking sport would in this way give us a chance not only to improve sustainability but also to address collateral issues such as economic disparity. Why not privilege sports that require less equipment and facilities, eliminating those, such as equestrian sports, accessible only to the wealthy? The guiding principle for reforming sport need not be original. It can be intrinsic sporting values such as fairness; they just need to be rethought globally. It is encouraging that the Olympic motto was modified in 2021 to add a final word: "together."[27]

The values required to implement environmental sustainability integrate well with the internal virtues and values of sport. In his foreword to the Olympic Movement's *Agenda 21* statement on sport for sustainable development, Klaus Topfer of the United Nations Environment Program (UNEP) points out that environment is like sport in that it knows no borders, transcends ideological cleavages, and does not recognize artificial distinctions between North and South or East and West, but is one and indivisible.[28] It is not enough to say that sport, like the environment, needs to be open to everyone. Foundational sports principles such as equal opportunity and the level playing field need to be reconceived globally. This entails an effort to overcome social inequities by working to improve the socioeconomic condition of the least advantaged.

The first objective of *Agenda 21* states that "sustainable development is only conceivable if accompanied by the satisfaction of those cultural and material needs that are essential for all individuals to live with dignity and play a positive role in the society to which they belong."[29] Likewise, *Agenda 21* asks sport to battle social exclusion by "promoting sports activities by groups of individuals who are excluded from them for reasons of economic resources, sex, race or caste."[30] Not only is inclusion part of the logic of sport—because the most able victor can only be found if all candidates compete—but also it is fundamental to sustainability, which demands that resources are managed in a way that all persons are able to live with dignity. Sport's international visibility puts it in an ideal position to model sustainable values—values that in any case are characteristic of sport.

PEACE: THE GOAL

The political goal of the Olympic Movement and, ultimately, all international sport is peace. This goal is viewed as an inheritance from the ancient Olympic Games that, as we have already seen, declared an effective truce to protect travelers and played an important role in the unification and internal pacification of the Hellenes. I have argued that this association between the Olympic Games and peace was probably more a by-product of the social dynamics of sport and human contact than a conscious goal of the ancient festival.[31]

Specifically, the athletic festival required people to set aside their conflicts, at least for a limited period of time. It required them to treat strangers and rivals as equals—at least with respect to the rules of a particular contest. And it encouraged them to tolerate their differences, at least well enough to inhabit a small river valley at close quarters during the summer heat. In short, the ancient Olympic Games used sport to motivate people to make a special effort to live together in a small space. Insofar as globalization represents the virtual shrinking of social space, the values of Olympic sport may help us to deal with this challenge. But what does this really mean in a practical sense?

The first element is the demarcation of a common space within which governmental conflicts are put aside. As we saw in the comparison of sport and art in chapter 6, such extraordinary spaces are part and parcel of play activities—that is, they are set off from the ordinary workaday world. In ancient Olympia, the relevant space was religious, a sanctuary bounded by a wall known as the *Altis*. The modern Games use decoration and pageantry—in particular, the opening and closing ceremonies along with the burning of the Olympic flame—to transform whole cities, at least temporarily, into special kinds of places. Anyone who has ever attended an Olympic Games can attest to this change. In the future, the relevant space may be virtual rather than physical. The important thing, however, is that it is recognized as a place where worldly conflicts are temporarily set aside and a special effort is made to interact both competitively and cooperatively despite human differences. Hopefully, we will come to appreciate these differences, or at least to learn from them, as we occupy this intercultural space. Most important, as on the field of sport, we must treat others as equals under the rules no matter our personal feelings of like and dislike.

Critics point out that as a peacemaking endeavor, sport is limited—at best—to the psychological dimension.[32] Even this aspect of peace promotion could be better served by engaging athletes, coaches, officials, and even spectators in it. As Bruce Kidd observes, very few athletes are encouraged to take part in the extraordinarily rich opportunities the Olympic Movement provides for cultural education and exchange.[33] Athletes with early events routinely skip the opening ceremony and often leave town before the closing ritual. Many refuse to live in the Olympic Village, which itself could be better integrated by having athletes of different countries room together. Some are even advised by medical staff to avoid shaking hands with competitors for fear of contracting illness. The Olympic Games staged during the COVID-19 pandemic incorporated whole new levels of isolation—yet, somehow, participants still traded pins and made friends.

The obvious obstacle is that many athletes are so focused on their performance that they eschew anything that might interfere with it, no matter how culturally valuable. Ironically, some of the star professional athletes for whom the Olympics is not a primary athletic objective seem to take best advantage of the cultural opportunities of the Games. It is not all the athletes' fault, however. As Kidd points out, "Relatively little effort is made to use the common language and experience of Olympic sports as a first step toward helping participants consciously navigate the divides of culture, be they structured by religion, ethnicity, class, or gender."[34]

As a solution, Kidd proposes an "Olympic curriculum" that would focus not just on competition but also on education, emphasizing intrinsic sport values such as fair play; including competitors from different backgrounds; instructing athletes on the health risks of intensive training; cultivating an awareness of the history, geography, and environmental influence of their sports; and developing the skills of intercultural communication, including foreign language. The curriculum would include community service, and honors and ranks would be based on overall achievement rather than mere athletic performance.[35]

Those who find such a transformation of sport implausible should ask themselves why, given the curricular demands already placed upon athletes in universities. The obvious objection is, again, that elite athletes are too focused on performance to take advantage of the intercultural opportunities that international sports provide. This, of course, begs the question of the *purpose* of international sport. If its goal is peace and if its peace-promoting ability depends on intercultural communication, why are we neglecting that in order to achieve ever greater performances? What good does adding another centimeter to the pole vault record really do for society? If it is, indeed, too much to ask of elite athletes to focus on high-level sport and peace politics, too, perhaps the Olympic Movement is to some degree wasted on them. The Youth Olympic Games, inaugurated in 2010, realizes several aspects of Kidd's educational vision by attempting to educate participants about Olympic philosophy and the realities of elite sport both within and alongside athletic competition.[36]

Another successful form of peace-promoting education is offered by the International Olympic Academy (IOA). This organization, housed in ancient Olympia, Greece, brings together students from all over the world to live and play together for extended periods each summer. I have participated in the academy's session for postgraduates on several occasions, and I can say from experience that the peace-promoting ideals of international sport are ably disseminated there.

First of all, the academy is an extraordinarily beautiful campus set apart from ordinary life at the foot of the ancient Mount Chronion. Students know to put aside their differences while they are there. Roommates often come from countries with a history of conflict and rivalry. Mornings are generally spent in the classroom; afternoons involve various sports activities. Students treat each other as equals in these activities, regardless of their differences in academic preparation or language capacity and their level of athletic ability. At the IOA, unlike the Olympic Games, men and women compete together. The evenings are devoted to cultural exchange, with students presenting their home countries' history, traditions, food, and drink. They don't always like one another, but they learn to live together and even appreciate their differences, often forming close bonds that last well beyond their time at the academy.

The point here is that sport's response to globalization need not be limited to the utopian image of the Olympic closing ceremony. More specific things can be done. Globalization provides not just great opportunities for sport but also serious challenges. A key sport value is equal opportunity, but globalization has historically favored the rich and powerful. Sport needs to be intentional about countering this tendency by providing opportunities for those less fortunate and by including those conventionally excluded. Another key risk of globalization is the loss of diversity, the homogenization of sport and culture more generally. Sports can be understood metaphysically as communities, and as communities, sports are capable of valuing and promoting diversity. Soccer should continue to celebrate different styles of play, and multisport festivals such as the Olympic Games should seek to promote nontraditional sports. Further, cultural differences, such as Muslim women wearing appropriate head scarves, should be tolerated so long as these differences do not interfere with the fundamental principles of sport.

Sport should be a partner and a model for global projects such as sustainable development. This entails less emphasis on records at the narrow end of the sport-selection cone and more emphasis on inclusive participation at the wide end of the cone. Finally, sport should work toward peace by providing an appropriate space where people can meet as equals, setting aside conflicts and tolerating—maybe even celebrating—their differences. Athletes should be encouraged to take advantage of these opportunities for cultural exchange; and at the same time, these opportunities should not be limited to athletes. As the example of the International Olympic Academy shows, the international political potential of sport may be best expressed through the play and interaction of nonelite athletes or even nonathletes who nevertheless can take part in the Olympic dream.

DISCUSSION QUESTIONS

1. Beach volleyball has relaxed its requirement that women compete in bikinis. This shows concern for cultural diversity, in particular, the more modest standards of dress found in many Muslim countries. Does such a change reflect or resist the forces of globalization? Do you think it is good for the sport? For women?
2. Multiculturalism in sport means valuing diversity, not only in styles of play but also in the variety of sports offered—but space and funding are always limited. Looking at the list of sports offered by your school or those on the Olympic program, identify one sport to remove and one to add in order to increase diversity.
3. Making global sport more sustainable means making it more complex and less expensive. Soccer is a great example of a complex and inexpensive sport. How could other sports change to become more sustainable? Are some sports simply unsustainable?

4. The examples of competitors being discouraged from shaking hands or living in the athletes' village at the Olympics shows how the peace-promoting potential of the Olympic Games can be compromised by athletes' overemphasizing performance. What should Olympic committees do to resolve this problem? Should Olympians be trained and selected for their ability as ambassadors as well as athletes?

NOTES

1. John Ian Wing, "Letter Saved the Games," National Library of Australia, Papers of Sir Wilfred Kent Hughes, NS 4856/series 19, accessed December 5, 2011, http://www.johnwing.co.uk/.

2. William Scheuerman, "Globalization," in *The Stanford Encyclopedia of Philosophy*, ed. Edward N. Zalta, Summer 2010, accessed December 5, 2011, http://plato.stanford.edu/.

3. Heather L. Reid, "Sport, Philosophy, and the Quest for Knowledge," *Journal of the Philosophy of Sport* 36, no. 1 (2009): 42.

4. Baron Pierre de Coubertin, quoted in Foundation for the Hellenic World, "The Revival of the Ancient Olympic Games," From Ancient Olympia to Athens of 1896, accessed December 12, 2011, http://www.fhw.gr/.

5. International Olympic Committee, "Tokyo 2020 Watched by More Than 3 Billion People," Olympic.org, December 12, 2021, accessed February 16, 2022, https://olympics.com/ioc/news/olympic-games-tokyo-2020-watched-by-more-than-3-billion-people.

6. Martin Heidegger, *Poetry, Language, Thought* (New York: Harper & Row, 1971), 166.

7. International Olympic Committee, *The Olympic Charter* (Lausanne, Switzerland: IOC, 2021), 8.

8. Victor D. Cha, *Beyond the Final Score: The Politics of Sport in Asia* (New York: Columbia University Press, 2009), 10.

9. A key example is Kant's categorical imperative; for a detailed argument, see Heather L. Reid, "East to Olympia: Recentering Olympic Philosophy between East and West," *Olympika: The International Journal of Olympic Studies* 19 (2010): 59–79.

10. Reid, "East to Olympia," 61.

11. Jim Parry, "Sport and Olympism: Universals and Multiculturalism," *Journal of the Philosophy of Sport* 33, no. 2 (2006): 194.

12. Scheuerman, "Globalization."

13. Parry, "Sport and Olympism," 197.

14. International Olympic Committee, "Olympic Solidarity Commission," *Olympics.com*, 2022, accessed February 16, 2022, http://www.olympics.com/.

15. Andrew B. Bernard and Meghan R. Busse, "Who Wins the Olympic Games: Economic Resources and Medal Totals," *Review of Economics and Statistics* 86, no. 1 (2004): 413–17.

16. Thomas Erdbrink, "FIFA Bans Headscarves for Iranian Women's Soccer Team," *Washington Post*, June 6, 2011, http://www.washingtonpost.com/.

17. Parry, "Sport and Olympism," 191.

18. Parry, "Sport and Olympism," 202.

19. Nigel Crowther, "The Ancient Olympics and Their Ideals," in *Athletika: Studies on the Olympic Games and Greek Athletics*, ed. W. Decker and I. Weiler (Hildesheim, Germany: Weidemann, 2004), 11.

20. For more on this aspect of the ancient Olympic Games, see Heather L. Reid, "The Political Heritage of the Olympic Games: Relevance, Risks, and Possible Rewards," *Sport, Ethics and Philosophy: Special Issue on the Olympic Games* 6, no. 2 (2012): 108–20.

21. World Commission on Environment and Development, *Our Common Future* (Oxford: Oxford University Press, 1987), 8.

22. Scheuerman, "Globalization."

23. Scheuerman, "Globalization."

24. International Olympic Committee, "Sustainability and Legacy Commission," *Olympics.com*, 2022, accessed February 16, 2022, http://www.olympics.com/.

25. Sigmund Loland, "Record Sports: An Ecological Critique and a Reconstruction," *Journal of the Philosophy of Sport* 27, no. 2 (2001): 130.

26. Loland, "Record Sports," 138.

27. International Olympic Committee, "The Olympic Motto," *Olympics.com*, updated 2021, accessed February 21, 2022, https://olympics.com/ioc/olympic-motto.

28. International Olympic Committee (IOC), *Olympic Movement's Agenda 21: Sport for Sustainable Development* (Lausanne, Switzerland: Author, 1999).

29. IOC, *Agenda 21*, 23–24.

30. IOC, *Agenda 21*, 26–27.

31. Heather L. Reid, "Olympic Sport and Its Lessons for Peace," *Journal of the Philosophy of Sport* 33, no. 2 (2006): 205–13.

32. For a critical overview, see Ramón Spaaij and Cindy Burleson, eds., *The Olympic Movement and the Sport of Peacemaking* (New York: Routledge, 2013).

33. Bruce Kidd, "Taking the Rhetoric Seriously: Proposals for Olympic Education," *Quest* 48 (1996): 85.

34. Kidd, "Taking the Rhetoric Seriously," 86.

35. Kidd, "Taking the Rhetoric Seriously," 89.

36. For more on the philosophy behind the Youth Olympic Games, see Sigmund Loland, "The Youth Olympic Games and the Olympic Ideal," in *The Youth Olympic Games*, ed. Dag Vidar Hanstad, Milena M. Parent, and Barrie Houlihan (New York: Routledge, 2014).

Conclusion

Ten Intrinsic Values of Sport

When I teach courses in the philosophy of sport, I usually ask students to introduce themselves by describing their sports experience. At the beginning, it seems to them as though the differences between their sports will yield big differences in their philosophies of sport, but by the end even the football players and dance team members have discovered how much they have in common. Despite the metaphysical difficulties in defining sport, despite the ethical ambiguity of concepts such as fair play, and despite the diversity of political beliefs that link themselves with sport, the philosophy of sport does lead us toward some unifying ideas. Although it might be incorrect to say that "sport" has certain values, I think we can say that people who value sport and understand it philosophically should also value certain things because they are somehow intrinsic to sport. As a conclusion to this exploration of the philosophy of sport, let me attempt to gather a variety of ideas from the text and assemble them into a list of ten intrinsic values of sport.

AUTOTELICITY

We begin, as Plato and Aristotle did, with an appreciation of sport's auto-telicity—the notion that it is (at least ideally) an end in itself, done for its own sake, without the need of external purpose or justification. In sport, we invent unnecessary obstacles and try to overcome them just because it makes the activity possible. This internal purposelessness of sport—what scholars sometimes call its "gratuitous nature"—resists attempts to reduce it to nothing more than a means toward such external goods as power, fame, or fortune. Match-fixing scandals such as the one we discussed in sumo, as well as similar cases in soccer and cricket, are not condemned because players profit; they are *already* professionals. The problem is that such scandals instrumentalize the game, selling out its internal principles for the sake of external goods. A true professional, one who values and identifies with a particular activity, will

275

not reduce that activity to mere means toward other ends. Like art, poetry, and staring at sunsets, sport is an activity that should be valued primarily for its own sake.

BOUNDARIES

The match-fixing scandals' violation of autotelicity can also be understood as a violation of sport's boundaries—a transgression of the limits that mark it off from everyday practicalities and of the rule-based constraints that carve out a space dedicated to open responsiveness. When a referee blows the whistle three times to mark the end of a soccer game, we know that a special piece of time has come to a close and, with it, the extraordinary senses of freedom and possibility that characterize sport. Real boundaries, such as whistles and court outlines, act like theater curtains or temple doors, as signals to adopt a particular attitude or to "frame" the upcoming experience—whether as an athlete, an official, or a spectator—in a special way. By keeping sport conceptually separate from the ordinary activities of life, we can temporarily relieve ourselves from workaday concerns and carve out a space within which to test and transcend our normal limitations, to explore the best of ourselves.

FREEDOM

Within the boundaries of sport, we also discover a paradoxical sense of freedom. This freedom derives not from the absence of constraints; to play a sport we must subject ourselves to an intricate network of rules. Because we voluntarily accept these rules, however, we gain the psychological feeling of freedom. Further, because we collectively accept these rules, the community of sport achieves the liberty identified by John Stuart Mill as foundational to creativity and thriving. We discovered that the absence of constraints in sport—such as the repeal or lax enforcement of doping regulations—can diminish athletes' sense of freedom, in that case by making them feel coerced to dope. Meanwhile, the rules' definition of simple tasks, such as running 100 meters, gives us the freedom to go all out within that task—setting the stage for the perfect alignment of skill and ability that causes the extraordinary experience of freedom known as "flow" or being in "the zone."

CHALLENGE

Many of sport's internal benefits derive from the challenges it presents. Sport challenges are characteristically unnecessary and contrived (to get from the start to the finish line of a 400-meter race, it is hardly necessary to run around the track). But it is precisely sport's prescription of artificial inefficiencies that creates the challenges that produce such goods as enjoyable absorption in the game and the cultivation of virtues. Valuing challenge in sport entails a sincere effort to win because competitors provide much of the challenge for their opponents. But victory should not be sought through technological efficiencies that reduce athlete agency. As the saga of the hydrodynamic swimsuits showed, undermining the inherent challenges of a sport potentially erodes its value. It is the process of training and hard work that gives the faster swimming time its worth—gaining the same thing instantly by a magic suit or any other trick ultimately robs the performance of its value (and, once the trick is widely used, of its exclusivity) by undermining the challenge inherent in the sport.

FAIRNESS

We observed, in fact, that it was illogical to seek equipment advantages in sport because, once such an action is willed universally, according to Immanuel Kant's categorical imperative, any advantage gained is neutralized immediately. Equal opportunity and reward according to merit—the basic principles of fairness—are inscribed in sport's rules and logic. Winning can only imply athletic superiority if the contest itself was fair and no potentially superior athlete was excluded from it. For this reason, competition classifications based on race, sex, and disability can challenge sports' fairness or they can enhance it by making the competition closer. Fairness is also a property of human beings and communities. In golf, we found players calling penalties on themselves to safeguard the game's fairness—a tradition that derives from community expectations as much as individual virtue. Other sports communities tolerate or even encourage intentional fouls, deception of referees, or deliberately mismatched contests that risk humiliating the losers. As baseball's "pine-tar incident" showed, fairness is an ethos that must go beyond written rules in order to express a human appreciation of the nature of a good contest.

UNCERTAINTY

Uncertainty of outcome is a primary quality of good contests. Mismatched competition was condemned in activities as diverse as Roman gladiatorial fights, martial arts matchups, and high-school basketball. We saw that sincere doubt about the outcome was a key innovation of Olympic-style sport in ancient Greece—one that might have inspired the advent of philosophy. Further, uncertainty is what absorbs us in sport and makes it a welcome relief from everyday predictability. College football teams often schedule much weaker opponents for the first game of the season for strategic reasons, but these games are rarely good experiences for the teams or the spectators. Crowds often leave stadiums once the outcome of a game seems decided. Insofar as the aesthetic value of the event depends on a sense of possibility, that value diminishes as the predictability of outcome increases. That 2006 Rose Bowl where my father had hoped for a blowout turned out to be a closely fought game that wasn't decided until inside the final minute. We got the "good game" he didn't want (and the result he didn't want), but the enduring uncertainty made it a great contest.

LEARNING

Uncertainty is also the foundation of learning, as Socrates's famous insistence on his ignorance so ably shows. Philosophy begins in wonder and uncertainty and, like sport, it seeks truth and knowledge. Just as scholars test theories through questioning and scientists test drugs using double-blind trials, sport tests athletic performance using the open and impartial mechanism of contest. So, sport itself is a kind of truth-seeking process, but we also learn things through the experience of sport. They say you can learn a lot about people from the way they play games—we can also learn about ourselves. In sport, we learn experientially, in a holistic way that integrates mind and body. Ethical concepts are manifest in behavior, giving sport the educational potential to function as a moral laboratory. The world is even learning from sport about globalization. But learning from sport is not automatic, and its lessons are not always positive. Education through sport can transcend the theoretical, but it has to be intentional. We need to make learning a primary goal of sport—one not so easily sacrificed in the name of increased performance.

EXCELLENCE

The difference between performance and excellence is important to understand. As Plato's distinction between *technē* (skill) and *aretē* (virtue) showed, the former derives its value from the latter. In other words, the tennis player's ability to hit a high-speed serve is less humanly valuable than the humility, courage, self-control, and persistence that were required to achieve that skill. Excellence in sport demands virtue; in fact, virtue and excellence are both translations of *aretē*, the Greek ideal prized in athletics and education. *Aretē* is a disposition for good actions that must, on Aristotle's terms, be actualized through their performance. Being the best and outperforming all others, what Homer called *aristeia*, is valued in sport not because sport-specific skills are worthwhile but, rather, because the virtues that contribute to that performance can be transferred to other human endeavors. As my student-athlete example showed, positive qualities exhibited in sport such as focus and endurance are not virtues at all if the athlete is incapable of exercising them in other activities. Further, sport may perpetuate injustice by attributing social worth to merely athletic excellence. When athletes strive for Olympic gold medals, what they really should seek is to become the kind of person who deserves the gold medal—one with virtues that can produce good in many activities and not merely sport.

COMMUNITY

The cultivation of virtue through sport was further shown to be a community activity. Alasdair MacIntyre's theory of social practices reveals the important sense in which sports are ultimately communities. We acquire virtue through sport not so much by training and improving our individual performances but, rather, by participating actively and thoughtfully in sports communities with histories, traditions, and shared standards of excellence. Becoming a great cyclist involves more than pedaling a bike: you must enter into a community and learn its history and standards of excellence; you must humbly subject yourself to coaching from recognized experts; and you must take responsibility for the effect your own actions have upon that community. This community aspect of sport contrasts with what William Morgan identified as the hyper-individualism that some athletes exhibit with the encouragement of the market. Pretensions of athletic autonomy are quickly unmasked. What would a hotshot sports star be without his team? Without his youth league coaches? Without the great players of the past who brought his sport into the public eye? Understanding sports as communities with sport-specific values allows them to resist the instrumentalizing tendencies of institutions and to exhibit such values as diversity, equality, opportunity, and collectively enjoyed internal goods.

BEAUTY

It is notoriously difficult to articulate the internal goods of sport because their appreciation depends upon a sport-specific understanding acquired primarily through the experience of participation. In this sense, they are not unlike beauty—indeed, beauty may be an appropriately amorphous description of an intrinsic value with diverse expressions. We have discussed a variety of examples, from the record flight of the Olympic ski jumper, to Roger Bannister's four-minute mile, to Rulon Gardner's retirement gesture in Athens, and to the simple sense of achievement gained through perfecting a spike move in volleyball. We have also discussed events that were less than beautiful—often because they lacked "fairness," a word with aesthetic as well as moral connotations: Ben Johnson's steroid-laced sprint victory, Diego Maradona's "hand of god" goal, and Sarra Besbes's refusal to raise her foil. Beauty in sport is not just a matter of aesthetic pleasure. As Seneca's account of ancient Roman games and the example of Michael Johnson's duck-like running style show, athletic beauty derives at least partly from a philosophical understanding of sport.

In a sense, all of the values listed above relate to beauty in sport. Sport's beauty derives partly from its autotelicity; like most of the arts and even some sciences such as philosophy, it is practiced primarily for its own sake. Part of sport's beauty comes from its framing—from our marking it off from ordinary life and expecting extraordinary, wonderful things to happen within that frame. There is beauty in the freedom experienced as a heightened awareness of possibility, or perhaps through the flow of a perfectly executed movement, such as Nadia Comaneci's "perfect 10" performance on the uneven parallel bars.

Fairness can be a synonym of beauty, and it reveals the ethical aspect of aesthetic value; the ancient Greek ideal of *kalokagathia* linked beauty and goodness not just in art but also in athletics and education. Uncertainty gives sport its dramatic beauty, perhaps more authentically than plays or literature because the final outcome is truly unknown. Sport's drama, in turn, is central to our learning; an aesthetic appreciation of virtuous action in sport is important for moral education. Athletic beauty is not merely skin deep but ideally a reflection of the virtues that training and competition demand. Finally, there is beauty in the athletic community—not least in the image that international sport can give us of a harmonious yet diverse global community.

The philosophical study of sport not only can help us to learn and explain important concepts in metaphysics, ethics, epistemology, and social-political philosophy but also gives us a better understanding of a significant human activity. People like to say that sport mirrors society, and it is true that sport contains myriad reflections of human nature—both good and bad. What we have learned, however, is that sport also has its own nature and logic—one that deserves to be understood, appreciated, and protected so that sport can be not only a significant human activity but a meaningful and valuable one as well.

Glossary

amateurism. The belief that activities such as sport should be performed out of love for the game rather than any external reward, especially money. Contrast **professionalism**.

aretē. Greek word for excellence, both mental and physical, often translated as virtue.

aristeia. Heroic idea of "being the best and outdoing all others," often cited in Homer.

athla. The labors or feats of heroes such as Heracles, which are imitated in athletic competition.

autotelic. Quality of being an end in itself; needing no external purpose or justification. Contrast **instrumentalism**.

broad internalism. Ethical approach to sport that takes its guiding principles to be embedded within sport itself. Contrast **conventionalism**.

consequentialist. Category of ethical theories, such as utilitarianism, that focus on the consequences of actions rather than principles or virtues. Contrast **virtue ethics**; **deontological**.

constitutive rules. Rules thought to define a game and distinguish it from other games.

conventionalism. Metaphysical approach to sport that understands it as a social agreement or convention without universal or eternal principles; linked with the ethical approach known as social practice theory. Contrast **essentialism, formalism**.

cosmopolitanism. Theory that people should consider themselves citizens of a world community, in addition to their particular nation or state.

deontological. Category of ethical theories, such as that of Immanuel Kant, which focus on moral laws or principles rather than virtues or consequences. Contrast **virtue ethics**; **consequentialist**.

dualism. Theory that minds and bodies are metaphysically distinct. Usually the body is thought to be material; the mind, immaterial.

ekecheiria. The ancient Greek ban on attacking travelers to the Olympic Games, which sometimes extended to a suspension of military hostilities known as the Olympic Truce.

empiricism. Theory that knowledge is acquired primarily through the senses. Contrast **rationalism**.

epistemology. Branch of philosophy that deals with knowledge and belief.

essentialism. Metaphysical approach that takes sport to have its own distinctive essence. Contrast **conventionalism**.

ethics. Branch of philosophy that examines theories of right and wrong, also known as moral philosophy.

ethos. The social expectations and conventions within sport, as opposed to its formal rules.

eudaimonia. Aristotle's term for an ethical person's final good or end, a happiness or thriving that can only be understood in terms of a complete lifetime.

external goods. Goods, such as wealth or fame, that are not specific to a particular practice but can be achieved through a variety of activities. Contrast **internal goods**.

fair play. A sport-specific understanding of justice often taken to be a deontological principle.

flow. A feeling of perfect control and effortlessness; also described as being "in the zone."

formalism. The understanding of sports as games defined exclusively in terms of their formal rules; linked to metaphysical essentialism. Contrast **broad internalism**.

globalization. The process of change in travel and communication technology that increases contact between people despite geographical and cultural distance.

golden mean. The middle state between excess and deficiency that represents virtue in Aristotle's ethics; for example, courage is the golden mean between foolhardiness and cowardice.

gymnastikē. Greek word for athletic training and exercise associated with the gymnasium.

hegemony. The imposition of a more powerful class's values and worldview upon others as a societal norm.

holism. A metaphysical approach that focuses on the connections between things rather than their distinctions. Contrast **dualism**.

hylomorphism. Metaphysical theory of persons based on the Greek *hyle* (matter) and *morphē* (the form or structure given to matter by the mind) that understands sport in terms of the mind reshaping the body to achieve excellence (*aretē*).

idealism. Metaphysical theory that affirms only the existence of ideas, denying that of matter.

instrumentalism. The belief that games should be used to achieve external goods, such as prizes and salaries. Contrast **autotelic**.

internal goods. Goods experienced through achievements according to the standards of excellence within a particular social practice. Contrast **external goods**.

internal logic of sport. The characteristic of setting up unnecessary or gratuitous obstacles for the sake of creating games—as in soccer's prohibition on handling the ball.

isēgoria. Greek word for equal opportunity, a concept that sport and democracy share.

isonomia. Greek word for equality before the law, a concept that sport and democracy share.

kalokagathia. Educational ideal of ancient Greek gymnasia that combines beauty and goodness.

logical incompatibility thesis. The claim that one cannot intentionally break a rule and play a game at the same time. Because games are just sets of rules, according to formalism, intentionally violating a rule amounts to intentionally failing to play the game.

lusory attitude. In Bernard Suits's account of games, the attitude exhibited by players that enables them to adopt less efficient instead of more efficient means of achieving the game's goal.

lusory goal. In Bernard Suits's account of games, the state of affairs that constitutes winning a game.

metaphysics. Branch of philosophy that examines the fundamental nature of things.

moral relativism. Belief that ethics has no universal truths but, rather, that moral principles are relative to particular communities, or perhaps individual opinion.

multiculturalism. Belief that diversity should be valued and preserved despite the homogenizing forces of globalization.

Olympism. Set of philosophical principles behind the modern Olympic Games.

ontological. Of or relating to the nature or being of a thing.

paternalism. The restriction of a person's liberty against his will, especially for his own protection.

phenomenology. Philosophical approach focused on the structure of human experience.

philosophical anthropology. Philosophy concerned with the nature and status of humanity.

physicalism. Theory of mind and body that asserts both to be nothing more than matter.

Platonic love. Intense affection that excludes sexual intercourse and focuses instead on education and *aretē*.

politics. Branch of philosophy that deals with social and community issues and organization.

postmodernism. Philosophical approach that is skeptical of objective explanations claiming to be valid for everyone.

professionalism. Excellence in the performance of a skill, often associated with a person's main activity.

psychē. Greek word for the soul; encompasses the ideas of life, mind, spirit, and emotion.

rationalism. Theory that knowledge is based primarily upon internal reasoning. Contrast **empiricism**.

segregation. The practice of separating athletes into different classes based on social categories such as sex or race. Desegregation is the removal of such classes.

social practice theory. An understanding of sports (and other activities) as communities based on the shared pursuit of excellence within a mutually valued practice.

sōma. Greek word for the physical body, conceived as lifeless matter in the absence of *psychē.*

sustainability. The ability to meet our present needs without compromising the ability of future generations to meet their needs.

technē. Greek word for a practical skill or art, to be contrasted with moral qualities such as *aretē.*

telos. Greek word for the end or goal that characterizes the motivation and purpose for an activity.

utilitarianism. A moral philosophy that focuses on consequences, striving to achieve the greatest good for the greatest number affected by any action.

virtue ethics. Moral philosophy that focuses on the character of the agent (i.e., the person who acts) rather than principles or consequences.

wu-wei. Eastern philosophical term that expresses the strength of nonaction or effortlessness.

Bibliography

Abanazir, Cem. "Institutionalisation in E-Sports." *Sport, Ethics and Philosophy* 13, no. 2 (2019): 117–31.

Alves, Ryan. "Real Life Lessons from the Gridiron." *Eastern Progress*, October 12, 2011. Accessed October 20, 2011. http://www.easternprogress.com/.

American Israeli Cooperative Enterprise. "The Nazi Olympics." Jewish Virtual Library, 2001. Accessed November 25, 2011. http://www.jewishvirtuallibrary.org/.

Ansaldo, Marco. "Immobile in pedana, tunisina boicatta Israele ai Mondiali." *La Stampa*, October 11, 2011. http://www3.lastampa.it/.

Aristophanes. "Clouds." In *The Comedies of Aristophanes*, translated by William James Hickie. London: Bohn, 1853.

Aristotle. *The Athenian Constitution*. Translated by Sir Frederic G. Kenyon. Washington, DC: Merchant Books, 2009.

———. *Complete Works*. Edited by Jonathan Barnes. 2 vols. Princeton, NJ: Princeton University Press, 1984.

———. *Nicomachean Ethics*. Translated by Terence Irwin. 2nd ed. Indianapolis: Hackett, 1999.

———. *Poetics*. Translated by Malcom Heath. London: Penguin, 1997.

———. *Politics*. Translated by C. D. C. Reeve. Indianapolis: Hackett, 1998.

Arnold, Peter J. "Democracy, Education and Sport." *Journal of the Philosophy of Sport* 16 (1989): 100–110.

———. "Sport and Moral Education." *Journal of Moral Education* 23, no. 1 (1994): 75–90.

Associated Press. "FINA Moves Up Bodysuit Ban." *ESPN Olympic Sports*, July 31, 2009. Accessed October 20, 2011. http://sports.espn.go.com/.

Athenaeus. "The Deipnosophists." In *The Smell of Sweat: Greek Athletics, Olympics, and Culture*, edited by W. B. Tyrell. Wauconda, IL: Bolchazy-Carducci, 2004.

Bäck, Allan. "The *Way* to Virtue in Sport." *Journal of the Philosophy of Sport* 36 (2009): 217–37.

Barnes, Colin. "Understanding the Social Model of Disability: Past, Present and Future." In *The Routledge Handbook of Disability Studies*, edited by Nick Watson and Simo Vehmas, 14–31. 2nd ed. New York: Routledge, 2019.

Beck, Owen N., Paolo Taboga, and Alena M. Grabowski. "Sprinting with Prosthetic Versus Biological Legs: Insight from Experimental Data." *Royal Society Open Science* 9, no. 1 (2022). DOI:10.1098/rsos.211799.

Becker, Carl B. "Philosophical Perspectives on the Martial Arts in America." *Journal of the Philosophy of Sport* 19, no. 1 (1982): 19–29.

Berkeley, George. *A Treatise Concerning the Principles of Human Knowledge.* Stilwell, KS: Digireads, [1734] 2006.

Bernard, Andrew B., and Meghan R. Busse. "Who Wins the Olympic Games: Economic Resources and Medal Totals." *Review of Economics and Statistics* 86, no. 1 (2004): 413–17.

Best, David. "The Aesthetic in Sport." In *Philosophic Inquiry in Sport*, edited by W. Morgan and K. Meier, 377–89. 2nd ed. Champaign, IL: Human Kinetics, 1995.

Bok, Derek. "Can Higher Education Foster Higher Morals?" In *Social and Personal Ethics*, edited by W. H. Shaw, 494–503. Belmont, CA: Wadsworth, 1996.

Boxill, Jan, ed. *Sports Ethics*. Malden, MA: Blackwell, 2003.

Bradley, Bill. *Values of the Game*. New York: Broadway Books, 1998.

Branch, Taylor. "The Shame of College Sports." *Atlantic Monthly*, October 2011. http:/www.theatlantic.com/.

Brand, Myles. "The Role and Value of Intercollegiate Athletics in Universities." *Journal of the Philosophy of Sport* 33, no. 1 (2006): 9–20.

British Broadcasting Service. "FINA Extends Swimsuit Regulations." *BBC Mobile Sport*, March 19, 2009. Accessed October 20, 2011. http://news.bbc.co.uk/.

Brittain, Ian. *The Paralympic Games Explained*. 2nd ed. New York: Routledge, 2016.

Brown, Ben. "Homer, Funeral Contests and the Origins of the Greek City." In *Sport and Festival in the Ancient Greek World*, edited by David J. Phillips and David Pritchard, 123–62. Swansea: Classical Press of Wales, 2003.

Brown, W. M. "Paternalism, Drugs, and the Nature of Sports." *Journal of the Philosophy of Sport* 11, no. 1 (1985): 14–22.

———. "Practices and Prudence." *Journal of the Philosophy of Sport* 17, no. 1 (1990): 71–84.

Brownell, Susan. *Training the Body for China*. Chicago: University of Chicago Press, 1995.

Burkert, Walter. *Greek Religion*. Translated by J. Raffan. Cambridge, MA: Harvard University Press, 1985.

Busbee, Jay. "Davis Calls Penalty on Himself, Gives Up Shot at First PGA Win." Yahoo Sports, April 18, 2010. Accessed October 21, 2011. http://sports.yahoo.com /.

Butcher, Robert, and Angela Schneider. "Fair Play as Respect for the Game." *Journal of the Philosophy of Sport* 25, no. 1 (1998): 1–22.

Cable News Network. "Sumo 'Fixing' Scandal Rocks Japan." CNN International Edition, February 4, 2011. Accessed October 21, 2011. http://edition.cnn.com/.

Caillois, Roger. *Man, Play, and Games*. Translated by Meyer Berlash. Urbana: University of Illinois Press, [1958] 2001.

Camus, Albert. *The Myth of Sisyphus and Other Essays*. Translated by Justin O'Brien. New York: Random House, 1955.

————. "The Wager of Our Generation." In *Resistance, Rebellion, and Death*, translated by Justin O'Brien. New York: Vintage, 1960.

Carr, David. "What Moral Educational Significance Has Physical Education?" In *The Ethics of Sports: A Reader*, edited by Mike McNamee, 306–15. London: Routledge, 2010.

————. "Where's the Merit If the Best Man Wins?" *Journal of the Philosophy of Sport* 26, no. 1 (1999): 1–9.

Cassiodorus. "Variae." In *The Roman Games*, edited by Alison Futrell, 74. Malden, MA: Blackwell, 2006.

Cheng, Chung-Ying. "On the Metaphysical Significance of *ti* (Body-Embodiment) in Chinese Philosophy: *benti* (Origin-Substance) and *ti-yong* (Substance and Function)." *Journal of Chinese Philosophy* 29, no. 2 (2002): 145–61.

Ching, Gene, and Gigi Oh. "Where Wushu Went Wrong." *Kungfu Magazine*, November 3, 2006. Accessed October 21, 2011. http://ezine.kungfumagazine.com/.

Cicero, Marcus Tullius. *Tusculan Disputations*. Translated by J. King. Cambridge, MA: Loeb, 1927.

Clarey, Christopher. "A French Revolution in the Fast Lanes." *International Herald Tribune*, November 18, 2011. Kindle edition.

Confucius. *Analects*. Translated by E. Slingerland. Indianapolis: Hackett, 2003.

————. *The Analects of Confucius*. Translated by Arthur Waley. New York: Vintage, 1989.

Cordner, C. D. "Grace and Functionality." In *Philosophic Inquiry in Sport*, edited by W. Morgan and K. Meier, 407–14. 2nd ed. Champaign, IL: Human Kinetics, 1995.

Cordner, Christopher. "Differences between Sport and Art." In *Philosophic Inquiry in Sport*, edited by W. Morgan and K. Meier, 424–36. 2nd ed. Champaign, IL: Human Kinetics, 1995.

Coubertin, Pierre de. *Olympism: Selected Writings*. Edited by Norbert Müller. Lausanne, Switzerland: International Olympic Committee, 2000.

————. "The Olympic Games of 1896." In *The Olympic Idea: Pierre de Coubertin—Discourses and Essays*, edited by Carl-Diem Institut, 10–14. Stuttgart, Germany: Olympisher Sportverlag, 1966.

Crowther, Nigel. "The Ancient Olympics and Their Ideals." In *Athletika: Studies on the Olympic Games and Greek Athletics*, edited by W. Decker and I. Weiler, 1–11. Hildesheim, Germany: Weidemann, 2004.

————. "*Euexia, Eutaxia, Philoponia*: Three Contests of the Greek Gymnasium." *Zeitschrift für Papyrologie und Epigraphik* 85 (1991): 301–4.

Cudd, Ann E. "Sporting Metaphors: Competition and the Ethos of Capitalism." *Journal of the Philosophy of Sport* 34, no. 1 (2007): 52–67.

Curtis, Thomas P. "Amusing Then Amazing: American Wins 1896 Discus." *Technology Review*, July 24, 1924. Reprinted in *MIT News*, July 18, 1996. http://web.mit.edu/.

DaCosta, Lamartine. "A Never-Ending Story: The Philosophical Controversy over Olympism." *Journal of the Philosophy of Sport* 33, no. 2 (2006): 157–73.

D'Agostino, Fred. "The Ethos of Games." In *Philosophic Inquiry in Sport*, edited by W. Morgan and K. Meier, 48–49. 2nd ed. Champaign, IL: Human Kinetics, 1995.

Danto, Arthur. "The Artworld." *Journal of Philosophy* 61 (1964): 571–84.

Davis, Paul. "Ethical Issues in Boxing." *Journal of the Philosophy of Sport* 20–21 (1993–1994): 48–63.

Dean, Jeffry. "Aesthetics and Ethics: The State of the Art." *Aesthetics Online*, 2002. Accessed November 1, 2011. http://aesthetics-online.org/.

Delattre, Edwin J. "Some Reflections on Success and Failure in Competitive Athletics." *Journal of the Philosophy of Sport* 2, no. 1 (1975): 133–39.

Descartes, René. *The Philosophical Writings of Descartes*. Edited by J. Cottingham, R. Stoothoff, and D. Murdoch. 2 vols. Cambridge, UK: Cambridge University Press, 1985.

Diogenes Laertius. *Lives of Eminent Philosophers*, vol. 1. Translated by R. D. Hicks. Cambridge, MA: Harvard University Press, 1972.

Dixon, Nicholas. "On Sportsmanship and Running Up the Score." *Journal of the Philosophy of Sport*, 19 (1992): 1–13.

———. "On Winning and Athletic Superiority." *Journal of the Philosophy of Sport* 26, no. 1 (1999): 10–26.

———. "Why Losing by a Wide Margin Is Not in Itself a Disgrace." *Journal of the Philosophy of Sport* 25, no. 1 (1998): 61–79.

Dombrowski, Daniel. *Contemporary Athletics and Ancient Greek Ideals*. Chicago: University of Chicago Press, 2009.

Drewe, Sheryle Bergmann. *Why Sport?* Toronto: Thompson, 2003.

Durà-Vilà, Víctor. "Why Playing Beautifully Is Morally Better." In *Soccer and Philosophy: Beautiful Thoughts on the Beautiful Game*, edited by T. Richards, 141–48. Chicago: Open Court, 2010.

Eassom, Simon. "Games, Rules, and Contracts." In *Ethics and Sport*, edited by Mike McNamee and Jim Parry, 57–78. London: E & FN Spon, 1998.

Eaton, Marcia Muelder. *Merit, Aesthetic and Ethical*. New York: Oxford University Press, 2001.

Edelman, Robert. *Serious Fun: A History of Spectator Sports in the USSR*. New York: Oxford University Press, 1993.

English, Jane. "Sex Equality in Sports." *Philosophy and Public Affairs* 7 (1978): 269–77.

Epstein, David. "Double Amputee Pistorius Keeping Olympic Sprinting Dreams Alive." SI.com, June 11, 2011. Accessed November 22, 2011. http://sportsillustrated.cnn.com/.

Erdbrink, Thomas. "FIFA Bans Headscarves for Iranian Women's Soccer Team." *Washington Post*, June 6, 2011. http://www.washingtonpost.com/.

Evangeliou, C. *Hellenic Philosophy: Origin and Character*. Burlington, VT: Ashgate, 2006.

Feezell, Randolph. *Sport, Play, and Ethical Reflection*. Urbana: University of Illinois Press, 2006.

Fischer, Norman. "Competitive Sport's Imitation of War: Imaging the Completeness of Virtue." *Journal of the Philosophy of Sport* 29, no. 1 (2002): 16–37.

Fisher, Marjorie. "Sport as an Aesthetic Experience." In *Sport and the Body: A Philosophical Symposium*, edited by Ellen Gerber, 315–21. Philadelphia: Lea & Febiger, 1974.

Foundation for the Hellenic World. "The Revival of the Ancient Olympic Games." From Ancient Olympia to Athens of 1896. Accessed December 12, 2011. http://www.fhw.gr.

Fraleigh, Warren P. "The Ends of the Sports Contest." In *The Ethics of Sports: A Reader*, edited by Mike McNamee, 106–15. London: Routledge, 2010.

———. "Performance-Enhancing Drugs in Sport: The Ethical Issue." *Journal of the Philosophy of Sport* 11, no. 1 (1985): 23–29.

———. "The Philosophic Society for the Study of Sport, 1972–1983." *Journal of the Philosophy of Sport* 10 (1984): 3–7.

———. *Right Actions in Sport: Ethics for Contestants*. Champaign, IL: Human Kinetics, 1984.

Francis, Leslie Pickering. "Competitive Sports, Disability, and Problems of Justice in Sports." *Journal of the Philosophy of Sport* 32, no. 2 (2005): 127–32.

Franke, W., and B. Berendonk. "Hormonal Doping and Androgenization of Athletes: A Secret Program of the German Democratic Republic Government." *Clinical Chemistry* 43, no. 7 (1997): 1262–79.

Futrell, Alison, ed. *The Roman Games*. Malden, MA: Blackwell, 2006.

Futterman, Matthew. "Another Double Amputee's Fight for the Olympics Is Dealt a Major Setback." *New York Times*, October 27, 2020. Accessed November 11, 2021. https://www.nytimes.com/2020/10/27/sports/blake-leeper-prostheses-ruling.html.

———. "Track and Field Aimed for Inclusion. Instead It Sidelined Star Athletes." *New York Times*, July 30, 2021. Accessed November 11, 2021. https://www.nytimes.com/2021/07/30/sports/olympics/track-field.html.

Gerber, Ellen, ed. *Sport and the Body: A Philosophical Symposium*. Philadelphia: Lea & Febiger, 1974.

Gleaves, John. "Too Fit to Fly: How Female Nordic Ski Jumping Challenges the IOC's Approach to Gender Equality." In *Rethinking Matters Olympic: Investigations into the SocioCultural Study of the Modern Olympic Movement*, edited by International Center for Olympic Studies, 278–88. London: University of Western Ontario, 2010.

Golden, Mark. *Greek Sport and Social Status*. Austin: University of Texas Press, 2008.

———. *Sport and Society in Ancient Greece*. Cambridge, UK: Cambridge University Press, 1998.

———. *Sport in the Ancient World from A to Z*. New York: Routledge, 2004.

Goldman, Tom. "Athlete's 'Nope to Dope' Became 'No to Sports.'" National Public Radio, 2011. http://www.npr.org/.

Groos, Karl. "Play from the Aesthetic Standpoint." In *The Play of Man*. New York: D. Appleton, 1901. Reprinted in Gerber, *Sport and the Body*, 302–4.

Grue, Jan. "The Problem with Inspiration Porn: A Tentative Definition and a Provisional Critique." *Disability and Society* 31 (2016): 838–49.

Guttman, Allen. *From Ritual to Record: The Nature of Modern Sports.* New York: Columbia University Press, 1978. Reprinted 2004.

Hanley, Elizabeth A. "A Perennial Dilemma: Artistic Sports in the Olympic Games." Unpublished manuscript, 2000.

Hardman, Alun, Luanne Fox, Doug McLaughlin, and Kurt Zimmerman. "On Sportsmanship and Running Up the Score: Issues of Incompetence and Humiliation." *Journal of the Philosophy of Sport* 23 (1996): 58–69.

Heidegger, Martin. *Poetry, Language, Thought*. New York: Harper & Row, 1971.

Herodotus. *Histories*. Translated by A. D. Godley. Cambridge, MA: Harvard University Press, 1920.

Herrigel, Eugen. *Zen in the Art of Archery*. Translated by R. F. C. Hull. New York: Vintage, 1999.

Hoberman, John. *Darwin's Athletes: How Sport Has Damaged Black America and Preserved the Myth of Race*. Boston: Houghton Mifflin, 1997.

———. *Mortal Engines: The Science of Performance and the Dehumanization of Sport*. New York: Free Press, 1992.

Holowchak, M. Andrew. "'Aretism' and Pharmacological Ergogenic Aids in Sport: Taking a Shot at the Use of Steroids." *Journal of the Philosophy of Sport* 27, no. 1 (2000): 35–50.

———. "Fascistoid Heroism Revisited: A Deontological Twist in a Recent Debate." *Journal of the Philosophy of Sport* 32, no. 2 (2005): 96–104.

———, ed. *Philosophy of Sport: Critical Readings, Crucial Issues*. Upper Saddle River, NJ: Prentice Hall, 2002.

Holowchak, M. Andrew, and Heather L. Reid. *Aretism: An Ancient Sports Philosophy for the Modern Sports World*. Lanham, MD: Lexington, 2011.

Homer. *The Iliad and Odyssey*. Translated by Robert Fagles. New York: Penguin, 1990.

Huizinga, Johan. *Homo Ludens: A Study of the Play Element in Culture*. Boston: Beacon Press, [1944] 1955.

Hume, David. *A Treatise of Human Nature*. Edited by L. A. Selby-Bigge. 2nd ed. Oxford, UK: Clarendon, 1978.

Hyland, Drew A. "Competition and Friendship." *Journal of the Philosophy of Sport* 5, no. 1 (1978): 27–37.

———. "*Paidia* and *Paideia*: The Educational Power of Athletics." *Journal of Intercollegiate Sport* 1, no. 1 (2008): 66–71.

———. *Philosophy of Sport*. New York: Paragon, 1990.

———. *The Question of Play*. Lanham, MD: University Press of America, 1984.

———. "The Stance of Play." *Journal of the Philosophy of Sport* 7, no. 1 (1980): 87–99.

Iamblichus. *The Pythagorean Life*. Translated by Thomas Taylor. London: Watkins, 1818.

Ilundáin-Agurruza, Jesús. *Holism and the Cultivation of Excellence in Sports and Performance: Skillful Striving*. London: Taylor and Francis, 2016.

Inoue, Akio. "Critique of Modern Olympism: A Voice from the East." In *Sports: The East and the West*, edited by G. Pfister and L. Yueye, 163–67. Sant Agustin, Germany: Academia Verlag, 1999.

International Olympic Committee. *Factsheet on the Olympic Programme*. Lausanne, Switzerland: Author, 2007.

————. "The New Exhibition at the Olympic Museum on the Theme of Hope." *Olympics.com*, March 28, 2011. Accessed November 25, 2011. http://www.olympics.com/.

————. *The Olympic Charter*. Lausanne, Switzerland: Author, 2010.

————. *Olympic Movement's Agenda 21: Sport for Sustainable Development*. Lausanne, Switzerland: Author, 1999. http://www.olympics.com/.

————. "Olympic Solidarity Commission." *Olympics.com*, 2011. Accessed November 28, 2011. http://www.olympics.com/.

————. "The Sport and Environment Commission." *Olympics.com*, 2009. Accessed December 5, 2011. http://www.olympics.com/.

International Paralympic Committee. *IPC Athlete Classification Code*, November 2015. Bonn: IPC, 2015.

————. "Powerlifting on an Upswing." Paralympian Online, 2000. Accessed November 21, 2011. http://www.paralympic.org/.

Jackson, Phil. *Sacred Hoops: Spiritual Lessons of a Hardwood Warrior*. New York: Hyperion, 1995.

Jackson, Susan A., and Mihaly Csikszentmihalyi. *Flow in Sports*. Champaign, IL: Human Kinetics, 1999.

Jespersen, Ejgil, and Mike McNamee. "Introduction." In *Ethics, Dis/Ability and Sports*, edited by Ejgil Jespersen and Mike McNamee, 1–10. New York: Routledge, 2009.

Jones, Carwyn. "Character, Virtue, and Physical Education." *European Physical Education Review* 11, no. 2 (2005): 140–42.

Jones, Carwyn, and P. David Howe. "The Conceptual Boundaries of Sport for the Disabled: Classification and Athletic Performance." *Journal of the Philosophy of Sport* 32, no. 2 (2005): 133–46.

Kant, Immanuel. *Groundwork for the Metaphysic of Morals*. Translated by H. J. Paton. New York: Harper and Row, 1948.

Keating, James W. "Sportsmanship as a Moral Category." *Ethics* 75 (October 1964): 25–35.

Kennell, Nigel M. *The Gymnasium of Virtue: Education and Culture in Ancient Sparta*. Chapel Hill: University of North Carolina Press, 1995.

Kidd, Bruce. "Taking the Rhetoric Seriously: Proposals for Olympic Education." *Quest* 48 (1996): 82–92.

King, Martin Luther, Jr. *I Have a Dream: Writings and Speeches that Changed the World*. New York: HarperCollins, 1992.

King, Winston. *Zen and the Way of the Sword*. New York: Oxford University Press, 1993. University of Pennsylvania Press, 1981.

Kretchmar, R. Scott. "Beautiful Games." *Journal of the Philosophy of Sport* 16, no. 1 (1989): 34–43.

————. "Ethics and Sport: An Overview." *Journal of the Philosophy of Sport* 10, no. 1 (1984): 21–32.

294 *Bibliography*

———. "From Test to Contest: An Analysis of Two Kinds of Counterpoint in Sport." *Journal of the Philosophy of Sport* 1 (1975): 23–30.

———. *Practical Philosophy of Sport*. Champaign, IL: Human Kinetics, 1994.

Kuhn, Anthony. "Chinese Martial Art Form Sports Less Threatening Moves." *Los Angeles Times*, October 16, 1988. Accessed October 21, 2011. http://articles .latimes.com/.

Kupfer, Joseph. "Sport: The Body Electric." In *Philosophic Inquiry in Sport*, edited by W. Morgan and K. Meier, 390–406. 2nd ed. Champaign, IL: Human Kinetics, 1995.

Kyle, Donald G. *Spectacles of Death in Ancient Rome*. New York: Routledge, 1998.

———. *Sport and Spectacle in the Ancient World*. Malden, MA: Blackwell, 2007.

Lacerda, Teresa, and Stephen Mumford. "The Genius in Art and in Sport: A Contribution to the Investigation of Aesthetics of Sport." *Journal of the Philosophy of Sport* 37, no. 2 (2010): 182–93.

Lao-Tzu. *Tao Te Ching*. Translated by S. Addiss and S. Lombardo. Indianapolis: Hackett, 2003.

Laozi. "Daodejing." In *Readings in Classical Chinese Philosophy*, edited by P. Ivanhoe and B. Van Norden, 161–206. 2nd ed. Indianapolis: Hackett, 2001.

Lapchick, Richard. *2010 Racial and Gender Report Card*. Chicago: Institute for Diversity and Ethics in Sport, 2010.

Lasch, Christopher. "The Degradation of Sport." *New York Review of Books* 24, no. 7 (1977). Reprinted in *The Ethics of Sports: A Reader*, edited by Mike McNamee, 369–81. London: Routledge, 2010.

Lehman, Craig. "Can Cheaters Play the Game?" *Journal of the Philosophy of Sport* 8 (1981): 41–46.

Lenk, Hans. "Towards a Philosophical Anthropology of the Olympic Athletes and the Achieving Being." In *International Olympic Academy Report*, 163–77 (Ancient Olympia, Greece: 1982).

Levy, Glen. "British Athletes Told to Avoid Shaking Hands at the Olympics." *Time* Newsfeed. March 6, 2012. Accessed March 7, 2012. http://newsfeed.time.com/.

Litke, Jim. "Black Athletes Eased Obama's Presidential Path." *NBC Sports*, November 5, 2008. Accessed November 21, 2011. http://nbcsports.msnbc.com/.

Livingston, Gretchen, and D'Vera Cohn. "Childlessness Up among All Women, Down among Women with Advanced Degrees." Pew Research Center, June 25, 2010. Accessed November 21, 2011. http://www.pewsocialtrends.org/.

Locke, John. *An Essay Concerning Human Understanding*. Oxford, UK: Clarendon, 1975.

Loland, Sigmund. "Classification in Sport: A Question of Fairness." *European Journal of Sport Science* 21, no. 11 (2021): 1477–84.

———. "The Ethics of Performance-Enhancing Technology in Sport." *Journal of the Philosophy of Sport* 36, no. 1 (2009): 152–61.

———. "Fairness in Sport: An Ideal and Its Consequences." In *The Ethics of Sports: A Reader*, edited by Mike McNamee, 116–24. London: Routledge, 2010.

———. *Fair Play in Sport: A Moral Norm System*. New York: Routledge, 2001.

————. "Record Sports: An Ecological Critique and a Reconstruction." *Journal of the Philosophy of Sport* 27, no. 2 (2001): 127–39.

Lopez, Frías, and Francisco Javier. "Does Play Constitute the Good Life? Suits and Aristotle on Autotelicity and Living Well," *Journal of the Philosophy of Sport* 47, no. 2 (2020): 168–82.

Loy, John W., Jr. "The Nature of Sport: A Definitional Effort." *Quest* 10, no. 1 (May 1968): 1–15. Reprinted in Holowchak, *Philosophy of Sport*, 16–28.

MacIntyre, Alasdair. *After Virtue*. Notre Dame, IN: University of Notre Dame Press, 1981.

————. *Whose Justice? Which Rationality?* Notre Dame, IN: University of Notre Dame Press, 1989.

Maglo, Koffi N. "The Case against Biological Realism about Race: From Darwin to the PostGenomic Era." *Perspectives on Science* 19, no. 4 (2011): 361–90.

Mandell, Richard. *The Nazi Olympics*. Champaign: University of Illinois Press, 1987.

McBride, Frank. "Toward a Non-Definition of Sport." *Journal of the Philosophy of Sport*, 2 (1975): 4–11.

McCurry, Justin. "Sumo Threatened by Scandal and Crime." *Guardian*, July 4, 2010. Accessed October 21, 2011. http://www.guardian.co.uk/.

McDonagh, Eileen L., and Laura Pappano. *Playing with the Boys: Why Separate Is Not Equal in Sports*. New York: Oxford University Press, 2008.

McFee, Graham. "Spoiling: An Indirect Reflection of Sport's Moral Imperative?" In *The Ethics of Sports: A Reader*, edited by Mike McNamee, 145–52. London: Routledge, 2010.

————. *Sports, Rules and Values: Philosophical Investigations into the Nature of Sport*. London: Routledge, 2004.

McNamee, Mike, ed. *The Ethics of Sports: A Reader*. London: Routledge, 2010.

————. "Hubris, Humility, and Humiliation: Vice and Virtue in Sporting Communities." *Journal of the Philosophy of Sport* 29, no. 1 (2002): 38–53.

————. "Olympism, Eurocentricity, and Transcultural Virtues." *Journal of the Philosophy of Sport* 33, no. 2 (2006): 174–87.

————. "*Schadenfreude* in Sport: Envy, Justice, and Self-Esteem." *Journal of the Philosophy of Sport* 30, no. 1 (2003): 1–16.

————. "Sport, Ethics and Philosophy: Context, History and Prospects." *Sport, Ethics and Philosophy* 1, no. 1 (2007): 1–6.

————. "Sporting Practices, Institutions and Virtues: A Critique and Restatement." *Journal of the Philosophy of Sport* 22, no. 1 (1995): 61–82.

————. *Sports, Virtues and Vices: Morality Plays*. London: Routledge, 2008.

Meier, Klaus V. "An Affair of Flutes: An Appreciation of Play." *Journal of the Philosophy of Sport* 7, no. 1 (1980): 24–45.

————. "Triad Trickery: Playing with Sport and Games." *Journal of the Philosophy of Sport* 15, no. 1 (1988): 11–30.

Mengzi. *Mencius*. Translated by Irene Bloom. New York: Columbia University Press, 2009.

Merleau-Ponty, Maurice. *The Phenomenology of Perception*. Translated by Colin Smith. London: Routledge and Kegan Paul, 1962.

Metheny, Eleanor. "The Symbolic Power of Sport." Presented to the Eastern District Association for Health, Physical Education and Recreation in Washington, DC, April 26, 1968. Reprinted in *Sport and the Body: A Philosophical Symposium*, edited by E. Gerber and W. J. Morgan, 231–36. Philadelphia: Lea & Febiger, 1979.

———. "This 'Thing' Called Sport." *Journal of Health, Physical Education, and Recreation* 40 (March 1969): 59–60.

Mikalson, J. *Ancient Greek Religion*. Malden, MA: Blackwell, 2005.

Mill, John Stuart. *On Liberty*. Indianapolis: Hackett, 1978.

Miller, Stephen G. *Ancient Greek Athletics*. New Haven, CT: Yale University Press, 2004.

———, ed. *Arete: Greek Sports from Ancient Sources*. Berkeley: University of California Press, 1991.

———. "Naked Democracy." In *Polis and Politics*, edited by P. Flensted-Jensen and T. H. Nielsen, 277–96. Copenhagen: Festschrift, 2000.

Moller, Verner. "The Athlete's Viewpoint." In *The Ethics of Sports: A Reader*, edited by Mike McNamee, 160–68. London: Routledge, 2010.

Moore, Eric. "Was Armstrong a Cheat?" *Sport, Ethics and Philosophy* 11, no. 4 (2017): 413–27.

Morgan, William J. *Sport and Moral Conflict*. Philadelphia: Temple University Press, 2020, 219. Kindle edition.

Morgan, William J. "Cosmopolitanism, Olympism, and Nationalism: A Critical Interpretation of Coubertin's Ideal of International Sporting Life." *Olympika* 4 (1995): 79–91.

———. *Leftist Theories of Sport: A Critique and Reconstruction*. Chicago: University of Illinois Press, 1994.

———. "The Logical Incompatibility Thesis and Rules: A Reconsideration of Formalism as an Account of Games." *Journal of the Philosophy of Sport* 14, no. 1 (1987): 1–20.

———. "Multinational Sport and Literary Practices and Their Communities: The Moral Salience of Cultural Narratives." In *Ethics and Sport*, edited by Mike McNamee and Jim Parry, 184–204. London: E & FN Spon, 1998.

———. *Why Sports Morally Matter*. Abingdon, UK: Routledge, 2006.

Morgan, William J., Klaus V. Meier, and Angela J. Schneider, eds. *Ethics in Sport*. Champaign, IL: Human Kinetics, 2001. 2nd ed., 2007.

Morris, Ian. "Equality and the Origins of Greek Democracy." In *Ancient Greek Democracy*, edited by Eric W. Robinson, 45–73. Malden, MA: Blackwell, 2004.

Mouratidis, John. "Heracles at Olympia and the Exclusion of Women from the Ancient Olympic Games." *Journal of Sport History* 11, no. 3 (1984): 41–55.

Mumford, Stephen. *Watching Sport: Aesthetics, Ethics, and Emotion*. Abingdon, UK: Routledge, 2011.

Murray, Hugh. "Review of Hoberman's *The Olympic Crisis*." *Journal of Sport History* 16, no. 1 (1989): 104–8.

Murray, Sarah C. "The Role of Religion in Greek Sport." *A Companion to Sport and Spectacle in Greek and Roman Antiquity*, edited by Paul Christesen and Donald G. Kyle, 309–19. Malden, MA: Wiley-Blackwell, 2014.

Nagy, Gregory. *The Ancient Greek Hero in 24 Hours*. Cambridge, MA: Harvard University Press, 2013.

National Collegiate Athletic Association. *2009–2010 Student Athlete Ethnicity Report*. Indianapolis: Author, 2010.

———. "Estimated Probability of Competing in Athletics beyond the High School Interscholastic Level." NCAA.com, 2011. Accessed November 21, 2011. http://www.ncaa.org/.

Nicholson, Nigel James. *Aristocracy and Athletics in Archaic and Classical Greece*. Cambridge, UK: Cambridge University Press, 2005.

Nielsen Company. "Beijing Olympics Draw Largest Ever Global Television Audience." Nielsenwire, September 8, 2008. Accessed April 10, 2012. http://blog.nielsen.com/.

Nietzsche, Friedrich. *The Birth of Tragedy*. Translated by Shaun Whiteside. London: Penguin, 1994.

———. "Thus Spoke Zarathustra." In *The Portable Nietzsche*, edited by Walter Kaufmann, 146–47. New York: Viking, 1982.

OlympicTalk. "Blake Leeper, Olympic Hopeful Double Amputee, Has Prosthetics Ruled Ineligible." *NBC Sports*, February 27, 2020. Accessed February 1, 2022. https://olympics.nbcsports.com/2020/02/27/blake-leeper-double-amputee-prosthetic-legs-ineligible/.

Osterhoudt, R. G. "The Term 'Sport': Some Thoughts on a Proper Name." *International Journal of Physical Education* 14, no. 2 (1977): 11–16.

Parry, Jim. "E-Sports Are Not Sports." *Sport, Ethics and Philosophy* 13, no. 1 (2019): 3–18.

———. "Sport and Olympism: Universals and Multiculturalism." *Journal of the Philosophy of Sport* 33, no. 2 (2006): 188–204.

———. "Sport, Ethos and Education." In *The Ethics of Sports*: *A Reader*, edited by Mike McNamee, 316–26. London: Routledge, 2010.

Patel, Seema. *Inclusion and Exclusion in Competitive Sport*. New York: Routledge, 2015.

Pausanias. *Description of Greece*. Translated by Peter Levi. 2 vols. New York: Penguin, 1979.

Pawlenka, Claudia. "The Idea of Fairness: A General Ethical Concept or One Particular to Sports Ethics." *Journal of the Philosophy of Sport* 32, no. 1 (2005): 49–64.

Penberthy, Macallan. "Rio Olympics' Special Guest: Asthma." *Foundation for Biomedical Research*, August 2, 2016. Accessed November 11, 2021. https://fbresearch.org/rio-olympics-special-guest-asthma/.

Percy, William A. *Pederasty and Pedagogy in Archaic Greece*. Urbana: University of Illinois Press, 1996.

Pike, Jon, and Sean Cordell. "Armstrong Was a Cheat: A Reply to Eric Moore." *Sport, Ethics and Philosophy* 14, no. 2 (2020): 247–63.

Pindar. *The Complete Odes*. Translated by Anthony Verity. Oxford: Oxford University Press, 2007.

———. *Olympian Odes, Pythian Odes*. Translated by William H. Race. Cambridge, MA: Harvard University Press, 1997.

Pinter, Stanislav, Tjasa Filipcic, Ales Solar, and Maja Smrdu. "Integrating Children with Physical Impairments into Sports Activities: A 'Golden Sun' for All Children?" *Journal of the Philosophy of Sport* 32, no. 2 (2005): 147–54.

Pinto, Barbara, and Olivia Katrandjian. "Wrestler Joel Northup Forfeits to Female Opponent in Iowa State Championships." *ABC News*, February 18, 2011. Accessed November 21, 2011. http://abcnews.go.com/.

Plato. *Apology*. Translated by G. M. A. Grube. Indianapolis: Hackett, 1980.

———. *Complete Works*. Edited by John M. Cooper. Indianapolis: Hackett, 1997.

———. *Laws*. Translated by Trevor Saunders. London: Penguin, 1970.

———. *Republic*. Translated by G. M. A. Grube. Indianapolis: Hackett, 1992.

———. *Symposium*. Translated by Alexander Nehamas and Paul Woodruff. Indianapolis: Hackett, 1989.

———. *Two Comic Dialogues: Ion and Hippias Major*. Translated by Paul Woodruff. Indianapolis: Hackett, 1983.

Postow, B. C. "Masculine Sports Revisited." *Journal of the Philosophy of Sport* 8, no. 1 (1981): 60–63.

———. "Women and Masculine Sports." *Journal of the Philosophy of Sport* 7 (1980): 51–58.

Rawls, John. *A Theory of Justice*. Cambridge, MA: Harvard University Press, 1971.

Reid, Heather L. "Amateurism, Professionalism and the Value of College Sports." *Journal of Intercollegiate Sport* 14, no. 3 (2021): 67–79. https://doi.org/10.17161/jis.v14i3.15676.

———. "Aristotle on the Beauty of Fair Play," *Estetica: Studi e Ricerche* 11, no. 1 (2021): 201–10.

———. "Aristotle's Pentathlete." *Sport, Ethics and Philosophy* 4, no. 2 (2010): 183–94.

———. "Athletic Heroes." *Sport, Ethics and Philosophy* 4, no. 2 (2010): 125–35.

———. "Athletic Virtue and Aesthetic Values in Aristotle's Ethics." *Journal of the Philosophy of Sport* 47, no. 1 (2020): 63–74.

———. "Athletic Virtue: Between East and West." *Sport, Ethics and Philosophy* 4, no. 1 (2010): 16–26. Reprinted in McNamee, *Ethics of Sports*, 340–47.

———. *Athletics and Philosophy in the Ancient World: Contests of Virtue*. London: Routledge, 2011.

———. "Boxing with Tyrants." *Sport, Ethics and Philosophy* 4, no. 2 (2010): 146–56.

———. "East to Olympia: Recentering Olympic Philosophy between East and West." *Olympika: The International Journal of Olympic Studies* 19 (2010): 59–79.

———. "The Ecstasy of *Aretē*: Flow as Self-Transcendence in Ancient Athletics." *Studies in Sport Humanities* 15 (2014): 6–12. Reprinted in *Olympic Philosophy*, 147–60.

———. "The Epicurean Spectator." *Sport, Ethics and Philosophy* 4, no. 2 (2010): 195–203. Reprinted in *Athletics and Philosophy in the Ancient World: Contests of Virtue*, 81–89. London: Routledge, 2011.

―――. "Heroic *Mimēsis* and the Ancient Greek Athletic Spirit." *CHS Research Bulletin* 7 (2019). Published online at http://nrs.harvard.edu/urn-3:hlnc.essay: ReidH.Heroic_Mimesis_and_the_Ancient_Greek_Athletic_Spirit.2019.

―――. "Of Sport, Service, and Sacrifice: Rethinking the Religious Heritage of the Olympic Games." In *Cultural Imperialism in Action: Critiques in the Global Olympic Trust*, edited by N. Crowther, R. Barney, and M. Heine, 32–40. London, Ontario: International Centre for Olympic Studies, 2006.

―――. "Olympia: Running towards Truth." *Sport, Ethics and Philosophy* 4, no. 2 (2010): 136–45.

―――. *Olympic Philosophy: The Ideas and Ideals behind the Ancient and Modern Olympic Games.* Sioux City: Parnassos Press, 2020.

―――. "Olympic Sport and Its Lessons for Peace." *Journal of the Philosophy of Sport* 33, no. 2 (2006): 205–13. Reprinted with revisions in *Olympic Truce: Sport as a Platform for Peace*, edited by K. Georgiadis and A. Syrigos, 25–35. Athens: International Olympic Truce Center, 2009.

―――. "Performing Virtue: Athletic *Mimēsis* in Platonic Education." In *Politics and Performance in Western Greece*, edited by Heather L. Reid, Davide Tanasi, Susi Kimbell, 265–77. Sioux City: Parnassos Press, 2017.

―――. *The Philosophical Athlete.* Durham, NC: Carolina Academic Press, 2002.

―――. "Plato on Women in Sport." *Journal of the Philosophy of Sport* 47, no. 3 (2020): 344–61.

―――. "Plato's Gymnasium." *Sport, Ethics and Philosophy* 4, no. 2 (2010): 170–82.

―――. "The Political Heritage of the Olympic Games: Relevance, Risks, and Possible Rewards." *Sport, Ethics and Philosophy: Special Issue on the Olympic Games* 6, no. 2 (2012): 108–20.

―――. "Sport and Moral Education in Plato's *Republic*." *Journal of the Philosophy of Sport* 34, no. 2 (2007): 160–75.

―――. "Sport, Philosophy, and the Quest for Knowledge." *Journal of the Philosophy of Sport* 36, no. 1 (2009): 40–49.

―――. "Was the Roman Gladiator an Athlete?" *Journal of the Philosophy of Sport* 33, no. 1 (2006): 37–49.

―――. "Wrestling with Socrates." *Sport, Ethics and Philosophy* 4, no. 2 (2010): 157–69.

Reid, Heather L., and Mike W. Austin, eds. *The Olympics and Philosophy.* Lexington: University Press of Kentucky, 2012.

Reid, Heather L., and Georgios Mouratidis. "Naked Virtue: Ancient Athletic Nudity and the Olympic Ethos of *Aretē*." *Olympika* 29 (2020): 29–55.

Riordan, James. *Sport, Politics, and Communism.* Manchester, UK: Manchester University Press, 1991.

Roberts, Terence J. "Sport, Art, and Particularity: The Best Equivocation." In *Philosophic Inquiry in Sport*, edited by W. Morgan and K. Meier, 415–525. 2nd ed. Champaign, IL: Human Kinetics, 1995.

Rogge, Jacques. "An Apologia for Professionalism." *Olympic Review* 26, no. 4 (1995): 52.

Roochnik, David L. "Play and Sport." *Journal of the Philosophy of Sport* 2, no. 1 (1975): 36–44.

Russell, Bill. *Second Wind: The Memoirs of an Opinionated Man.* New York: Random House, 1979.

Russell, John S. "Are Rules All an Umpire Has to Work With?" *Journal of the Philosophy of Sport* 25, no. 1 (1999): 27–40.

———. "Resilience." *Journal of the Philosophy of Sport* 42, no. 2 (2015): 159–83.

———. "Robert L. Simon on Sport, Values, and Education." *Journal of the Philosophy of Sport* 43, no. 1 (2016): 51–60.

———. "Striving, Entropy, and Meaning." *Journal of the Philosophy of Sport* 47, no. 3 (2020): 419–37.

———. "The Value of Dangerous Sports." *Journal of the Philosophy of Sport* 32, no. 1 (2005): 1–19.

Sabo, Donald F., et al. "High School Athletic Participation, Sexual Behavior and Adolescent Pregnancy: A Regional Study." *Journal of Adolescent Health* 25, no. 3 (1999): 207–16.

Salemi, Vicki. "Shining a Spotlight on National Disability Employment Awareness Month." *Forbes*, October 29, 2021. Accessed November 11, 2021. https://www.forbes.com/sites/vickisalemi/2021/10/29/shining-a-spotlight-on-national-disability-employment-awareness-month/?sh=64144802348f.

Sansone, David. *Greek Athletics and the Genesis of Sport.* Berkeley: University of California Press, 1988.

Sapora, Allen V., and Elmer D. Mitchell. *The Theory of Play and Recreation.* New York: Ronald Press, 1961.

Sartre, Jean-Paul. *Being and Nothingness.* Translated by Hazel E. Barnes. New York: Philosophical Library, 1956.

Scanlon, Thomas F. *Eros and Greek Athletics.* New York: Oxford University Press, 2002.

Scheuerman, William. "Globalization." In *The Stanford Encyclopedia of Philosophy*, edited by Edward N. Zalta. Summer 2010. Accessed December 5, 2011. http://plato.stanford.edu/.

Schmid, Stephen. "Reconsidering Autotelic Play." *Journal of the Philosophy of Sport* 36, no. 2 (2009): 238–57.

Schnee, Steven, and Astrid Rodrigues. "The Amputee Wrestler: Rohan Murphy Can Take You Down." *ABC Sports*, December 9, 2010. Accessed November 21, 2011. news.go.com/.

Schneider, Angela J. "Fruits, Apples, and Category Mistakes: On Sport, Games, and Play." *Journal of the Philosophy of Sport* 28, no. 2 (2001): 151–59.

———. "On the Definition of 'Woman' in the Sport Context." In *Values in Sport*, edited by T. Tännsjö and C. Tamburrini, 123–38. London: Routledge, 2000.

Schneider, Angela, and Robert Butcher. "Why Olympic Athletes Should Avoid the Use and Seek the Elimination of Performance-Enhancing Substances and Practices from the Olympic Games." *Journal of the Philosophy of Sport* 20–21 (1993–1994): 64–81.

Searle, John. *Speech Acts: An Essay in the Philosophy of Language.* Cambridge: Cambridge University Press, 1969.

Seneca, Lucius Annaeus. *Letters from a Stoic (Epistulae Morales ad Lucilium).* Translated by R. Campbell. London: Penguin, 1969.

Senn, Alfred Erich. *Power, Politics and the Olympic Games.* Champaign, IL: Human Kinetics, 1999.

Sheets-Johnstone, Maxine. "Rationality and Caring: An Ontogenetic and Phylogenetic Perspective." *Journal of the Philosophy of Sport* 29, no. 2 (2002): 136–48.

Shildrick, Margrit. "Critical Disability Studies: Rethinking the Conventions for the Age of Postmodernity." In *The Routledge Handbook of Disability Studies*, edited by Nick Watson and Simo Vehmas, 32–44. 2nd ed. New York: Routledge, 2019.

Simon, Robert. "Does Athletics Undermine Academics? Examining Some Issues." *Journal of Intercollegiate Sport* 1, no. 1 (2008): 40–58.

———. "Internalism and Internal Values in Sport." *Journal of the Philosophy of Sport* 27, no. 1 (2000): 1–16.

———. *Fair Play: Sports, Values, and Society.* Boulder, CO: Westview, 1991. 2nd ed., *Fair Play: The Ethics of Sport*, 2004.

———. "Good Competition and Drug-Enhanced Performance." *Journal of the Philosophy of Sport* 11, no. 1 (1985): 6–13.

Singer, Peter. "Is It Okay to Cheat in Football?" Project Syndicate, June 26, 2010. Accessed April 10, 2011. http://www.project-syndicate.org/.

Slusher, Howard S. *Man, Sport, and Existence.* Philadelphia: Lea & Febiger, 1967.

Smith, Brett, Andrea Bundon, and Melanie Best. "Disability Sport and Activist Identities: A Qualitative Study of Narratives of Activism among Elite Athletes with Impairment." *Psychology of Sport and Exercise* 26 (2016): 139–48.

Smith, Nicholas D. "Plato and Aristotle on the Nature of Women." *Journal of the History of Philosophy* 21, no. 4 (1983): 467–78.

Snell, Bruno. *The Discovery of the Mind in Greek Philosophy and Literature.* New York: Dover, 1982.

Spivey, Nigel. *The Ancient Olympics: A History.* Oxford: Oxford University Press, 2004.

Stecker, Robert. *Aesthetics and the Philosophy of Art.* Lanham, MD: Rowman & Littlefield, 2005.

Stoll, Sharon K., and Jennifer M. Beller. "Do Sports Build Character?" In *Sports in School: The Future of an Institution*, edited by John Gerdy, 18–30. New York: Columbia University Press, 2000.

Strabo. *The Geography of Strabo.* Edited by H. L. Jones. Cambridge, MA: Harvard University Press, 1924.

Suits, Bernard. "The Elements of Sport." In *Philosophic Inquiry in Sport*, edited by W. J. Morgan and Klaus V. Meier, 39–48. Champaign, IL: Human Kinetics, 1988.

———. *The Grasshopper: Games, Life, and Utopia.* 2nd ed. Peterborough, Ontario: Broadview, [1978] 2005.

———. "The Tricky Triad: Games, Play, and Sport." *Journal of the Philosophy of Sport* 15, no. 1 (1988): 1–9.

———. "Venn and the Art of Category Maintenance." *Journal of the Philosophy of Sport* 31, no. 1 (2004): 1–14.

———. "What Is a Game?" *Philosophy of Science* 34, no. 1 (June 1967): 148–56.

———. "Words on Play." *Journal of the Philosophy of Sport* 4, no. 1 (1977): 117–31.

Sun Tzu. *The Art of War*. Translated by Lionel Giles. Hong Kong: Forgotten Books, 2007.

Tamburrini, Claudio. "Sport, Fascism and the Market." *Journal of the Philosophy of Sport* 25, no. 1 (1998): 35–47.

Tamburrini, Claudio, and Torbjörn Tännsjö. "The Genetic Design of a New Amazon." In *Genetic Technology and Sport: Ethical Questions*, edited by Claudio Tamburrini and Torbjörn Tännsjö, 181–98. New York: Routledge, 2005.

Tännsjö, Torbjörn. "Against Sexual Discrimination in Sports." In *Values in Sport*, edited by T. Tännsjö and C. Tamburrini, 101–15. London: Routledge, 2000.

———. "Is Our Admiration of Sports Heroes Fascistoid?" *Journal of the Philosophy of Sport* 25, no. 1 (1998): 23–34.

Thucydides. *History of the Peloponnesian War*. Translated by B. Jowett. Oxford, UK: Clarendon, 1900.

Torres, Cesar. "Furthering Interpretivism's Integrity: Bringing Together Ethics and Aesthetics." Presidential address to the International Association for the Philosophy of Sport, Rochester, New York, September 2011.

Ungerleider, Steven. *Faust's Gold*. New York: St. Martin's, 2001.

Valavanis, Panos. "Thoughts on the Historical Origins of the Olympic Games and the Cult of Pelops in Olympia." *Nikephoros* 19 (2006): 137–52.

Van Hilvoorde, Ivo, and Laurens Landerweerd. "Disability or Extraordinary Talent?" In *The Ethics of Sports*, edited by Mike McNamee, 231–41. London: Routledge, 2010.

Van Hilvoorde, Ivo, and Niek Pot. "Embodiment and Fundamental Motor Skills in eSports." *Sport, Ethics and Philosophy* 10, no. 1 (2016): 14–27.

Vannata, Seth. "A Phenomenology of Sport: Playing and Passive Synthesis." *Journal of the Philosophy of Sport* 35, no. 1 (2008): 63–72.

Von Schiller, Friedrich. "Letter XV." In *Essays and Letters*, vol. 8, translated by A. Lodge, E. B. Eastwick, and A. J. W. Morrison. London: Anthological Society, 1882. Reprinted in Gerber, *Sport and the Body*, 299–301.

Voy, Robert. *Drugs, Sport, and Politics*. Champaign, IL: Human Kinetics, 1991.

Wafi, Aymen. "Sarra Besbes: je m'en fiche . . . j'ai fait mon devoir." Koora.com, October 19, 2011. Accessed October 20, 2011. http://www.koora.com/.

Waley, Arthur. *Three Ways of Thought in Ancient China*. Stanford, CA: Stanford University Press, 2002.

Walton, Gary M. *Beyond Winning: The Timeless Wisdom of Great Philosopher Coaches*. Champaign, IL: Leisure Press, 1992.

Weaving, Charlene, and Jessica Samson. "The Naked Truth: Disability, Sexual Objectification, and the ESPN Body Issue." *Journal of the Philosophy of Sport* 45, no. 1 (2018): 83–100.

Weinberg, Rick. "Pine Tar Nullifies Home Run, So Brett Goes Ballistic." *ESPN*, 2009. Accessed October 20, 2011. http://sports.espn.go.com/.

Weiss, Paul. *Sport: A Philosophic Inquiry*. Carbondale: Southern Illinois University Press, 1969.

Wertz, Spencer K. "The Capriciousness of Play: Collingwood's Insight." *Journal of the Philosophy of Sport* 30, no. 1 (2003): 159–65.

———. "Is Sport Unique? A Question of Definability." *Journal of the Philosophy of Sport* 22, no. 1 (1995): 83–93.

———. "Representation and Expression in Sport and Art." *Journal of the Philosophy of Sport*, 12 (1985): 8–25.

Wing, John Ian. "Letter Saved the Games." National Library of Australia, Papers of Sir Wilfrid Kent Hughes, NS 4856/series 19. Accessed December 5, 2011. http://www.johnwing.co.uk/.

Wolbring, Gregor. "Paralympians Outperforming Olympians: An Increasing Challenge for Olympism and the Paralympic and Olympic Movement." *Sport, Ethics and Philosophy* 6, no. 2 (2012): 251–66. Reprinted in *Olympic Ethics and Philosophy*, edited by Mike McNamee and Jim Parry, 149–64. New York: Routledge, 2013.

World Commission on Environment and Development. *Our Common Future*. Oxford: Oxford University Press, 1987.

Wright, Lesley. "Aesthetic Implicitness in Sport and the Role of Aesthetic Concepts." *Journal of the Philosophy of Sport* 30, no. 1 (2003): 83–92.

Young, David C. *A Brief History of the Olympic Games*. Malden, MA: Blackwell, 2004.

———. "Mens Sana in Corpore Sano? Body and Mind in Greek Literature." *Proceedings of the North American Society for Sport History* (1998): 60–61.

———. *The Olympic Myth of Greek Amateur Athletics*. Chicago: Ares, 1984.

Yuasa, Yasuo. *The Body, Self-Cultivation and Ki-Energy*. Albany: State University of New York Press, 1993.

———. *The Body: Toward an Eastern Mind-Body Theory*. Edited by Thomas P. Kasulis. Albany: State University of New York Press, 1987.

Zeigler, Earle F. *Philosophical Foundations for Physical, Health, and Recreation Education*. Englewood Cliffs, NJ: Prentice Hall, 1964.

Index

AAU. *See* Amateur Athletic Union
ableism, 236
Abrahams, Harold, 19
absorption, 46–48, 120
Academy (Plato), 11–13, 17n26, 89–91, 97, 140, 172
Achilles, 22
advantages, 144–46
aesthetics: aesthetic sports, 87; of beauty, 82–83; commercialism of, 88–89; of culture, 169n17; ethics and, 166–67; Nietzsche on, 84; of spectatorship, 81–86; value of, 84, 91–92, 163–64, 169n24
Aesthetics and the Philosophy of Art (Stecker), 87
African Americans, 205–9. *See also* racism
After Virtue (MacIntyre), 68–69
agency, 134–35
Agenda 21 (Olympic games), 268–69
Amateur Athletic Union (AAU), 201
amateurism: doping and, 117–18, 122; in Olympic games, 24–25, 71, 117–18, 189, 211n6; philosophy of, 19, 112; professionalism and, 189–91, 194–95; skill in, 19; of student-athletes, 189–91
Americans with Disabilities Act, 235

Anaximenes, 6
ancestry, 82–83, 103
ancient Greece: academic gymnasiums in, 11–13, 17n26; *aretē* in, 62, 172, 176–77; beauty in, 165–66; cheating in, 211n5; China and, 104, 139–40; class in, 210n3; culture of, 1–4, 7–9, 15n8, 81, 211n6, 248; education in, 9–11; Egypt and, 203; ethics of, 90, 147–48; females in, 214–15; Gods of, 7; identity in, 210n1; ideology in, 280; myths from, 41; Olympic games in, 77, 171–72, 189–90, 262; Olympism in, 5–7; philosophy of, 13–15; race in, 211n12; Rome and, 245–46, 278; spectatorship in, 91, 162; United States compared to, 187; virtue in, 25, 153n8
Apple, 254
"Are Rules All an Umpire Has to Work With?" (Russell, J.), 61–62
aretē: in ancient Greece, 62, 172, 176–77; Aristotle on, 140; leadership from, 6; in Olympic games, 9–10; philosophy of, 5, 13; skill and, 279; social class and, 7–8, 247; to Socrates, 12; *technē-aretē*, 179; as virtue, 4, 70, 104, 132
Aretism (Holowchak and Reid), 151

305

equality, 8–9, 15, 17n23, 39–40,
69–70, 204, 269
Erving, Julius, 164
erythropoietin (EPO), 53
eSports, 56
essentialism, 111–12, 126
essential rules, 59
ethics: aesthetics and, 166–67; of
ancient Greece, 90, 147–48; of
Aristotle, 13–14, 141, 143–44,
163, 182, 279; in athletics, 43–44,
111–12; breaches of, 170n37; broad
internalism, 126; in collegiate
sports, 192–95; in deontology,
125–26; of education, 83, 182–84;
in epistemology, 215; in football,
73; framing, 160–62; Groos on, 89;
in modernity, 25; moral goodness,
92; moral obligations, 132–33;
moral principles, 24; Olympism
and, 24–26; politics and, 131–32;
psychology of, 131–33; of purists,
159–60; rules and, 64n25; skill and,
136; social activism and, 219–20;
of spectatorship, 157–59, 165–68;
strategy and, 130; in utilitarianism,
140; virtue and, 13, 76–77, 214
ethnocentrism, 264
Europe, 262–65. *See also*
specific countries
European Enlightenment, 20
Evert, Chris, 254
excellence, 62, 75, 137n26, 254, 279
exercise, 71–72
experiential education, 182–83
exploitation, 192–95
external goals, 48
external goods, 71–73, 75, 77
extraordinary play, 41–42, 47
extraordinary seriousness, 117–19
extrinsic values, 119–21

failure, 74
fairness, 195, 223, 233–34, 277, 280

fair play: deontology and, 125–26, 128–
29; philosophy of, 131–33; rules for,
126–29, 133–36; virtue of, 129–31
Fair Play (Simon), 62
fans. *See* spectatorship
fascism, 249–51
Feezell, Randolph, 38, 40, 43,
45–46, 117, 119
females: in ancient Greece, 214–15; in
athletics, 213–14; in communism,
252; education of, 12–13, 175–76;
with men, 227n50; in Olympic
games, 9, 22–23, 90; in *Republic*,
217; rules for, 223; sexism against,
197–98, 210n4, 221; in skiing,
224n2; social activism for, 208–10.
See also gender; sex
feminism, 221
fencing, 125–26, 131–32
Fielding, Henry, 23
FIFA, 57, 127–28, 202, 222
FINA, 133–34
Fischer, Norman, 147
Fisher, Marjorie, 84
flow, 120–21, 276
Floyd, George, 202, 209
football: college, 278; ethics in, 73;
National Football League, 35, 209,
262; rules of, 61; spectatorship of,
146; violence in, 79n28
foreign languages, 191, 196n8
formalism, 58–61, 126–29
Fosbury, Dick, 164
Fraleigh, Warren, 62, 116, 131
framing, 83–86, 160–62
Francis, Leslie Pickering, 231
freedom, 8, 39–41, 114–17, 161, 276
free play, 37, 39, 114–17
fun, 45–46, 48
"Fundamental Principles of
Olympism," 21–24

gambling, 164
games: broad internalism from, 61–63;
formalism of, 58–59; goals of,

About the Author

Heather L. Reid is scholar in residence at the Exedra Mediterranean Center in Siracusa, Sicily, and professor of philosophy emerita at Morningside College in Sioux City, Iowa. A competitive cyclist in her youth, she won a national intercollegiate championship and qualified for the final Olympic trials in 1984 and 1988. She is a 2015 Fellow of the American Academy in Rome; 2018–2020 Fellow of Harvard's Center for Hellenic Studies in Washington, D.C.; and 2019 Fulbright Scholar at the Università degli Studi di Napoli Federico II. She has written numerous books and articles on ancient philosophy, philosophy of sport, and Olympic studies. She also has been invited to lecture on these topics in Beijing, London, Rome, Seoul, and at the International Olympic Academy in Olympia, Greece. She is past president and recipient of the distinguished service and distinguished scholar awards of the International Association for the Philosophy of Sport. She serves on the boards of the *Journal of the Philosophy of Sport*, *The International Journal of Applied Philosophy*, and *Sport, Ethics and Philosophy*. Her books include *Olympic Philosophy* (2020), *Introduction to the Philosophy of Sport* (2012), *Athletics and Philosophy in the Ancient World: Contests of Virtue* (2011), and *The Philosophical Athlete* (2002; 2nd ed., 2019). She is coauthor of *The Olympics and Philosophy* (2012), *Aretism: An Ancient Sports Philosophy for the Modern Sports World* (2011), and *Filosofia dello Sport* (2011).